Northwestern University

STUDIES IN *Phenomenology &*

Existential Philosophy

On Heidegger
and Language

Edited and translated by

On Heidegger
and Language

JOSEPH J. KOCKELMANS

Northwestern University Press

1972   Evanston

Joseph J. Kockelmans is Professor of Philosophy
at The Pennsylvania State University.

Contents

Preface

HEIDEGGER IS CERTAINLY RECOGNIZED as one of the greatest thinkers of our era, and it is well known that the question concerning the meaning of Being is central to all of his thinking. His main interest is in trying to understand Being's finitude and historicity considered as such as well as in all of their consequences. Heidegger's original point of departure was an analytic of man's Being taken as *Da-sein, lumen naturale*—that is, as eksistence, standing out, and thus as Being-in-the-world. He used phenomenological and hermeneutic methods in order to let the "things themselves" become manifest, interpreting them from the preontological understanding of Being which is inherent in man's Being as such. Heidegger hoped that a careful analysis of man's Being would help him find a way to make our preontological understanding of Being explicit. In his later works he continued to struggle with the same basic problem but approached the question from the viewpoint of the different forms, or "expressions," in which Being manifests itself in the various epochs of Being's own history, notably from the viewpoint of the world in which we find ourselves today. This "turn" in Heidegger's approach to the main problem took place between 1929 and 1935; its effect is reflected in the profound difference between Heidegger's earlier and later publications. We must keep in mind, however, that both approaches are necessary and that they belong together, although insights gained from the later works have necessitated some changes in the original approach.

Throughout both his earlier and later periods Heidegger has maintained a great interest in the problem of language. Here, too, is found a marked difference between Heidegger's original and later reflections on the subject; but again we must keep in mind that, in his view, both considerations are necessary and that they, too, somehow belong together.

The enormous difference between Heidegger's conception of language and what is currently found in books on "philosophy of language" is readily apparent. In interpreting this difference many people have assumed that Heidegger adopts a completely negative attitude toward classical philosophy of language, but this assumption can easily be disproved by Heidegger's own remarks on the issue. He does not criticize the classical conception of language as much as he concerns himself with finding a foundation for its underlying assumptions and reinterpreting it from the viewpoint of philosophy's basic concern: the problem concerning the meaning of Being.

In his earlier works, notably in *Being and Time,* Heidegger says very little about language taken as a system of signs and symbols embodying a certain totality of meaning. He is mainly interested in examining the *presuppositions* that underlie the various interpretations dealing with the relationship between speech and language as found in classical philosophy. Among these presuppositions, the ones that concern him the most are: (1) the conception of man that is at the base of these ideas; (2) the basic relationship between man's original praxis (as concernful dealing with things and care for his fellow men) and theory (whether scientific or prescientific); (3) the precise relationship between the constitution of meaning and the articulation of meaning; and finally (4) the relationship, within the process of the constitution of meaning, between "emotive" intuition and articulating, discursive understanding. In evaluating Heidegger's view it is of the greatest importance to bear in mind that everything he says about speech and language must be understood within the context of the general concern of *Being and Time:* to clarify the *question* concerning the meaning of Being.

In Heidegger's later works his attention turns from a concern for language from the viewpoint of man's speech to a concern for language's essential contribution to the very possibility of man's speech. Here, too, it is extremely important to realize that everything that is said in this connection is to be understood in light of the question that dominates Heidegger's thought as a whole: the question concerning the meaning of Being. His later reflections on language are particularly difficult to understand and are objected to by many philosophers. It seems, however, that most of the criticism rests on a basic misunderstanding of Heidegger's deepest intention.

In reading Heidegger's reflections on language one must keep in mind that by *language* he does not mean the whole body of words and methods of combining words used by man or a group of men; nor is he concerned with what Ferdinand de Saussure aptly called the structural system of diacritical oppositions necessary and sufficient for a system of sounds to constitute a system of communication. Heidegger uses the term in its broadest possible sense; thus by *language* he means everything by which *mankind* brings meaning to light *in an articulated way*, regardless of whether it is done concretely, by means of the sentences of a language in the narrow sense of the term, or through a work of art, a social or religious institution, and so on. Correspondingly, the term *speech*, or *speaking*, is used for the most part in a very broad sense so as to include such expressions as "This symphony speaks to me," "This painting says something to me," "This religious ceremony communicates meaning to me." Concerning this use of the terms *language* and *speech*, it is to be noted that it is by no means contrary to our common way of speaking.

Although the ideas that have been briefly touched upon here constitute the main subject matter of the papers collected in this anthology, I feel that I should further inform the reader as to what he should and should not expect to find in this book. Most of the papers are meant to explain Heidegger's conception of language to readers who already have a solid insight into his philosophy as a whole. Some papers comment on certain of Heidegger's basic texts, whereas others attempt to extend Heidegger's view to areas where Heidegger himself has never applied his thoughts. In order to compensate for the one-sidedness of such an approach to Heidegger's conception of language, critical reflections, introductory papers, and purely linguistic reflections have been added in an endeavor to place Heidegger's original ideas within the broadest possible perspective.

The first part of the book contains two introductory papers. The first of these indicates the two principal areas in which Heidegger has attempted to make a positive contribution to a philosophical reflection on language. The second gives a clear but critical exposition of Heidegger's original conception of speech and language as found in *Being and Time*. It is the only paper that deals explicitly with Heidegger's original view, although in the others this view is certainly always preunderstood.

The second part of the book contains six essays that were presented at the International Colloquium on Heidegger's Conception of Language held at The Pennsylvania State University, September 18–21, 1969. The discussions following the papers have been included also, at least insofar as the commentators and speakers have signified a desire to have them so included. Some of the questions and comments of a more informative nature have been incorporated into the footnotes.

Finally, the third part of the book contains two papers of a predominantly linguistic nature. Erasmus Schöfer's essay deals with the linguistic particularities of Heidegger's language use and style. I have added this essay, which constitutes just one section of an important book completely devoted to Heidegger's use of language, in order to show how Heidegger's linguistic particularities are to be understood from a linguistic point of view and how they are related to the main problem of his own thought on language. Finally, Johannes Lohmann's article has been included for the purpose of clarifying Heidegger's view on the relationship between thought and the particular language in which it becomes expressed.

All of the papers combined do not give an adequate idea of Heidegger's conception of language, for it is not possible at this point in time to do so. Heidegger's view is still in the process of development, and many of his publications on the subject are not yet available. In view of this situation, it seems that this book points to many basic problems for which Heidegger has tried to find an acceptable solution.

In translating the papers (with the exception of Professor Marx's and my own) I have attempted to remain as close to the original texts as the English language would allow. Instead of endeavoring to produce a literary work of art, I have attempted to present Heidegger's thought and that of his commentators as accurately and completely as possible. All of the translations have been checked by the authors in order to avoid misunderstandings on important issues. However, I assume the responsibility for inadequacies in the translations which critical readers will certainly find in many instances.

Footnote references are to the German editions of Heidegger's works. Translations of direct quotations from Heidegger are for the most part my own. Where existing English translations have been referred to, the page numbers are included in parentheses in the footnotes. This has not been done, however, in references to *Being and Time*, since the English translation includes the German page numbers in the margin of the text. Translator's notes clarifying the translations are indicated by asterisks.

Grateful acknowledgment is made to the authors for their cooperation throughout the work and to those publishers who have granted permission to reprint selections from copyrighted material. I would like to thank Robert Henricks for his assistance in transliterating the Chinese. Finally, I would like to express my sincere appreciation to Mr. Ralph Carlson and the entire staff of Northwestern University Press for endorsing the project and for their consistent cooperation from beginning to completion.

Joseph J. Kockelmans
The Pennsylvania State University

Acknowledgments

Some of the essays in this volume have already appeared in print. The following material is reprinted with permission of the publishers:

Joseph J. Kockelmans, "Language, Meaning, and Ek-sistence," in *Perspectives in Phenomenology*, ed. F. Joseph Smith (The Hague: Nijhoff, 1970), pp. 94–121.

Jan Aler, "De taal bij Heidegger," *Algemeen Nederlands Tijdschrift voor Wijsbegeerte en Psychologie*, LIII (1961), 241–60.

Walter Biemel, "Dichtung und Sprache bei Heidegger," *Man and World*, II (1969), 478–514.

Otto Pöggeler, "Heideggers Topology des Seins," *Man and World*, II (1969), 331–56.

Heinrich Ott, "Das Gebet als Sprache des Glaubens," in *Wirklichkeit und Glaube* (Göttingen: Vandenhoeck & Ruprecht, 1969), Vol. II, *Der persönliche Gott*, 94–121.

Werner Marx, "The World in Another Beginning: Poetic Dwelling and the Role of the Poet," in *Reason and World: Between Tradition and Another Beginning* (The Hague: Nijhoff, 1971), pp. 97–112.

Erasmus Schöfer, "Metalogische Denkformen und grammatische Besonderheiten," in *Die Sprache Heideggers* (Pfullingen: Neske, 1962), pp. 196–217.

Johannes Lohmann, "M. Heideggers 'Ontologische Differenz' und die Sprache," *Lexis*, I (1948), 49–106.

List of Abbreviations

WORKS BY HEIDEGGER

ED	*Aus der Erfahrung des Denkens*
EM	*Einführung in die Metaphysik*
FD	*Die Frage nach dem Ding*
HB	*Brief über den Humanismus*
HD	*Erläuterungen zu Hölderlins Dichtung*
HH	*Hebel—Der Hausfreund*
HW	*Holzwege*
ID	*Identität und Differenz*
KB	*Die Kategorien- und Bedeutungslehre des Duns Scotus*
KM	*Kant und das Problem der Metaphysik*
N I,II	*Nietzsche,* Vols. I and II
PT	*Phänomenologie und Theologie*
PW	*Platons Lehre von der Wahrheit*
SD	*Zur Sache des Denkens*
SG	*Der Satz vom Grund*
SZ	*Sein und Zeit*
UP	*Die Lehre vom Urteil im Psychologismus*
US	*Unterwegs zur Sprache*
VA	*Vorträge und Aufsätze*
W	*Wegmarken*
WD	*Was heisst Denken?*
WG	*Vom Wesen des Grundes*
WM	*Was ist Metaphysik?*
WW	*Vom Wesen der Wahrheit*

See Selected Bibliography for full citations of these works.

PART I

1 / Language, Meaning, and Ek-sistence

Joseph J. Kockelmans

WHEREVER ONE ENCOUNTERS human beings one finds language. It is only natural then that man, as soon as he begins to reflect on what he is, will meet the phenomenon of language. Speech itself, one soon sees, also asks that man reflect thoughtfully and try to understand language from the viewpoint of that which immediately manifests itself in language.

For many centuries thinking mankind has been trying to form an idea of what "language in general" could be. The general characteristics that allegedly hold true for all languages are often said to constitute the very essence of language. Accordingly, to speak and write thoughtfully about language with the intention of delineating the proper characteristics of "language in general" means to form an idea of the essence of language and to distinguish it from other possible ideas about language. All through the years a correlative study of man's speech has occupied a central place in any study concerning the very essence of language.[1]

What then is speech, properly speaking? Within the conception of language that, as just briefly indicated, focuses its main attention on the question of what "language in general" is supposed to be, speech is defined for the most part as the putting into action of our speech organs. In this view to speak is to utter and communicate one's thoughts and emotions through audible words, that is, with one's voice. In this conception three insights

1. *US* 11–12.

are tacitly presupposed to be true and certain. First, speech is the utterance of what was hidden in man's "inmost soul" and now becomes manifested. However, to conceive of speech as the utterance of what was originally contained and hidden in man's heart makes language into something that is "outward," or "external." Second, speech is conceived of here as an activity of man. According to this view one might say that man, and only man, speaks and that through his speech language comes into being in one way or another. Third, it is supposed that the verbal expression, by which man "materializes" thought, is always a presentation or re-presentation of reality, or eventually of "ideal" entities.

This view of language is not a new one. We can read in Aristotle's *Peri Hermēneias* that

> spoken words are the signs of the soul's experiences, and written words are the signs of spoken words. Just as all men have not the same writing, so all men have not the same speech sounds; but the soul's experiences, which they immediately signify, are the same for all, as also are those things of which our experiences are the images.[2]

Here Aristotle ascertains the fact to which one usually adheres when adopting this general view of language—namely, that the written letters and words of a language signify sounds, that the sounds, in turn, are signs of the thoughts of the soul, and that the latter, finally, signify the relevant things or state of affairs. In this view of language the sign quite obviously occupies a central place. It is the sign which in many ways, now revealing, now concealing, brings things to light. As long as the sign continues to be experienced as essentially connected with an immediate pointing to, as was the case in classical Greek thought, no great difficulties are necessarily attached to this conception. However, when the sign is no longer conceived of as a pointing to in the sense of an immediate bringing to the fore, as has generally been the case since the time of the Stoics, then great problems arise. Such problems are connected not only with the essence of language but also with man's knowing and thinking.

Notwithstanding the many and often substantial changes in this conception of language and speech, it has succeeded in maintaining itself in the Western world since the time of the

2. Aristotle *Peri Hermēneias* c. I. 16a3–8.

Stoics. If one limits oneself to the heart of the matter, one may find this view not only in the language theory of Wilhelm von Humboldt but also in the language conception of George von der Gabelentz, Ferdinand de Saussure, and others as well. In contemporary views of language analogous ideas are still frequently met. A few quotations from a recent essay by Anton Reichling may serve to clarify the point. Attempting to indicate in a few words what "language" and "speech" really are, Reichling says:

> My speech takes the place of . . . a series of my activities. But my speech is itself an activity as well. It is an activity of a special kind: it is a "substituting" activity which saves me much trouble. . . . The sounds of speech are a means, an instrument. Thus we are dealing here with a substituting, instrumental activity. . . . Speaking is essentially a "cooperative" instrumental activity. . . . However, speech is not merely substituting, instrumental, and cooperative, but it is also "symbolic": we produce sounds, but in so doing we know that we are dealing with "things." . . . Speaking is a form of signalizing, of giving signs . . . ; in what is said we "know" the "things" that we talk about. . . . And because it is absolutely unnecessary that the "things" that we are dealing with fall within the realm of our immediate experience at this very moment, . . . it is clear . . . that speaking and listening are forms of thinking. And that the same thing holds good for writing and reading, that needs no argument. . . .
> Language is the totality of system, of vocabulary as well as of systematically built and employed constructs, which respectively both make possible and in each concrete case of usage constitute the universal, cooperative, instrumental sign-behavior of man." [3]

We must therefore conclude that in the different sciences of language certain fundamental insights concerning language and speech have remained essentially unaltered, notwithstanding all the profound and far-reaching changes and renewals that undoubtedly have taken place during the last two centuries. One can take this situation as a conclusive argument for the correctness and exactness of these fundamental insights. Hence it is not part of my plan to argue that this characterization of language and speech is wrong or to be rejected as altogether meaningless. On the contrary, this view of language is right; it is oriented

3. Anton Reichling, *Verzamelde studies over hedendaagse problemen der taalwetenschap* (Zwolle: Tjeenk Willink, 1962), pp. 14–15, 46.

toward, but also limited to, what can be brought to light about linguistic phenomena by empirical investigation. The only aspect which should be mentioned in connection with the view briefly outlined above is that the proper meaning of speech here—and in connection with it, the very essence of language too—apparently does not come genuinely to the fore, since there are still too many elements that ask for a further interpretation and a more radical foundation. In the final analysis this conception of language seems to remain in the air as long as one is not able to clarify and clearly indicate what is meant by "man" and how the mode of being characteristic of man is necessarily connected with the very essence of language.[4] This is what I have chosen to make the main theme of my essay.

It is well known that the view of language and speech, described above in much too brief a fashion, became philosophically acceptable during the course of years in a number of different ways. Taking Merleau-Ponty's lead, it is perhaps possible to characterize the two most important currents in the philosophy of language in the following terms.[5]

The first view, taken in its extreme form, reduces man's speech to the production of words with the help of the vocal organs under the influence of certain activities of the brain and nerves; these activities are excited by external stimuli that propagate themselves in the nervous system and are coordinated through the mysterious mechanism of association. Notwithstanding the fact that speech is conceived as an activity of man, man is fundamentally passive in speaking insofar as his speaking is causally determined by stimuli from the outside. If such a view were true, it would show at best, not that I am speaking, but that this determinate language "comes over me" in a passive way.

The second view has its starting point in an inner thought which is rooted only in itself. Language is simply a conventional but coherent system of signs and symbols that has as its purpose the communication of inner ideas to other people without any influence of the means of communication on the speaker's way of thinking. In this view one admits that words and combinations

4. US 243–50, 14–16, 202–7.
5. Maurice Merleau-Ponty, *Phénoménologie de la perception* (Paris: Gallimard, 1945), pp. 204–10 (English translation by Colin Smith, *Phenomenology of Perception* [New York: Humanities, 1962], pp. 175–81).

of words are "physical" in nature; but the only important thing is to what these physical signs refer, which as such transcends this "physical" reality.

At first these two conceptions of language seem to be completely different. On closer examination, however, it becomes clear that these views actually agree in several fundamental ways. Both conceive of language as exclusively a means of communication—a vehicle for the exchange of thoughts which are already formed or for the communication of a meaning which is already there. What is to be said already exists before it is expressed. Either the meaning that is communicated through speech exists in the world (and man must accept that meaning in one way or another), or meaning is constituted exclusively within the domain of the mind or consciousness. In both cases this meaning is to be uttered at a later moment by means of language. In so doing man uses perceptible signs or symbols that in essence are merely conventional. In both views the multiplicity of the existing languages can be explained easily. In both instances speech is a sensory motoric phenomenon which in itself contributes nothing to the constitution of meaning. A word taken in itself is empty; it is effective either as a physical stimulus or as a perceptible sign that is added to the meaning from the outside without being essentially related to it. Speech expresses meaning; it does not reveal or disclose it. Language is merely a means of communication in and through which man can convey meaning; but it can never be a source of meaning and of light.

Most phenomenologists do not agree with either of these conceptions of language; neither do they agree with certain views that are implicit in these conceptions of language and speech. Merleau-Ponty in particular has taken great pains to show, in many detailed analyses, how far both views are right and acceptable and in what sense they are one-sided. To escape one-sidedness phenomenologists try to show that speech is primarily a creative activity that brings meaning to light and sometimes even originates it. In so doing they strongly stress that the source of all difficulties in linguistic philosophies of the past is to be found in the view of man underlying these philosophies. This is the main reason why so many phenomenologists speak extensively about the relation between language and "meaning-giving ek-sistence." This new view of man, as proposed here, necessarily requires a new conception of language and speech and, at the same time, can give us an admissible solution for different problems that the classical philosophies of language have left unsolved.[6]

In this paper I shall begin by discussing certain fundamental insights concerning man which are generally accepted in the realm of existential phenomenology. It is assumed that the reader will be familiar with developments in the philosophy of language within this realm.[7] Within such a general perspective I will try to answer *some* basic questions which are immediately connected with the problem concerning the exact relationship between language and man's speech. This problem is considered first from the viewpoint of man's speech. Special attention is devoted to the question of how the meaning of things is connected with the signification of words. In dealing with this problem I follow relevant sections of Heidegger's *Being and Time* as closely as possible. Second, the question is examined from the viewpoint of language. I indicate a set of problems that are of the utmost importance for a philosophy of language. Although the direction in which a possible answer to these questions may be found is indicated, a definitive solution is not given. In formulating these problems and indicating a possible solution I have been inspired to a very great extent by Heidegger's *On the Way to Language*.

6. *Ibid.*, pp. 203–32 (174–99). Cf. Alphonse De Waelhens, *Une philosophie de l'ambiguïté: L'existentialisme de Maurice Merleau-Ponty* (Louvain: Nauwelaerts, 1951), pp. 150–62; *idem, Existence et signification* (Louvain: Nauwelaerts, 1958), pp. 123–41; Remy C. Kwant, *Fenomenologie van de taal* (Utrecht: Het Spectrum, 1963), pp. 14–21.

7. In addition to the literature mentioned in the preceding notes, see also: Edmund Husserl, *Logische Untersuchungen*, 3 Vols., 3d. ed. (Halle a.d.S.: Niemeyer, 1921–22), II, sec. 1, 294–342 (English translation by J. N. Findlay, *Logical Investigations* [New York: Humanities, 1970]); *idem, Formale und transzendentale Logik: Versuch einer Kritik der logischen Vernunft* (Halle a.d.S.: Niemeyer, 1929), pp. 16–23 (English translation by Dorion Cairns, *Formal and Transcendental Logic* [The Hague: Nijhoff, 1969]); *idem,* "Die Frage nach dem Ursprung der Geometrie als intentional-historisches Problem," *Revue Internationale de Philosophie*, I (1939), 203–25; H. Pos, "Phénoménologie et linguistique," *ibid.*, pp. 354–65; Maurice Merleau-Ponty, *Signes* (Paris: Gallimard, 1960), pp. 49–122 (English translation by Richard C. McCleary, *Signs* [Evanston, Ill.: Northwestern Univ. Press, 1964]); Alphonse De Waelhens, "De taalphilosophie volgens M. Merleau-Ponty," *Tijdschrift voor Philosophie*, XVI (1954), 402–18; B. Brus, "De taal bij Merleau-Ponty," *Nederlands Tijdschrift voor de psychologie en haar grensbebieden*, XVI (1958), 26–80; SZ 130–67.

EK-SISTENCE AND LANGUAGE

ONE OF THE MOST FUNDAMENTAL INSIGHTS of existential phenomenology consists in the fact that the proper mode of being characteristic of man is conceived as "ek-sistence." This term is to be understood to mean "to ek-sist": "to stand out." Man is subject, but he is an ek-sisting subject that places itself outside itself in the world; he "stands out toward" the things in the world and the world itself. Such a conception of man's "essence" cannot be derived from other more fundamental insights. It can be made acceptable only by showing that no real mode of man's Being can be conceived which is not a mode of Being in and toward the world.

Ek-sistent man is essentially a worldly reality that "gives meaning." As *lumen naturale* man originates meaning in everything he does—in every act, in his concern for his fellow men and things, in his work, thought, and games. Speaking is one of the ways in which man originates meaning. But, if man's speech always functions within the whole of his "meaning-giving ek-sistence," it is impossible to talk about speech without explicitly dealing with this "meaning-giving ek-sistence." On the other hand, thinking about man as "meaning-giving ek-sistence" will necessarily lead to speech and language. There cannot be any doubt that there is a special relationship between speaking and all other forms in which man's ek-sistence reveals meaning. It is precisely this special relationship that demands particular attention in this inquiry concerning the very "essence" of language. About this special connection one can say immediately that the meaning which was brought to light in one way or other by man's ek-sistence outside the realm of speech proper can be revealed in a new way by man's speaking. The main question now is in precisely what this new element consists. In order to be able to explain this we shall have to examine further some basic insights of existential phenomenology.

By saying that man as ek-sistent is a "meaning-giving being," existential phenomenology tries to demarcate its own position in regard to two other possible philosophical views of the origin of meaning. One could say that man finds meaning in the world and does not have to contribute anything to its origin or genesis.

In this view the world is already a domain of meaning; the only thing man has to do is to take cognizance of this meaning. Meaning is therefore in this case an "objective datum" found and encountered by man, but not constituted or projected by him. There is no question here of a "meaning-giving act," but only of a reception of meaning. In speech man merely re-presents this pregiven meaning; in his speech man utters this meaning, expresses and communicates it.

One could also say that man's consciousness is the exclusive source of meaning. According to this conception consciousness creates or projects meaning outside itself in things in a purely active way. What is called "a real thing" is, in this view, no more than the correlate of the activity of consciousness or of pure spirit as creative of meaning.

Although existential phenomenology in many respects prefers the second conception to the first, it nonetheless contends that it is not consciousness or pure spirit which is the source of meaning, but man as ek-sisting. Furthermore, it argues that man's ek-sistence is the source of meaning if and only if man as ek-sistent is in living dialogue with the other (*das Andere*). Existential phenomenology also holds that man is a source of meaning in his dialogue with his fellow men and things in the world, not only in his reflexively conscious activities, but primarily in his non-reflexively conscious and preconscious activities. Finally, existential phenomenology argues that even in his reflexively conscious giving of meaning man appears to himself not as a *res cogitans*, or a "thinking substance," but as an ek-sisting originator of meaning.[8]

We have said that man can bring meaning to light in many ways; but, whatever these ways may be, man always brings meaning to light *as* ek-sistent. In order to be able to answer the question of how man gives meaning in his speech (and how from this perspective language is to be understood) it will first be necessary to try to answer two questions: What is the most original and primordial way in which man gives meaning, and precisely what has to happen before the meaning, which was already brought to light, can be uttered and expressed by man? A few brief remarks may suffice to clarify the viewpoint of existential phenomenology in this regard.

8. Kwant, *Fenomenologie van de taal*, pp. 22–52 *passim*.

In the history of philosophy there is a very old tradition according to which the most fundamental manner in which man gives meaning is in speculative thought. Existential phenomenology rejects this view if *thought* means the theoretical knowledge which for many centuries has occupied a central place in Western culture. According to existential phenomenology, man establishes meaning in every form that his ek-sistence can concretely adopt. If one now asks what the most fundamental form is in which man reveals meaning, it will be clear that this question coincides with an inquiry into the primary mode in which man ek-sists. Existential phenomenology contends, on the basis of immediate experience, that man does not experience himself primordially as an "I think" but as an "I can," "I am able to do." In other words, man primarily "materializes" his ek-sistence, not in his theoretical knowledge, but in his concrete doing, acting, and making—in his "practical" concern with things and with his fellow men. The most primordial form that man's Being-in-the-world can adopt is that in which man concernfully deals with things that thereby become his "materials" and "tools," with the help of which he produces "utensils." Inseparably connected with this, and equiprimordially, man is also concerned with his fellow men; but this concernful dealing with his fellow men also comes about first and foremost on a primarily "practical" level.[9]

This view, often misunderstood as a form of irrationalism, has been the subject of much criticism. Without a doubt this criticism is sound and valid if in this context the terms *practical* and *praxis* are taken in a narrow sense. However, if these terms are understood as they were originally meant, that is, if they are taken to mean everything in our culture which cannot be called "mere theory" in the generally accepted sense of this term, then the view seems to present no serious difficulties whatsoever. Genetically, historically, and from our own immediate experience here and now, it can easily be shown that all meaning found in our theoretical knowledge refers back to a "primordial praxis" in which it originated. It is from the viewpoint of the "primordial praxis" (understood in a very broad sense) that all forms of "theory" are to be understood. Furthermore it is of great importance to realize that within our "primordial praxis" a distinction is to be made between the "primordial praxis" of a not yet

9. SZ 52–62.

conscious subject and the "primordial praxis" of a reflexively conscious subject. One must realize also that in all forms of "praxis" there is already a certain "seeing" and "understanding," which Merleau-Ponty aptly refers to as *practognosie*. What in our culture is called "knowing" is almost exclusively that procedure in which one takes distance from the light that was already present in the "primordial praxis," transforms it by means of a conscious and sometimes even reflexively conscious cognitive act, and lets things appear, which—insofar as their meaning is concerned—were already given purely in the "primordial praxis," in the way they appear (*in ihrem Aussehen [eidos]*).[10]

In all forms that the "praxis" can assume, man is always related to a determinate and concrete being or to a determinate group of things.[11] Yet in the "primordial praxis" a certain "whole" is also always given as that in which each concrete thing can appear as meaningful. This whole of relationships, within which things mutually refer to one other and can manifest themselves as meaningful, is called "world." The relationship of man toward this "totality," which manifests itself mediately in man's concernful dealing with things, does not yet imply a special theoretical activity—at least not originally. The essential relationship between man and world, which mediately comes to the fore in each concernful dealing with this or that concrete thing, is contained in an "original mood" that is necessarily connected with each concrete interpretation of meaning and with each understanding characteristic of the "primordial praxis."

It is difficult to say precisely in what the ontological structure of this "original mood" consists because our thematic knowledge of all that is connected with man's "frame of mind" always falls short. Undoubtedly mood communicates something to us about our own mode of Being in relationship to the other as a whole; but it is very difficult to determine why one is disposed, or "tuned," in a determinate way and what this disposition tells us about ourselves and the other. The "original mood" informs man about his position in the midst of things in the world. Contained in this

---

10. Alphonse De Waelhens, *La philosophie et les expériences naturelles* (The Hague: Nijhoff, 1961), pp. 41–58, 71–106; SZ 62; Joseph J. Kockelmans, *Phenomenology and Physical Science* (Pittsburgh: Duquesne Univ. Press, 1966), pp. 49–69.

11. With regard to the following, see SZ 134–40.

"insight" are different elements that must be carefully distinguished.

First, in his mood man is aware of his own being, of the fact that he is. Without wanting to be, and without freely having chosen to be, man *is*. His being appears to him as a being "thrown"; he appears to himself to be thrown among things. In mood man becomes conscious not only of the fact that he *is* but also of the fact that he *has to be*, that his being has to be realized by himself as a task.

Second, the fact that man is in this or that mood depends on the modalities of the involvement which he always has with things in the world. Mood is an implicit, continuous "judgment" regarding man's self-realization. Hence man can be disclosed to himself in a primordial way more through mood than through theoretical reflection. However, if man ek-sists, is as Being-in-the-world, then mood must also disclose to him not only his own being as being "thrown" but also the being of other men and things.

It was mentioned previously that man, in his everyday concern, encounters intramundane things as things emerging from the horizon of the world taken as a referential totality. But this is possible only if the world has been disclosed as such beforehand. Precisely because the world is given to man beforehand, it is possible for him to encounter intramundane things as such. This prior disclosedness of the world is constituted by one's mood; the fact that man is openness in the direction of the other in the world is given to man in the most original way, through that fundamental and primordial feeling of his "being there."

Not only does man possess an existential possibility of being always "in a mood"; his mode of Being is determined equiprimordially by his "understanding." [12] This "understanding" is to be conceived of not as a concrete mode of knowing but precisely as that which makes all concrete modes of knowing possible. On the level of the "original praxis" this primordial understanding always is already present in mood, and all understanding in its turn is connected with mood.

This original understanding has reference not so much to this or that concrete thing or situation as to the mode of Being

12. SZ 142–60.

characteristic of man as Being-in-the-world. In original under-standing the mode of Being characteristic of man manifests itself as a "being able to." However, man is not something present-at-hand that possesses its being able to by way of an extra; he him-self is primarily a being able to be. This being able to be, which is essential for man, has reference to the various ways of his being concerned for others and for things and of his concern with the world. But, in all this, man always realizes in one way or another his being able to be in regard to himself and for the sake of him-self.

Original understanding thus always pertains to man's Being-in-the-world as a whole. That is why man's moodful understand-ing brings to light not only man himself as being able to be but also the world as a referential totality. By revealing the world to man, his primordial understanding also gives him the possibility of encountering intramundane things in their own possibilities. That which originally was ready-to-hand (zuhanden) is now ex-plicitly discovered in its "serviceability," its usability, and so on.

Accordingly, primordial understanding always moves in a range of possibilities; it continuously endeavors to discover pos-sibilities, because it possesses in itself the existential structure of a "project." In his primordial understanding man projects him-self onto his ultimate "for the sake of which"; but this self-projec-tion necessarily implies at the same time—and equally originally —a world-projection. In his original understanding man thus opens and frees himself in the direction of his own Being but, at the same time, also in the direction of the world. For this reason primordial understanding implies essentially a certain view—a "sighting" of things, of fellow men, of the world as a whole, and evidently also of man's own mode of Being. To the extent that man's view is concerned with "equipment," fellow men, himself, or the world as a whole, this "sight" appears in a different mo-dality.

Thus primordial understanding, which is always inseparably connected with mood, always has the character of an interpreta-tive conception in which man discloses himself as being able to be in the different modalities that are possible for him. This in-terpretative conception, which is equiprimordially oriented to the other, is as such not yet explicitly articulated in understanding. However, it can develop in that direction by means of explana-tion (Auslegung). In and through explanation understanding appropriates comprehendingly that which is already understood by it. In explanation understanding does not become something different; it becomes itself. Man does not acquire further information about what is already understood. Explanation is, rather, the development of the possibilities that were projected in understanding.

Perhaps what is meant here can best be explained by taking one's starting point in man's everyday concernful dealing with things. In each concrete form that can be adopted by the "original praxis," man's concernful dealing with intramundane things implies an original understanding of those things and of man himself as Being-in-the-world, an understanding which at first is not articulated. However, this form of understanding can be further explained so that the ready-to-hand comes explicitly into that sight which understands it. In this case the "circumspection" characteristic of man's concernful dealing with things discovers intramundane things by unraveling and thereby explaining them. In the final analysis all preparing, arranging, repairing, and improving are enacted in such a way that what was ready-to-hand circumspectively in its serviceability, that is, in its "in order to," now is taken apart, unraveled, and thus ex-plained. That which has been taken apart in this way, in regard to its in order to, thereby receives the structure of "something as something." To the circumspective question as to what this particular ready-to-hand thing may be, the circumspectively explanatory answer is that it serves such and such a purpose. By explicitly pointing to what a thing is for, we do not simply designate that thing; what is designated is understood as that *as* which we are to take that particular thing. The *as* constitutes the structure of the explicitness of each thing that is understood. It is the constitutive element of what we call explanation. If in dealing with what is environmentally ready-to-hand we explain it circumspectively, we "see" it, for instance, as a hammer, a table, a door, a car, a bridge. However, what is thus explained need not necessarily be taken apart in an explicit enunciation (*Aussage*). Any mere prepredicative using and thus "seeing" of what is ready-to-hand is in itself already something that understands and explains. The articulation of what is understood in the explaining and bringing close of each intramundane thing—with the help of the guiding clue "something *as* something"—is there before any explicit statement is made about it. Thus the *as* does not emerge for the first time in the explicit statement but only gets expressed and enunciated. This is possible only because that which is enunciated was as such already at man's disposal.

If we never perceive intramundane things which are ready-to-hand without already understanding and explaining them, and if all perception lets us circumspectively encounter something *as* something, does this not mean that at first something purely present-at-hand is experienced and is later interpreted as a door, a house, and so on? Evidently this is not the case. Man's explanation does not throw a meaning over some "naked" thing that is present-at-hand, nor does it place a value on it. The intramundane thing that is encountered as such in the original understanding, which is characteristic of man's concernful dealing with things, already possesses a reference that is implicitly contained in man's co-understanding of the world and thus can be articulated by explanation. In our original understanding what is ready-to-hand is always already understood from a totality of references which we call "world"; but this relationship between what is ready-to-hand and the world need not be grasped explicitly in a thematic explanation, although such an explanation is evidently, at least in principle, always possible. If the thematic explanation occurs, it is always grounded in the original understanding. In this sense one can say that our "having" intramundane things—as well as any sighting of them and the conception of them to be found in the explanation—is founded on an earlier having, on an earlier sighting, and in pre-conception, all of which are characteristic of our original understanding.

At any rate, in the pro-ject (*Ent-wurf*) characteristic of original understanding, a thing is disclosed in its possibility. The character of this possibility corresponds in each case with the mode of Being of the thing which is understood. Intramundane things are necessarily projected upon the world—that is, upon a whole context of meaning, a totality of references with which man's concern as Being-in-the-world has been tied in advance. When an intramundane thing and the mode of Being characteristic of man is discovered and comes to be understood, we say that it has meaning. But what is understood is, strictly speaking, not the meaning but the thing itself. Meaning is that in which the intelligibility of something maintains itself. Thus, meaning is that which can be articulated in the disclosure of understanding. The concept of meaning contains the formal framework of what necessarily belongs to that which can be articulated by our understanding. Meaning is a project's "upon-which," which can be structured by our original understanding and from which each thing *as* this or that becomes understandable. Meaning is therefore the intentional correlate of the disclosedness which necessarily belongs to our original understanding. Thus only the mode of Being characteristic of man "has" meaning insofar as the disclosedness of Being-in-the-world can be "filled" by the things which are discoverable in that disclosedness. There can be a question of meaning only within the dialogue between man and things in the world. Because meaning is the disclosure of the openness characteristic of man, his original understanding always has reference to his Being-in-the-world as a whole; in other words, in each understanding of the world man's ek-sistence is co-understood and vice versa.

All explanation is rooted in the original understanding of our "primordial praxis." That which is articulated in this explanation and thus was already predelineated in the original understanding as something articulable is what we call "meaning." Insofar as enunciation as a derivative mode of explanation is also grounded in our primordial understanding, it too has meaning; but this meaning cannot be defined as that which is found "in" the enunciation along with the enunciating act.

An explicit analysis of an enunciating act can take different directions. One of the possibilities consists in showing how in an enunciating act the structure of the *as*, which is constitutive for understanding and explanation, is modified; in so doing one is able to bring both understanding and explanation into a new light. If the enunciating act is considered from this perspective, it soon becomes clear that one must attribute three meanings to the enunciating act; these are interconnected and originate from the phenomenon which is thus designated.

In the first place *e-nunciating* means "pointing out," "showing." In this we adhere to the original meaning of *logos* as *apophansis*, that is, as letting things be seen from themselves. In the enunciating statement "This hammer is too heavy," that which is discovered is not a meaning but a thing manifesting itself as ready-to-hand. Even if the thing is not close enough to be grasped or seen, man's pointing out refers to the thing itself and not to a representation of it. What is pointed out is thus neither a "merely" represented thing nor a psychic state of the one who does the enunciating.

Enunciating also means "attributing." In each statement or enunciation a "predicate" is attributed to a "subject"; the subject is determined by the predicate. However, that which is enunciated is not the predicate but the thing itself—in the example given, the hammer. That which determines is found in the "too heavy." That which is shown in the enunciation taken in this second signification of enunciation (that which is determined, the thing, the hammer) has undergone a narrowing of content as compared with what is shown in the enunciation taken in the first sense of the term (the too heavy hammer). That is why each attribution as such necessarily presupposes a pointing out, so that the second signification of enunciation has its foundation in the first. Therefore, the elements of the attributing articulation, namely, subject and predicate, arise only within this pointing out. The determination does not, in the first place, consist in a discovering, but as a mode of the pointing out it restricts our seeing to what manifests itself there; by this explicit restriction of our view, that which was already manifest (the hammer) may be made manifest explicitly in its being determined. The determination must, in the first instance, take a step backward when confronted with that which is already manifest (the too heavy hammer) in order to be able to let that which was already manifest be seen in its further determinable determinateness. Thus, the positing of subject and predicate, as well as the attribution, are thoroughly "apophantic" in the strict sense of the term.

Finally, *enunciating* means "communicating." As such it is related directly to enunciation taken in the first and second significations. It means letting someone see with us what we have pointed out, by determining it. Letting someone see with us means sharing with the other that thing which has been pointed out in its determinateness. In so doing we share the intelligibility of the mode of Being characteristic of such a thing by keeping it in that world in which what has been pointed out can be encountered. Therefore, any being expressed necessarily belongs as a correlate to enunciation as communication; for, as something communicated, that which has been shown in the enunciation is something that others who make the enunciation can share, even though the thing which has been pointed out and which has been determined is not close enough for them to grasp or see. Once a thing is expressed, it can be passed on in a further re-telling; but in that case what has been shown may become veiled again, although even then one still has the thing itself in view and does not affirm some "universally valid meaning" which has been passed around.

Summarizing, we may conclude that a statement or "enunciation" is a determining and communicating pointing out. Obviously one may object to this view on the ground that enunciation is not very likely to be a derivative mode of explanation. Furthermore, it is not clear just what in the explanation must change for explanation to become enunciation. In order to cope with these difficulties it is necessary to make the following observations.

That enunciation is a derivative mode of explanation is evident from the fact that explanation does not come about originally in a theoretical, predicative judgment but is already present in our concernful dealing with things in the "primordial praxis." The only problem remaining then is to identify the modification through which enunciation originates from our concernful explanation. In our "primordial praxis" an intended thing—a hammer, for instance—is at first ready-to-hand as a tool. If this thing becomes the ob-ject of enunciation in the sense indicated above, then along with the enunciation a modification of the character of the intentional orientation must first be enacted. The ready-to-hand with which we were originally concerned in our "practical" achievements changes now into something about which we are going to enunciate something. The necessary condition for this is that we orient ourselves intentionally in what is ready-to-hand toward a certain presence-at-hand. Through this new way of looking at, precisely that which at first was ready-to-hand becomes concealed as ready-to-hand. Within the discovering of a thing's presence-at-hand, which at the same time is a concealing of its readiness-to-hand, the thing which is encountered as present-at-hand becomes determined as present-at-hand in such and such a way. Only at this moment are we given any access to "properties" or the like, which evidently are drawn from that which is present-at-hand as such. In other words the *as* structure, which we have already met in the explanation, undergoes a typical modification in enunciation. The *as,* whose function was to appropriate what was understood, no longer refers to the totality of references within which the "primordial praxis" comes about. As far as its possibilities for further articulation are concerned, the *as* is now cut off from the referential totality that constitutes my world and is pushed back into the homogeneous domain of what is merely present-at-hand. Therefore the *as* characteristic of the enunciation has as its function only the determining letting be seen of what is present-at-hand. This leveling of the primordial *as* of our circumspective explanation to the *as* in which something is determined in its presence-at-hand is the specifying characteristic of enunciation. It is only in this way that the possibility of a pointing out which merely looks at comes about.

It is to be noted that between our concernful understanding of what is ready-to-hand (in which the explanation, as it were, is still completely implicit) and the extreme opposite, namely, the purely theoretical enunciation of what is merely present-at-hand (in which the explanation is clearly articulated) there are many intermediate forms; a careful analysis of these is of great importance for the philosophy of language. Although we will not deal with these forms at this time, there is one thing upon which we must focus attention because of its immediate pertinence to the main subject of this study.

It was stated several times in the preceding discussion that mood and original understanding are the fundamental existentials of that mode of Being which is characteristic of man as Being-in-the-world. It was also said that original understanding as such already contains the possibility of the explanation, that is, the explicit articulating appropriation of what is understood. What is called enunciation in the strict sense of the term appeared in the foregoing analyses as a derivative mode of explanation. Only where we dealt with the third meaning of *enunciation*, namely, the communication or expression, did we come across speech and language. Language was mentioned only there because it, too, via mood and original understanding, is ultimately rooted in the essential openness characteristic of the proper mode of Being of man as Being-in-the-world. In those analyses, however, we did not deal explicitly with the discursively articulating *logos* (*Rede*), which is the immediate, ontologico-existential fundament of language.

Discursive and articulating *logos*, viewed existentially, is as original as mood and original understanding.[13] Its essential function is to articulate discursively the intelligibility of something. Only when the intelligibility is explicitly articulated can the appropriating explanation come about, so that discursive *logos*, in the final analysis, constitutes the fundament of explanation and enunciation. What can be articulated in explanation is meaning. It appears then that, properly speaking, one ought to say that meaning is what can be articulated in and through *logos*. Furthermore, what becomes articulated in discursive articulation as such can be called the total meaning, which can be disclosed as a whole in various particular significations. Thus these significations, taken as articulations of the total meaning, always carry meaning.

However, if *logos* as the discursive articulation of the intelligibility of all that is implicitly contained in man's concernful dealing with things in the world is a primordial existential of disclosedness, which itself is primarily constituted by Being-in-the-world, then *logos*, too, must essentially have a specifically mundane mode of Being. This mode of Being consists in the fact that the totality of meaning of what is intelligible can be put into words in and through *logos*. It is in *logos* that words can be attributed to significations; thus it becomes immediately clear that the view according to which significations are to be attributed to "word-things" must be unacceptable.

The "enunciatedness" of *logos* is language. Taken as that in which language has its mundane Being, the totality of the words and of the other language structures that are systematically built up from them is, once it is constituted, something which one encounters as an intramundane reality, ready-to-hand for anyone who wants to speak. It is true that language can be conceived of also as the totality of all word-things that are present-at-hand, those which can be brought together in a dictionary and whose usage can be described in grammar and syntax. Existentially seen, however, language is the "enunciatedness" of the *logos*, because that being whose disclosedness is articulated by *logos* has the mode of Being of a Being-in-the-world that is entirely committed to the world.

Discursive *logos* is therefore the "signifying" articulation of

13. SZ 160–66.

the intelligibility of man's Being-in-the-world and of everything that is essentially contained in it. Being-in-the-world is essentially Being-with others. Through discursive *logos* this Being-with others takes the form of inviting, warning, assenting, refusing, pronouncing, consulting, promising, speaking in a person's behalf, and so on. However, speaking is always the enunciation in regard to each other of the discursive *logos* with respect to something. This *logos* does not necessarily have to refer to a determining assertion; a command or a wish can be the theme of *logos*, also. Whatever its concrete form may be, the *logos* always has an intentional structure because it co-constitutes the disclosedness of man's Being-in-the-world. In all forms of speaking there is something said as such, and this "something said" is what language communicates.

It must be repeated here that in this context the phenomenon of communication is to be taken in a very broad sense. Communication, insofar as it is explicitly enunciated—giving information, for example—is merely a special case of communication taken in the original meaning of the term. In the communication which is enunciated, our understanding of Being-in-the-world with others becomes articulated. Communication is therefore never anything like a conveying of experiences, opinions, or wishes from the interior of our subjectivity to the interior of another's. Our Being-with others is already essentially manifest in mood and understanding. In discursive *logos* our Being-with others only becomes explicitly articulated. In our discourse it becomes explicitly shared in an appropriate way.

In discursive *logos* the intelligibility of our Being-in-the-world, which is always connected with a certain mood, becomes articulated in significations. The constitutive elements of this articulation are: what our speaking is about, what receives its shape and form through it, communication, and making known to others. However, these are not properties empirically found in each language; they are, rather, the essential characteristics of the *logos* rooted in original understanding and primordial mood and making anything precisely like language possible. It is more than likely that in many factical linguistic forms some of these elements remain implicit and unnoticed. The fact that not all of them always receive verbal expression is merely an indication that in concrete cases we always deal with one of many possibilities.

Attempts to bring the essence of language to light have been limited for the most part to one or some of these elements. This is why language is often characterized as "expression," "symbolic form," "communication," "assertion," or "the making known of experiences." Clearly, even if these various characterizations were to be added together, nothing would be achieved in the way of a comprehensive conception of language. Such a conception can be reached only by means of an accurate analysis of the mode of Being characteristic of man as Being-in-the-world.

Thus far we have not shed much additional light on the subject of language. In approaching the subject, one question arises above all others: Precisely what mode of Being is characteristic of language? Is language only an intramundane tool which is ready-to-hand? Does it have a mode of Being analogous to the one characteristic of man, or does it have a mode of Being of its own? Furthermore, the relationship between language and man as source of meaning must be explained in a more precise and comprehensive way than it was in the foregoing analyses. Since a philosophical reflection on language would fall short of making the essential point if these questions were to remain unanswered, we must at least briefly deal with the fundamental problem touched upon in these questions. But here, too, we must limit ourselves to some general remarks.

Language and Ek-sistence

Man speaks. In so doing he usually remains within the realm of a language which is already constituted. This fact can be considered from different points of view. As was done in the foregoing analysis, one can first ask precisely what is to be understood by man's speech, how speech is connected with all other modes in which man is able to bring meaning to light, and how in speech a language becomes constituted. However, one can also focus attention on how man always speaks from a language which is already constituted and which he merely employs. On this level the relationship between man and language receives a new dimension.

In his speech man usually takes up a language that is already constituted. In his speech he listens to what that language "has to say." Does this mean that language itself speaks? In order to be able to answer this question, one must realize that the important issue for the philosophy of language is not so much that people speak but that something is said. Saying something and speaking are not identical. It is possible for one to speak much and say nothing. It is also possible to say much by keeping silent. Etymologically it seems that to say means to point out, to show, to let something appear, to let something be seen or heard. From this viewpoint, to say something to someone means to show one another what one wants to talk about, that is, to make that which is talked about appear of itself. Thus the very essence of language is to be sought not so much in speaking as in a primordial "saying" taken as "showing" and "making appear" (*Sage-Zeige*).

A first indication of the exactness of this supposition is found in the fact that speaking is at the same time also hearing and listening. Not only are speaking and listening found together in every dialogue between human beings, but taken "in themselves" they are identical—that is, speaking is a listening and vice versa. Speaking is initially a listening to the language "which one speaks." In this case speaking is not listening at the same time; listening to the language even precedes each speaking. We do not speak a language as much as we speak *from* a language. We are able to do this only because we have first listened to that language before we have started to speak that way. What we hear and listen to in this case is the "saying" of a language.[14]

Although one can say that a language cannot speak unless man has first made it sound by means of his speech organs, it is also true that language "speaks." It "speaks" insofar as it says something to us, points something out to us, shows us something. To be sure, its "speaking" originates in a saying that was once first spoken but until now has remained undiscussed, a saying in which the fundamental dif-ference, which seems to constitute the very marrow of the essence of language, has been enacted. Yet language itself "speaks" too, inasmuch as it points out and shows and thereby, penetrating all domains of what is present, lets what

---

14. *US* 145, 179–81, 198–202. What follows here is not intended to be a commentary on Heidegger's *On the Way to Language*, nor is it meant to serve as a brief summary of its content. I am fully aware that many important aspects of Heidegger's philosophy of language are not touched on in this paper and that some issues discussed here have been interpreted differently.

is already present manifest or hide itself. We must listen to a language in such a way that we let its saying "speak itself out" to us. This fundamental willingness to let a language speak itself out to us precedes all hearing and listening. In our own speaking, which essentially implies our listening to a language, we "say after" what we heard before. We let the "soundless voice" of language come over us and evoke the sound that is "locked up in us."

Our own speaking, which essentially implies our listening to a language, can allow language as "saying" (taken as pointing out) to speak itself out to us only insofar as our own Being was already open to such "saying." We hear the "speaking" of a language only to the extent that we belong within the domain which it discloses for us in "speaking." Only to those who "belong" to a language does the language grant the possibility of listening to it and, therefore, the possibility of speaking. This granting, which goes on continuously in each concrete act of man's speaking, is what lets us attain the possibility of speaking. In the granting of primordial saying the essence of language is to be found.[15]

As we have seen, primordial saying, properly speaking, means to point out, to show, to let appear, to offer, to hand over, to make free in both a revealing and a concealing way. That which is shown and handed down by language's saying is, in the final analysis, the world. The mode of being characteristic of this saying is a freeing of the world by means of a revelation and, at the same time, a concealing.[16]

How does this come about? Saying means showing. In everything which addresses itself to us, which concerns us as what is said or discussed, which "speaks itself out" to us, which still waits for us as something that is not yet discussed—in all of this, and also in our own active speaking, the pointing out, or showing, that lets what is present appear while it conceals what is absent holds sway. Primordial saying is thus in no way a linguistic expression of something manifested earlier that is now trotted out; each appearing and disappearing rests precisely on primordial saying as a pointing out. Saying frees what is present in the direction of being permanently present, just as it fetters what is absent in its being permanently absent. Saying thus "joints" (*fügen*) the openness of the "clearing" (*Lichtung*) for which all

15. *US* 11–15, 145–49, 199–202, 252–55.
16. *US* 20–22, 198–202. Cf. *HB* 69–80 (278–84).

manifestation looks and from which all concealing flees. Saying is the gathering together (*logos*) of a manifold pointing, "jointing" together any appearing and letting what was manifested remain by itself.[17]

Saying thus calls and brings what is called closer. However, this bringing closer does not bring what is called nearer in the sense of putting it down in the domain of the immediate. Although this calling calls hither what is called, what is called remains at a distance where it remains as absent. Saying therefore calls nearer what is called, but it does not withdraw it from the distance where it was and remains. Saying calls something, as it were, back and forth, calling it to become present and nevertheless summoning it to remain absent at the same time. What is called to the fore by this saying is not present in space as tables and chairs are present. Even the place which is co-summoned in this calling, and to which, therefore, what is summoned is called, has a mode of being present which includes its remaining absent. In the final analysis, this place is the world. It is to a world that saying calls the things which are summoned; it invites them as things to "concern" man. The summoned things gather a world around themselves. Saying summons things and lets them be what they are; but the thing is what it is only as a thing that "bears," so to speak, a world in which it remains as what it is, a world in which it can appear as meaningful. In the primordial saying of many specialized languages, the summoned things often cause only a limited domain of things to remain as world; and sometimes this world is solely an ideal world.

Just as saying summons things, so does it also summon a world. It entrusts a world to things and at the same time preserves things in the "luster of a world." This world grants things their proper modes of being, whereas things "bear" their own world. The saying of language therefore speaks; it makes things come to a world and a world to things. Because world and things can never be independent of one another, these two ways of "making something come" cannot be separated. They penetrate each other, and in so doing they cross, as it were, a middle point in which they are one. However, world and thing do not melt into a unity at this middle point; even there they remain distinct in their closeness. In an original dif-ference the saying of a language, in a

17. *US* 256–58.

manner of speaking, keeps apart from itself a middle point to which and through which world and thing are one toward each other. This saying makes the things be things and the world be world and thus carries them toward each other. Thus saying does not make the things and then the world be present in order to appropriate one to the other in a later phase by connecting them at the middle point. The dif-ference of saying, as the middle point, mediates world and things in their own and proper modes of Being and thus carries out their belonging together. Saying grants to world and things the "dimension" within which, in their closeness, they can be themselves in regard to each other. That which saying first summons is thus the difference between world and things in their essential correlatedness.[18]

In this way primordial saying makes world and things be what they are. It makes what is present and what is absent attain their characteristic modes of being from which they can manifest themselves and abide according to their own characters. It makes world and things achieve what is proper to them by ap-propriation. What this ap-propriation, which comes about through the saying of language, is cannot be explained by comparing it with the activity of a cause; neither can it be described as a certain occurrence. In the manifestation of saying it can be experienced only as that which grants. There is nothing to which this ap-propriation could be reduced or from which it could be explained. The ap-propriation is not the result of something else, but a most original granting that makes anything present a "there is. . . ." The only thing that can be said of this ap-propriation is that it appropriates: it lets things be what they really are; it makes the world come to the fore in its proper character and grants to man an abode in his own proper mode of Being so that he can manifest himself as speaking. Thus the only thing that man can do in speaking is to listen to the primordial ap-propriation which comes about in the saying of language and to try to respond to it in his own speech.[19]

In looking over what we have said about language, we must conclude that our results are still disappointing. Whether or not we have really traced the essence of language in this way and whether or not, in our "mythical" terminology, we have genuinely succeeded in expressing what we really intended to say, it is un-

18. *US* 20–28.
19. *US* 258–60. Cf. *ID* 28–32.

deniable that in the foregoing consideration many essential problems were not even touched on. Solutions for other problems were suggested which, on closer examination, seem to be unacceptable. Is it really possible to separate the saying of language from man's speaking? On the other hand, is it really necessary to build a bridge from the original saying of language to our own speech? One could say in regard to the second question that the original saying is much more like "the stream of silence" which bridges its own banks, that is to say, the original saying and our repetitive speaking. What would be the meaning of these additional considerations? Is it not true that in this view language is blown up to a fantastic monstrosity which, as long as we adhere to the "cold" facts, we never experience as such? There can be no doubt that all saying remains necessarily connected with man's speaking. No language says anything if man does not speak it. However, the question is of the precise nature of the link between language and speech. Language certainly needs man's speech, and yet it is not merely the product and result of man's speaking. In what does the very essence of language genuinely consist? In examining this further, we shall try to avoid all "mythical" expressions as far as possible. In order to have a good starting point for these considerations, we must first return to a few things touched on earlier.[20]

We have seen that man experiences himself immediately as Being-in-the-world. It is in the original dialogue between man and world that meaning originates, the meaning of things as well as the meaning of man's own Being. This meaning comes to light first in our concernful dealing with things and our fellow men. All merely theoretical interpretation is secondary in regard to this. At any rate, man's original understanding as well as all derivative modes thereof, in which man appropriates to himself the being of things and explicitly relates himself to his own proper mode of Being, are possible only on the basis of the fact that man as ek-sistent is essentially open in regard to all that manifests itself to him.

In view of the above, the understanding of Being as total meaningfulness is essential to man. In this understanding of Being, which is first found in man's "primordial praxis," there is given an understanding of things which has the character of a

20. *US* 255–56.

being able to deal with them, as well as an understanding of man through the many possible projects with regard to things in the world. Although we have not yet explicitly mentioned it, it becomes clear on closer consideration that this understanding of Being almost always takes place within a relative totality of meaning which always appears to be already there and which, in the culture to which we belong, comes to us from the past as well as the present. This totality of meaning comes to meet us to a great extent in the language we speak, since our familiarity with our culture comes about largely through listening and reading. Also, and especially in this language, our world appears to us as the already present totality of all possible references, within which each concrete thing can appear as this or that. Therefore, man and thing can be "connected" meaningfully only within the world that addresses itself to us in and through language. Only on this basis can man name things and express them. Within the horizon of a certain culture, which mainly in and through its language makes the world emerge from hiddenness and places it in "unconcealedness," man and things as well as man and fellow men are concretely related. Language as the "clearing" and "illuminating open space" grants man (and, through him, also things) the possibility of truth (*a-lētheia*). Therefore, language, in a certain sense at least, brings about the original interwovenness of man and things in the world, because this interwovenness can come about only if and as long as those who are interwoven are really "there" and come to light with regard to one another.

It is therefore necessary to accept the fact that in their mutual interwovenness man and thing are subject to a certain be-falling which itself contains meaning even though this "event" neither occurs nor manifests itself except from the interwovenness of man and world in all its concrete modalities. It is this ap-propriating event in which a certain culture be-falls man through language and which first gives man the possibility of founding meaning. In that sense, and in that sense only, is it that language manifests itself as that which comes first. It manifests, or "shows," itself in that it makes things "light up," and it can do this only by simultaneously calling man to the total meaningfulness. Ultimately Being itself shows itself in language. Thus, through language man is put into the service of Being, the total meaningfulness which shows itself in language, *and* man becomes interwoven with things within a world in a unique way.

Therefore, man as one who comprehends Being is separated from all other beings by an unbridgeable gap.[21]

Man "receives" what manifests itself in language from Being. What he receives in this way he can and must speak forth again. Thus meaning "comes to light" again. Although each man ultimately wants to enclose "all that is" in one way or another in his speech, all of man's speech is always permeated with a certain "naught." Unexpected possibilities of comprehending the meaning of things are always excluded once a determinate interpretation of their meaning is chosen, but in such a case unexpected possibilities still remain enclosed in the "matrix of hiddenness." Thus, a language taken up by one man is never completely identical to the same language taken up by other men, each of whom will do things in his own way. There is, therefore, much that cannot be understood from the "language of the one" but seems to announce itself in the "language of the other." It is sometimes said with some exaggeration that each man speaks his own language which others cannot understand.

What we have tried to indicate here is much more obvious in comparing languages of different cultures. For some primitive people certain trees were sacred objects. When they saw such a tree, it appeared to them as a dwelling place of a god. In our culture, however, a tree can no longer announce itself as that upon which our over-all well-being depends. Yet for the primitive man the god was as real as the tree he saw. The god as "thing" was woven into the language which at that time constituted "all that is" and made the god as "thing" come to light. The language, therefore, made up the "truth" for that time, and people had to remain in such a realm of speech if they wanted to be understood by others. One arrives at analogous results by comparing Western languages with the Indian, Japanese, or Chinese languages.[22]

A certain "naught" is also characteristic of the language of each cultural period. This manifests itself not only in what a language does not show but also in its mistakes, one-sided views, and errors. It is the task of man to make the truth come to light from this "domain of error." From this point of view, to care for truth means that man must watch Being itself as it shows itself in a certain language.

There is an original interwovenness of man and things in the

21. *HH* 10, 34.
22. *US* 85–155, 219.

world which necessarily belongs to a definite language of a particular cultural period and from which man ultimately derives all his possibilities of questioning and of founding meaning. If man brings meaning to light in an *authentic* way, then he takes "something" out of the night of hiddenness and posits it within a horizon of intelligibility which is already there and which is enclosed in the language spoken to him in a certain culture. In his authentic speech, time and again man occasions a "clearing" within the unconcealedness which language offers him and within which things as "re-created" can appear in the openness of their unconcealedness. Although man is always committed to a determinate language, his ek-sistence is thereby not necessarily conditioned. What a language speaks to man is always a starting point, but that onto which ek-sistence projects itself and the world is not yet determined. The new meaning that man can always force to "light up" therefore always originates, as it were, in a "realm of emptiness." On the other hand, not everything is possible. Even our authentic speech remains committed in one way or another to that language, one of the "houses of Being," in which man dwells and whose shepherd only he is.

However, here again one must realize that meaning does not originate primordially through words, in the strict sense of the term. Rather, it is already found in each form of human behavior, in gesture, mime, work, art, game—in man's "praxis." But in all these cases man's ek-sistence, which brings meaning to light, finds itself already in a relative totality of meaning that his culture speaks out to him in its language, as in the ebb and flow of the sea; in this "sea" ek-sistence is like a wave that crests and falls time and again in order to throw itself forward, even beyond the boundaries set to it by its language.[23] In so doing ek-sistence aims at Being itself, which manifests itself here as the horizon of all possible horizons of meaning.

From these considerations it becomes clear that different forms of "saying" must be distinguished. First there is the saying of each concrete man. Then there is the saying of a culturally and historically determined language which addresses itself to man. However, this language was "formed" by man in the very remote past, especially by great thinkers and poets. Thus, in and through a language which was once originally spoken by men, total mean-

23. Merleau-Ponty, *Phénoménologie de la perception*, 229–30.

ingfulness "speaks itself out" to modern men and in turn speaks to the world and things, in this way giving us "sight" of ourselves and of our world. The only thing we can do is to try to correspond to the saying of language as "pointing." This correspondence undoubtedly is first a listening to, but it surely is not a passive being delivered to. The saying of each concrete language is limited. Its "speech" can even degenerate. Then it is man's task to break through these limits and to correct any aberration by means of authentic speech. Philosophy has a very important task here. By reflecting on the essence of language the philosopher is able, taking his starting point in the concrete saying of his own language, to discover what that total meaningfulness is which language reveals and conceals at the same time, to find out what world and things genuinely are as they are "addressed" to him in and through the relative total meaningfulness characteristic of his own language. What language ought to bring to light contains many dimensions and regions. In regard to them, and especially in regard to the hierarchy among them, each language and each speaking man has many possibilities, positive as well as negative. It is man's task, within the language which is spoken to him, to gather together and to keep together in the proper way all these dimensions and regions. Only in this way can man "safeguard" his language, pursue unrestricted total meaningfulness, and, in so doing, reach his destination as man.[24]

24. *HB* 53, 79, 112–16 (270–71, 283, 298–300); *US* 19–32, 108–18, 194–96, 206–14; *HH* 10.

2 / Heidegger's Conception of Language in *Being and Time*

Jan Aler

REFLECTIONS ON LANGUAGE occupy an important place in twentieth-century philosophy due to the situation in which philosophy finds itself today. This is particularly true for Heidegger's work. Not only do Heidegger's reflections on language stand out, but also his use of language is especially remarkable. Two aspects of his use of language must be considered: his mode of expression and the manner in which he presents his argumentation using linguistic (or also literary) data.

It is worthwhile to analyze this complex issue in detail. Many of Heidegger's admirers, as well as some of his adversaries, fascinated by the Heidegger publications that have appeared since 1936 (written when Heidegger was almost fifty years old) are inclined to deal with *Being and Time* as if the work were only of minor importance. Such neglect is unjustifiable and, furthermore, constitutes a serious obstacle if one wishes to concentrate fruitfully on the later publications. There is no doubt that the idiomatic peculiarities as well as the conception of language found in *Being and Time* offer ample material for reflection. This essay will therefore be limited to an analysis of Heidegger's work from this perspective. It will deal with Heidegger's style, his attitude toward the history of language and toward literature, and his conception of language. It will become apparent how the relationship between language and understanding in Heidegger's conception of language becomes more complicated because of the role played by *logos* (*Rede*). By taking these considerations as a unity and reflecting on them from the viewpoint of Heidegger's analy-

[33]

sis of temporality, it will be possible to get a sharper picture of their genuine meaning.

HEIDEGGER'S STYLE

WHEN ONE IS FIRST CONFRONTED with Heidegger's analysis of man's Being, the linguistic peculiarities used in the explanations are among the most conspicuous aspects of the work. Not only are they found in some places in the book, but they pervade the work as a whole. However, the peculiarity of his mode of expression is most striking in one determinate sector of his language usage: in his effort to grasp the Being of man Heidegger's philosophical terminology particularly attracts our attention. A peculiar tension in the choice of words strikes the reader immediately. The formal connection of concepts in particular is indicated through the use of a Latin, or at least a Latinized, technical terminology; this underlines the strictly theoretical character of the exposition, which is intended to be a contribution to ontology. For example, Heidegger frequently uses common terms, such as *structure, mode, character,* and *constitutive,* and also words now more or less obsolete, such as *derivative, explicate, privatio,* and *deficient,* to structure his argument.

These technical expressions constitute the skeleton which Heidegger clothes with the fundamental concepts of man's Being. The latter concepts are indicated, however, if we disregard a very few exceptions, by words that have their origin in ordinary language or at least could have easily occurred there. One would expect such words to appear in lyric poetry or in edifying prose rather than in explanations of an intellectual nature in which the words are used in such a technical manner. Here we think immediately of *Dasein* and then of *Zeug, Bewandtnis, Befindlichkeit, Entwurf, Sorge, Schuld,* and *Gewissen* and finally of *gewärtigen, gegenwärtigen, geschichtlich,* and *Wiederholung,* to mention just a few. The key word *Existenz,* which delineates the context of this anthropological concept formation, still belongs to the formalizing terminology that (not by accident) is strongly reminiscent of Scholastic philosophy. But the titles of the concepts employed within this context—that is, the titles of the "existentials" (which, in contradistinction to the "categories," are immediately related to man's Being)—are remarkably German. Heidegger prefers to use complicated German expressions rather than the very common technical terms such as *functionality* or *instrument* (although, on the other hand, he deals with the formal structure of the concepts in a manner that is certainly not puristic). The term *facticity* seems to be an exception; but this term, via the adjective *factical,* has a closer relationship to the everyday German language than one would be inclined to think at first sight (for *faktisch* is as German as *success* is English).

No doubt this choice of words surprises the reader, especially in contrast with the technical language that naturally accompanies it throughout *Being and Time.* Within the terminology this opposition of abstractness and a closeness to everyday life marks Heidegger's explanation. However, in this contrasting phenomenon a basic unity of purpose manifests itself, saving the whole from ambiguity. This must occupy our attention next.

In the technical idiom previously mentioned, which is bound so strongly to a very old tradition, a certain freedom in regard to that tradition is manifested. The most obvious illustration of this freedom is found in the fact that Heidegger complements the existing vocabulary with a new term whenever it seems desirable for the clarity of his formulation. In addition to the adjective *existentiell* one finds *existential,* which plays an important role as a noun. In opposition to the immediacy of a concrete, individually lived existence, it refers to the concept of man's existence which has been formalized to abstract generality.[1]

Such an addition, although not always completely new, is incorporated into the technical language and used throughout Heidegger's work—for example, *ontic* in addition to *ontologic.* Anyone who reflects on these additions will note that such renewals adhere to the idiom: the differentiation of *existentiell* and *existential* completely corresponds to a tendency in this direction that is common in German. Such an addition is a taking of liberty but not a sign of arbitrariness.

The regauging of an existing term such as *existence* goes even further, and yet this, too, is not arbitrary; it closely follows the word form itself, which indicates a "going out towards." This attention to the suggestion contained in the parts of words ac-

1. Heidegger is applying here a differentiation commonly used in German to a new case; in German one finds *rationell* and *rational, funktionell* and *funktional.*

cordingly becomes manifest in the syllabized spellings *ek-sist* and *ek-stasis,* which recall the Greek origin of these words. Such a splitting up of the unity of the word intensifies the plasticity of the idiom. Although in this case the word form does not become absolutely meaningful, the word nonetheless gains signification; it no longer appears as a completely contingent label for the concept but, to a certain degree, shows a natural relationship with the concept. Once the spelling of a word is made conspicuous, one experiences himself as grasping an original connection between term and concept. Furthermore, the syllabizing process increases the emphatic character of the linguistic usage; an idea is hammered home with the aid of words that have been made more plastic. Such a usage of technical terminology searches for accuracy of language as the instrument of thought and, at the same time, enlivens the use of language by closely connecting itself with the "spirit" of the language.

The possibilities of using such a procedure are naturally still greater in the author's living native language, and Heidegger has grasped every opportunity his language has to offer him in this regard. He lets himself be led by the language and is as frank as he is cautious in so doing. Concretely, one may point to the following:

First, in his terminology Heidegger systematically avoids expressions which are current in these kinds of considerations. At the very beginning of *Being and Time, man* is replaced by *Dasein,* and the book only incidentally employs such expressions as *consciousness, spirit, mind,* and *soul.*

Second, Heidegger often strictly sets apart—and thus distinguishes between—synonyms of the everyday language, specializing them by means of definitions. In this way he distinguishes between *fear (Furcht)* and *anxiety (Angst),* disregarding the less strict, common usage.[2] By *Mitsein* he means something different from *Mitdasein.*

Third, Heidegger expands his well-considered stock of words

---

2. In the common and current distinction between *Furcht* and *Angst,* among other things the more bodily concentrated tendency of *Angst* (oppression, tightness of the chest) plays an important role; in the case of *Furcht,* in addition to the objective relationship underlined by Heidegger, one can establish, on the other hand, a more transcendental nuance due to the indeterminateness of the word. For example, the following differentiation occurs in common language usage: "Man ängstigt sich vor dem Kettenhund, und man hat Furcht vor dem Schicksal."

by specifying and varying them with prefixes and suffixes, which he uses in a very strict sense. In this way he can create new words that are nonetheless wholly German, such as *Zuhandenheit*. In other cases an ancient word comes into play again—for instance, *Befindlichkeit*, which was used in the sixteenth and seventeenth centuries. When the author combines such variants in one determinate context, the radical word is uncommonly accentuated; this is particularly the case when the variants are accumulated. (The type which is found very often is "Das sich überhörende Hinhören.")

Fourth, notwithstanding the fact that in this way it is possible to originate linguistic forms that are as much like current words as possible, in Heidegger's terminology the systematic signification of such derivations sometimes differs completely from the one commonly used. For instance, *zeitigen* is perfectly good German, but in common usage it never signifies "to create time structures." It indicates, rather, that *in* time certain processes bring something about. It pertains specifically to a vegetative development ("to ripen," "to make something become ripe") or to a causal connection analogously associated with such development. It suggests that something is propelled to completion by the stream of time and reaches this completion when the time is ripe. All of this is intratemporal (*innerzeitlich*), whereas, in Heidegger, time (chronological time) is itself a temporalization (*Zeitigung*)—that is to say, one among others. The existential-aprioric structure of temporality temporalizes itself (*zeitigt sich*) in this way (or in another). Heidegger's term penetrates much more deeply into all of this. It makes us become aware of that which constitutes the foundation of the *Zeitigung* in the common sense of the term and nonetheless somehow gives it the emotional value that the current signification possesses.

A striking example of such a creation of language, one that completely adheres to the rules of word derivations (etymology) and yet offers us a new word that can be recognized at first sight, is *Entfernung*. Heidegger uses it in the most literal sense conceivable—namely, as "making distance disappear." Prefix and radical are employed correctly; and yet the result is a word signification that is the exact opposite of what one customarily understands by this word—namely, "distance."

In all of these cases Heidegger enlivens the use of language by means of etymology. But this linguistic virtuoso achieves the same effect by following the opposite road also—by isolating the simple form from its compounds. *Zeug*, for example, in itself, rarely has the signification that it often possesses in compounds —namely, "tool" or "piece of equipment."

The result of these and similar manipulations is a style of writing that is especially accurate, plastic, lively, emphatic, and original. There is seldom a case as paradoxical as that of *Entfernung*. Heidegger openly violates the rules of the language only once; namely, at a most central point in the explanation he departs, in his linguistic renovation, from the grammatical system of the German language by using the form *gewesende*. The gigantic battle over Being really leads here to disruption: *gewesen* is a perfect participle; with this ending, however, it is used as a present participle and is made active.

Heidegger surrounds this bold venture with excuses—which are found elsewhere in connection with a number of more common changes in signification. Such excuses are not as superfluous as the almost coquettishly emphasized introductory apology for the awkwardness of his explanation. For, next to Scheler, Heidegger is certainly the best stylist in modern German philosophy. He handles the most variegated figures of speech with greatest ease. Sometimes one suspects a kind of professional pleasure on his part—for instance, in his preference for the paradoxical connection of opposites in the oxymoron. The deliberate weightiness of many of his formulations can serve not only to clarify thought but to hinder it also. When the latter occurs, a laboriously controlled pathos breaks through, placing the reader under the pressure of its expressive force. The summaries following the careful and detailed descriptions are, in a sense, crushing. When one reads how the "there of the there-is stares man in the face with inexorable mysteriousness," and how man "is shipwrecked on that mystery," then one is prepared to experience as an oppression the concatenation (*Verklammerung*) of the existentials, to which Heidegger has rightly given the greatest possible attention.

Without anticipating Heidegger's reflection on language, it is possible to understand the tendencies mentioned from the perspective of the range of ideas found in *Being and Time*. First of all, in the introduction Heidegger explains his plan to develop a scientific philosophy that would fulfill an old desideratum— namely, the development of the idea of the natural world—and to do this with the assistance of phenomenology. Phenomenology describes phenomena, that is, those things that show themselves the way in which they themselves are. Now the combination of a scientific philosophy and a philosophy that remains close to life is what is so striking in his choice of words. And the philosophy is close to life, also, in the sense that its formulation forcefully influences life itself.

Second, in his analysis of man's Being Heidegger always distinguishes between authentic and inauthentic Being. The latter is characterized by, among other things, a conventionality that never comes to self-activity. This is why Heidegger's close affiliation with the German idiom reserves for itself a language-creating freedom in opposition to the conventional.

LITERATURE AND THE HISTORY OF LANGUAGE

UPON REACHING THIS POINT one is able also to account for Heidegger's position regarding the history of language and for his usage of linguistico-historical data. The inauthentic way of living, which does not appropriate the possibility of self-realization, similarly does not obtain that which, in the handing down of a cultural tradition, could serve that purpose. The possibility of self-realization is not even recognized in its authentic meaning. However, for a living tradition such a testing self-activity is a necessary condition. Heidegger's critical attitude toward the current use of language, which he sees as an eminent factor in the governing conventions, is thus complemented by his selective openness with respect to the history of language, which he sees as a branch of utmost importance of the history of the mind.

Heidegger's bold but by no means arbitrary use of the German language certainly seems to "make" new expressions, but upon closer inspection all of these appear to be not so "new." It is, rather, a renewal of the "old." This "old," the original, is therefore essential to the quest for a natural conception of world, a conception which is directed against the conventional. In the course of the mind's history the becoming aware, insofar as man himself is concerned, has obviously not become more "natural" in the conceptual elaboration of reflection. That natural conception of world has become sedimented in language. It is still there, at one's disposal, but one must uncover it.

Let us suppose that someone wishes to clarify the fact that in the structure of *Being-in-the-world* the existential *Being-in* is not identical with the categorial *Being-in*. In clarifying this one can appeal to data of the history of language—for instance, to the origin of *in* as a prefix and to the etymology of *I am*.[3] These data suggest that originally *Being-in* was understood, or at least was conceived of, as a "Being-with," a "Being familiar with." These data obviously do not "prove" that "indeed" the Being of man is to be characterized by this relationship toward reality. At the most they provide a hint of the original awareness of this relationship within a determinate linguistic community—and this awareness, given the line of development of the mind's history, is important enough in itself. But the ancient usages of words obviously do not possess the value of an argument (because . . . therefore . . .) and are not employed in that way in Heidegger's explanation. Rather, they serve the purpose of orientation; they constitute a valuable indication of the direction to take in uncovering a structure[4] which one sees oneself and to which one wishes to draw the attention of others ("See what I mean there").

It is possible that the attention one pays to a certain state of affairs was aroused by these or similar data from the history of language. To this extent the explanation is circular, and this is by no means kept secret. Heidegger conceives of *alētheia*, for instance, as "unconcealment" and then uses this conception to confirm his explanation of what truth taken as an existential is —namely, "Being discovering." This confirmation plays a part in the framework of the detailed explanation of this existential.[5]

Much earlier, in Heidegger's introductory remarks concerning his method, his use of the Greek word hints in this direction.[6] The initial explanation is not much more than an assertion ("dogmatic interpretation") concerning the Greek idiom.[7] But the later phenomenological descriptions focus attention on relationships which constitute support for these "assertions" concerning the Greek idiom. The explanation of the Greek terms suggested earlier is now clarified insofar as their content is concerned. In this regard the explanation can be objectively justified. But is this suf-

---

3. SZ 54.
4. SZ 53–54.
5. SZ 219–26.
6. SZ 32–34.
7. SZ 220.

ficient for a historical proof? Certainly not; but, on the other hand, it at least justifies searching for a solution in this particular direction—that is, such an explanation is phenomenally justified. If the explanation can be deepened in this context, and if, further-more, by taking a special view of the mind's history it is possible to clarify how it could ever happen that this original intention gradually came to be forgotten, then one's explanation of the Greek idiom is in turn reinforced.[8]

Such a striking case shows not only the illustrative but also the inspirational value of a word's history. However, one can experience at the same time the limitations which, in such an argument, are to be placed on the value of such an inspiration. Yet there is a third important aspect for delineating the limits of the function of linguistico-historical data. This aspect is con-nected with the whole nature of the transcendental-phenomeno-logical argumentation. In each case such an argumentation, along very general lines, develops a structure in its constitutive mo-ments. Then it proceeds from this most general horizon to more detailed explanations within the projected context. In this way the context becomes clarified at the same time. This road from the general via the particular back to the general does not have the character of a deductive foundation; if it did, this particular way of proceeding would be absurd. The phenomenologist does not want to deduce but rather wants to bring to light and make mani-fest.[9]

This relationship between the general and the particular is found in each case to be the relationship between transcendental structure and concrete mode. After the structure is described initially, the connection that was so developed is put to the test with the help of a concrete mode (*Bewährung*). Will one succeed, for instance, in using the structure of the mood of finding one-self in (*Befindlichkeit*) as a guiding clue in analyzing a concrete mood—namely, that of fear? [10] If this is the case, then the analy-sis has confirmed the general scheme: the scheme itself is ten-able. Can the structure of original understanding (*Verstehen*) be applied generally to concrete assertions? [11] If so, one has shown that this construction is not merely a figment of the imagination;

8. SZ 220 ff.
9. SZ 8.
10. SZ 140–42.
11. SZ 148–53.

for it has proved its usefulness in the clarification of our experience. This experience, this concrete mode, is then a variation of the theme of the transcendental structure; and this structure in turn becomes more richly developed in such variations. This principle of verification is found in no other way in the further course of these trains of thought. Concrete verification (*konkrete Bewährung*) [12] is desirable after the proof (*Nachweis*) of an ontological fundament is given. An existential project is in need of an attestation to be given by the analytic of Dasein (*daseinsmässige Bezeugung*).[13] A thesis that can be tested in this way, on concrete facts of life,[14] and can stand the test has become phenomenally accessible. It is in this way, also, that the analysis of the traditional concept of truth develops the relationship between assertion and phenomenon.[15]

The linguistico-historical data can in their own way very well serve a purpose in verifying a general theory on the basis of the phenomena. That is why, the data also appear to confirm the phenomenological results. Confirmation by means of the sources cited means that the results are not arbitrary constructions, that they did not come about forcibly. The analogy between this linguistico-historical argumentation and Heidegger's use of language is, within the perspective of the phenomenological method, self-evident: in both cases Heidegger tries to unveil original meanings, to bring the past to life again, and to free once more the forces that have produced the past. The quest for the natural conception of the world is set in motion by suggestions from language. The results of this search in turn confirm and clarify these suggestions. Because of the value that is necessarily attached to the elementary original, such a confirmation is not without meaning for the tenability of the structure that was developed in this way.

Heidegger announces his use of *alētheia* as follows:

The ultimate business of philosophy is to preserve the force *of the most elemental words* in which Dasein expresses itself, and to keep the common understanding from levelling them off to that unin-

12. SZ 234.
13. SZ 301.
14. SZ 331 ff.
15. SZ 214–19.

telligibility which functions in turn as a source of pseudo-problems.[16]

His warning against "uninhibited word-mysticism" means in this connection that, on the basis of the results of his investigation concerning the content (*Sache*), he sees through the word in its signification. He concludes: "When Dasein so expresses itself, does not a primordial understanding of its own Being thus make itself known?"[17] Heidegger thus recognizes in linguistico-historical data what he has found in the analyses in *Being and Time*. "What is ontologically 'new' in this interpretation is ontically quite old. . . . We are conceptualizing existentially what has already been disclosed in an ontico-existentiell manner."[18] With the help of the insight thus acquired, Heidegger tests the vocabulary and distinguishes the irrelevant data from the relevant in a manner such as we have dealt with here. This explains why he calls *validity,* as it is used in the terminology of logic, an "idolized word."[19] Yet, with the help of the etymological data for this word, it would have been easy enough to accentuate the ancient religious-ethical nuances in its signification. If one were offended by the development of the signification of *Geld* ("money"), he could still turn to the ennobling term *Gilde* ("guild"). But logical validity (as a further characterization of the truth of a judgment) does not fit at all in this conception. The concept does not speak; in this case the history of the word does not come into action. Thus *Being and Time* does not mention the data that are available here but are not actual.[20]

Heidegger also finds fruitful points of departure in the history of ontology. But for that purpose ontology, too, must first be judged in regard to its tenability on the basis of the phenomenal structure. This leads to a revision, the ontological "destruction." The genuine experiences that gave rise to the concepts handed down become then rediscovered: namely, as the existential starting point of the existential-ontological theory.

16. *SZ* 220.
17. *SZ* 222.
18. *SZ* 196.
19. *SZ* 155–56.
20. See note 2 above. In this connection it may be pointed out that, according to German philology, *Angst* might very well be a relatively young derivative from Latin (*angustus, angor*). In judging the method outlined, one must take into consideration this kind of complication also.

But it is not only the vocabulary in general that can mediate this starting point; Heidegger incidentally taps yet another source of preontological becoming aware of man's Being. This source comprises literary documents that can confirm his existentials such as "care," "death," "authentic Being": the ancient *Cura* ("Care") fable, Pindar's as well as Goethe's "Become what you are," the enactment of the experience of death in a Renaissance poem, and a work by Tolstoi. While Heidegger conceives of the question of Being as the radicalization of a tendency that essentially belongs to man's Being taken as ek-sistence—that is, as the radicalization of man's preontological understanding of Being—at the same time he shuns conventions and searches for original experiences. His confrontations with poets thus have a function analogous to that found in linguistic foundations: they confirm what was already established.[21] In both cases the phenomenologist apparently feels a need to legitimate the results as being already predelineated in order to show that they are not merely constructions and figments of the imagination.

The explanation given in connection with the *Cura* fable calls such a conclusive force "merely historical" (*nur geschichtlich*).[22] The expression, which Heidegger purposely puts within quotation marks, is a fine example of irony in a thinker who, at the moment he first delineates his investigation, posits that man's Being is essentially like time, and thus necessarily possesses historicity, so therefore each concrete mode of Being—including the ontologically questioning mode—is characterized by this fact. With this "merely historical" (*nur historisch*) the full weight of Heidegger's theory is thrown behind the *Cura* fable as well as behind the literary documentation that follows.

Language and Understanding

Once Heidegger's appeal to language and literature is recognized and the quality of his command of the language is known, it is to be expected that his theory will attach an especially important significance to language as existential and in so doing will pay particular attention to the word in its meaning with

21. SZ 183.
22. SZ 197.

regard to thought. Let us therefore examine this aspect in greater detail.

It is well known that *Being and Time* is mainly concerned with man's Being in order to lay the foundation for a general ontology. This preparatory reflection is performed in two phases. First, a number of structures of man's Being are developed in an "analytic," which in itself is again "preparatory"; second, these structures are explained as modes of temporality. Temporality is the essence of man's Being; thus, time is comprehended as the horizon of that understanding of Being which is characteristic of man.

In the preparatory analytic of man's Being, one obviously expects also to find an explanation of language. Heidegger realizes who this man is who, in his Being, always comports himself with this Being in one way or another. The essence of man consists in this peculiarity, in the mode of Being as Being towards, in his ek-sistence. In man's ek-sistence his Being is disclosed to him; he himself discloses to himself the there of his Being-there. Two different things are found in this disclosedness. The fact that I know that I am there implies that in being-there I have to be thrown into a Being in which I always already find myself. But ek-sistence also means, on the other hand, that in being-there it is left to my own ek-sistence to decide what I will make out of it: this is the project of self-realization in which, anticipating the goals and returning from the goals to the means with which they could be achieved, I will never be able to escape from this thrownness. The chasm of such a conflicting twofoldness is the heart that Heidegger's analytic tries to make explicit in a way as tenacious as it is cautious. Its point of departure is man's ek-sistence as concernfully being in the world together with others, and from this it develops this structure as a coherence of existentials.

But there is still another, equally essential dualism that determines the train of thought, and, at least for the time being, it must be distinguished from the first. This duality involves an opposition that we have already mentioned—namely, that of authentic and inauthentic being. Again, this distinction cannot be carried through as an absolute separation in the factual existence of man, but on the other hand it is necessary for clarifying the structure of this existence. It is true that in principle this distinction rests on an ontological structure which is neutral in

regard to this contrast and which gives to both of these modes of
Being as such their foundation. In fact, however, this neutral
structure is practically identical with the inauthentic one. The
thinker who, as we have seen, at all costs wishes to avoid the
semblance of finally coming out with "an idea of [his] own
contriving," does not wish to deduce this anthropological structure from an "Idea," either.[23] His phenomenological clarification
is oriented toward man in his everyday doing, toward the most
ordinary data concerning man. With this attention to this first
and for the most part (*zunächst und zumeist*), to the everyday
indifference (*alltägliche Indifferenz*), the difference between the
neutral structure and its inauthentic variant is blurred; they
sometimes blend imperceptibly into one another, and the inauthenticity, the fallenness, is an extreme form of appearance
with regard to the indifferent point of departure.

Only relatively late—in the next to the last chapter of the
preparatory analytic—is language even mentioned. The analytic
concentrates least of all on this anthropological, pre-eminently
fundamental phenomenon. It does not deal with language as the
range of systematized possibilities of expression by means of
symbols which appear in the possible combinations of vocal
sounds; it is concerned, rather, with speech as that form of human behavior in which these possibilities become materialized.
In this analytic, linguistic phenomena are dealt with in the same
way as other basic forms and principles of man's Being—for
instance, consciousness, intuition, thinking,[24] and even experience (*Erlebnis*), that key word in the philosophy of life.[25] Heidegger's investigation goes "behind" such phenomena in search
of some primary mode of man's Being as their ontico-ontological
condition. This mode is reached here not via the basic forms
mentioned but from the phenomenological characteristic of
man's Being-in-the-world, which is to be developed with the help
of the average everydayness of man's ek-sisting and is guided by
the idea of a transcendental foundation of the immediate living
reality.

In the introductory description of the disclosedness of Being-
in-the-world Heidegger mentions language, among other things,

23. SZ 196, 43.
24. SZ 142–48.
25. SZ 134–40.

as one manifestation of an existential called *logos* (*Rede*). Earlier, he briefly touches on this theme in mentioning the relationship between observation of objects (*Vernehmen des Vorhandenen*) and language.[26] Corresponding to this cursory indication in the investigation of ek-sistence is a passage in the methodological prelude to the investigation: in characterizing the *logos* of phenomenology, Heidegger also considers the relationship between *logos* and *phōnē*.[27]

Both of these earlier passages give rise to the supposition that language will come to the fore only in a much later phase of the transcendental derivation and, as the first passage confirms, as an ontological derivative of *logos*. However, when in *Being and Time* the structure of man's disclosedness is brought to light in greater detail, it appears that in the final analysis language is reached in the continuing explicitation of man's understanding. We must dwell on this subject somewhat longer.

Language as found in words and sentences appears as a communicating speaking forth and constitutes the third and most accidental [28] moment in the structure of the assertion—namely, a mode of the predication in our judgment. This predication is, at this point, by no means thought of explicitly as a linguistic phenomenon. It is true, however, that in the predication there comes about the transition from being occupied with something to speaking to others about something, about something which merely occurs. Such a determination presupposes the indication of the this-here about which one wishes to speak. From such an indication the members of the predication grow forth; [29] for, in order for one to be able to indicate the this-here and point it out, he must dwell with it. On the other hand, the pointing out of something that is to be further determined presupposes some meaning or signification which, in the judgment, is formally attributed to what has been pointed out; but this signification must also belong to what was pointed out. These conditions for the possibility of a pointing out as the origin of a speaking out are fulfilled by the interpretative explanation (*Auslegung*).

26. SZ 59–62, 130–34.
27. SZ 32–34.
28. "Aussage ist mitteilend bestimmende Aufzeigung" (SZ 156). The adverbial (undeclined) form makes "communication" strongly peripheral in the definition.
29. SZ 155.

With this existential we have penetrated one layer deeper into our derivation of language from the disclosedness of man's ek-sistence. The meaning which, in our concernful dealing with (characteristic of our concern for our own Being), is to be attributed to a thing is laid out in interpretative explanation. This explanation comes about in such a dealing with. It does not consider, but instead it handles. When someone gets something ready in order to use it later, he lingers with that piece of equipment. The tool becomes conspicuous to him *as such*, delineates itself in its meaning. In all other cases one keeps moving within the routine of the mutual relationships, a routine in which the things used refer to one another and in this way acquire and grant meanings. Signs are not the only bearers of meanings. They refer explicitly; namely, their usefulness is in referring to a context of usages as to a world in which one lives. Signs make us aware of their use and of the course of action we have to take in their regard; but all tools refer in their serviceability for to this for-what.

This functional referential context always reaches finally beyond the tool to man himself. He ek-sists. In the world his own Being-in-the-world is at stake for him. The tools are therein at his service and constitute the realm of his possibilities. Man does not just encounter them; he does not just passively run into them. He discovers these possibilities in bringing them to the fore. In this way his meaning-giving behavior, his project of his own Being-in-the-world, co-constitutes the world of his labor, this equipmental totality. Within this project the things present themselves in their meanings. Interpretative explanation develops these possibilities projected by man's understanding; it unfolds these meanings. Explanation grasps the meanings that understanding has established. This totality of references, this whole that has been articulated before all explanation, this multifarious unity of meanings, is disclosed primarily by understanding. It is only on this third layer that the foundation, the ontological ground, of language is reached in the structure of man's ek-sistence. Then the long road from assertion to understanding comes to an end. But was it not said that language is a derivative of the existential *logos*? Yet *Being and Time* develops the context that has been briefly outlined here in minute detail in order to be able finally to dwell on language as a late derivative mode of the speaking forth of *logos*.

THE ROLE OF *Logos*

WITHIN THE FRAMEWORK of the analytic this way of dealing with language is an intended consequence of the phenomenological method and is by no means a "jumbled" explanation to be straightened out afterward. The description repeatedly distinguishes a multiplicity of ontological determinations as the moments of a correlativity which, forced to its extremes, underlines the equivalence of the moments as well as their mutual determinateness. Heidegger's explanation describes the structural unity in which the ontological determinations are to be understood, beginning with a nucleus which is always carefully adhered to. Again in a circular movement such a description passes through the moments of the structure almost with desperate tenacity, guarding against its splintering.[30]

But what is the case here with disclosedness? It consists of the basic mood of finding oneself in (the realization and emotional experience of the thrownness), understanding (the capacity to project), and *logos*. The first two in this sequence are dealt with separately, but they are understood together and through one another. Moodness has its understanding, and understanding always has its mood.[31] In this way the threads are knit to and fro, back and forth. This procedure is repeated for these two moments in regard to *logos*, although there is some difference insofar as this strict interdependence is established explicitly only at the very end and not, as it unambiguously appears, as the guiding clue throughout the train of thought.[32]

In the meantime, however, the activity of *logos* is co-thought in the whole series of existentials derived from understanding and extending to assertion. For our discussion it is important that this occurs as well in regard to aspects characteristic of language: the understandability, although it is in principle wordless, is nonetheless articulated, comprising a context of significa-

30. *SZ* 180, 351.
31. *SZ* 142.
32. *Logos* is indeed as primordial as moodness and understanding (*SZ* 161), but it is not always mentioned together with them in the same breath as a mode of Being-there. Therefore, it so happens that *logos* is lacking altogether in the encompassing, repetitive formula for resoluteness (*SZ* 182).

tions; the disclosedness of ek-sistence is articulated by *logos* in the original sense of the word. This, in turn, constitutes the ground for the possibility of the derivative modes of understanding with which Heidegger deals. Parallel to this, it is always shown how fundamental moodness is articulated—for instance, in the coherence of the relating elements in a concrete mood [33] or as a sequence of distinguishable nuances in our being tuned (disposition) [34]—and thus how *logos* plays its part here also.

Language came to the fore as an accidental moment in the structure of assertion—namely, "speaking forth" (*Heraussage*), "statement" (*Aussagesatz*).[35] *Logos*, however, is a constituent of assertion as prelingual but articulated explanation. Thus it is consistent that this same moment appears accordingly as expressedness (*Hinausgesprochenheit*).[36] In this way language approaches, functions (in both aspects of foundation) in our Being with others in the world with things. Language is thus in every respect constitutive of our ek-sistence. That it is an ontological derivative phenomenon by no means excludes this fact. But the mode of ek-sistence in which Heidegger's exposition reveals the constitutive character of language is, within the general perspective of the preparatory analytic, the average everydayness: language is a tool to be used in social intercourse.

We employ this instrument because we are essentially in the world and committed to it: language is a consequence of man's thrownness. Understanding, of which language is an ontological offshoot, was fundamentally explained, however, in its meaning-giving project character as the counterpart of original moodness, representing the thrownness in the structure dealt with. This understanding is prelinguistic. With the significations, it lays the existential-ontological foundation for language. However, as soon as understanding manifests itself as a phonetic expression of significations—as an expression in words—one can observe that the project appears in its being thrown. Looking back one notes how, with the introduction of the speaking forth (*Heraussage*), a transition is completed—one that could not be sufficiently elucidated earlier. Is this why the transition took place so incidentally and almost reluctantly? Although one believes

33. SZ 134–42.
34. SZ 136.
35. SZ 155, 157.
36. SZ 161.

that he is dealing with linguistic phenomena, the issue remains one of ontological foundation. This is why Heidegger needs a distinction such as that between *assertion* (*Aussage*) and *speaking forth* (*Heraussage*), a distinction between words that at first sight appear to mean the same thing. A corresponding reservation, although expressed in another way, characterizes the mention of language in connection with the observation of objects.[37] However, is it perhaps possible that, when the transition from *logos* to language expressly constitutes the theme of the exposition, the precision of the analytic increases?

Meanwhile, this can scarcely be contended in regard to the formula that introduces such an analysis: "To significations, words accrue." [38] This is metaphorical language. However, in view of Heidegger's subtle use of language, this figurative representation of the phenomenal context should not be taken merely as a "flower of speech." There is still another reason to take this metaphor seriously. As we have seen, it appears earlier,[39] and there is objectively the closest possible connection between these passages. In the first reference the issue is the appearance of significations within the indication when interpretative explanation discloses the equipmental context in its meaningful articulation; in the later reference the issue is the manner in which these significations become word significations.

The presupposition common to both these indications is a process of growth, a thought-less (unpremeditated), and yet teleological, "organic" occurrence of immanent lawfulness. But this presupposition is not approached both times in the same way. In the genesis of the significations, indication unfolds itself, as if it were to differentiate itself and begin to flourish (*erwachsen*). The process of the growth of the words, on the other hand, adds these words to the significations (*zuwachsen*), and at the same time the significations are on their way to the words (*zu Worte kommen*). The organic lawfulness comprises a wider occurrence within which this process of enrichment (*Zuwachs*) comes about. But the reader remains uncertain as to the nature of this organic compass. *Being and Time* is silent about the origin of this enrichment.

The reader is puzzled not only by the incompleteness of the

37. *SZ* 59–62.
38. "Den Bedeutungen wachsen Worte zu" (*SZ* 161).
39. *SZ* 155.

metaphor but also by its organicistic character. How can this metaphor be applied to an instrument, to a factor in the equipmental context? On the other hand, in his preparatory reflection on the analysis of man's ek-sistence Heidegger has clearly spoken against a vitalistic easygoingness in philosophical anthropology.[40] His existentials certainly cannot be interpreted in that sense. At a decisive moment in the analytic this becomes fully clear: In his analysis of man's finitude Heidegger rejects among other things the conception of life as a kind of "ripening process," "completed" by death.[41] By applying the organicistic metaphor to language, its genesis and relationship with man's Being become problematic.

The perspective that is opened here is surprising within the framework of the analysis. Would it be better still—keeping in mind the peculiar "coloring" of what is perhaps the most fundamental existential, namely, "temporalization" (*Zeitigung*)—to take such metaphoric suggestion as incidental and strictly accidental? This is forbidden, however, by the accurate rebuttal of the passage with which we have just dealt, which certainly excludes all accidentalness. For, in the same way that *Being and Time* introduces the analysis of language, it also drops the subject again. A number of questions that present genuine challenges to linguistics and philosophy of language keep the horizon open. Heidegger reminds us of three phrases about language in which language is conceived of as a living being.[42] The applicability of such metaphors illustrates the basic problem formulated therein: Does language have the character of a tool, does it have an anthropological character, or is there a third possibility? In the light of our foregoing reflections, the direction in which Heidegger searches for the answer is clear.

This interpretation, however, concerns merely the "marginal phenomena" that surround Heidegger's analysis. In more direct descriptions his analysis develops a structural connection between *logos* and language that better harmonizes with the main lines of the exposition. In a certain respect, however, this connection offers a remarkable contrast to the characterization of the nexus between understanding and language. For, as far as the word *assertion* (*Aussage*) is concerned, one is dealing with

40. SZ 45–50.
41. SZ 244.
42. SZ 166.

an ontological fundament of the wording, although one believes that the issue is the wording itself. Conversely, the term *logos* (*Rede*) refers repeatedly to speech phenomena and linguistic phenomena although, on the basis of the meaning introduced, one expects to hear more about the prelingual existential. German promotes this obscuring even more strongly than English.[43] Heidegger's terminology is guided by this tendency, although his exposition precisely underlines the distinction.[44]

Such an obscuring contrasts with the foregoing pertinacity but nevertheless is also a symptom of the same intrinsic difficulty: the construction of the transition from existential to linguistic phenomena remains a point of concern. If this explanation is correct, the ontological description must confirm it.

In the description found in *Being and Time* Heidegger devotes his attention to the aprioric structure of *logos*. In the complex of phenomena to which this structure is related, one can distinguish four moments. In a conversation: (1) I say (2) something (3) to some one (4) concerning certain events that happened. These moments constitute the structure if all four of them are indispensable and irreducible. In this, "neo-realism" (4) obviously fulfills these requirements. Since *Bekundung* (1) and *Mitteilung* (3) cannot be reduced to wording, they likewise fulfill these requirements. Heidegger even calls attention to the fact that their essential realization is at stake in such an independence. Genuine understanding is something completely different from giving information.[45] When listening attentively, one does not concentrate on the acoustic phenomenon (*Verlautbarung*) but on what the other intends to say; one is not "with" the linguistic phenomenon but "with" the thing. Insight into the thing does not follow from but forms the foundation of our attention. What

43. The German word *Rede* does not mean "ratio" (*Vernunft*) but "*oratio*," "speech," "conversation," or "discourse," "that which is said," "oration" or "address," "phrase" or "expression," "rumor." Heidegger uses the term in this context (1) to indicate the founding existential ("Rede liegt der Auslegung und Aussage schon zugrunde." "Die Hinausgesprochenheit der Rede ist die Sprache") and (2) as *nomen actionis* in addition to the infinitive made into a noun ("Reden ist Rede über"). Even when (2) is introduced (*SZ* 161), (1) nonetheless keeps resounding in the phrases. That is why the conception of "Rede als Aussage" (*SZ* 165) can be rejected. Otherwise Heidegger very often, although never in section 34, uses *Rede-Redewendung* to mean "phrase" or "expression" (for example, *SZ* 180, 186, 189).

44. *SZ* 153–60.

45. *SZ* 162.

is genuinely expressive in language is precisely that which strikes us in the wording but nonetheless does not possess a word character. How meaningful silence can be! Such reflections all point in the same direction: these two constitutive moments of *logos*—namely, (1) and (3)—come to the fore most conspicuously extralingually and prelingually and in doing so possess the same relationship to language as the situation or event, the "subject matter" (4). They found the possibility of language usage; but they do not form the correlate of language and certainly not its result.

Developing the irreducible character of these necessarily presupposed moments with the help of such experiences is obviously performed at the cost of the wording factor. The indispensability of this factor then becomes positively doubtful; the lingual element in speech seems to become ontologically irrelevant. Another reflection also leads to this conclusion. The correlation between moodness and understanding is constitutive of the structure of disclosedness. Both existentials find full expression in the structure of *logos* through expressing and understanding.[46] But in this way the latter is completely present in *logos* (as the articulation of disclosedness), and there is no need to appeal to a lingual moment (*das Geredete* [2]).

The opposite procedure, however, is found in Heidegger's dealing with *logos* in the mode of inauthenticity, where the wording is of prime importance and places its mark on speech. In a very colorful way Heidegger describes manifold variants of small talk (*Gerede*), in which the objective fundament (4) is lacking and where, without understanding (3) and without personal involvement (1), the word (2) dominates.[47] In "*Gerede*" the structural moment of "*das Geredete*" has made itself independent and absolute at the cost of what is ontologically constitutive in *Rede*.[48]

Within the framework of this analysis we may note that (1) *logos* founds language, (2) that in the neutral structure of *logos*

46. SZ 162, 164.
47. SZ 167–70.
48. Here the quality of Heidegger's usage of language is particularly outstanding. The terminology expresses uncommonly well the exact results of the structural analysis. On the other hand, this analysis is a fine example of Heidegger's capacity to clarify implications of the German idiom.

language is mentioned as a constitutive moment, (3) that the description of the structure disqualifies this moment, and (4) that language, however, dominates in one particular mode of *logos*. This complexity is a result of the modal variability that characterizes the structure of man's Being-in-the-world. In their variation and transition the different modes show a dynamic orientation. Thrownness tends toward fallenness. Man's Being-in as a Being-with is inclined toward Being away from. The neutral ontological structure is fundamental in regard to this event but is also abstract. Viewed from the standpoint of *logos*, it suffices to distinguish three constitutive moments within the ontological structure. *Logos* then is not language, and consequently there is no language *in logos*. But, when we are in the world with others and with things, we express our insights in mutual understanding. Language then appears as the expressedness of *logos*, and in this way *logos* is existentially language. Language as "the totality of words" [49] is a means toward mutual understanding and is at one's disposal as an element in the equipmental context. This phenomenon, with which we were concerned earlier in connection with the relationship between understanding and language, compels us to suppose a constitutive moment in *logos* which enables *logos* to manifest itself as speech (and therefore as language). The structure of *logos* then becomes (reluctantly on the part of Heidegger) enlarged.

If such a moment is lacking in the neutral aprioric structure, then the transition from *logos* to language cannot be accomplished. However, when one introduces that fourth element, the structure that is so constituted is no longer purely neutral, and one prepares in it the mode of inauthenticity. In this way an essential determination is introduced into the structure of disclosedness, giving us an opportunity to consistently develop from this structure the fallenness. Man employs equipment within a system of references and is thus committed to this equipment also. In-the-world he is permanently exposed to the temptation of being taken up by the world, of losing himself in it—of losing himself in, among other things, language as the mundane mode of Being of *logos*.[50] When *logos*, which is already exteriorized in speech, is furthermore taken up with language, then it *is* lan-

49. SZ 161.
50. SZ 161.

guage.[51] *Logos* taken in this verbal form of fallenness is mere banter, small talk.

It is in this manner that, in the changing determination of the relation between *logos* and language, the mode of Being of man decides the ontological character of language. Then one may posit that the mode of authenticity implies a characteristic of language that is fundamentally different from all of this. From the discussion of the phenomenon of language, what has been stated generally in the introduction to this investigation is manifested in detail: the neutral ontological structure is concretely never so neutral that it can keep itself outside the alternative of inauthenticity and its counterpart. If one approaches a structure in its everydayness, the everydayness determines its concretization. The disqualification of the moment of wording cannot remedy this; the structure of *logos* is merely made ambiguous by this disqualification.[52] Furthermore, the transition to the fourth element does not solve the puzzle that occupied us in the organicistic metaphors. Just the opposite is the case: the fourth factor rests on this puzzle. Without words it is impossible to get to linguistic phenomena. Such phenomena cannot be derived from the significations and thus not from understanding as *logos* articulates it. *Logos* taken in its fundamental function in the structure of disclosedness is therefore not a sufficient foundation for the significations of the words. There are words, and this phenomenon must be recognized; that is why *Being and Time* mentions them. But at the same time the hint concerning their origin transcends the horizon of the transcendental analysis of man's Being. Word and language transcend man's ek-sistence. In the constitution of *logos* as speech this phenomenon is taken into consideration. But does not *logos* equally transcend this ek-sistence?

51. *SZ* 167.
52. To illustrate this once more with another example: the term *communication* (*Mitteilung*) changes, as far as content is concerned, depending on the phase of the exposition in which it occurs. (1) In the foundation of assertion in understanding, "communication" is synonymous with "speaking forth" (*SZ* 155). (2) In the structural analysis of *logos*, "communication" is the aprioric foundation of the possibility of such a speaking forth, which, as "communication," is a special case (*Sonderfall; SZ* 162). (3) In the characterization of small talk, "communication" is again *logos* which speaks itself forth (*SZ* 168). It becomes clear that, as early as in section 33, the last derivative of understanding constitutes the mode of inauthenticity, even though it is not mentioned.

CARE, TEMPORALITY, AND LANGUAGE

IN CONCLUSION I wish to call attention to the way in which the continued investigation in *Being and Time* confirms the characterization that has been developed here. The general scope of *Being and Time* implies, as we have seen, that the same phenomena will be discussed again with greater clarification and that language, too, will again be dealt with. This occurs first in the conclusion of the preparatory analytic and, much later, in connection with the temporality of disclosedness.

In the concluding part of the preparatory analytic the various series of constituents are integrated into the structure of care (*Sorge*). This structure is finally clarified—naturally in the mode of inauthenticity—with the help of the problematic of the current reality and truth conceptions.[53] Truth as *adaequatio* is just as equally a third-rate phenomenon in regard to the fundamental existential of revealment (*Entbergung*) via discoveredness (*Entdeckt-sein*) as was language in regard to the existential principles of understanding via interpretative explanation and of *logos* via speech. Like understanding and *logos*, truth is found in the realm of assertion and small talk—that is, in the realm of man's inauthenticity. The fact that in characterizing language we have focused our investigation in this direction begins to bear fruit. After the recapitulating description of disclosedness,[54] the exposition mentions fallenness as being essential but says nothing about *logos!* When *logos* is finally mentioned,[55] one comes to know it on this basis, consistently and one-sidedly, as small talk (*Gerede*). The recapitulation thus does not completely parallel the preparatory analysis, in which the fallenness of disclosedness was thematized only after the structure of language and was illustrated with the help of an extremely deficient mode. This narrowing of the theme is taken for granted in advance in the concluding part of the preparatory analytic.

The same process occurs with regard to disclosedness and *logos* in the explanation of the temporality of the structure of care. What until this point was included in disclosedness as

53. SZ 212–30.
54. SZ 220.
55. SZ 223.

constitutive moment because of the mode of "everydayness"[56] is now mentioned as an integral part of its "completeness."[57] In addition to understanding and moodness there is fallenness. This is why the temporal structure employed in the explanation of the phenomenon of "*logos*" is that of fallenness (*gegenwärtigen*).[58] In the latter, man alienates himself from his genuine life-possibilities.[59] Immediately before this passage, small talk was again central in the temporalization of fallenness—namely, when it became clear that this phenomenon could not yet be temporalized because of the anticipation (in the reversed order of the exposition).[60] It appears that in a more general sense, too, the *logos* structure cannot be made visible in its own temporality within the context of an interpretation of man's ek-sistence precisely set up for that purpose.[61] The extremely careful formulation of the relationship between disclosedness and *logos* as found in the preparatory analysis clearly gives its tone away.

In addition to the direct confirmation of the interpretation developed in this paper, an indirect confirmation is equally important. In *Being and Time* linguistic phenomena are brought up a third time—and in this case for the first time in the mode of authenticity. The authentic ek-sistence does not hover above everydayness but is a special mode of rooting therein, of appropriating Being to oneself. Thrownness inevitably tends toward inauthenticity and fallenness. Thrownness and fallenness both express an ontological conception of motion, a continuous and oriented course of motion. He who finds himself again, retrieving himself from this fallenness, radically changes the character of the motion. In the mode of authenticity one is indeed concerned with a movement against the grain. This is successfully suggested by such terms as *pull, push, plunder,* and *violation,* which help Heidegger to characterize the authentic mood.[62]

Accordingly, all attention is drawn (as far as *logos* is con-

---

56. See, for example, SZ 167.
57. SZ 249; see also SZ 350.
58. SZ 349–50.
59. SZ 348.
60. SZ 346.
61. SZ 349.
62. These terms clearly suggest the fact that this mood has a discontinuous character, that of the leap. Just as genuine knowledge leaps into the circle of understanding (*SZ* 310–16), so man leaps into authentic being.

cerned) to the "call" (*Ruf*), a phenomenon that stands in sharp contrast to the endlessly babbling chatter of everyday talkativeness. The call is a way of speaking that possesses a concentrated intensity. The existential possibility of Being-one's-Self comes to the fore in Heidegger's analysis and is furthered by an explanation of the phenomenon of "conscience." The "voice of conscience," which makes us understand something, presupposes language. But this *logos*, the genuine *logos*, is wordless.[63] The response to the call of conscience obviously is merely small talk. Such a response is an attitude within the world: man projects himself resolutely and silently toward the most proper possibilities of Being.[64]

The authentic mode of *logos* thus does not properly belong to language, just as was the case with its counterpart, the effective dealing with equipment. The reflection on language becomes caught and pressed between the characterization of speechless dealing with and the picture of a speechless Being-one's-Self. Conversely, where *Being and Time* deals with language more fully, for the most part it depicts the empty talk of fallenness.[65] The authentic Being of man (*das eigenste Seinkönnen*) is brought up only once in connection with language and *logos*. There, in the midst of an exposition that is extremely objective and abstract, the intimate and sensitive indication concerning "the voice of the friend whom [*den*] every man carries with him" surprises us.[66] In using these metaphors the author sometimes gives only half a word "to the wise." If the reader strains his ears, he accomplishes exactly what the passage wished to teach him and illustrates the point that listening is constitutive of speaking. After one finishes reading *Being and Time*, he no longer needs to be a "wise one" to recognize the presence of the voice of conscience as early as on page 163.[67] The subject was touched on there in order to shed light on the prelingual and extralingual aspects of man's understanding in the ontological

63. The silent call of conscience (SZ 296) alarms man, pushes him into anxiety, confronts him with his fallenness (SZ 276). Conscience summons us to be quiet and to listen.
64. In this connection *Verschwiegenheit* is persistently brought to our attention. See SZ 297, 301, 305, 382.
65. SZ 167–70.
66. SZ 163.
67. That is why *Verschwiegenheit* (belonging to resoluteness) appears familiar to us when we look back at section 34.

characterization of speech. The entire terminology, from *logos* via interpretative explanation to speaking forth, tends directly toward language and speech; but in so doing Heidegger expresses for one series of derivatives a thesis which he then posits as a general rule: namely, that, ontologically viewed, all origination is degeneration. The series from *logos* as articulation to language as expression in sounds illustrates this.

The cause of this remarkable twist in the reflection on language is obvious. If in methodically striving for phenomenal accessibility one concentrates so attentively on that which "in the first place and in general" is the case, then phenomenology substantially examines man's Being in the mode of appearing of everydayness. If in addition "a factical ideal of Dasein" [68] promotes the one-sided focusing on the criticism of culture in the description, then one gives a strong voice to the inauthenticity found in everydayness. In this way method and tendency converge. If one still adds to all of this the fact that, with respect to a number of statements, the reflection on language has to remain within the framework of the substance of fundamental ontology, then the exposition of language as found in *Being and Time* is being considered with some understanding of the relativity of these statements, just as their functional determination implies.

A certain discrepancy between the reflection on language and Heidegger's actual practice is thus explained. His characterization of language usage cannot be applied without adaptation to his own style of writing. It also seems difficult to combine the role given to language and literature in the method of *Bewährung* with the disqualification of the word which we have discussed earlier. Yet one must also learn to notice the discord with respect to the governing language convention, a discord which manifests itself in Heidegger's choice of words. This is positively in accordance with the reservation in regard to language that appears in section 34 and the sarcasm of section 35. Such a style goes against the grain. Heidegger's linguistico-historical documentation travels upstream, back to the source. It undoes that degeneration in the same way as was done in the struggle with the use of language. Heidegger obviously does not resign himself to the available language tool. In the process of gradually becoming aware of things, he does not let himself be

68. *SZ,* 310.

guided by that tool; he does not understand man from his equipment but forges linguistic means in order to make a new insight communicable. Viewed in this way—that is, from the creativity of an original writer—the assertion that words accrue to significations receives a new emphasis from within. What is at stake here, just as in the case of silent self-realization, is the undoing of fallenness; what is at stake is thus an aboriginal experience that forces itself on us in dealing with our familiar equipment.

If one considers the restrictions which are placed on this reflection on language by the function that this reflection has in *Being and Time,* then such an assertion receives a meaning that transcends its immediate contribution to the exposition. In conjunction with cognate indications, such a remark moves away from the periphery to which these indications were pushed by the plan of the book to a somewhat more central position. It is true, however, that even then the vegetative suggestion of the formulation (*zuwachsen*) does not match the grandeur suggested by the style of writing. But is it not a question of whether or not both of these aspects are characteristic of creativity? Does this vegetative suggestion not have much in common with the "struggle for a gift"?

In light of the functional determinateness of the exposition of *Being and Time,* another remark from section 34, this one concerning literature, is of special importance for an adequate explanation of Heidegger's conception of language. Precisely how literature appears as a linguistic work of art is not explained.[69] This is quite consistent; for otherwise Heidegger would be dwelling on the linguistic tool (albeit as plaything). What literature is able to accomplish is what Heidegger is concerned with: literature discloses ek-sistence; it communicates possibilities of moodness. It brings man to the there of his Being-there. The ontological rank of such language usage then becomes evident. One must take into account the epistemological valuation of moodness, which in its unveiling capacity reaches much further than theoretical knowledge.[70] The primary discovery of the world takes place in moods.[71] From this point of view the essential signifi-

69. However, the context focuses all attention upon tone, modulation, speech tempo, thus upon those kinds of nuances which linguistics knows how to suggest so compellingly.
70. SZ 134.
71. SZ 138.

cance of literature is already delineated in the explanation found in *Being and Time*. This again throws light on language and word. In linguistic art the sensitive (by no means to be taken yet as "filled with feeling") explanation of our Being-in-the-world takes place in such a way that it also speaks to others. If this had not been touched on in principle, it would then have been impossible in *Being and Time* to develop the phenomenon of being united by a common fate within the framework of man's historicity.[72]

In such cases the harmony between Heidegger's reflection on language and his style of writing stands out. The author not only repeatedly demonstrates his ability to create such a harmony but also deals with the harmony explicitly in its own nature. *Being and Time* concentrates on a very special series of moods: fear, anxiety, concern, guilt. But, in reading the passages that follow the discussion of these moods, we are urged to distinguish in this respect the restriction imposed by the function of the book and therefore, to understand not only Heidegger's conception of language in a broader perspective but also the living reality he wishes to disclose. In the development of the instrumental perspective in regard to reality, all attention is focused on nature as equipment. This is obviously something other than nature in its pure being-present-at-hand but also different from nature as power of life: "it is Nature as that which 'stirs and strives,' which assails us and enthralls us as landscape." [73] Here the reader is again confronted—in passing, but nonetheless unmistakably—with a third possibility, the possibility of linguistic interpretation.

72. *SZ* 382–87.
73. *SZ* 70.

PART II

PART II

3 / Poetry and Language in Heidegger

Walter Biemel

THERE ARE TWO WAYS of dealing with the difficulties presented by Heidegger's thought: either it can be analyzed and criticized from the outside, or an effort can be made to understand it from the inside.

Let us look closely at the first possibility. It is in no way difficult to pin Heidegger's position down to certain theses and then to argue that these theses are untenable because they do not harmonize with the way of questioning one has adopted. This approach suggests itself especially if one tries to measure Heidegger with traditional conceptual schemes. In that case it soon becomes clear that this cannot be done; but this can mean two things: either that Heidegger's position is indeed untenable or that such an approach is intolerable. Obviously, the interpreter will most likely defend the first alternative; otherwise he would have to give up his own position and thus revoke his own interpretation. The difficulty which hides behind this approach, however, is even greater. When a thinker, in carefully considering tradition, tries to call it into question, his gradual abandoning of the language of tradition is inherent in his attempt. This can be shown very clearly in Heidegger; in *Being and Time* there already is no longer room for the traditional subject-object problematic, and a new way of understanding man is inaugurated, with the concept of "Dasein." It can be shown further that such concepts as "phenomenology" and "ontology," which are found in *Being and Time*, are later avoided. In fact, in *Being and Time* the concept of phenomenology is already substantially modified.

[65]

The questioning back for the ground, which governs Heidegger's thought for such a long time, is finally superseded too in his last writings. All of this is merely meant to explain how, while thought proceeds, the language of thought changes. If an interpretive assessment is attempted from the viewpoint of traditional language, precisely that which constituted progress will be reproved by the interpreter because it does not harmonize with his position.

This difficulty must not be underestimated. We necessarily seek access to Heidegger from the standpoint of the tradition of Western metaphysics in which we stand. We are so biased by this tradition that we do not see how he moves away precisely from it. This moving away finds its linguistic expression in the phrase "the overcoming of metaphysics." In an interpretation based on this tradition Heidegger can easily be reproached with what, from his point of view, is precisely the advantage of his presentation, and his language, which frees itself from metaphysics, can be unnotedly retranslated into the language of metaphysics. As we have noticed already, this retransformation, although it seems to facilitate understanding, in fact makes understanding impossible; for that which is then "understood" is no longer what Heidegger means but that from which he pushes himself away. It is then not difficult to advance criticisms, but these (in the final analysis at least) miss the point.

What about the second possibility? Here an attempt is made to arrive at Heidegger's position with a leap and then to remain there. What Heidegger says is no longer translated into a "foreign" language and thus alienated, but now another difficulty arises—namely, that it is no longer apparent what explanatory steps were necessary in order to move into this new position. There is a false impression that Heidegger simply jumped out of the tradition one day and forcibly started something new; at the same time there is an impression of a relapse into the archaic —something new that is opposed to what is genuinely new. Such an interpretation is usually limited to repeating what Heidegger has said already, so the question immediately arises: What is the value of such an interpretation? Is it not merely a poor copy of the original?

There is also the question of whether the interpreter is really speaking from Heidegger's attitude or whether he merely believes he is doing so. There is thus a certain presumption in this way of speaking. The interpreter passes himself off as Heidegger, knows what is meant by this concept and that one, and can therefore save himself the trouble of traveling the laborious route over which Heidegger has gone. The interpreter even seems to be more fully informed of Heidegger's thought than Heidegger is himself. Strictly speaking, however, his interpretation is no more than a toilsome stuttering in which, however, neither the toil nor the stuttering are admitted. The movement in Heidegger's attempt at thinking from the very beginning until this very moment is thus denied; the interpreter acts as if Heidegger's insights sprang straight from a sudden inspiration, whereas Heidegger continually refers explicitly to the necessity of the movement and the execution and even wishes his entire thought to be understood as pathway. Hegel has already rebuffed the presumption of wanting to possess the results without traveling the road that leads to them. However, Heidegger cannot be hastily identified with Hegel; the characteristic of absolute certainty, which Hegel's philosophy possesses, is not found in Heidegger, and this is certainly not just by chance. Heidegger is not pretending modesty when he allows a questionableness to hover over all his searching. We are here not in the position of absolute subjects for whom knowledge and truth coincide. This way of interpreting in which the interpreter argues that he stands within Heidegger's thought and is fully acquainted with it, would be rejected by Heidegger because it is not in harmony with the caution of his proceeding and the movement of his thought. Moreover, this kind of speaking about Heidegger contains a precipitance that contradicts the style of his thought.

If both possibilities of interpretation—the one that alienates from the outside and the one that overleaps from the inside—are inadequate, what are we then to do? We must begin by admitting that we are wholly unable to give an interpretation. An interpretation must be revealing. It must be able to show what lies hidden in a thought, on what that thought is grounded, what dimensions are opened up by it, and thus what margin for questioning is freed by it; and, where possible, the interpretation must be able to show what kind of change in understanding is brought about by that thought. None of this can be done as long as Heidegger's thought is the issue at stake. We can present criticisms of his thought, we can rebel against it, and we may try to unmask it or find delight in it; but in the final analysis all of this remains unimportant. To this day a genuine dialogue with Heidegger has never taken place because the partner for such a dialogue is lacking and because, strictly speaking, we remain strange to his thought. It is more honest to admit this strangeness than to pretend that what is said here is already known and familiar.

In this paper I will try to make some of this strangeness visible. This paper is not an interpretation; it cannot lay claim to such a title. If it should succeed in coming somewhat closer to Heidegger, I will be satisfied. It will not hide the difficulties that reading Heidegger has in store for us, but it will not act as if Heidegger is necessarily to be blamed for them. If a genuine discussion with Heidegger is ever to take place, preparatory work must be done; this text may be understood as a contribution to such preparatory work.

In order to experience something of the movement that is inherent in Heidegger's thought and to avoid the impression that his last and most strange insights emerged like a flash of lightning, I would like to pursue the following course. First I will briefly discuss the conception of language in *Being and Time*. Then, corresponding to the theme of this essay, I will describe language and poetry as found in "The Origin of the Work of Art" and "Hölderlin and the Essence of Poetry," texts which stem from the period of the mid-1930s. Finally, a discussion of the later texts on language will consider those aspects of Heidegger's thought which are the most difficult and most strange.[1]

1. Wolfgang Zucker made the following comments, with which Professor Biemel expressed agreement: "Professor Biemel correctly warns against any fixation of Heidegger's thought into theses to be accepted or rejected by the reader and, in contrast, correctly demands an openness of the reader for the 'strangeness' of Heidegger's way of thinking and a readiness for a dialogue beyond assent or dissent. Has not Heidegger demonstrated this very *methodos*, this sharing of the way, in the introduction to his own attempt at translating-interpreting the strangeness of the Anaximander fragment? Is not his analysis of the process of thinking as *nach-denken, an-denken*, and *danken* precisely the necessary attitude and activity by which, according to Professor Biemel's lucid presentation, the reader may approach an understanding? Furthermore, is not any attempt at translating Heidegger's German sentences into any other language perhaps one of the best ways of training in this 'following on the road of thought' (*nach-denken*), in this use of strangeness as crystallization point (*an-denken*), and in this recognizing of strangeness as a favor (*danken*)?"

LANGUAGE IN *Being and Time*

LANGUAGE PLAYS AN IMPORTANT PART already in *Being and Time*. In accordance with the existential-ontological formulation of the question which aims at freeing the structure of Dasein and which shows that the structural moments possess a constitutive function in regard to Dasein, language is shown to be such a structural moment (*Existenzial*). We need not elaborate here on the character of this analysis or on how Heidegger conceives of Dasein as Being-in-the-world. In chapter 5 of *Being and Time* the meaning of "Being-in" is explained: Da-sein as moodness (sec. 29), Da-sein as primordial understanding (sec. 31), and Da-sein as *logos*—language (sec. 34).

Heidegger says at the beginning of section 34 that "the fundamental *existentialia* which constitute the Being of the 'there,' the disclosedness of Being-in-the-world, are primordial mood and primordial understanding." [2] He leaves *logos* out of consideration in order to be able to make visible first what is characteristic of the immediate openness of Dasein in primordial mood and then the peculiarity of primordial understanding which belongs to Dasein in such an original way that Dasein can ek-sist only as understanding. Therefore, primordial understanding comprises the entire complex of Being-in-the-world— that is, the meaningfulness as basic structure of the world and the possibility of Dasein's own power to be. In so doing Heidegger shows that primordial understanding dwells always in the dimension of possibilities, because it is not a particular act of man but something that is founded in Dasein's original project—and the project constitutes the leeway of the power to be. "As long as it is, Dasein always has understood itself and always will understand itself in terms of possibilities." [3] Without understanding there is no Dasein.

Dasein possesses the possibility of expressly appropriating to itself the understanding within which it keeps itself; for this Heidegger uses the term *interpretation* (*Auslegung*). "Interpretation [is not] the acquiring of information about what is understood; it is rather the working-out of possibilities projected in

2. SZ 160.
3. SZ 145.

understanding." Heidegger further defines *assertion,* in contrast with *interpretation,* as "a pointing-out which gives something a definite character and which communicates." [4] Assertion is possible only on the ground of that which is already made accessible in understanding. The question of how far Heidegger considers assertion to be a derivative mode of interpretation need not be dealt with here. What is important is the fact that it is founded in primordial understanding.

What new element emerges with *logos* when Heidegger attributes to *logos* such significance that he introduces it as being equiprimordial with moodness and understanding? [5] *Logos* is first determined as "the articulation of intelligibility." In order to forestall misunderstanding *logos* as something supplementary in regard to interpretation and assertion (something like the mere report of what was already "thought"), Heidegger says expressly that it is at the root of interpretation and assertion. What becomes articulated in *logos* is its meaning (*Sinn*). "The intelligibility of Being-in-the-world—an intelligibility which goes with a mood, *expresses itself as logos.*" [6] Original mood, understanding, and *logos* constitute a structural unity. Any context of meaning that was disclosed in primordial understanding is now spoken out in words. Primordial understanding always moves within contexts of meaning (cf. the concept of world as total meaningfulness). For these meanings words are created; words are necessary for one to utter meanings. Words do not exist for themselves as things to be supplied with meanings, but their Being is justified by the fact that they can manifest meanings. Since meanings and contexts of meanings become accessible in understanding, words are needed to make them comprehensible. It is in *logos* that "the 'significant' articulation of the intelligibility of Being-in-the-world" occurs. [7]

What must first be maintained in this determination is the relationships among moodness (original being open for . . .), understanding, and *logos* (articulation of moodlike understanding); they form a unity, articulated in a threefold way, in which Dasein ek-sists. *Logos* is in no way to be equated with language. In this period of Heidegger's thought *logos,* in contradistinction

4. *SZ* 148, 156.
5. *SZ* 161.
6. *SZ* 161.
7. *SZ* 161.

to the usual meaning of the word, is the constitutive moment, and language is merely "the way in which *logos* gets expressed." [8] Language is that through which *logos* makes itself mundane; through language it becomes an element of the world and can be treated like other things found in the world.

Let us briefly consider the conception of *logos* as communication. The presupposition of communication is Being-with. Dasein is always with other Dasein and need not first secure the existence of its fellow men by means of artificial operations. In this Being-with Dasein understands itself and the other, as well as the world in which they, in each case, are; the other is at the same time given to Dasein in its own moodness as "being tuned," although this giving might very well be subject to illusion. This sharing of the common experience that is immediately lived is expressly articulated in communication. Only because Dasein is Being-with, in Heidegger's view, is communication— that is, the explicit utterance of the gained experience in which Dasein in each case finds itself—possible. For this reason also, strictly speaking, communication is only possible among Dasein having a common experience of world. A report of the extreme living conditions on an exploring expedition becomes communication only if the reader is able to picture the conditions as possibilities that eventually could happen to his own existence. If this is impossible, then what is accessible through reading is not genuinely understood, does not become communication, but remains a "foreign matter" (*Fremdkörper*). Communication thus does not create community but presupposes a lived community which through communication merely experiences its explicit articulation. Dasein expresses itself in communication; this is not an uttering of something that was inside but an articulation of Dasein's Being-outside; it brings into work the original mood in which fellow men and environment encounter one another, as well as fellow men's understanding of environment and Being-with.

The leading idea in Heidegger's arguments about *logos* is the following: "In *logos* the intelligibility of Being-in-the-world (an intelligibility which goes with moodness) is articulated according to significations; and *logos* is this articulation." [9] Heidegger

8. *SZ* 161.
9. *SZ* 162.

thus does not take as his point of departure a subject which has the ability to speak, to disclose with words what is inside; his point of departure is the basic structure of Dasein as Being-in-the-world. *Logos* is considered from the viewpoint of this basic structure; it is nothing but the articulation of each concrete Being-in-the-world and implies all of the moments that belong to Being-in-the-world. As far as *logos* is concerned, utterance is not the decisive moment; each utterance is founded in the specific mode of Being-in-the-world.

Heidegger distinguishes four moments in *logos*: the "about which" (that which the talk is about), the announcement (that which is said in the talk), the communication (taken here in the narrow sense), and the manifestation (that which is uncovered by *logos*). In *Being and Time* this distinction is only briefly mentioned; later, particularly the moment of manifestation (in the sense of uncovering or freeing) comes more and more to the fore, and this element then leads to the connection between *logos* and truth. But here we wish to draw attention only to the relation between *logos* and listening. Dasein is able to hear because it is determined by openness. In listening, Dasein is with the other and what he says; here we pay attention primarily not to words and speech but to that which is uncovered by them. Modulation, rhythm, and everything that can be said to belong to the modes of speech are subordinated to a manifestation, or, it can also be said, to the engagement, of the speaker to the thing which is at stake. In other words, the manner of saying is heard also, not in order to stick to it, but in order to make understandable the relation, the attitude of the speaker in regard to the events brought forth. Thus, via *logos,* we are with the thing itself and immediately with the attitude of the speaker in regard to the thing. In *Being and Time* Heidegger reproaches linguistics because, in its conception of *logos* as utterance (*Aussage*), it attempts to conceive of language by taking the present-at-hand as guiding clue, as if language were a present-at-hand mundane thing, and because the mode of Being characteristic of language is therefore not expressly thematized. This is an idea which governs *Being and Time,* an idea which circles around the differences among the Being characteristic of man, the intramundane ready-to-hand, and that which is merely present-at-hand. This distinction is the presupposition which is necessary in order genuinely to ask the question concerning the meaning of Being.

This brief characterization of *Being and Time*'s formulation of the problem in no way exhausts what is said there about *logos* and language but is intended to be merely an introduction to the context in which *logos* is seen there and what it means to understand *logos* as an existential of man's being-in-the-world.

LANGUAGE AND POETRY

IN "THE ORIGIN OF THE WORK OF ART," which was written in 1935, expanded in 1936, and published in *Holzwege* in 1950, Heidegger says, "All art, as the letting come to pass of the advent of the truth of beings as such, is in essence poetry." [10] An explanation of this sentence will be presented which, it is hoped, will show a development in Heidegger's thought about language. It is necessary in this regard to give a comprehensive presentation of the truth concept, a central concept of Heidegger's thought.[11]

In "On the Essence of Truth," the first draft of which originated in the early 1930s and which may thus be drawn upon here, Heidegger begins with a description of the current concept of truth: truth as conformity. This conformity can be understood in two ways. (1) The thing tallies (*stimmt*); it can be seen as that which corresponds with what we possess of it as foreknowledge. The thing upholds, as it were, the scheme in which it is thought. True friendship, for instance, fulfills all conditions that we connect with the concept of friendship. (2) The proper place of truth, however, is preferably put in the realm of judgment; one may say that this has been done since Aristotle, although there is still another conception of truth in Aristotle, just as Heidegger has shown. According to this conception, what is stated in the assertion conforms to reality (to the thing). "Veritas est adaequatio rei et intellectus," as it has been said in medieval philosophy. The term *adaequatio* can be understood in a twofold way. Man's intellect conforms to the things created by

10. HW 59 (693–94).
11. Some of the following material is taken from the introduction to the French translation of "On the Essence of Truth," by Alphonse De Waelhens and Walter Biemel, which appeared in an expanded form in *Symposium*, III (1952). Cf. Ernst Tugendhat, *Der Wahrheitsbegriff bei Husserl und Heidegger* (Berlin: de Gruyter, 1967).

God; on the other hand, things conform to the *intellectus*—not man's, however, but God's, since they come into Being according to God's Idea. "Both concepts of the essence of *veritas* always mean a conforming to and thus conceive truth as correctness." [12] That man's intellect is able to conform itself to things is shown by the fact that both man and thing are mutually coordinated on the ground of the divine plan of creation.

Heidegger is not satisfied with this concept of truth, which is maintained even in modern times, although the Christian system of the world no longer possesses authority as ultimate truth. Heidegger asks more fundamentally for that which makes conformity at all possible. In order for an assertion to conform with the thing, the thing itself must be in the realm of the open, appear as something manifest, be present. The one who makes the assertion must in turn take his domicile in the same domain so that the relevant thing may encounter him. In Heidegger's formulation, "The assertion must derive its correctness from the openness [*Lichtung*] of the comportment." [13] Truth is thus understood from the viewpoint of the openness in which both the thing and the man who comports with this thing find themselves. This openness, however, is in no way to be seen as a pure clearing in which what was in the dark before becomes gradually brighter and brighter, the eventual goal being maximum brightness. It might be understood, rather, as a medium that at each time lets certain determinate traits come to the fore so that the being is able to show itself according to the openness that has been achieved. Therefore, the openness is subject to change. The openness of classical Greek thought (that is, of the Greek world) is different from the openness of the medieval world view, and the modern openness is, once again, quite different from both. This change is, for Heidegger, the fundamental change of history.

In the passage quoted earlier from "The Origin of the Work of Art," Heidegger defines art as "the letting come to pass of the advent of the truth of beings as such"; by this he means that art is the "bringing about" of the openness. "It is from the poetizing essence of art that it comes to pass that [art] erects in the midst of beings an open place in whose openness everything is different

12. WW 8.
13. WW 11.

from usual." [14] By speaking of "letting come to pass" rather than of simply "positing" or "creating," Heidegger implies that in the final analysis the taking place of the openness is not merely an achievement of man but that, as it were, man can receive only what Being itself sends him and may open himself to or shut himself off from this. Art is eminently a possibility for opening, for meeting.

What until now has been the genuine poetizing element of art thus becomes the change of the openness by which being is able to show itself, to appear. At the end of his interpretation of the Greek concept of *alētheia*, Heidegger also uses the term *unconcealment* instead of *openness*. "The effect of a work does not consist in a working. It consists in a change in the unconcealment of beings which comes to pass through the work, and this means a change in the unconcealment of Being." [15] *Being* means here "Being-ness"; how beings in the ensemble become accessible depends on the unconcealment. What comes to pass in poetry is not the inventing of occurrences and events, as this is attributed to our poetizing fantasy, but the openness in whose open being makes its appearance, shows itself, is. The change is here conceived of as "clearing project"—a project in which what is projected is the clearing (the openness). Later, Heidegger clearly specifies the character of this project in such a way that it is not man who "throws out," but Being itself. The expression "letting come to pass," which was quoted earlier and which also appears in the following sentence, points in the same direction. "What poetry as clearing project unfolds in the way of unconcealment and pro-jects to the rift of the form is the open which lets the unconcealment come to pass in such a way that in the midst of beings the open makes the beings shine and sound forth." [16]

If what is poetized in poetry is the openness, and if poetry is the essence of art, it may be understood that all other arts are to be reduced to poetic art in the narrow sense of poetry. However, this is not what Heidegger means in "The Origin of the Work of Art." He conceives of poetry here so broadly that it is the basic condition of all art, including the art of language (*Sprachkunst*). But why draw upon this essay if our main interest is in language? The reason is that in a second move Heidegger ex-

14. *HW* 59 (693–94).
15. *HW* 59 (693–94).
16. *HW* 60 (694–95).

pressly shows interest in the art of language, to which he grants "a privileged position in the whole of the arts." That is why we must first overcome the current conception of language as "communication." "Language is not only and primarily a phonetic and written expression of that which is to be communicated." Heidegger is criticizing the view that language forwards by means of words what is already manifest. He confronts this view with his interpretation that "language first and foremost brings being as a being into the open." [17] In naming a being one first makes it appear. Where there is no naming, there is no openness. Therefore, Heidegger equates saying with the project of the clearing; through saying, unconcealment comes into being.

Thus, what Heidegger stated previously in regard to art as poetry (taken in a broad sense) he now concretizes with the help of the example of naming. Through naming, beings first become accessible as beings; it is the condition necessary for them to be recognized and used as determinate beings. This becoming accessible of beings as beings, this uncovering of their beingness, is unconcealment. This must not be understood as if beings were present before but in a state of concealment; unconcealment means, rather, the entering into Being as appearance. Through unconcealment there is being for man; being is integrated into the project of world. According to the way in which this happens the history of a certain nation comes to pass, and its essence becomes materialized.

Something peculiar is taking place here. Heidegger starts with poetry in the broad sense of the term in order to proceed to poetry in the narrow sense. But even before he speaks of poetry in the narrow sense, it becomes clear that what comes to pass in language coincides with the essence of art as poetizing which was first outlined. The explanations concerning language thus do not bring us anywhere other than where we were already in the first delineation of the essence of art; on the contrary, we have returned to it. This circumscription of the essence of art becomes concretized to the extent that language is that through which openness (unconcealment) comes to pass. "This naming first nominates a being to its Being, and from this Being. Such a naming is a projecting of lighting in which is expressed the manner in which being comes into the open." [18]

17. *HW* 60 (694–95).
18. *HW* 61 (695).

Heidegger does not go into detail as to how in the various languages different worlds come to the fore; that would be beyond the scope of this reflection on art. In his lectures, however, he refers repeatedly to the differences between the Greek and the Roman worlds in relation to the differences between their languages.

The train of thought of Heidegger's essay on the work of art undergoes a change when he asks "whether art, specifically taken in all its modes from architecture to poesy, exhausts the essence of poetry." [19] Here he is pointing out that we may not limit ourselves to art in order to experience what poetry means but that we must appeal to thought in order to comprehend what occurs in poetry. This idea occupies Heidegger through his latest works. [20]

Let us now return to language. "Language itself is poetry in the essential sense. Because language is that event in which for the first time being as being is disclosed to man, poesy [poetry in the narrow sense] is the original poetry in the essential sense." [21] How is this statement to be understood? To understand it, we must explain the relationship between language and poesy. For poesy to be possible, man must move in the realm of language, must disclose to himself being through the medium of language. Within this domain poesy occupies a privileged position; it is expressly and exclusively dedicated to the disclosure of being. Poesy completes what is set up in language, that at which language aims. The arts which do not realize themselves in the realm of language presuppose the disclosure of being through language. "Each of them is a special poetizing within the clearing of Being, which, wholly unnoticed, already came to pass in language." [22]

We must therefore distinguish an original clearing such as that which comes to pass in language from that which, within the clearing that already has taken place, establishes itself in a determinate way and gains a foothold there. Heidegger limits himself in this regard to concise remarks. One only wishes that his analysis of this distinction were more concrete—for instance, showing how the Greek world, founded by its language,

19. *HW* 61 (695).
20. See pp. 82–93 below.
21. *HW* 61 (695).
22. *HW* 61 (695).

finds expression and reaches its completion in architecture. Without a doubt Greek architecture supposes a determinate conception of the essence of the gods and of the relationship of man to the gods. If the divine had not first been said in language, it would have been meaningless, even impossible, to erect memorials to the gods. In these memorials, sacred woods and temples, a certain measure is revealed, an order having an effect on the lived self-understanding of the Greek man and influencing him by forming him. Within the history of a nation, one form of art can temporarily occupy a privileged position and can give new impulses, whether this be architecture, painting, or music; but in each case language is already there. The question now is whether language can decay in a certain way and whether one of the arts can guard the openness.

We have seen that the essence of art is poetry. The essence of poetry, in turn, is establishing the truth, the articulated clearing in which Being comes to pass. In "The Origin of the Work of Art" this establishment is seen in a threefold manner: as bestowing, founding, and beginning. *Bestowing* is understood as the making available of what is new, which "never can be compensated or equaled by what is present-at-hand and available," and thus possesses the character of abundance. *Founding* frees the historical ground on which a nation stands. *Beginning* is the instigation of the agonistic essence of truth. "The genuine beginning, as a leap, is always a leap forward in which all that is to come is already overleaped, albeit as something which is still veiled." [23]

This digression has shown how Heidegger understands language as poetry in connection with the essence of truth; that which comes to pass in art is "an excellent manner in which truth is—that is, historically comes to be." As historical, art is "the creating preservation of the truth in the work." [24] When art comes to pass, a nation begins a new epoch in its history.

In 1936, approximately one year after writing "The Origin of the Work of Art," Heidegger takes up the theme of poetry again, in his lecture "Hölderlin and the Essence of Poetry." For Heidegger, Hölderlin is the poet par excellence. Because he poetizes the essence of poetry, he can be questioned about it.

23. HW 62–63 (695–97).
24. HW 65, 64 (698, 697).

Heidegger borrows five sayings from Hölderlin and, in explaining them, presents the essence of poetry and that of the poet.

1. [Poetizing is] that most innocent of all occupations.
2. Therefore language has been given to man as the most dangerous of possessions . . . in order that he may testify to what he is.
3. Man has experienced many things
   And many of the heavenly ones has he named
   Since the time we are a dialogue
   And able to hear from one another.
4. But what remains is established by the poets.
5. Full of merit, and yet poetically, dwells man on this earth.[25]

Since my intention here is not to present the relationship between Heidegger and Hölderlin but to deal with language and poetry, I will draw attention only to those passages of explanation which contribute something to this purpose.

In Heidegger's explanation of the second saying, the following statement is found: "In order that history be possible, language has been given to man." [26] This is completely in harmony with the explanation from "The Origin of the Work of Art." In language man may testify as to who he is; in language the constitution of a world comes to pass. Heidegger maintains the relation between language and openness also when he says: "But now it is only by virtue of language at all that man is exposed to what is open, which *as* being besets and inflames man in his Dasein and as not-being deceives and disappoints him." [27] Without language there would be no experience of being; there would be no realm of what is open, in which all doing and undergoing of man takes place. Heidegger sees the danger that Hölderlin attributes to language in several ways. The first of these is to be understood from Heidegger's basic statement "Danger is the menace of being to Being." [28] Language as danger can also mean that what is freed and at the same time preserved in language by no means needs to be the most noble; it can just as well be

25. Johann Hölderlin, *Sämtliche Werke,* ed. N. V. Hellingrath (Munich: Müller, 1923), III, 337; IV, 246, 343, 63; VI, 25 (editor's translation).
26. *HD* 34.
27. *HD* 34.
28. *HD* 34.

the most vulgar. Language can also become an illusion—the unessential can pretend to be the essential.

All of these latter statements constitute a resumption of the arguments central to "The Origin of the Work of Art":

> Language is not a mere tool that man possesses in addition to many others; on the contrary, it is only language that affords man the very possibility of standing in the openness of Being. Only where there is language is there a world, i.e., the perpetually changing environment of decision and work, of action and responsibility, but also of arbitrariness and noise, of decay and confusion. Only where world holds sway is there history. . . . Language is not a tool which is at man's disposal but rather that event which disposes of the supreme possibility of man's being.[29]

In this manner Heidegger wishes to remove the common comprehension of language as a means of communication and to make language the basic event of man's Being.

In the third saying language is conceived of as a dialogue in which the gods get a hearing and a world appears. Being able to talk and being able to hear are seen as equiprimordial, just as the naming of the gods and the appearance of the world are also simultaneous with language. In this connection the naming of the gods is possible only if they address themselves to us. (This parallels Heidegger's conception of Being—that it can be experienced only if it addresses itself to us.) This dialogue is mediated by the poets. In these comments a distinction must be made between what Heidegger has Hölderlin say—for instance, about conflict, intimacy, and the gods—and what Heidegger himself says about language and unconcealment.

In the discussion of the fourth saying Heidegger says, "Poetry is establishment by and in the word." The idea with which we are already familiar—namely, that what is established is the open—is further developed as follows: "That which supports and holds sway over all that is must become manifest. Being must be disclosed in order that beings may appear." That which is open of the Open is here explicitly called "Being"; and Heidegger refers to the way in which Being is in need of man, is entrusted to man, in the same way as in Hölderlin everything heavenly is "entrusted to the poets as a matter of care and service. . . . When the poet speaks the essential word, being is

29. HD 35.

by this name first nominated as that which it is. Poetry is the establishment of Being by means of the word." [30] Taking up what was said in "The Origin of the Work of Art," Heidegger sees the establishment of the open as simultaneous and somehow identical with grounding. "The saying of the poets is establishment not only in the sense of the free bestowal but at the same time in the sense of the firm grounding of man's Dasein on its ground." [31] Heidegger later overcomes this idea of establishment as positing, as we shall see, and considers it to be a hidden echo of the philosophy of German idealism.

We started with the view that poetry needs language in order to be able to be; it appears that in the course of this presentation a change has taken place. Poetry that makes what is open possible at the same time makes language possible. The essence of language must be understood from the essence of poetry. Heidegger therefore calls poetry the aboriginal language—that is, what is at the root of language. In this connection poetry is then understood in the specific sense, as the disclosure of unconcealment, not as poesy. It can thus be maintained that in this period of Heidegger's thought the essence of language is understood from the essence of poetry. "The ground of human Dasein is the dialogue in which language does truly come to pass. The aboriginal language is poetry as establishment of Being." [32]

From poetry understood as aboriginal language, Heidegger then comes to see the poets as Hölderlin sees them—namely, as the mediators between gods and men. The poet's establishing is hereby conceived of as an independent act but, at the same time, as an act of highest necessity. The naming of the gods presupposes that the gods grant themselves to be known through signs mediated to the nation by the poets. On the other hand, however, the poets are bound also to the myths of a nation, in which the historical good is preserved; and it is their duty to explain these myths. In Hölderlin's definition of the essence of the poet, Heidegger sees a verification of his interpretation of poetry as a coming to pass of the truth; the idea is taken from Hölderlin but is formulated by Heidegger in his own language.

Heidegger experiences yet another point in Hölderlin in which the two meet one another. Hölderlin's definition of the

30. *HD* 38.
31. *HD* 39.
32. *HD* 40.

essence of poetry cannot be atemporal, for man's existence is historical. Therefore, the time for which this definition holds good is specified, namely, the time in which the gods have flown and the coming of God is expected. Heidegger uncovers the kinship between this point of Hölderlin's and his own thought, which is understood as the revealing of Being's forgottenness—of Being's withdrawal—and as preparation for a possibly new approach. The expression "needy time" also holds true for the way in which Heidegger interprets metaphysics and its being overcome. The coming to an end of the epoch of metaphysics and the preparation for the time of thought is the "needy time" of that philosophizing which prepares for the transition to thought.[33]

POETIZING AND THOUGHT

WE MUST NOW ATTEMPT the leap to Heidegger's later texts on language, written in the 1950s, two decades after the Hölderlin lecture. In his introduction to three lectures entitled "The Essence of Language," Heidegger formulates the issue: "to gain an experience with language." This cannot mean that we should engage in experiments with language but that, "once we become attentive to our relationship to language," we should reflect on our abode in language.[34] In other words, we should become fully aware of something that immediately concerns our own Being. Heidegger refers expressly to the fact that the issue is not to gather knowledge about language in the sense of metalanguage and metalinguistics. The question is therefore not merely one of criticism of another possibility of dealing with language. Heidegger makes it clear from the beginning that his questioning concerning the essence of language will no longer take place within the perspective of modern metaphysics and that the investigations in the sense of metalanguage remain

33. Erling W. Eng made the following comments which, according to Professor Biemel, certainly indicate an important task for the poet in our time: "Is the poet perhaps limited to disclosing to us the uncanny character (*das Unheimliche*) of the machine? Since the meaning of the machine lies in its functionality, does it have any sense as phenomenon? Perhaps Brecht's 'estrangement effect' (*V-Effekt*) is aimed precisely at the machinal as such, to expose it."

34. *US* 159.

dominated by that perspective. "Metalinguistics is the metaphysics of the universal technification of all languages into the only functioning interplanatory instrument of information." [35] In opposition to the scientific and philosophical knowledge of language, he proposes "to gain an experience with language." It might be added here that the issue is to try to get close to language in a thoughtful way; for in Heidegger's view philosophy and thought are basically different ways of approach.[36]

In the experience with language one must try to have language bring itself up for discussion. Language has the special characteristic that we live in it, are familiar with it, and deal with it without catching sight of it. We continuously heed what becomes accessible to us through language and thereby overlook language itself. In order to get out of this position Heidegger again appeals to the poet, not merely because he has a privileged relationship to language but because he brings this relationship up for discussion. Whereas Hölderlin poetizes the essence of the poet, Stefan George poetizes the relationship with language, our experience with language. This is why at the center of these explanations Heidegger interprets George's poem "The Word" (published in 1919).

> I brought to the border of my country
> Miracles from afar or dreams
> And waited until the fierce Fate (Norne)
> Found their name in her well.
> Thereupon I was able to grasp it tight and strong
> Now it blooms and shines through this mark. . . .
>
> Once after a good journey I arrived
> With a gem rich and tender

35. *US* 160.
36. L. J. Ferguson questioned Professor Biemel as to the difference between the approach of philosophy and the approach of thought to language. Biemel answered: "By philosophical dealing with language Heidegger means the metaphysical approach which in our century is embodied in metalinguistics; by thoughtful dealing Heidegger does not mean to force language into the channels of metaphysics and to fasten it there, but rather to lead us to 'make' an experience with language, as he explains in *On the Way to Language,* or, more carefully formulated, to think about language from the e-vent not as something that rules over man but as that to which he is exposed, that about which he must think." (For the difference between philosophy and thought, see also Heidegger's illuminating text "Das Ende der Philosophie und die Aufgabe des Denkens," *SD* 61 ff.).

She searched for a long time and told me,
"There is nothing like it among the things
    which sleep in these depths."
Thereupon it escaped from my hand
And my country never gained that treasure. . . .
Thus I sadly learned the renunciation:
"No thing be there where the word is lacking." [37]

One could immediately object that George's way of writing poetry, which tends to what is "pathetically precious," no longer has anything to offer us. He is scarcely known, let alone read, by today's youth. His way of writing poetry is barely possible today, just as it is no longer possible to compose in the manner of Wagner. However, although George is obviously not "up to date," it is possible that in his poem something of our experience with language becomes manifest, something that outlasts and surpasses his pretentious style of writing. Art can never be measured in terms of its popularity.

This poem is dedicated completely to the poet's experience with the word. The first stanza describes the power of the poet. He is able to collect astonishing things, as well as what has been seen in dreams, for which the Fate goddess grants him names. In this way the being which already is becomes fully manifest through its word, manifest also for others. Through the names, the poet secures what he has seen. A climax of the poetic activity is shown here. What the poet is able to grasp is hereby also accessible to others. Even the exceptional ("Miracles from afar or dreams") is brought close to his fellow men, albeit only with the help of the Fate goddess. By ending the stanza in the present tense ("Now it blooms and shines through this mark"), the poet shows the persisting, the presencing, which comes to pass in this poetizing in which the names receive power over the things.

In contrast with this, in the second stanza the poet mentions an experience in which he brings to the name-giving not something that comes from afar but something that lies in the hand (*auf der Hand liegendes*), which he calls "a gem." A gem is that through which the Being of the wearer becomes manifest. But it is precisely for this thing that the Fate goddess does not find a name. In view of the fact that until now she has found a name for every being, it might be assumed that what is presented is

37. *US* 220 (editor's translation).

something which is not-being. On the other hand, however, it is designated as a gem, as being particularly precious, and thus as a being of a special kind. When the word for it fails to appear, the gem disappears; the poet is unable to retain it. Here a new mode of Being of the word comes to the fore. The word not only is able to yield the name for a being that is already there—"it is not merely the naming grasp for that which is already present and proposed as such" [38]—but also grants the being present.

How is the final line of the poem to be understood? According to Heidegger, it names not what is renounced but the domain into which the renunciation must enter. "What the poet learned to renounce is the view that he formerly subscribed to concerning the relationship between thing and word." The word *be* (*sei*) must be understood as imperative; more carefully formulated, the renunciation of his former understanding implies a command. "The word addresses itself to the poet as that which keeps and maintains a thing in its Being." [39]

The poet experiences himself as the custodian of the word. A limit experience for which the word does not suffice (the Fate goddess does not find a name) must not be understood merely negatively; for, with the poet's learning to renounce, it also becomes clear what the word is able to do. Heidegger sees in the mood of sadness "the mood of composure in regard to the nearness of what is withdrawn but at the same time saved for an original advent." [40] This mood can also be considered the basic mood for Heidegger's thought. Let us draw attention to the concept of "needy time," to Heidegger's thought concerning Being's withdrawal, in which a possible new advent announces itself when the withdrawal is experienced as such, and which, at the same time, makes Heidegger's position in regard to metaphysics understandable. The history of metaphysics is thought of as the epoch of the forgottenness of Being. This epoch is not immediately overcome in Heidegger's thought, but in it the absence of Being is for the first time expressly thought; this epoch is conceived of as the time of Being's farness. In this way the possibility of a reversal is given, as this is expressed in the quotation above. Heidegger returns to the original thinkers, for in their thought the originating is still alive. From that, we wish to

38. *US* 227.
39. *US* 167, 168–69.
40. *US* 169.

gather only the following: the considerations of language—the word of the poet—are problems in which Heidegger's basic experience collects; in them a purified retrieval of the Being question takes place.

As far as Heidegger's way of proceeding is concerned, what matters for him is to listen to the address (*Zusage*) of language. "Language must in its own way address itself—that is, its essence—to us." [41] If we succeed in this listening, we will be able to gain a thoughtful experience with language. The preparation for such an experience is being able to catch sight of the proximity of poetizing and thought, even being able to settle in this proximity.

Heidegger's explanation will show that, notwithstanding the important statements about language in the realm of thought, notwithstanding the exciting data found in what has been composed in language, the essence of language "everywhere does not bring itself to word as the language of Being." We have seen first that in speech language recedes on behalf of what is said in it. This recession can find its ground in the fact "that language with its origin holds itself back [*an sich hält*] and thus denies its essence to our current pro-posing representation." The difficulty is not immediately to personify the state of affairs expressed in this way; the formulation can certainly tempt us to do so. Heidegger points to a possible reason why the essence of language withholds itself: "that the two privileged modes of saying —poetizing and thought—were not searched for expressly, that is, in their proximity." [42] This is exactly what Heidegger wishes to do in the second of the three lectures entitled "The Essence of Language."

Heidegger's interpretation of the final stanza of "The Word" was to show that the issue is to be found in the relationship between thing (being) and word—specifically, that the word helps the thing to its Being and keeps it therein. Thus the word is not merely related to the thing; it is that "which maintains the thing as thing," that which Heidegger calls "the relationship" (*das Verhältnis*). The word is thought of not as a mere reference or relation but as that which keeps and maintains (*das Haltende*) in the sense of that which grants.

41. *US* 180.
42. *US* 186.

What poets and thinkers have in common is the element "language"; but we do not yet know how "element" is to be understood and how it varies in meaning depending on whether the word is used poetically or in thought. At the beginning of the interpretation of George's poem it seemed as if the proximity of poetizing and thought was reached: that which has been composed must become accessible through thought. But, as Heidegger says in the second lecture, something essential is lacking in this interpretation—namely, the comprehension of proximity *as such*, the proximity which the interpretation takes as its point of departure. In both poetizing and thought we dwell already in language, but to catch a glimpse of this sojourn is most difficult. Since this sojourn determines man in his essence, the return "into the region of our being human" [43] is our main task and that which, within Heidegger's dimension of thought, governs all his pains and efforts. This region is not to be understood as a "stationary place" to which man is nailed down but as the abode in which the possibility of developing is given to him.

Heidegger has never conceived of the return to this abode as an arbitrary archaization; that is impossible because Dasein is understood to be essentially historical, and history never goes backward. Indeed, Heidegger's comparison of "the step backward to the abode of man's essence" with "the step forward to the essence of the machine"—where the latter obviously is meant critically—is governed by the conception that, as long as man does not know in what his essence consists, in what it is grounded, progress in the sense of technical mastery is questionable. The one who progresses in this way can measure his progress only in regard to his progressing ability to master nature; he need not know anything about the position in which he finds himself there.

In the interpretation of George's poem it was left undecided how the gem is to be understood. But now Heidegger proposes that the gem for which the Fate goddess does not find a word is nothing but the word itself. According to Heidegger the limit manifests itself here for the poet. In the domain of the poet no word can be found for the word itself. Can that perhaps take place through thought? The word is not a thing. If we search for it among things, we shall never find it. The word "is" not, if

---

43. *US* 190.

we reserve the word *is* for the realm of things; but nevertheless it "is" in a more privileged way than all things. Heidegger expresses this in the following way: "As far as the word is concerned (if in thought we wish to do justice to it) we should never say 'it is' [*es ist*] but rather 'it gives' [*es gibt*]." [44]

Es gibt must not be understood here in the sense of being present-at-hand, in which one can say, "There are [*es gibt*] beautiful apples this year," but in the sense of giving as granting. The word, according to its very essence, is granting. What it gives is *Being.* This is not to be understood in the sense that the word lets the thing come into being just as, according to the medieval conception, everything originated from God's thought. We must recall here the concept of clearing in which all being can appear without its being created by the clearing. The question remains as to how we are to conceive of the word as that which gives; that is precisely the task of our thoughtful concern for the word.

In searching for the proximity of poetizing and thought we have, so far, only reached the point of understanding that their nearness is to be conceived of on the basis of language. In the following statement a decisive shift is expressed: "For man is man only insofar as he is devoted to the address of language, is used for language, to speak it." [45] Until now the determination of man's essence was the main issue, and we came across language as the abode which, although nearest to man, remains hidden from him; but here man suddenly steps backward, and language comes to the fore. This statement represents the extreme pole of the conception of language as merely a means of communication, a commodity. Man suddenly appears as the one who is used—by language. Is this not an impermissible hypostatization of language? How is language to be understood as the essential element with man merely at its service?

In order to proceed, Heidegger assumes that the essence of language is to be found in the saying (*Sage*). "Saying [*sagan*] means to show: to let appear, to free in a way which is at the same time clearing and hiding, taken in the sense of pro-offering of what we call world." [46] This is first of all the consistent continuation of the conception of language as found in "The Origin of the

44. *US* 193.
45. *US* 196.
46. *US* 200.

Work of Art," where the letting appear is seen in its twofold character of freeing and holding back, of revealing and concealing, and as mentioned there also in connection with the explanation of truth.[47]

In order to get closer to the essence of language Heidegger takes the following guiding principle for his experience with language—the essence of language: the language of Being (*das Wesen der Sprache: die Sprache des Wesens*). In this guiding principle a change takes place which—once we have understood it, once it has taken place with us—will lead us to the extreme.

In the first part of this principle "essence" (*Wesen*) is understood as quiddity (*to ti estin*). "Language" is the subject; what is at stake is understanding the *essentia* of the subject. "The essence which is thus understood is delimited to that which is later called the concept, the representation with the help of which we bring close to ourselves and grasp what a thing is."[48] (This refers back at the same time to the first stanza of "The Word" by Stefan George.) The essence which is understood in this way keeps us in the domain of the proposing representation of metaphysics.

In the second part of the principle it is in no way permitted merely to bring a change of terms about so that *Wesen* thus becomes the subject and "language" is attributed to it; this change must bring about a turn from the proposing representation of metaphysics to a thought which is no longer metaphysical. Since we have grown up wholly within the representation of metaphysics and have inherited from it one mode of representing, this new way of speaking must appear strange to us.[49]

In the first statement *Wesen* means quiddity; in the second statement it must be understood as continuing and lingering, not as mere duration, but as that which concerns us, strikes us, touches and moves us. "Language belongs to this continuous abiding and is inherent in that which moves everything as that which is most characteristic of it."[50] However, how are we to think of that which moves everything? In one of Heidegger's most recent publications [51] it is thought of as the Fourfold, as the

47. *WW* 41 ff.
48. *US* 201.
49. See pp. 65–68 above.
50. *US* 201.
51. Cf. *VA* 176–81.

four regions of world—earth, heaven, men (mortals), and gods —which in their interplay constitute the world.

In his interpretation of some lines from the fifth stanza of Hölderlin's "Bread and Wine" Heidegger sees "the word . . . as the region which lets earth and heaven, the flowing of the depth and the power of the highest, encounter one another, and which determines earth and heaven as the world regions." [52] Language is thus understood as that which governs the interplay of the four world regions. In this mutual interplay nearness takes place. Nearness and saying as that which lets appear are what continuously abide from language—they are the same (*das Selbe*).

> Language as the Fourfold of world is no longer merely such a thing with which we, the speaking men, have a connection in the sense of a relation which exists between man and language. Language as the saying which moves the world is the matrix of all relationships. It relates, supports, and enriches the "opposition to one another" of the world's regions, maintains and guards them while it—the saying—holds to itself [*an sich haltet*].[53]

In this connection Heidegger no longer understands the sounding forth of language as a result of physiologico-physical processes. "The sounding forth of language is detained in the tuning which chimes the regions of the world structure to one another by playing them onto one another." [54]

Heidegger has reached here, in regard to language, a summit in the realm of saying which touches upon the limit of that on which we can reflect and which must evoke astonishment. Language is thought of as the original source which keeps the world regions together, which keeps them opposite one another. We are constantly in danger of falling back into the usual representations, according to which language is like an external link, and one cannot understand from where this link comes or from what it derives its linking power.

If Heidegger is understood in an approximately appropriate way, language is nothing separate, found outside the Fourfold of the world (where else then should it be?); it is the relatedness

52. *US* 207.
53. *US* 215.
54. *US* 208.

of the Fourfold in the Fourfold itself. It is not a transcendent power, for that would be a metaphysical representation; it is, rather, the proximity that governs in the Fourfold, for which Heidegger uses the word *nearness* (*Nahnis*). Formulated in a different way, it is the original gathering (*Versammlung*). Here Heidegger agrees with Heraclitus and his idea of the *Logos,* which Heidegger for years has explained as the original gathering. Language as the original gathering is soundless. Through language, seen in this way, it is given to man to say "is"; and Heidegger has thought about this from the start. The gathering and soundless language of the silence is the language of abiding Being (*Wesen*)—of Being provided it is not represented metaphysically. In the last line of George's "The Word," Heidegger sees a poetic reference to the breakdown of the word as we are familiar with it and to thought's comprehension of language's stillness. This is possible only because poetizing and thought possess their proximity in language as nearness.

In order to avoid the impression that the issue here is about decreed theses through which the truth concerning language is fixed and not about a tracking of the unsayable or about always new traces which could lead to further approximation, another idea will be presented for consideration. This idea is taken from Heidegger's "The Road to Language," which is the most recent of his texts on language. In this lecture Heidegger considers how man's speaking, man's language, is related to the language of the stillness. To understand *Ereignis,* a word which is at the center of this text, we must first briefly indicate the context in which the word emerges.

Language speaks by pointing. "Language speaks in that it is the one that points; and, reaching into all the regions of the world, it lets that which comes to presence out of each region appear and disappear." [55] The connection between language and letting appear is found in all texts about language, starting with *Being and Time;* but of course how this letting appear is to be thought of and what it is that speaks change. According to Heidegger, the speaker (man) can speak only because he listens to language, and he is able to hear only because he belongs to language. "Only to those who belong to [language] does the saying grant the possibility of listening to language and thus of

55. *US* 255.

speaking." [56] Thus Heidegger sets off this granting as a fundamental trait of language. The relationship between the speaker and language recalls the relationship between Dasein and Being that Heidegger mentions earlier, when he says that Dasein can be only by the grace of Being, but on the other hand Being is in need of Dasein.[57] "Language is in need of man's speech and is nevertheless not the mere product of his speech activity." [58]

The basic language, which Heidegger calls saying, makes all appearing possible. "The saying governs and joints the 'Free' of the clearing, for which all appearing must search and from which all disappearing must flee, whereunto each being present and being absent must point itself, must announce itself." [59] From what takes place in saying, conceived of in this way, Heidegger comes to the *Ereignis*. It makes something be suited for (*ereignet*), that is, it grants "the Free of the clearing in which what is present can abide and from which what is absent can escape and, in withdrawal, can keep its abiding." [60] This granting must not be understood according to the cause-effect schema. "There is nothing else to which one could still reduce the e-vent and with the help of which it could be clarified." [61] It is the last thing that our glance comes across as it tries to unravel saying's granting. In another essay Heidegger says of Being, "it gives [*es gibt*]"; here he says that the *Ereignis* also grants this *es gibt,* "of which Being, too, is still in need in order (as presence) to arrive at what is proper to it." [62]

The manifold possibilities of showing refer to the saying as that which shows, and this, in turn, refers to the *Ereignis*. It may be appropriate here to remember that we are not permitted to hypostatize the *Ereignis* as a power which is beyond everything and which holds sway over Being; we must rather try to grasp the *Ereignis* as that which governs in language and which we run into in our questioning back concerning language's pointing. In our attempt at thinking the *Ereignis*, by no means do we leave language behind. A new aspect of language offers itself here: the way in which language lets man himself speak

56. *US* 255.
57. Cf. *HB* 74–76 (281).
58. *US* 256.
59. *US* 257.
60. *US* 258.
61. *US* 258.
62. *US* 258.

by making available to him the clearing in which each being will appear. Again, this connection must not be understood in the sense that man is subject to a power to which he must submit himself; Heidegger wishes to show what man owes to language as saying. Through language man is able to speak in the sense of the *logos* that expresses itself with spoken words. (A change has taken place here which, in regard to *Being and Time,* is radical.) Genuine speech is for Heidegger a cor-responding to the saying and to the appropriating e-vent. The relationship between Dasein and Being, which we mentioned earlier, returns when Heidegger says, "Man is used in order to bring the voiceless saying to sounding." [63]

In genuine speech nothing takes place but a manifestation of the appropriating e-vent, which remains hidden, however, for the one who speaks. That is why, according to Heidegger, the thinking experience of the essence of language is nothing but the freeing of the movement that leads from the appropriating e-vent to man's speech. Language is able to grant the clearing because in its very essence language is a granting and an appropriating e-vent. The historical moment, which Heidegger's thought never leaves, is present here too. The appropriating e-vent is not a unique occurrence. It is able to reveal itself, to show or to hide itself; according to this showing or hiding, language comes to pass, and man's speech is something that changes.

> All language of man comes to pass in the saying, and as such it is genuine language in the strict sense of the word, although in each case the nearness to the appropriating e-vent will be different. Each genuine language, because it is assigned to man by the movement of the saying, because it is sent to him, is therefore fateful [*Geschick-lich*].[64]

In what way does this surprising idea at all pertain to the subject of this paper, which is poetry and language? Heidegger says, "All pondering thought is poetry, but all poetizing is thinking." [65] In Heidegger's view, what genuinely poetizes is the appropriating e-vent, which remains appropriated also to language; in his earlier texts it can therefore be addressed as poetry.

63. *US* 260; cf. p. 91 above.
64. *US* 264.
65. *US* 267.

Discussion

LASZLO VERSÉNYI: I would like to begin by commenting on Professor Biemel's introductory remarks concerning the difficulty of entering into a dialogue with Heidegger. Professor Biemel prefaces his paper with a warning: Since Heidegger tries to overcome tradition, we must not attempt to translate his words into the language of traditional philosophy and must not criticize his thought from the point of view of traditional metaphysics. "We must begin by admitting that we are wholly unable to give an interpretation" of Heidegger's philosophy and that we can neither reveal its hidden ground nor understand the dimensions opened up by it. Since to this day we remain strange to this thought, says Professor Biemel, we cannot enter into a genuine dialogue with Heidegger. The most we can do is to prepare the ground for the time, if that time should ever come, when a genuine discussion with Heidegger might take place.

In contrast to this approach I would like to suggest that the time has indeed come for us to enter into a dialogue with Heidegger, that this is not only possible but necessary if we are to do justice to his philosophy, and that in the process of this dialogue we may find that his thought is less strange and less nontraditional than we first suspected or Heidegger claims. To support this suggestion I would like to take a look at the three stages of Heidegger's thought discussed by Professor Biemel and indicate briefly some of the questions that I think can and must be raised at each of these stages.

First, in *Being and Time* language is the articulation of intelligibility. Its function is to put into words our understanding of the entire complex of Being-in-the-world, and this disclosure of Being-in-the-world is at the same time our function, our essential mode of Being, as existing Dasein.

If we accept this characterization of language and Dasein, it seems to me entirely possible to enter into a dialogue with Heidegger by raising the question of whether his articulation of the structure of Being-in-the-world reveals rather than obscures this structure. After all, this basic structure is our own, and its disclosure is the essence of our own existence. Therefore, by raising this question we are not doing something alien to us but are essentializing and radicalizing our own mode of Being. In view of this, *Being and Time* invites us to rather than forbids us from the dialogue.

In the second stage of Heidegger's philosophy there is a hermeneutic shift away from the interpretation of our everyday understanding of Being; yet, for all this, Heidegger's view of language does not greatly change. Although it is a more essential language that is being analyzed in this stage, the essence of language is still world- and self-disclosure. It is still language that "first brings beings qua beings into the open," [66] that names things and by this naming brings them to word and makes them shine forth. Though language is now called poetry, the essence of poetry is still truth—the disclosure of world and earth, the disclosure of the ground on which a historical nation stands as well as a disclosure of what abides and endures in and through all historical change. Without language there is still no experience of Being, no world, no history, and no essential existence for man, whose Dasein is firmly grounded on language's ground only through the poet's word.

If we accept this view, it is no more difficult and no less necessary for us to enter into a dialogue with Heidegger than it was in the first stage. Although we deal here not with the everyday understanding of Dasein but with the rare and exceptional understanding and disclosure of world and earth that happens in great poetry, we can and must raise the same question as before: Is it truth or untruth, disclosure or concealment, that takes place in these works? Do Heidegger's interpretations of Sophocles and Rilke, Anaximander and Heraclitus, reveal or conceal, enrich or impoverish, the world that is opened up by their saying? Is Heidegger's selection of these poets and thinkers justified by the essential truth of their work, that is, by the fact that their words reveal better than those of other poets and thinkers what is most essential in our tradition and most abiding in our world? Since the poets' greatness consists in disclosing, founding, and opening up the historical ground on which we stand, their works still invite us to rather than forbid us from a thoughtful reflection, a reflection on them as well as on our Being. Not only is Heidegger engaged here in a dialogue with tradition, but we too must enter into this dialogue; for, in the words of Hölderlin, the poet from whom Heidegger is so fond of quoting, we are essentially that dialogue.

66. *HW* 6o.

Professor Biemel might agree with what I have said thus far about the possibility of a dialogue, but in the third stage the situation changes radically in his view. "We must now attempt the leap to Heidegger's later texts," he counsels; the leap is necessary, in his opinion, because in these texts philosophy and thought diverge so greatly as to become basically different ways of approach to the disclosure of Being. Philosophy remains metaphysical, while essential thought attempts to overcome metaphysics and therefore must not be translated into the language of traditional philosophy. However, as far as Professor Biemel's description of this stage goes, it is hard to see why a leap is necessary; certainly the difference between the second stage of Heidegger's view of language and the third one does not seem to justify a claim of radical discontinuity.

In *Holzwege* language first brought being qua beings into the open; by naming them, language made them appear as the beings they were. In the last three essays of *On the Way to Language*, language does exactly the same: the word brings into the open and maintains the thing as thing. In *Holzwege* the work of art gathered all the strands of a world together and revealed a whole world in its opposition to the earth's self-refusal. In the essays in *On the Way to Language* the role of language is essentially the same: "Language, as the world-moving saying, is the relation of all relations. It relates, supports, presents, and enriches the opposition to one another of the world's regions." [67] It holds them together in their opposition and preserves them as such. Like the Heraclitean *logos*, language is still an "original gathering" of all that is disparate into a complex unity and an unfolding of this unitary whole into all its disparate yet related strands. "Ek pantōn hen, ek henos panta," where *hen panta* is not what the *logos* says but what the *logos* does, the way in which the *logos* is. [68]

This view of language represents no essential departure from the view expressed in the essays of the second stage. What is more important, and the point I want to make here, is that this view in no way supports Heidegger's claim to have overcome metaphysics and broken the bounds of traditional philosophy in order to initiate an entirely new way of thinking. In what way is language as this type of essential disclosure, as

67. *US* 215.
68. *VA* 219.

this Heraclitean gathering of all into one, different from what language has always been and done in the history of Western thought? Was not Plato's *dialegesthai* a careful gathering and holding apart, a weaving together and distinguishing in their unity, of all the strands of Being? Was not the function of Plato's forms the Heraclitean *hen panta*? Was not Plato's *Agathon* the source of all being and shining forth, the ground of all disclosure and visibility, in much the same way as the *logos* to which all language corresponds is in Heidegger? I suggest that, if Heidegger had read Plato as sympathetically as he did Heraclitus, he would have seen this.

At any rate, even in this third stage, both Heidegger's language and language in Heidegger remain to a large extent metaphysical. Since the function of language is still "to reach into all the regions of the world and in each case to let appear and disappear that which comes forth out of this region," [69] language cannot dispense with *ta physika onta.* Language is still their unfolding and opening up, and it is still in and through this unfolding that Being grants itself in language to us.

So far, I would say, Heidegger's thought about and use of language is neither very strange nor as nonmetaphysical and nontraditional as he likes to claim. On the contrary, this thought lives on a historical ground and is nourished by tradition. Heidegger's merit is not that he breaks with tradition but that he revitalizes it by drawing from its deepest wells of inspiration and returning to the sources that gave it life and substance.

It is, of course, true that there is a strange strain in Heidegger's latest thought, a strain that is truly nonmetaphysical and as such resists interpretation and forbids rather than invites philosophical dialogue. Yet even this strain is far from being novel or nontraditional. In Heidegger's latest essays there is an increasing emphasis on a new hermeneutic that is not an interpretation of the poets' understanding of Being or of ours but is rather an uninterpretive transmission of the mission (*Geschick*) of Being. Language becomes more and more a mysterious "bringing of message and tiding," a silent hearkening to the ineffable voice of Being, and a "making manifest of that which is wholly Other." [70] Since we speak in "another tongue" in transmitting

69. *US* 255.
70. *US* 122, 128.

this Message that uses us as messengers, the message can no longer be translated into the language of metaphysics. Since the ground on which we now stand is a groundless ground, a "ground without why," any philosophic questioning on our part is out of order, and only silent submission to the self-granting mystery remains open to us. Since language is now essentially a monologue, "speaking alone and lonesome to itself," [71] we can no longer enter into a dialogue—with Heidegger or with each other—but can only perform the lonely leap into the abyss of this groundless thought. Professor Biemel is certainly right in saying that we cannot overcome the strangeness of Heidegger's message here. The reason we cannot do so, however, is not because Heidegger is saying something new or unfamiliar but because strangeness is the very essence of what Heidegger is now saying, just as it has always been the essence of all thought attempting to overcome metaphysics.

All such attempts to say the unsayable are attempts to overcome not just metaphysics but language itself. Since language cannot be overcome by language, these attempts are doomed to fail, doomed to end in ambiguity, strangeness, mystery. This does not make them fruitless or unnecessary; their very failure teaches us something about language by pointing to the limits beyond which all must remain strange to us, bound to language as we are. Thus, while these attempts disclose nothing beyond language, they do disclose the boundaries of language, and this is a most necessary disclosure. Straining language to its breaking point (*wo das Wort gebricht*) may be the most difficult and dangerous task imposed on us, but as this thrust against language alone makes us aware of the precariousness of the ground on which we stand—namely, language—the task must be undertaken.

The task must be undertaken because it is one that language imposes on us, as Heidegger emphasizes. That he is right is witnessed by the fact that this attempt to do with language what language cannot do was made again and again, not just by poets and mystics but by all great philosophers in the history of Western thought. From Plato's vision of the Good beyond the dialectic, through Kant's idea of the unconditional ground which reason cannot understand yet must attempt to think, to Wittgen-

71. *US* 241.

stein's ethical nonsensicalities "beyond significant language"—
all these dangerous and daring exercises in creative thought
were attempts at precisely what Heidegger is attempting. Reason
can never find rest and satisfaction within its own boundaries
(Kant); and "the urge of man to thrust against the limits of
language" (Wittgenstein) and "to discover something that
thought itself cannot think" (Kierkegaard) has always been
present in Western thought. Reason, thought, language—call
it what you will—has continually brought itself into question,
beginning long before Heidegger. Even the path Heidegger has
taken in his philosophy of language—from our everyday disclosure of world, through the extraordinary world of poetic
disclosure, to the limits of world and word—is a well-trodden
path, taken again and again by all the great thinkers and poets in
the history of thought.

All of this is hardly surprising. Language is one continuous
whole; from the most practical to the most abstract, from the
most technological to the most mystical, it ranges back and forth
through its own expanse whether we expressly will it or not. It
is in this way that "language uses us" (Heidegger) in accordance
with its own nature. No philosophy is worth much unless it encompasses all these uses—the ways in which we use language as
well as the ways in which it uses us—because to do this is precisely the function of language, the function of thought. If we
disregard this function, we fail to fulfill not just the demand of
language but our own essential nature, which is precisely to live
up to this demand—to live in and cultivate the house of language, our only abode on earth. If we are to do this we must
remember that we do not, and are not called upon to, erect this
abode at this historical moment out of nothing. For almost three
thousand years philosophy and poetry have been at work, building and preserving it. Therefore, we can best carry on this work
not by denying our historical partnership but rather by entering into it thoughtfully, that is, by appropriating our tradition
and engaging in an ever ongoing dialogue with the thinkers and
poets of the past—just as Heidegger has done in all his work,
from *Being and Time* to his latest writings.

BIEMEL: I should like to begin with the remark which, I believe,
has elicited Professor Versényi's opposition—namely, that my
explanation is not intended as an interpretation of Heidegger's

philosophy. In the statement "We are wholly unable to give an interpretation," the word *we* refers mainly to myself. It should be noted here that it would be advantageous if Professor Versényi and I were able to come to a mutual understanding concerning the term *interpretation*. I, for example, distinguish between *explanation* (*Auslegung*) and *interpretation* (*Deutung*). An explanation is an attempt to work out clearly the structure of a text, its construction, its articulation, so that we may get into the text and understand it. An interpretation attempts more; here we wish to understand what the text, be it a philosophical or literary one, is really about, what it changes in our horizon of understanding, and the extent to which the text itself thus occasions a change in our own horizon. This change must be understood in explicit terms. In order to be able to do this we should have succeeded, strictly speaking, in transcending the relevant text (of the philosopher in question). An example of such an interpretation is Heidegger's interpretation of Kant, in which Heidegger attempts to bring to light what had remained unsaid in Kant's thinking.

I am not attempting here to establish something like this, and in fact I do not know of anyone who has succeeded in giving such an interpretation of Heidegger. I feel it is better and more sincere to admit this and then to undertake the preparatory work for such an interpretation. I consider my contribution here to be such a preparatory work. However, one could misunderstand my position if he were to interpret my statement as meaning that I think it impossible for anyone to come to such an interpretation at some future time.

Another concept that leads to misunderstanding is the concept of "strangeness." When I spoke of the strangeness of Heidegger's thought, I did not mean that his thought does not concern us and that we do not have to commit ourselves to it. I meant, rather, that the experience of this strangeness constitutes a decisive step in the direction of possibly becoming familiar with his thought. If we do not come to the point where we experience this strangeness, if we do not live through it, then, in my view, we are in danger of placing Heidegger right back in that domain, precisely in that dimension which he wishes to overcome. This could be formulated dialectically so that, with the strangeness as the negative moment, the presupposition for a becoming familiar as the positive moment is given also.

Professor Versényi consistently formulates his objection by arguing that Heidegger's thought is less surprising, and equally less different from the tradition (which obviously constitutes that with which we are familiar), than what I meant to indicate by my remark and what Heidegger would have us believe. He therefore makes an effort to show the extent to which Heidegger remains bound to the tradition by discussing, precisely from this perspective, the three phases that I have elaborated.

One remark is in order here. I agree with Professor Versényi that Heidegger indeed maintains a continuous dialogue with metaphysics. In this respect Heidegger differs considerably from Husserl, who wishes to materialize a radical new beginning in philosophy and therefore places the tradition between brackets. Because Husserl does not need the tradition for his new beginning, he is able to manage with a minimum of traditional knowledge—Descartes, the English empiricists, Kant, and certain ideas from Brentano. On the other hand he thoroughly takes issue with the psychological and logical literature of his time. Wittgenstein, too, takes a negative stand in regard to the tradition; for him it is something like a trap that prevents him from getting ahead. The philosophical problems of the tradition are quasi problems; in his view what matters is to set in motion an original questioning. Heidegger, however, knows the tradition. Renouncing it would contradict his conception of historicity. The question is merely whether he remains bound to the tradition or indeed succeeds, through understanding the tradition and interpreting it, in opening up a new dimension not yet found in the tradition.

Heidegger's interpretation of metaphysics is the first to bring metaphysics to a self-contained unity, showing connections which had never before been anticipated. One can obviously argue as to whether or not Heidegger always does justice to individual philosophers.

I should now like to remark on some specific issues. Professor Versényi says that *Being and Time* invites rather than prohibits a dialogue. I, too, believe that *Being and Time* has been a work of revolutionary influence during the first part of our century, that almost no philosopher can avoid its influence, and that virtually everyone must come to terms with the book. If one calls any attempt whatsoever at such understanding a dialogue, then I agree with Professor Versényi; however, if we look back and examine, for instance, Husserl's copy of *Being and Time* and the comments he made there, we can evaluate how strange and unusual this work has been for Heidegger's contemporaries. The theses and insights contained in this book are so widely propagated today that we can scarcely understand that in its time the work fell like a bombshell. We need only think, however, of value philosophy, epistemology, or philosophy of consciousness and the influence which *Being and Time* had on these currents in order to remind ourselves of its impact.

Today *Being and Time* has lost much of its strangeness because it has changed us. Nevertheless, a genuine dialogue with it has not yet been brought about, as far as I can see. For such a dialogue to take place, an equally independent thinker must take a position in regard to the work and interpret it accordingly. Even a systematic explanation of the book is still lacking, although some good starts have been made in that direction.

Let me say, therefore, that *Being and Time* was surprising and strange at the time it first appeared; however, it has changed us in such a way that it no longer appears strange to us. We must add here that this important book still remains closest to the tradition, as Heidegger himself pointed out.

As far as the second section of my essay is concerned, I would like to point out that Heidegger's interpretation according to which art is an outstanding mode in which truth abides—that is to say, is historical—has indeed had such an influence also that we no longer experience its novelty. On the other hand, however, this view has not been experienced in the same way within the tradition, with the exception of Schelling, whose interpretation comes very close to Heidegger's.

In order to avoid making this rejoinder too long I should like to move immediately to the third phase, Heidegger's latest publications on which we have relied for his interpretation of language. For Professor Versényi there is no difference between Heidegger's view in this stage and what he says about language in his earlier writings. Therefore, according to Professor Versényi, Heidegger remains within the perspective of the metaphysical interpretation of language here too.

First an incidental remark is in order. According to Hei-

degger, Heraclitus is not a thinker who stands in the tradition
of metaphysics but rather an original thinker who genuinely
thought about what was later to be buried in the tradition. Just
because Heidegger establishes a relationship with Heraclitus, as
I have tried to do also, is no argument for the thesis that Heidegger remains within the metaphysical tradition.

When Professor Versényi suggests that Heidegger merely
takes up the Platonic tradition (for instance, where the Idea of
the *Agathon* occupies the place Heidegger attributes to Being),
we must remind ourselves that, in Heidegger's view, it is precisely in Plato that a decisive step away from the original experience of Being has been taken. Heidegger explains this step
by pointing out that, in Plato, *alētheia* is "brought under the
yoke" of the Idea. This means in turn that, although truth is
still present as unveilment, the tendency toward concealment
which is to be thought of simultaneously with unveilment is no
longer found here. Consequently, the idea of reception comes
to the fore. Furthermore, the Idea becomes that which makes
this reception of the truth possible. This means (formulated in
an exaggerated way) that a start has been made toward the
interpretation of *logos* as man's reception—an interpretation
which, in Heraclitus' view, is impossible. Thus, according to
Heidegger, the fundamental interplay of concealing and revealing becomes, in Plato, a one-sided revealment.

Another characteristic should be mentioned to clarify the
separation of the Platonic position from the position defended by
Heidegger—namely, the moment of historicity. There is no
room for this moment in Plato's interpretation. On the other
hand I willingly grant that the characteristic trait of the revealment, of the letting becoming manifest, which we find in Plato
reminds us of Heidegger's characterization of language. A
thorough analysis, however, can easily demonstrate that this is
just a reminder, something like a resonance.

I completely agree with Professor Versényi that Heidegger's
thought has a historical ground and is nourished by the tradition,
that he revives the tradition and leads us back to the original
sources; but I disagree with him when he argues that Heidegger's
thought exhausts itself in this revival. Heidegger's success in
showing and interpreting metaphysics as a uniform movement
is possible only because he is able to stand within metaphysics
and, at the same time, take a position outside it. In other words,

by going back to the ground of metaphysics he is able to lay something bare which remained hidden from metaphysics itself. In following the unfolding of Heidegger's thought we can convince ourselves how the return to the ground of metaphysics is abandoned and transcended in his most recent publications.

In "Time and Being," Heidegger says:

> To think Being without being, means to think Being without any reference to metaphysics. Such a reference, however, is still maintained in any attempt to transcend metaphysics. This is why we must refrain from any attempt to transcend it and must leave metaphysics to itself. If a transcendence (of metaphysics) continues to be necessary, then it concerns that kind of thought which expressly focuses its attention on the e-vent (*Ereignis*) in order to address (*sagen*) It (the e-vent) from itself (thought) to itself.[72]

Here Heidegger interprets in his own way first the overcoming of Being in the sense of Beingness (*ousia*)—the point in question is to understand that Being can be thought of differently from the way it is in metaphysics—and second the insight that this Being which is thought of in a nonmetaphysical way remains bound to metaphysics precisely through the fact that it pushes itself away from metaphysics. Thus, this step too is to be abandoned, which is precisely what Heidegger does in this text where Being is conceived of in terms of the e-vent (*Ereignis*).

Professor Versényi grants that in Heidegger's later publications a nonmetaphysical trait manifests itself, but his thesis is that even this trait is not new or nontraditional. The references to Plato, Kant, and Kierkegaard are examples that remain within the realm of metaphysics and are even typical examples of the metaphysical attitude. To say that Heidegger's thoughtful attempt in regard to language has been made repeatedly by the great philosophers and poets is, in my view, yet to be justified. If Professor Versényi means that these writers and poets have discovered the limit of language, and thus that the limit has been experienced, I agree with him. However, Heidegger does not limit himself merely to that experience; he attempts to change language. This change, taken from the viewpoint of metaphysics, may be characterized as an overcoming of this

72. *SD* 25.

limit, a new attaining of a language for which we do not yet have a name. According to Heidegger this language is the language of thought as language of the e-vent. It seems to me that this language sounds strange to us today because it is unfamiliar to us.

4 / Heidegger's Topology of Being

Otto Pöggeler

ON THE PERIPHERY of Heidegger's work there is a remarkable booklet entitled *From the Experience of Thinking*, which presents some isolated sayings resembling short poems in form. In this booklet, written in 1947 by a thinker in his secluded mountain cabin, there appears the saying: "But thinking poetizing is truly the topology of Beon (*Seyns*)." * To prevent objections to this saying, Heidegger elucidates it with other pertinent phrases. Summarizing Heidegger's thought, one can perhaps state that topology indicates to Being the place of its essence; and, since the poetic character of thought is still hidden, one sees today in such a saying the "utopia of a half-poetic understanding." However, as the topology of Being, this poetizing thinking is the task which modern thought must undertake. Heidegger mentions topology again in his dialogue on nihilism with Ernst Jünger. In Heidegger's view Jünger gives us merely a topography of nihilism, of its proceedings and its overcoming, and this topography should be preceded by a topology, by "the providing of space (*Ort, topos*) for" (*eine Erörterung*).[1] One could summarize Heidegger's many lectures, essays, and letters which

---

* Following Hölderlin, Heidegger occasionally uses the older German spelling *Seyn* instead of *Sein*. We render it by an equally antiquated form that comes from the Anglo-Saxon: *Beon*. In Heidegger's view the antiquated form designates the difference that holds sway between Being and beings, that is, the ontological difference. (William J. Richardson: *Heidegger: Through Phenomenology to Thought* [The Hague: Nijhoff, 1963], pp. xvi, 457, 554).
1. ED 22; W 240.

have been published during the last decades as fragments of a topology of Being, as fragments of an effort to lead the mere topography of the "metaphysical" thought of Being over into a topology of Being. Heidegger's attempt at founding ontology in a fundamental ontology, of overcoming metaphysics in a metaphysics of metaphysics, becomes adequately materialized only in this topology.[2]

The sayings which appear in *From the Experience of Thinking* should be reflected upon here. These phrases indicate that thought taken as the saying of the place of the "abiding coming to pass," that is, as the saying of the truth of Being, together with poetizing, belongs in the domain of language. However, this poetizing thinking is offensive and scandalous to what is considered thought today. In point of fact today's philosophy, which has awakened and sobered down, claims that this metaphysical speculation is no more than a poetic or pseudopoetic dream. This is the case whether the proof for this view is along the lines of the linguistico-analytic criticism of meaning characteristic of the Anglo-Saxon tradition or along the lines of the German historical tradition, which, through the history of ideas and the criticism of ideologies, tries to unmask what—as half-poetic and metaphorical talk, necessarily bound to a certain point of view—was once called philosophy. The point in question is whether Heidegger's thought is no more than a last exaggeration of pseudopoetic speculation, something like a bewildering dream that wakes one in the morning, or whether it is a legitimate attempt to question back to the presuppositions of metaphysical tradition, to maintain thereby the genuine concern of this tradition, and even to uncover this concern. Precisely what is this topology of Being which must almost appear to be the utopia of a half-poetic understanding?

2. Erling W. Eng raised the following questions: "Does the formulation 'topology of Being' not require that it be meaningful in the Greek philosophical tradition to speak of a *logos* of *topos* or *topoi*? Can this position be sustained? Is it not possible that such a formulation makes sense only in terms of ancient Hebrew religion?"

Heinrich Ott asked: "Is Being the last and most encompassing theme of Heidegger's thought? Or does the concept of Being appear only within the perspective of an engagement with the Western philosophical tradition? Or is there perhaps an even more encompassing theme in Heidegger's thought, namely, the 'hermeneutic'? (For instance, in Heidegger's dialogue with the Japanese in *On the Way to Language,* the concept of Being plays no part at all.)"

I

Let us briefly recall that from the very beginning the "saying" of Being—or better, perhaps, the problem concerning "Being," "Language," and "Being and Language"—has occupied a central position in Heidegger's thought. Heidegger has often pointed to the fact that the Being question of Brentano's dissertation *Von der mannigfachen Bedeutung des Seienden nach Aristoteles* can be found at the very beginning of his own road toward thought. *Being and Time* was to prepare, if not to give, a "science *of Being as such*, . . . its possibilities and its derivatives." [3] The author of *Being and Time* believes that he has been able to trace a fundamental, inherited prejudice of all speaking about Being —namely, when one speaks of the Being of a being, one apparently takes Being as something that is continuously present. Therefore, in this being present (of the *ousia*) one can distinguish between the *that* of the being present (the *existentia*) and the differing *what*, that is, the way that what is present looks thus, (*eidos; the essentia*). Regardless of whether one takes the *essentia* or the *existentia* as primordial—or even if one should prove that the *existentia* is by no means a "real predicate"—one remains nevertheless within the domain of a form of thought that conceives of Being as continuous presence and from there distinguishes between essence and existence. Man in his own mode of Being, that is, man as *de facto* historical "existence," can in no way be understood from the viewpoint of this conception of Being and from this distinction between essence and existence. There is therefore a need for new qualifications of Being, for "existentials" in addition to the categories that have been handed down. But how can the former qualifications be distinguished from the latter? Is there a principle for this distinction, this division of "Being"? The author of *Being and Time* is of the opinion that tradition points toward such a principle: when tradition conceives of Being as something that is continuously present, then it conceives of the meaning of Being in the light of presence and present-ness, thus in the light of a dimension of time. Our task is to determine the meaning of Being not merely from a one-

3. SZ 230.

sidedly stressed and hypostatized dimension, namely "continuous presence," but from the full and originally experienced time as a whole.[4]

How is it even possible to speak of Being? The question concerning Being is at the same time the question about the right "way of saying," about "logic" in a broad sense of the word. In his dissertation Heidegger joins the battle against psychologism in logic and demands a philosophic investigation of the doctrine of judgment as found in mathematical logic. "One would have to show," says Heidegger about mathematical logic, "how its formal character keeps it far from the vital problems of the judgment meaning, of its structure, and of its cognitive significance."[5] Heidegger has tried to deliver what is required here in section 33 of *Being and Time*. He tries to understand the meaning and cognitive significance of the assertion using the example of simple predications, taking Aristotle's definition of the assertion as *apophansis* ("showing letting be seen") as his point of departure. What an assertion achieves becomes clear when one distinguishes it from a request, a wish, or a command. Request, wish, and command intervene in the human "with one another" and try to establish something in it. If one asks for the specific meaning that the assertion has for this "with one another," it manifests itself as *apophansis:* it shows something as something. In this letting something be seen as something the synthetic character of the assertion is founded, forcing itself so much to the fore that one no longer asks for the "meaning" of the assertion. The philosophical or "ontological" interpretation that questions the *is* of the assertion taken as Heidegger tries to deliver it has to show that the achievement meaning of the assertion is a derivative one: in this showing letting be seen, what is becomes object, a thing which is identical to itself and to which predicates now become attributed. However, the world in which we live is

4. Walter Biemel made the following comments: "In Heidegger's view existentials are structural moments that are not historically determined. Formulated differently, one might say that existentials belong to the essence of Dasein as such; the question of how they are materialized concretely is indeed a historical issue. It seems to me, also, that our concernful dealing with what is ready-to-hand does not constitute a genuine existential for Heidegger."

5. *UP* 97 n. For what follows, cf. Ernst Tugendhat, *Der Wahrheitsbegriff bei Husserl und Heidegger* (Berlin: de Gruyter, 1967), esp. pp. 331 ff. Tugendhat, critically joining Husserl and Heidegger, tries to extend the concept of truth and to transcend the concept of propositional truth.

not merely a world of objects—of what is present-at-hand, as Heidegger says—but a world of what is ready-to-hand, a world in which something encounters us to which we correspond more properly through request, wish, and command than through mere assertions. Heidegger distinguishes between the apophantic *as,* which is characteristic of the letting something be seen as something, and the hermeneutic *as,* which is proper to our concernful dealing with that which is.

Thus within the whole of language the syntheses of the assertions have only a limited, if not an entirely derivative, significance. It is above all questionable whether that thinking which as a connection of assertions has reference to a world of objects or quasi objects asks the question of Being and thus asks how in our world being encounters us and in that sense "is." It could very well be that in our world a "meaning" manifests itself to the philosopher only when he engages in the living process in which such a meaning has been brought to the fore historically. In that case philosophy would have reference to methodically developed theories or contexts of assertions but would not reassume these theories in a final "theory." But what *Logos,* what language, would philosophy then follow? If it could not be merely assertion, would it not then become request, wish, command, or even conjuring gesture, prophecy, or perhaps poetry? If this question is to be clarified, we must ask, What precisely is language? In his *Habilitationsschrift* Heidegger is still trying to cope with this problem with the help of the speculative, aprioric grammar of the medieval treatises and of Husserl's phenomenology. The order of language corresponds, via the order of our knowledge of the objects, to the order of the things themselves, to "Being."

While Heidegger was still relating Being and language to one another by means of such metaphysical suppositions, the whole approach became problematic to him. "At that time," he reports, "what was mainly and specifically on my mind was the question concerning the relationship between the word of Holy Scripture and theologico-speculative thought. It was, if you like, the same relationship, namely, the one between language and Being." [6] The word of Holy Scripture is message, demand. In the hour of grace this claim places man before a decision: it grants to the one who accepts and preserves the word in faith a new

6. *US* 96.

"Being." However, this claim, as a revelation which lets all that is be seen in a new Being, is historical. It places an earlier revelation, an "old" testament, in the right light; it refers to a future, more complete revelation. Although this new Being is a Being in the direction of time, it is not the standing present of a continuous presence. When the word of the Scriptures speculatively and dogmatically becomes unfolded, either Being that has been granted toward time becomes philosophically perverted into Being as continuous presence, or traditional speculative thought breaks down (just as this should have happened, according to *Being and Time,* in the faithful questioning of the young Luther). However, Heidegger is not a theologian; the Christian faith is for him merely a model of an experience of life and world, an experience that must be able to receive its philosophical legitimation without this model, also.[7] The following question thus remains: Can the Being of being—for instance, the Being (the "abiding coming to pass") of poetry with its historical character —be understood merely as the essence of the poetry of a determined epoch? Is the relationship of poetry to philosophy or technicity, for instance, not also a historical constellation? Is

7. Since the 1930s, Heidegger has developed his thought on the basis of another model: namely, on the basis of that "tragic" world experience as Greek tragedy has developed it and as Hölderlin has tried to reactivate it. Thus, Heidegger has developed his thought on the basis of the happening of truth that comes to pass in an art which is seen from the viewpoint of Greek tragedy and Hölderlin's hymns, not from the viewpoint of the aestheticism of the modern trend. Hans-Georg Gadamer has tried within an epistemological reflection on the achievement of the sciences of man (*Geisteswissenschaften*) to bring Heidegger's motives to bear (*Wahrheit und Methode* [Tübingen: Mohr, 1960]). Jürgen Haberman later incorporated these hermeneutic and linguistico-analytic positions in a reflection on the "logic" of the social sciences which is not in the least formed by the Marxist conception of history (*Zur Logik der Sozialwissenschaften* [Tübingen: Mohr, 1967]). These attempts were rejected as pseudo-theological by philosophers oriented toward positivism, for instance, by Hans Albert in *Traktat über kritische Vernunft* (Tübingen: Mohr, 1968). The question of whether or not the issue here is about pseudo-theology, pseudo-mythology, and pseudo-poetry can certainly not be answered by referring to the fact that there is a historical connection with theological, mythological, and poetic ideas. The question is, rather, whether or not the concept of philosophy authorizes us from the start to reject as unphilosophical, pseudo-theological, pseudo-mythological, and pseudo-poetical a thought which feels that, in the final analysis, it cannot maintain a distinction in certain disciplines between ascertainable facts and evaluations, between Being and Ought, between historical investigation or philological explanation and "application."

the meaning of Being, or, as Heidegger has said since the 1930s, the truth of Being from which all possible significations of Being separate themselves, a happening that withdraws itself from and at the same time grants itself to man? [8] Is this happening *Ereignis*?

When philosophy is related to such a happening, what manner of speaking, what "logic," does it have to follow? Heidegger says that then "the fate of the domination of 'logic' within philosophy" becomes decided; the "idea of logic" dissolves "in the whirl of an original questioning." [9] The word *logic* is placed within quotation marks here, signifying that Heidegger does not mean that formal logic dissolves; to advance such a meaning would obviously be sheer nonsense. What is dissolved is the

8. I speak here of the meaning of Being as well as of significations of Being merely to obtain a plural for the word *Sinn* (other distinctions between *Sinn* ["meaning"] and *Bedeutung* ["signification"], such as Frege's, are not taken into consideration here). In his dissertation, Brentano speaks of the manifold *Bedeutungen* of "being," and Heidegger in this sense asks the question concerning the *Bedeutung* of Being in *An Introduction to Metaphysics*. In *Being and Time* Heidegger speaks of the *Sinn* of Being. However, just as in his *Habilitationsschrift* (*KB*) Heidegger introduces the *Bedeutungen* as components of the *Sinn*, in *Being and Time* he seems to have conceived of the *Bedeutungen* as articulated moments of the *Sinn* (cf. *SZ* 83, esp. 160–61). Later Heidegger substitutes for talk about the *Sinn* of Being, which obviously belongs to the viewpoint of modern historicism and epistemological reflection, talk about the truth of Being, whereby he feels that he has to understand truth as unconcealment in a philological way. Undoubtedly, to speak about the *Sinn* of Being does not imply a nominalist position any more than to speak of the truth of Being implies a realist position. In *An Introduction to Metaphysics* Heidegger indeed distinguishes between the *Bedeutung* of a word and what is named (*das Genannte*), thus between the *Bedeutung* of Being and the essence (*Wesen*) of Being, or Being itself; but then he stresses immediately that Being itself is not a "thing" and, furthermore, that Being itself "is dependent upon the word in a completely different and more essential sense" than each being. It is obviously nonsense to conceive of that Being about which Heidegger speaks as a hypostasis in the sense, for instance, of a Platonizing exaggerated realism (which, unfortunately, is quite often customary in linguistico-analytic philosophy).

9. Cf. *W* 14, 17, 103 ff. The question of whether Heidegger, in a kind of phenomenological blindness, misconceives the achievement meaning, that is, the greatness as well as the limits of this reckoning, in his polemic against "reckoning" has been developed by Oskar Becker. Cf. "Mathematische Existenz," *Jahrbuch für Philosophie und phänomenologische Forschung*, VIII (1927); *Grösse und Grenze der mathematischen Denkweise* (Freiburg and Munich: Alber, 1959); *Dasein und Dawesen* (Pfullingen: Neske, 1963); *Untersuchungen über den Modalkalkül* (Meisenheim: Hain, 1952). In regard to Becker, cf. Otto Pöggeler, "Hermeneutische und mantische Phänomenologie," *Philosophische Rundschau*, XIII (1965), 1–39.

"idea" of logic, the achievement meaning of the assertion which is one-sidedly maintained, hypostatized into idea, and given the command over philosophy—in other words, the apophantic. Heidegger opposes the tendency to conceive of philosophical speech one-sidedly from the viewpoint of the assertion as showing letting something be seen as present-at-hand—the tendency to let truth be considered merely as the evidence of something that is brought into view or at least can be brought into view; the tendency to oblige philosophy to try to possess the "naked," unveiled truth or at least to promise to lead to such a possession, the required verification. The "Being" of poetry obviously cannot be established and determined in a definitive way; above all, the meaning of the truth of Being (within which the Being of poetry, for instance, is distinguished from the Being of philosophy) can be an unlimited happening, a "history."

When we now (as Heidegger at least for a time has done) call the meaning of the truth of Being "Being"—namely, "Being itself," Beon (*Seyn*)—it becomes clear that Being, this "basic concept" of metaphysics, can by no means be a concept. Therefore, Heidegger has pointed out that, as an address to thought which withdraws itself from every definitive fixation, the "voice" of Being (the tune called by Being) becomes accessible only in an understanding "attunement." This occurs, for instance, in anxiety, which dumbfounds us and in which each "saying *is*" keeps "silent"; in the call of conscience, whose mode of calling or speaking is keeping silent; in awe (the Greek *aidōs*), which is able to let what encounters it stand in its "numinous" abysmalness.[10] When traditionally philosophical speech is understood from the viewpoint of the apophantic saying, the philosophical speech that tries to correspond to the tune called by Being is always different from and more than such a saying. It is at the same time a not-saying, a keeping silent, which can be very eloquent, which has much to say but nevertheless has to reassume all saying into a growing dumb in the presence of a happening that transcends all that is sayable in its indeterminateness and undeterminableness. The keeping silent that Heidegger demands is precisely an accomplishing of something by keeping silent (*Erschweigen*), an accomplishing of this indeterminateness and undeterminableness. The "logic" of that

10. Cf. W 9, 103; SZ 296.

philosophy which unfolds itself as topology of Being is "sigetics" (*Sigetik*), the lawfulness of that activity which, accomplishing something by keeping silent, accomplishes in all contexts of assertions the indeterminateness and undeterminableness of the happening of the "truth of Being" by keeping silent.[11]

That philosophy debouches in keeping silent is something which, strictly speaking, should excite all those diagnosticians who have already aroused endless talk about the fact that today poetry leads to dumbness, the brightness of the painting disappears, and so on. At the same time the parallelity of the most opposite tendencies of contemporary thought, namely, the Continental European speculative tradition and the English analytic tradition, appears to become tangible here. Does Wittgenstein's *Tractatus* not finish with the statement: "Of that about which one cannot talk, one must keep silent"?[12] This treatise, too, speaks very eloquently of those things about which it should have kept silent, since its six main theses formulate statements about the world as a whole. Should not the seventh thesis, namely, the demand for silence, be subject itself to the silence commandment? If there is talk of that about which one, properly speaking, should keep silent, then it is obviously preunderstood that traditional philosophical speech is able to cancel itself as meaningless. However, is this keeping silent a last act? Does it stand under the line which today is drawn to philosophy (*den Schlusstrich ziehen*)? Or is this keeping silent the origin

11. *Sigetics* is from the Greek verb *sigan*, which means "to keep silent." In the not yet published essays *Beiträge zur Philosophie*, which stem from the late 1930s, Heidegger speaks of sigetics as the "logic" of that philosophy which asks for the truth of Being. Cf., in this connection, Otto Pöggeler, *Der Denkweg Martin Heideggers* (Pfullingen: Neske, 1963), p. 276. When Heidegger conceives of language as the "chime of silence" and, thus, as the gathering together of the distinction of world and thing into the mystery, in other words, from the viewpoint of the *Ereignis* (*US* 29 ff.), his main concern is about that lawfulness of the saying of Being's truth to which the title "sigetics" points from the outside.

12. Karl-Otto Apel has tried to determine philosophically the relationship between Heidegger and Wittgenstein and in this way to take opposite philosophical paths, in regard to the task of thought today, back to an encompassing starting point. Cf. esp. "Sprache und Wahrheit in der gegenwärtigen Situation der Philosophie," *Philosophische Rundschau*, VII (1959), 161–84; "Wittgenstein und Heidegger," *Philosophisches Jahrbuch*, LXXV (1967), 56–94; "Heideggers philosophische Radikalisierung der 'Hermeneutik' und die Frage nach dem 'Sinnkriterium' der Sprache," in *Die hermeneutische Frage in der Theologie*, ed. O. Loretz and W. Strolz (Freiburg: Herder, 1968), pp. 86–152.

from which philosophy is to live from now on? Is philosophical speech altogether meaningless, or is it merely misleading in the sense that it has been misleading and will remain so? Before one is able to look for an answer to such questions, one must realize the task which Heidegger attributes to that topology whose mode of saying should be "*das Erschweigen.*"

II

WHAT IS THE ISSUE in the "science of Being" which Heidegger strives for in *Being and Time* and later presents as the topology of Being? Extrinsically and schematically, within the realm of traditional representations, one can perhaps indicate the goal of this topology in the following manner. Not only is it necessary in the individual regions of being to examine being in regard to the basic conception (*Grundverfassung*) of its "Being"; it is also necessary (insofar, at least, as this is possible) to place a general ontology, a science of being as being, in front of or, eventually, beside the regional and special ontologies such as these are elaborated in the sciences and the individual philosophical disciplines, as well as (in a "preontological way") in extraphilosophical understandings. Furthermore, one must ask in what element or on what fundament the ontologies mentioned can on the whole be developed and related to one another. In the topology of Being the issue is not so much the regional ontological work itself as the "fundamental ontological" question —how, generally speaking, does the development of "ontologies" come to pass, or how is ontology possible? Therefore, the author of *Being and Time* is interested primarily in the foundational crises of the sciences, that is to say, in the sciences insofar as they become problematic to themselves.[13] The individual modes

13. Heidegger points to the fact that mathematics, physics, biology, the sciences of man, and theology have met foundational crises (*SZ* 8–11). As far as mathematics is concerned, for instance, Heidegger could at that time point to the dispute between intuitionism and formalism, the goal in which was to find and secure the "primary mode of approach to that which should be the object of this science." Is intuitionism correct in feeling that the existence of mathematical objects is guaranteed when these objects can be constructed by certain means? Or is formalism correct in feeling that the existence is secured when these objects can function without contradiction in a mathematical theory? Oskar Becker has worked out these problems (see note 9 above). He applies Heidegger's

of man's knowledge and behavior—the various sciences, as well as art, technique, morality, faith—must be reassumed into an encompassing context of questions. How can such a context of questions be understandable in itself? Can it be further developed into an "apophantic" context of assertions, into a "theory"? If such a context cannot be developed into a theory, into what can it be developed?

Heidegger attempts to unfold this question by distinguishing, for instance, between the apophantic *as,* characteristic of the assertion that determines something as something, and the hermeneutic *as* of our practical concern with things, which takes something as something in a way that is related to man's interest and concern. I will only briefly recall Heidegger's analyses. A thing—a hammer, for instance—is (as Heidegger tries to show) in the "environment" of our everyday life not present-at-hand but ready-to-hand. The hammer, as a piece of equipment, is there in order to pound; it serves a certain praxis and, through its serviceability, refers to something else—to the leather that is to be pounded, to the shoes that are to be made. As a piece of equipment that is ready-to-hand, the hammer stands within the totality of a context in which the one piece of equipment refers to the other, within which it has a determinate relationship and significance with each individual other piece of equipment. The whole of this matrix of relations, destinations, and significations, the world as the environmental world of our everyday life, depends on the last "for-what" in which Dasein, Dasein's own Being, is at stake; in which man "comports himself" in a manner that is in many ways predestined; and in which man is "thrown" to himself, to his fellow men, and to the things. Heidegger calls this "comportment," which belongs to the "for-what" just mentioned, "care," precisely because he wants to avoid a term such as *praxis* and, for that matter, the traditional opposition of theory and praxis. Therefore all the patterns that theory and praxis may enter must thus be understood as modifications of care.

---

formulation of the problem to the sciences of man (Gadamer), poetics (Staiger), psychiatry (Binswanger), anthropology (Bollnow), and jurisprudence (Maihofer). This way of being effective (*Wirkung*) belongs to the history of the effectiveness of Heidegger's thought as well as to the further development of the speculative question concerning Being and world, or rather the metaphysico-historical clarification of this question and the association of Heidegger's calling in question of philosophy with the new approach of philosophers such as Wittgenstein and Marx.

Praxis is not without theory; it has its own mode of "vision," namely, "circumspection," and can make theory enter its service. By the same token, theory can emancipate itself largely from practical interests and apply itself to a disinterested wanting to see. The ready-to-hand then becomes the mere present-at-hand. The environment within which the ready-to-hand belongs becomes robbed of the dynamism of its references; a "demundanization" materializes. The hammer is then no longer there in order to pound. Of course, the mere presentation of a hammer as a thing which is present-at-hand, too, can at first be motivated by determinate interests; an investigation concerning the composition of the metallic hammer head, for instance, can be motivated by the interest to produce a good and powerful hammer. However, the presentation of what is present-at-hand can always be further stylized to pure theory. This theory can make the praxis enter its service; for instance, it can make the praxis construct apparatus for the theory's investigations. Praxis and theory, concern for what is ready-to-hand and presentation of what is present-at-hand, are tendencies of care that can interpenetrate one another in many ways. Dasein, however, is able to apply itself only to concern with what is ready-to-hand or to presentation of what is present-at-hand because, as Heidegger shows in the second division of *Being and Time*, it can ek-sist authentically or can forget this authentic ek-sisting. Even when the praxis takes into account the fact that active people get old and die and thus must be replaced by others, it forgets the ek-sisting in which Dasein takes upon itself its fate as its own in advancing toward its death and in wanting to have a con-science.

Heidegger does not limit himself to describing the presentation of what is present-at-hand, our concern with what is ready-to-hand, and man's ek-sisting proper. He also tries to show how these modifications of Dasein must be understood in their difference from the temporality of Dasein. Dasein is essentially temporal, namely, temporalizing time. Dasein can make a point of taking the temporalization of time upon itself; in its historicity it then expressly endures its destiny of having to temporalize time as mortal and finite man and, thus, of having to ek-sist in an authentic way. However, Dasein can also forget that it temporalizes time when, as temporal entity, it finds itself in a temporal horizon. Even the scientists—the natural scientists and the historians—would have been unable to say that the world has existed for billions of years, that there have been human beings for some hundreds of thousands of years, that there have been high cultures for several thousands of years, if in the uniqueness of their here and now they did not temporalize time. Conversely, man would have been unable to take upon himself his destiny (*Schicksal*) if he had not always already found himself in a temporal leeway according to his "inner temporality." "Historicity" and "inner temporality" are also tendencies of Dasein that interpenetrate one another in manifold ways. The turning toward historicity makes authentic existence possible, whereas the turning toward inner temporality makes possible the "self-forgotten" concern with what is ready-to-hand and the presentation of what is present-at-hand. Inner temporality is again modifiable; if the orientation toward what is in the future is largely eliminated in favor of the orientation toward what is present or even constantly toward what is making something present, the mere presentation of what is present-at-hand drives out the concern with what is ready-to-hand.[14] The temporality of Dasein in its modifiability thus proves itself to be the principle for the distinction of Dasein's possible modes of comportment.

When Dasein presents what is present-at-hand, deals with what is ready-to-hand, and ek-sists authentically, is it not necessarily already familiar with Being present-at-hand, Being ready-to-hand, and Being as ek-sistence? How is one to understand these distinctions in Being itself? When the temporality of Dasein is the principle for the division of Dasein's modes of comportment, could it not be that time, which is temporalized by Dasein, is the principle for the division of the meaning of Being into possible significations of Being, for instance, Being present-at-hand, Being ready-to-hand, Being as ek-sistence? Heidegger calls the time that is taken in this way "temporality," a name that is derived from Latin. He apparently wishes to name the dimensions, or "ecstases," of time with terms also derived from Latin; for instance, he calls the present (*Gegenwart*) "*Präsenz.*" The presentation of the various interplayings of the dimensions of temporality should then give us the guiding clue for the division of the meaning of Being. If, for instance, time is temporalized with "present" as the priority, Being has a "presentlike" (*präsenzialer*) meaning; temporalizing temporality, Dasein places

14. Heidegger has unfolded these modifications in a doctrine of the "ecstases" of temporality. Cf. esp. *SZ* 325–31, 336–39, 353, 360, 364–66.

itself in the inner temporality, which lets being be encountered in a pregiven temporal leeway as something that is present. Being can show itself in this way, for instance, in a Being present-at-hand and a Being ready-to-hand through which, by means of a shifting in the interplay of the dimensions of temporality, a difference emerges again in the "presentlike" meaning of Being, even a distinction between Being present-at-hand and Being ready-to-hand. In the third division of *Being and Time*, which as yet has not been published, Heidegger wished to show how time as temporality is the place, or domain, in which the meaning of Being becomes divided into the different meanings of Being.

Why does Heidegger take time as temporality [15] as the guiding clue for dividing Being into Being present-at-hand, Being ready-to-hand, and Being as ek-sistence, and for distinguishing the contents of the categories and existentials that are attributed to the individual "modes of Being"? The introductory section 6 of *Being and Time* gives us the answer. In the ontological tradition "Being" is understood predominantly as *ousia* or *parousia,* as presence-at-hand of what is present-at-hand, or as continuous presence—thus, from one dimension of time, namely, the present. It is the task of today's ontological questioning to take the one-sidedly accentuated presence, which is perverted even further into "continuous" presence, back into a full and pluri-dimensional time and then to understand the meaning of Being from the originally experienced time, that is, from temporality. Ontology's history thus places us before the decisive question.

The second division of *Being and Time,* namely, the phenomenological "destruction" of the ontological tradition, is meant to elucidate that the first division, namely, the phenomenological description and construction, is borne by ontology's history. The hermeneutic circle in which the investigation takes place should be paced (*Ausschreiten*) in this way.[16] However, in *Being and*

15. I will not deal here with the fact that, strictly speaking, time in connection with space supplies the guiding clue, in other words, that the temporal domain of the "world" is the building structure for the meaning of the truth of Being.

16. This circle is later called "reversal" (*Kehre*). Through some misleading formulations, Heidegger has contributed to the opinion that the reversal comes into play between the second and third divisions of *Being and Time,* that is, between the analytic of Dasein and the development of the question concerning time and Being (concerning temporality as the guiding clue for the articulation of the meaning of Being). However, the reversal comes to the fore in its full sharpness only in the transition from

Time Heidegger does not succeed in keeping this circle with all its tensions together; that is, from the very start he is unable to keep the leading suppositions and prejudices present. For this reason the course of the questioning breaks up into different questions. In the third part of the first division Heidegger should ask whether there is a main meaning of Being (Being as Being historical, corresponding to historicity as the genuine temporalization of time), a full and original meaning from which, through privation and derivation, all other meanings of Being can be gained. (This occurs, for example, in the doctrine of the *analogia entis* where the Being of each being becomes determined according to the degree to which this being participates in the highest and most perfect Being.) In the second division Heidegger should develop the question of whether or not this meaning of Being shows itself merely historically today and, perhaps, only today.

In the published parts of *Being and Time* the signification of "historicity" already breaks up into two significations that are not sufficiently thought together. In one place historicity is the genuine temporalization of time and, thus, the "principle" of the distinction between Dasein's modes of comportment. But in the introductory sections historicity is the medium in which each ontological investigation always moves and in which, therefore, the manifestation of historicity as the genuine mode of the temporality of time moves too. In the published parts of *Being and Time* it remains unclear whether the historicity of the understanding of Being has a suprahistorical structure to which the understanding of Being in early history, early cultures, and high cultures, as well as that in future epochs, must adapt themselves, or whether it is the "historicity" that is characteristic of the mature and "experienced" man of our time. (Is this historicity, the critics could certainly ask here, not a secularization of the Christian eschatology?) Is the readiness-to-hand, just as it has been developed in *Being and Time* in a "shoemaker perspective"

the first to the second division of *Being and Time,* that is, in the transition to the "destruction." There Heidegger goes back to the guiding supposition that the ontological tradition today forces us to ask authentically about what is forgotten in this tradition, namely, about time and Being. To present the reversal as a turn from a human Dasein to a hypostatized Being is sheer nonsense. As far as the reversal is concerned, it is just as little a matter of playing off Greek, or even a "pre-Socratic," thought against modern philosophy.

(which today is already historical), the readiness-to-hand of the craftsman's piece of equipment in a determinate epoch, or is it also the readiness-to-hand of the utensils of early culture or the readiness-to-hand of the products of technique? The investigations of *Being and Time,* however, not only remain in a realm of vagueness but also become entangled in an aporia. If historicity is the discoverable principle of the distinction between Dasein's modes of comportment, one cannot subsequently attribute historicity or historicality to this historicity (in the "destruction"); however, if historicity is the medium in which each question concerning the meaning of Being must remain, the question concerning the meaning of Being cannot lead to historicity as the final principle for the unfolding of the meaning of Being (that is, to an "idea" of Being, as Heidegger says).[17]

Heidegger eliminates the initial ambiguity that led him into the aporia by expressly trying to develop the way in which different significations of Being become differentiated in the meaning of Being and how temporality is, after all, the "principle" of the distinction. He shows in what sense, as he expresses it, the meaning of Being is the "ground" in which all significations of Being are rooted and from which all understanding of Being "nourishes" itself, as from the last towards-which of its Being project.[18] Heidegger heads off that "ontotheology" which first founds being in its Being and then founds this differentiated Being again in a standard being, the "god of the philosophers." (Even atheism can make use of this "god," because atheism relates all being to the mortality and historicity of man as a last reference point, that is, the god of the philosophers.) In opposition to this conception Heidegger determines the meaning of Being as abysmal groundless ground. One cannot indicate a ground for the fact that an understanding of Being emerges after all; grounding and founding always presuppose the meaning of Being, which therefore, as abyss, must turn away from itself the desire to found. While the meaning of Being lets a

17. One can obviously draw attention to the fact that Heidegger does not call historicity "principle" (namely, principle for the articulation of Dasein's modes of comportment), and that only in a very vague sense does he speak of an "idea" of Being. However, when his speaking remains vague, one should ask not what he says verbally but what he presupposes in his doing. One should ask, for instance, whether time in fact functions as "principle" for the articulation of the meaning of Being.

18. Cf. SZ 35–36, 151, 323–24.

determinate signification of Being (for instance, Being as presence-at-hand of what is present-at-hand, continuous presence) become the standard signification, it "groundlessly" (*ungründig*) bars other significations, and even itself, as the ground of manifold significations. The meaning of Being, experienced as abysmal groundless "Ground," is "truth" as unconcealment, whose coming into being must remain a mystery and whose happening is historical in a sense that cannot be understood from what we usually call history. The world as the building structure of this truth is that organized structure which is stratified in many ways and which constructs itself according to the manner in which time temporalizes itself.[19] This temporalization of time is, of course, now conceived of as a historical temporalization; thus, the stratification of the organized structure of Being's truth is a historical one that can be distinguished in epochs. For instance, when Heidegger sets forth the continuously available (*Gestell*) and the fourfold as the standard processes of organization, this "with one another" of the continuously available (the world of science and technology) and the fourfold (the world of art and religion) is thought of as a constellation that, historically, precisely determines our epoch. Indeed, only in our time is it possible for being to show itself in the world of what is continuously available as continuously available stock of resources; and yet technique was prepared by the "metaphysical" history of the West. The question of whether or not and how the world as fourfold can maintain itself together with the world as the continuously available is to be decided historically. This is still an open question.[20]

The topology of Being asks how a painting of Paul Klee, a poem of Trakl, what is observed in a physical experiment, the product of technique, an effective law of our jurisdiction, belong together in the whole of our world. Thus, it asks how in this

19. Heidegger speaks in *Being and Time* of a "transcendental horizon," that is, of that horizon in which being can be transcended toward its Being and in which Being at the same time becomes articulated in different significations (cf. *SZ* 39). Since world was at first understood from the open of the horizon, or "heavens," Heidegger proposes, in opposition to this understanding of world, an understanding of world as that which hides itself but which equiprimordially determines the building structure of the truth as "earth" (cf. *HW* 7–68 [649–701]). Later, Heidegger conceives of earth and heavens as structural moments of world.

20. Walter Biemel expressed some doubts regarding the combination of *Gestell* and *Geviert* into a unity.

world as the building structure of Being's truth the courses of Being are traced out and, therefore, how being can encounter us in different ways. Heidegger concludes that the individual courses, as well as the constellations in which these courses stand, are historical, that they are epochally changing. Heidegger even holds that Newton's laws began to be "true" with Newton, that a Galilean physical theory is not "more advanced" than a corresponding ancient doctrine in the same way that the poetry of Shakespeare is not "more advanced" than that of Aeschylus.[21] Does this mean, for instance, that in modern times a moving body behaves according to the axiom "Force is equal to mass multiplied by acceleration," but that in antiquity that body behaved (as premodern physics held) according to the axiom "Force is equal to mass multiplied by velocity"? Does this mean that the one axiom otherwise is not more right and more advanced than the other? There is something, indeed, in favor of the conception according to which the moving force and the velocity are proportional to one another: the faster one walks the more force one has to expend. To be sure, in riding a bicycle this situation becomes more problematic; and a satellite cannot be held in orbit with such a conception. The modern doctrine, however, is correct only if one distinguishes the forces having an influence on the motion, that is, only if the propelling force is separated by means of abstraction from the other influencing forces—friction and gravitation. Because there obviously was an aversion to resolving such a unitary phenomenon as the motion of a body into different components by means of methodical abstraction, the analytic experiment of modern physics remained unknown in antiquity and in the middle ages. This is the only state of affairs to which the topology of Being wishes to draw attention, thereby pointing to the fact that ancient and modern conceptions of motion cannot be immediately compared with one another.

It might appear that this topology is a historical science

21. Cf. SZ 226–27; HW 70–71. Heidegger's formulation of the problem receives its full sharpness only when one takes into consideration the possibility that being is found at the same time in a different "Being," that works of art, for instance, are not only found in early cultures in a different way than in the era of technique but can be met at a given time in different ways. For example, a church is aesthetically conceived by a tourist and at the same time, precisely as a work of art, is related to its religious origin by others.

which should strive for its own manner of exactness in the ascertainment of historical facts. However, the issue is not one of historical ascertainments but one of questions connected with historical decisions, questions that are still open. The issue is not primarily whether or not a physical theory is consistent in itself and verifiable, but what, for instance, the complex of atomic investigation, atomic armament, and atomic industry (which comes about in a remarkably irrational way) means in our world. Do we have to set limits on the future development and application of biological research and technique, which through agriculture and medicine make possible the present life of mankind? By means of what principles must we regulate the economical processes? What meaning do the sciences of man (*Geisteswissenschaften*) have in the whole of our lives? What is happening today with poetry and art? We are unalterably placed before these questions; but is it possible to develop such questions scientifically or philosophically? Rudolf Carnap has formulated the thesis that within a certain linguistic system one can ask meaningful questions about being or existence. For instance, within a system about numbers one may ask if there is a largest prime number. However, one is unable to question scientifically this system itself by asking if there are numbers. Such a question is meaningless as a theoretical question, although it does have a practical meaning when, in its context, one asks whether or not it is appropriate to apply a certain system to a determinate realm of entities. The question of whether or not a determinate linguistic system should be accepted is said to be a question of praxis.[22]

22. Cf. Rudolf Carnap, "Empiricism, Semantics and Ontology," *Revue Internationale de Philosophie*, XI (1950); L. Linsky, *Semantics and the Philosophy of Language* (Urbana: Univ. of Illinois Press, 1952). Can the unification in the direction of the structures of linguistic systems or in the direction of Wittgenstein's language games as forms of life again become the theme of philosophical reflection and, therefore, also of criticism? Or must such a unification always be presupposed as a unification that has been decided in praxis, so that philosophy taken as therapeutic language criticism merely supervises the functioning of the language games and leaves everything else the way it is? Heidegger, too, dismisses the idea of a philosophical "ultimate foundation"; nevertheless, in contrast to linguistico-analytic philosophy, he subordinates the unification above the structure of the individual "forms of life" to the critical question. Heidegger also has a maxim for this unification which, however, no longer (in an ontotheological manner) gives in a definitive way a privileged position to one determinate structure as far as content is concerned: the truth as "the truth of Being" can be brought to the fore and admitted

Are we to assume that the topology of Being changes practical questions into theoretical ones or into quasi problems? Heidegger surely attempts to cut the traditional distinction between theory and praxis and, in his own way, to develop the possibility of a knowledge for practical purposes. In the decade after he wrote *Being and Time,* Heidegger oriented himself more toward the *poiēsis* of art and poetry than toward praxis or even technique. However, this does not make his thought simply pseudopoetry; the difference between thought and poetry precisely is to be redetermined. His thought is not merely conjuring gesture when it is capable of showing how not merely the assertion but also, for instance, the question belongs to thought, how thought can be "way," and so on.[23] When this thought understands itself as *Erschweigen,* it makes other, although not necessarily "more untenable," assumptions than those that Wittgenstein makes in the concluding sentences of his *Tractatus.* In flowery and metaphorical language, as if all of this were self-evident, Wittgenstein speaks of elucidating, reciprocal understanding, the transcendence of language above itself, of a ladder and the throwing away of this ladder, of an overcoming and a "seeing the world rightly."

III

IN HEIDEGGER'S THOUGHT philosophy becomes a topology of Being, a saying of the word of Being's truth, which takes all "topographic" descriptions of the domains of truth back into itself. This topology is no longer capable of developing into a "theory" in the sense of an "apophantic" context of assertions;

---

only in such a way that the entire building structure of the truth does not collapse. (In Heidegger's view such would be the case in a universally extended technique, that is, if one were to make the world as the continuously available [*Gestell*] into something absolute.) We merely want to point to the fact that, in neo-Marxism, Heidegger's formulation of the problem is developed concretely in an analysis of the late capitalistic society. See, for instance, the attempts made by Jürgen Habermas to unmask technology itself as "ideology." Cf. Habermas, *Technik und Wissenschaft als "Ideologie"* (Frankfurt: Klostermann, 1968).

23. I have tried to develop provisionally, through an investigation of "explain" (*Erklären*), "elucidate" (*Erläuteren*), and "discuss" (*Erörteren*), how Heidegger answers the question of the saying by means of what he actually does in his later works. Cf. Pöggeler, *Der Denkweg Martin Heideggers,* pp. 280–99.

it takes all theories back into an unlimited and undeterminable happening of truth. Its logic is "sigetic"; its saying is at the same time a not-saying, an accomplishing something by keeping silent (*Erschweigen*). Is this topology hereby something other than the knowledge of knowing and not-knowing, which Socrates determined philosophy to be? Socrates is a philosopher not because in the realm of statesmanship, for example, he knows more than the statesmen. Socrates examines the statesmen, the poets, and the craftsmen (in our time, the politicians, the economists, and the lawyers; the men of letters and the theologians as the administrators of the tradition; and the scientists and the technicians) and proves himself to be a philosopher by the fact that he not only knows something but also attempts to find out what he knows and what he does not know. Not only does his knowledge aim immediately at the paths on which being encounters us in a "Being"; at the same time it aims at the constellation of these paths and, thereby, at the "Nothing" which belongs to that "Being" and which withholds from our knowledge a last self-evidence and assigns each individual science its limits. Kant tries in his *Critique* to place this knowledge of knowing and not-knowing on a sure path, the high road of science, by investigating the employment of reason and delimiting its single manner of employment.[24]

24. Theodore J. Kisiel made the following comments: "Professor Pöggeler's development of the sigetic character of the new topo-logic should now help us to understand the nature and aims of the various linguistic strategies that have become a part of 'Heideggeriana.' The thought that is to move the topology of Being from a metaphysical to a sigetic realm is still called upon to utter the place of this silent essence. The thinking that seeks a change in the very essence of the old language, attempting to overcome its metaphysical assumptions of substance and subject, its grammatical and subject-predicate relation, and its propositional logic, must still resort to a peculiar kind of proposition, a proposition (*Satz*) which is at once a leap (*Satz*) into the sigetic dimension and therefore a saying which is at once a not-saying. I wonder, then, if Professor Pöggeler might give some further specifications of such a sigetic logic by commenting further on some of the 'propositions' that Heidegger actually utilizes—for example, what Professor Pöggeler calls 'tautologies' and what I would prefer to call 'verbally iterative sentences': speech speaks, nothing nothings, the world worlds, the thing things, and so on. What light does such a linguistic strategy throw on the topology of Being? Of particular importance in this family is *das Ereignis er-eignet*. Is this the new 'principle' (*Satz*) of identity and distinction which is to articulate the new topology of Being in a temporal way, in place of, for example, the *analogia entis* of classical metaphysics? Is not this family of verbally iterative sentences Heidegger's way of expressing his new conception of

Does Heidegger do something different? He is obviously a believer in doing something different. He does not even seek the sure path, the highroad on which philosophy becomes genuine science; he merely seeks those forest trails which suddenly end up in the impassable and soon become overgrown again, leading to manifold errors. In this way does he not again gamble philosophy away to that groping about which Kant wanted to avoid, even to a groping about under mere concepts? Or does Heidegger only draw the consequences of the development of post-Kantian philosophy? Post-Kantian thought has asked in what medium the critical examination, delimitation, and legitimation of the employment of reason is effected. This medium was determined as language and history, and one thus projected a "metacritical" philosophy, using the question concerning language and history as a guiding clue. Hamann noticed that Kant's critique of reason comes to pass in the medium of language, but that language is historical; Herder and Humboldt pursued this metacritique, but the problematic gradually changed from a philosophical into an empirico-scientific one. Hegel attempted to take the modes of reason's employment that Kant distinguished back into the unity of a "transcendental" history of reason; Marx and Dilthey have certainly tried to show that this history, as a residue of a metaphysical semblance, is to be taken back into the "genuine" history. Positivism conceives of the failure of philosophy in regard to the "genuine reality" of those media, namely, language and history, as something definitive. Heidegger, on the other hand, interprets this failure as a freeing of philosophy into a new mode of thought; but he says, nevertheless, that this new mode must appear as pseudopoetry. Is it not true that, at least in this way, the leading currents of contemporary philosophy converge, that the one current conceives as a new possibility what the other forbids itself as subterfuge? Is not the impression of such a convergence fortified when one notices that analytic philosophy today is "linguistico-analytic" throughout, and that Heidegger, too, is of the opinion that thought should be a thought from language and that the world as the building structure of Being's truth should be arranged predominantly by language as the "house" of Being?

Regardless of whether or not such convergences exist, the

essence (*Wesen*) as verbal, his new way of regarding what it means to be in itself, as such (*an sich, als solches*)?"

degree to which Heidegger's "thought from language" differs from the linguistico-analytic philosophy becomes clear when one tries, for instance, to read Heidegger's *An Introduction to Metaphysics* with the eyes of a language analyst and then asks himself whether the discourse on Being, modes of Being, different significations of Being, and so on, is able to stand the linguistico-analytic criticism. Let us present a few theses pertaining to this conception of Being.

1. Parmenides places "Being," understood as continuous presence without becoming and perishing, in contradictory opposition to Nothing. Plato changes this opposition into a contrary one, so that the comparative, "more being," and the speaking about degrees of Being become possible. Aristotle tries to orient the manifold significations of Being toward one leading signification; and in the medieval conception of the *analogia entis* this orientation becomes a more strict and systematic classification.[25] This classification of Being's significations ultimately leads to the late medieval and modern attempts to conceive of the Being concept as a univocal concept or at least to delimit it to a few, clearly delineated meanings. While in this way the significations of Being become determined, philosophy loses the Being question as that question in which all other questions may converge; ontology becomes a science among other sciences, but an ontotheology—or even merely a topology of Being that takes all individual sciences back into an encompassing unity—is now no longer possible. The individual sciences must now take care of founding their work on sufficiently legitimated concepts. Heidegger resists this development. The *is* that is fixed to predication and existential assertion, for instance, becomes a mere "haze," since in this case there can no longer be a question of modes of Being and degrees of Being. Being becomes the object of arbitrary manipulations, while the sciences and these manipulations are no longer able to say in what encompassing context they belong.[26]

25. For the distinction between the Aristotelian and medieval doctrines of Being, see Pierre Aubenque, *Le problème de l'être chez Aristote* (Paris: Aubier, 1962). Heidegger as well as his teacher Franz Brentano obviously assume, because of their orientation toward the medieval conception, that Aristotle should have known a strict classification of the significations of Being as well as a guiding meaning of Being.

26. Kant tries to determine the distinction between the *is* of the predication and the *is* of the existential assertion in terms of a relative and an

2. In his reflections on the grammar and etymology of the word *Being,* Heidegger argues that the basic signification of *Being* which is generally accepted today came into being through an effacement and blending of the significations of those roots with whose help the verb *to be* (taken either defectively or suppletively) is conjugated. (At least for the philologist and linguist these roots are still immediately audible in the phonemes *ist, bin, gewesen*). Basically Heidegger wishes one to include in the *is* not only the significations of those verbs whose roots have contributed to the formation of the conjugated forms of *Being* but also the significations of all verbs. Linguistics takes as its point of departure the fact that the function of *is* as copula comes into being through abstraction from all significations and that in an existential assertion the *is* as principal verb is not a real predicate like, for instance, *to run* or *to sing.* In other words, the *is* does not give object-language information but metalinguistic information in an object-language form.[27]

3. In *An Introduction to Metaphysics* Heidegger gives a series of concrete examples which are supposed to show that in the word *is* Being opens itself "in a manifold way"; and yet the meaning of Being remains in the vicinity of presence and

---

absolute positing; in so doing he shares the view according to which the doctrine of the ambiguity of the *is* is to be abolished. Heidegger does not accept this orientation of Kant's thought; he requires, rather, that Kant elucidate the thesis of Being, not merely episodically, but "in accordance with its content and scope," to make it "the primary statement of a system" and unfold it "into a system" (W 275). To be sure, for Heidegger, the demand for a "systematic" unfolding holds true only within an epoch that requires that philosophy be a system. For Heidegger there is no thesis of Being, no system of Being, but rather the unterminated and interminable topology of Being.

27. On the one hand, Heidegger says that the word *Being* has a "floating, undetermined signification" (since even the significations of its roots are blurred). On the other hand, he argues that the word *is* has a highly determined signification and that we understand exactly the difference between Being and not-Being which is enclosed in it, "whether, for instance, the window there, which obviously is a being, *is* closed or *is not.*" From this, Heidegger concludes: " 'Being' proves to be a most highly determined and yet completely undetermined something. According to ordinary logic there is here a manifest contradiction" (*EM* 59–60 [66]). This is obviously out of the question. The *is* of the copula is not blurred in an indeterminate number of significations; it abstracts from significations as these are found in verbs such as *to run, to sing.* The determinateness that it possesses as connective is not in contradiction to its typical abstractness. On the contrary, precisely because the copula is a mere connective, it must be abstract.

present-ness (as it does in the metaphysical tradition). For this reason Heidegger believes that he can interchange the *is* of his exemplary sentences and synonymous expressions. A more precise analysis, however, shows that such an interchange is impossible and that speaking about manifold meanings of the *is* is untenable in the way originally assumed.[28]

28. The analysis of Heidegger's examples has been carried out in Helmut Gipper, *Bausteine zur Sprachinhaltsforschung* (Düsseldorf: Schwann, 1963), pp. 174 ff., and in Konrad Specht, *Sprache und Sein* (Berlin: de Gruyter, 1967), pp. 31 ff. In addition to existential assertions such as "God is" and ellipses such as "The farmer is in the field" (for "The farmer has gone into the field" ["ist aufs Feld" for "aufs Feld gegangen"]), Heidegger mentions the expression "Er ist des Todes [He is doomed, in the grip of death]." The *ist* should here be understood, Heidegger feels, as "to become the property (slave) of" (*verfallen*): "Er is dem Tode verfallen, er verfällt dem Tode [He has fallen in the grip of death]." If there were an interchangeability between *sein* and *verfallen,* one would be able to say, "Er verfällt des Todes." But we can only say, "Er verfällt *dem* Tode." The *ist* does not have the significance of *verfällt.* The idiomatic expression referred to (*ist* with the genitive *des Todes*) has a special signification. In a certain context the *ist* (like other verbs—*machen,* for instance) can function as *verbe à tout faire;* that is, in its abstractness and under quite special circumstances it can stand for a concrete verb. But this does not mean that *ist* assumes the signification of *verfallen;* one cannot say "Das Haus ist" instead of "Das Haus verfällt [The house falls into disrepair]." In addition to this, linguistic analysis must draw attention to the fact that one can definitely indicate that common and self-maintaining signification which comes about when the verb *machen* is used as *verbe à tout faire* (for it always means an activity that leads to a result), but that one runs into insurmountable difficulties when one tries to do the same thing with *to be* as *verbe à tout faire.* (The conception according to which the *is* as copula merely has a grammatically connective function and no proper signification leads Gipper and Specht to criticize also the interpretation of the copula given by several logicians who, to be sure, want to attribute different "significations" to the *is* of the predication and to the *is* of the identity assertion. Gipper and Specht object to this conception that the difference in significance which comes about rests on the difference in construction of the whole statement.) In the question concerning the signification of *Being,* Heidegger by no means takes only the *is* as his point of departure; he regrets explicitly that the verb *to be* is considered one-sidedly from the *it is,* because the *I am* and the *you are,* "just as much as the *is,* represent verbal inflections of *to be*" (*EM* 70 [77]). Indeed, when I say to myself, "I am happy," and thereby expressly identify myself with myself, this is something other than when I refer to myself using my name and say, "X is happy." When a man says to a woman, "You are beautiful," it is not his intention to make an assertion about a thing. (The fact that for the historico-philological sciences of man [*Geisteswissenschaften*] the "object" is not merely an object for an uninterested subject, and that, rather, object and subject belong together in an encompassing hermeneutic process, constitutes the basic problem of a reflection on history since the late works of Dilthey.)

4. The linguist who turns to the "question of Being" on the one hand and Heidegger with his Being question on the other cannot genuinely encounter one another, since their questioning moves in different directions. The linguist is immediately concerned with pinning down the word *is* to precisely delineated modes of usage. He will, for instance, put the following question to Heidegger: When you speak of *is*, do you mean the *is* of the predication, of the identity assertion, or of the existential assertion? Heidegger's answer will be: None of these. He searches for something different—namely, for that Being from which all possible modes of the *is, am,* and *are* originate and also for the difference, for instance, between an apophantic and a hermeneutic usage of *is* in the sense touched on in the foregoing. By means of the phrase "being is" Heidegger wants to direct thought into the originating from this origin, into the coming to pass of the truth. Heidegger, who feels elsewhere that tautologies (such as "Die Sprache spricht") are illuminating, finds himself referred back, through this phrase, to the basic question of philosophy.[29] The linguist in turn calls attention to the fact

---

Heidegger is inclined to assume that the deictic, indicating element of an assertion—such as "this here is . . . ," the identification with myself in the "I am . . . ," and the *you* reference in the "you are . . ."—is to be attributed to the *is, am,* and *are,* and thus to Being, not to the *this here, I,* and *you.* That is why, already in the introductory explanations of *Being and Time,* he can say that in Being, namely, in the transcendence of Dasein's Being, is found "the possibility and the necessity of the most radical individuation" (*SZ* 38). But when does an "assertion" (such as "You are beautiful") have not only an "apophantic" but, for instance, a "hermeneutic" achievement meaning? In *Being and Time* Heidegger speaks of "assertions" which not only are "theoretical statements" but remain contained in the "circumspective" explanation. The *is* of the copula, too, in Heidegger's view, cannot be conceived of merely as connective; it must manifestly be interpreted in such a way that in each case it shows a specific achievement meaning, for instance, the apophantic or the hermeneutic meaning (cf. *SZ* 157–60). It obviously is the linguistic situation and the context that causes the "assertion" to be not merely "theoretical statement." That is also why Heidegger concludes his lecture "Time and Being" with the remark that the saying concerning the happening (*Ereignis*) of Being's truth spoke "merely in statements" and in this way put an obstacle in its own way which is still to be overcome (cf. René Char, ed., *L'endurance de la pensée* [Paris: Plon, 1968], p. 68).

29. *An Introduction to Metaphysics* (by means of the question "Why are there beings rather than nothing?") searches for the "decision in the ground which grounds that being is being *as* such a being which it *de facto* is" (*EM* 2–3 [3]). Later, the why question, the searching for a why ground, is dismissed as a mode of unfolding philosophy's basic question which still misunderstands itself (cf. esp. *SG passim*). The formulation from the

that a phrase such as "being is" or even "being is being" is without information. Could being then also not be? Could one also find "being" among that which is? The linguist must also say that even sentences in which one finds the determination "is a being" are erroneously formed, insofar as in their formation one does not observe that the *is* is used in a completely different way from *sachhaltige* verbs. Of course Heidegger, too, understands the *is* not simply as a "real predicate." But, while the language analyst distinguishes the *is* from a real predicate, Heidegger argues that the distinction between real predicates and the *is* of the existential assertion certainly does not measure out the span of the meaning of Being, because *realitas*, the presence-at-hand of what is present-at-hand, is only one possible mode of Being. In Heidegger's view all possible significations of Being (Being present-at-hand, Being ready-to-hand, Being as ek-sistence), and also such distinctions as the distinction between real predicates and the *is* of the existential assertion within the domain of Being of the *realitas*, are co-thought in the phrase "being is." The traditional conception according to which in the

---

epilogue of *What Is Metaphysics?* is also significant: "Man alone among all beings, invoked by the tune called by Being, experiences the marvel of all marvels: *that* being is. Thus, he who in his essence is called toward the truth of Being is for that reason always attuned in an essential way" (*WM* 46–47; cf. *W* 103). The lecture series *What Is Called Thinking?* uses the statement "Being is" as a point of departure for a reflection on Parmenides as well as for a destruction of the definition of thought from the Greeks up to Nietzsche. It finds in this statement "the most fulfilled mystery of thought and that in a first hint of the saying." Heidegger says that in this statement the issue is not about the fact *that* something is or the question *what* it is, but perhaps about both at the same time (or, rather, about that which makes these and other modes of Being possible). Heidegger speaks of the "auxiliary verb" *is*, but then quotes a statement that employs the *is* as principal verb: "Space is." It certainly is not Heidegger's intention to distinguish the *is* of this statement, as the *is* of the existential assertion, from the *is* as auxiliary verb or copula; by no means does he conceive of this *is* as the *is* of the existential assertion. He argues, rather, that the *is* of this statement makes it possible for all assertions to have an *is* (such as "The tree is an apple tree"). He therefore conceives of this *is* as the origin of different modes of *is*, as that which makes all saying of "it is" possible and guarantees the order of the world. "Without that *is* in the sentence 'The tree is,' these assertions, along with the entire botanic science, would fall into bottomlessness. But not only this. Each human comportment to something, each human sojourn within this and that domain of being, would run off into emptiness if the *is* did not *speak*. A human being could not even run off into emptiness, for in order to make that possible the emptiness should already have been in the 'here' (*Da*)" (*WD* 106).

essentia, too, a "Being" is to be found is not done away with; it is only to be revised insofar as the traditional distinction between *essentia* and *existentia* is conceived one-sidedly from Being as continuous presence and, therefore, for instance, cannot be applied to human "ek-sistence." The doctrine of the *analogia entis* and, for that matter, the usage of the comparative "more being" are not completely meaningless for Heidegger; they are only "ontotheologically" misunderstood. Only because Heidegger adheres to the traditional metaphysical language game with respect to the word *Being* and does not give way to language analysis, which declares that this game is meaningless, is it possible that for him there is a topology of Being or, as it is called in *Being and Time,* a "genealogy" of Being.

5. When there is a tendency to pin down the usage of *is* (which is not even found in all languages) to precisely delineated modes of usage, Being loses the function that it had in Western metaphysics—namely, the function of being a guiding clue for the formulation of philosophical problems, a function as universal as it is radical. It is then no longer possible to attempt, as Heidegger does in *An Introduction to Metaphysics,* to advance from the Being question as the guiding question to the question that is philosophically basic—namely, the question concerning the truth of Being and concerning the world as the building structure of this truth. In any case one can then still ask for an encompassing meaning of *Being* and think with Kant, for instance, that this can be found in the absolute or relative positing; in this way, however, one will be led beyond ontology and forced from the dimension of Being into another dimension—the dimension of the positing or also the praxis. Heidegger's attempt to extend the meaning of Being—for instance, to extend this meaning beyond the realm of the presence-at-hand—must then appear as an overstretching into what is vague and indeterminate, which does not correspond to the actual language usage.[30]

30. Ernst Tugendhat, referring to Quine, Carnap, and Strawson, has developed the linguistico-analytic criticism of ontological questioning in this way. For him the dimension of our universal philosophical questioning is, in the final analysis, "no longer a dimension of Being but rather—between indicative, optative, and imperative—a dimension of the praxis" ("Die sprachanalytische Kritik der Ontologie," in *Das Problem der Sprache, Achter Deutscher Kongress für Philosophie,* ed. Hans-Georg Gadamer [Munich: Fink, 1967], p. 492). Tugendhat puts forward four arguments against employing the word *Being* as a guiding clue for a universal philosophical reflection: (1) a sentence like "Er schwimmt" cannot be

However, when Heidegger understands *Being* from the truth of Being, and the truth of Being as a truth that is to be brought about, he too is led into a dimension to which praxis and *poiēsis* belong; Heidegger prepares for the question of the way in which this dimension can be tackled with the help of guiding clues such as praxis, wanting to have a conscience, *poiēsis,* technique. To speak simply of a question of praxis or of a dimension of positing and praxis means to exhaust *one* guiding clue no less than Heidegger exhausts the guiding clue Being. The questions emerge of whether language after all has a word for what one could regard as the "speculative" middle of language and of whether a radical and universal philosophical questioning under "speculative" pressure always has to stretch a determinate guiding clue into something universal and to exaggerate it into something radical. Is it not true that one can only advance to such a "middle" by interchanging the guiding clues? And does this middle not always show itself differently when one approaches it from different points of the circumference? The destiny of the "metacritical" philosophy, as this has been developed since Kant, suggests this supposition.

Discussion

THOMAS LANGAN: The word *topology* is a term destined to as brilliant a career in philosophy as the now well worn *structure.* I am delighted that Professor Pöggeler has reaffirmed so forcefully the extent to which Heidegger's thought is a revelation of the essential space-time dimensions of Being's happening. One can scarcely exaggerate the point that Heidegger's philosophy, at least until its last phase, is devoted to the revelation of the *sense* of Being; this requires interpretation of the interrelation of dimensions of space that unfold along a time course, namely, that of a destiny of epoch-founding events. A basic question

---

changed (as is done in Aristotle) into the sentence "Er is schwimmend," therefore, into a statement with *Being* and participle, without a change of signification; (2) a relation cannot be understood as a determination of Being; (3) in the optative and imperative the issue is not about a "Being"; when I say, "Do not come," I do not deny a "Being"; traditional ontology limits itself to a "world of the indicative"; (4) an assertion according to which a "Being" is expressed in words like *and* and *all* would barely have any support in language.

raised in Professor Pöggeler's paper is how far one can push this notion of a historical space as the center of postmetaphysical thought. I propose here to set aside for a moment the ultimate development of Heidegger's thought, in which he seeks to think Being directly without relation to the beings (*Seienden*), in order to raise the possibility of developing Heidegger's earlier thought in what might be called, somewhat lightly, "the earthiest direction."

Consider the distance separating the notion of *place* when this word is used to describe the position of a concept or a function in a formal system and the notion of *place* when it is used to name our physical position. A topology of Being must be able to bring both poles together and make sense of both. By underscoring several dimensions of Heidegger's reflection, I would like to illustrate the extent to which this philosophy can be interpreted in a way that inevitably brings us back to the problem of the element of nature in thought.

In one of his later essays Heidegger speaks of "the essential space of an epoch" (*der Wesensraum eines Zeitalters*), the character of which is established by the fundamental way in which Being offers itself (*sich schickt*) in a particular epoch.[31] As Professor Pöggeler has indicated in his paper, Heidegger offers a particularly full and exact characterization of the way in which Being offers itself in our own epoch—the epoch of the planetary domination of technique. Heidegger has indeed sought to name the way, and that has proved difficult; the terms *Gestell* and *Geviert* are strained a bit indeed. But, for all their poetic ungainliness, the thought they signal is precious; nowhere else has Heidegger so thoroughly laid out an aspect of the topology of Being.

Let us recall three points within this particular *topos*. First, both the *Gestell* and the *Geviert* are ways in which the beings (*Seienden*) are related to each other and to that most crucial being, the human existent. Both affect the way the world is disposed; both influence the disposing of things according to a radically different, but correlative, space-time.

The second point, and a very important one, is precisely that correlativity; the *Gestell* and the *Geviert* are correlative because they are the two faces of the epoch-founding destiny (*Geschick*),

31. *ID* 44.

which, as always, is ambiguous—two-faced (*Zwei-deutig*), one might say. They are the improper (*uneigentlich*) and the proper (*eigentlich*) possibilities of the same epoch in Being's historical offering of itself. As always, the improper possibility seems to be a kind of starting point for the proper one. The landscape into which we are born is most strongly impressed with the industrial-bureaucratic way of disposing things; the shocking sameness and the crushing anonymity of it all awaken us, as never before, to the profundity of a caring relationship to things.

The third point is that this state of affairs, characteristic of our epoch, is no mere accident; nor is it "necessary," in the Hegelian sense. I regret to see Heidegger, in "Time and Being," backing away from the term *necessity* (*Notwendigkeit*), which he had earlier brought so effectively beyond metaphysics by thinking anew the sense of the turn (*wenden*) and the meaning of the *Not*. He had made it very clear that past revelations of Being do not necessitate the later ones in the sense that what happens later is implied in what happened earlier. Each essential step forward requires a creative leap (*Sprung*); but not just anything can happen at any time.

I would state this third point in the following way. From the foundation of metaphysics, through Being's gift of itself in the form of the question about Being, there is opened a definite range of possibility. Because this is an open range of possibility, prediction of what will happen is possible only on a level of great vagueness. What finally does happen is determined by actual concrete accomplishment, which is a further gift of Being. However, it is possible for the thinker to understand retrospectively what subsequently did happen as a possibility that was inherent in the structured indeterminateness of the earlier situation. To use a crude topological simile, from where I am now standing (in State College, Pennsylvania), and by virtue of my being here, I can move in quite a few directions, to many destinations. However, I can move only to a finite set of possible destinations in a limited number of directions. I cannot go to State College, nor can I go east to Pittsburgh or west to Bochum, unless I overthrow the canons of convenience and emulate Christopher Columbus. An interpretation along these lines could save both the essential element of the leap, which genuine creativity requires, and, at the same time, the intelligibility of what has happened. It remains meaningful to speak of the Sense of Being (*Sinn des Seins*).

Let us return to the second point, about the present epoch. As *Gestell,* the present epoch is the final phase of the metaphysical tradition. As *Geviert,* which somehow springs up out of the very groundlessness of the absurdity of the *Gestell,* the present epoch, because of a further gift of Being, is thought to be already somewhat beyond the metaphysical tradition although, in terms of the effect thus far on the world, potentially more than actually. (Or is it always that way with the authentic voice of Being? Is this voice perhaps always the voice of an individual crying in the wilderness?)

Our epoch, according to Heidegger, not only is the final phase of a tradition (*Endstadium*) but also is occidental (*abendländisch*). It is that moment of decline into the darkness of night which sees even the distinction between Occident and Orient effaced. It is the moment when the technical product of the occidental metaphysical tradition spreads over every distinction of place and time, covering not only the planet but even the solar system. Not only is the Hegelian march of Spirit from East to West present in Heidegger's thought; in his view it can hardly be taken too seriously. It is not a matter of indifference that philosophy began in Greece and moved in due course to Germany. Greece, Heidegger warns us, is not that piece of land between Sicily and the coast of Asia Minor which today sports many an archaeological digging, no more than Germany is Zähringen or Todnauberg. *But then it is, too.* One cannot further pursue the question of place (*Ortschaft*) and neighborhood (*Nachbarschaft*) without raising anew—and it ought to be raised again and again—the question of the interpenetration of world and earth. As I see it, this question is one with the question of the contribution of that in the being which is most "in itself" (*an sich*), to use the Hegelian manner of speaking. If anyone objects that Heidegger sees no such element in the beings, I can only invite him to reflect again on the questions posed at the opening of "Die Frage nach dem Ding" and on the very crucial point that Heidegger does not really answer those questions, either in the second part of the essay or, if my interpretation is correct, anywhere. The question—in Hegelian terms, the relationship between Spirit and Nature—remains a central difficulty in Heideggerian thought.

If authentic philosophy, then, is preliminary and preparatory hermeneutic interpretation, striving to comprehend man as situ-

ated, that is, man in a *topos*—if thought is in search of an endur-
ing Fundament—then philosophy will have to succeed in thinking of the spatiality-temporality of care as care for things. What
kind of a place is it where and when things are permitted to
dwell; where and when the light of the entire tradition is gathered together and allowed to throw a rich glow of appreciation
over all that is and can be; where and when the hysteria of the
moment is passed over for the serene wisdom of the abiding
ages; and where and when planetary domination of a degrading
sameness is replaced by appreciation of local tradition, and all
traditions respect each other mutually, leaving room for all to
live? The challenge of these questions is indeed a call for the
continued elaboration of a topology of Being.

JAMES M. EDIE: Heidegger has said so often and his commentators have repeated so insistently—that the essence of language
is to point out, to show, to reveal, to let being be seen, that we
have begun to wonder whether he was simply unaware of or
insensitive to the many other diverse and complex usages of
language. It is clear from Professor Pöggeler's paper that, in some
sense, Heidegger wishes to do justice to these other usages and
values as well. The manner in which Professor Pöggeler introduces these other usages is somewhat disconcerting, however;
this is perhaps due to the necessarily partial and oblique approach to this question, which appears almost as an obiter
dictum rather than as part of the central argument. I would like
Professor Pöggeler to clarify Heidegger's (and, eventually, his
own) thought on this matter.

Professor Pöggeler seems to give a linguistic criterion for
distinguishing the "apophantic *as*" from the "hermeneutic *as*."
Namely, he states that *apophansis* is a matter of asserting, pointing out, or stating something, but that there is another, more
fundamental, field of linguistic usage involved in our "concernful
dealing with that which is." This field of usage is expressed in
such linguistic forms as requesting, wishing, commanding, and
so on. He further relates this linguistic distinction to the ontological distinction between objects that are present-at-hand (*Vor-
handene*) and those that are ready-to-hand (*Zuhandene*). This
distinction becomes the even more encompassing distinction between the theoretical attitudes of consciousness (*theōria*) expressed in our apophantic uses of language and the practical and

"concernful" attitudes (praxis) expressed in nonapophantic and, presumably, "hermeneutic" uses of language for purposes other and wider than the mere stating of what is the case in judgments. Moreover, he argues—correctly, I think—that according to Heidegger our practical and "concernful" attitudes toward the world, things, and other persons are primary, and our apophantic attitudes, if one can call them that, of taking a distance (of contemplation, so to speak) are secondary and derived.

This distinction, if I have understood it correctly, leads me to make two remarks, on the basis of which I would like Professor Pöggeler to clarify and explain the meaning of this linguistic distinction in Heidegger's philosophy. My question concerns the explanation (*Auslegung*) of Heidegger's thought rather than its inner interpretation (*Deutung*). I am not asking for an internal justification in terms of Heidegger's motives for saying what he does, but for an external clarification for those of us outside the inner circle who want to know, first of all, precisely what Heidegger means and claims to say by means of this distinction. I am asking for an interpretation, if that is possible, which would be capable of addressing itself to our common philosophical problems rather than to the internal problems of strict Heideggerian exegesis.

The first remark is that this distinction, as a linguistic distinction between two categories or usages of speech, seems almost identical to that established by Austin in *How to Do Things with Words* between illocutionary expressions (apophantic ones, in Heidegger's language) and perlocutionary expressions (those which, over and above expressing a meaning, are meant to "work" in the world, to bring about an effect, to communicate evaluative or emotional attitudes, and so on).[32] Likewise, this distinction does not seem essentially different from the one that Husserl makes between presentational acts (of consciousness, of speech) and nonpresentational acts (such as desiring, willing, evaluating, and so on). If this is the case, there is nothing particularly startling in what Heidegger is saying; but there is a difficulty. Whereas Husserl argues that every nonpresentational act is "founded on" or "contains" a presentational act as its basis, and Austin (similarly, but of course without reference to Husserl)

32. John L. Austin, *How to Do Things with Words* (Cambridge, Mass.: Harvard Univ. Press, 1962).

argues that all perlocutionary expressions imply an illocutionary act while the inverse is not true, Heidegger seems to want to say the opposite—namely, to give the primacy to the perlocutionary and nonpresentational in experience. This would seem to commit him to something like a pragmatic theory of truth, and it has very serious consequences for philosophy. I am not at all objecting that such a framework for the discussion of meaning and truth cannot, perhaps, be well justified; but I would like to know if it is correct to assert that this is what Heidegger is claiming. A clarification of this question would help those of us who remain mystified by much of his language and terminology to understand where his notion of truth leads and whether or not it ultimately commits him to the relativism and pragmatism that seems to me to be lurking within it.

The second remark is more serious. If the basis for the distinction between the "apophantic *as*" and the "hermeneutic *as*" is linguistic, how can Heidegger and his followers claim that "the hermeneutic" gets us out of and breaks through the closed linguistic circle? I should think that it would be necessary for Heidegger, more than for any other philosopher, to place "the hermeneutic" aspect of experience (and at least some of our meaningful dealings with the world) outside of and prior to language as a whole. Does Heidegger admit any nonlinguistic (or prelinguistic, or extralinguistic) realm of meaningful experience or not? If he does not, we have here a more radical—and, some of us would feel, a more perverse—opposition to Husserl than we at first suspected; but at this juncture it is less important to attempt to judge the validity of what Heidegger is saying than to understand just what it is he means to say. If I have misconstrued the nature and consequences of the distinction Professor Pöggeler is making, I would be grateful for his corrections.

Pöggeler: The remarks made by Professor Edie have shown quite clearly and accurately how one must deal with Heidegger's thought and how one can learn from him. Heidegger understands his own thought as a "corrective"; he does not wish to develop a philosophy in general or determinate philosophical disciplines (such as a philosophy of art or a philosophy of language), but rather to search for a corrective, a necessary change for that thought which determines the beginning of philosophy as well as our contemporary knowledge and behavior. Therefore, anyone who wishes to learn from Heidegger must bring along something to be corrected if the occasion arises—for instance, a phenomenology such as Husserl's or a linguistic philosophy such as Austin's. He who approaches Heidegger from the viewpoint of linguistic philosophy must certainly be amazed that Heidegger attempts to include Western metaphysics taken as a whole, with all its problems, in contemporary discussion. Heidegger does this because he is convinced that these problems still determine a thought which remains hidden under the surface (*untergründig*) and with which he believes he no longer has a relationship. Must Heidegger's attempt not necessarily lead to a mystification of the traditional problems? And must this tradition not force its incorrect ways upon this thought? Does Heidegger not reintroduce all those hypostatizations which metaphysics used to discuss under headings such as "substance," "subject," and so on, when he not only distinguishes an "apophantic" from a "hermeneutic" attitude but also makes what is "ready-to-hand," what is "present-at-hand," and "ek-sistence" correspond to the apophantic and the hermeneutic attitudes (or eventually to the intentional concernful dealing with something)?

Furthermore, does Heidegger not fall into the tendency of metaphysical thought to consider a determinate characteristic trait of something as the only essential element and to separate it from what is merely accidental? For instance, in this sense Heidegger speaks of the "essence" of language. He seems to find this "essence" in pointing, letting be seen, and presenting and to hold other aspects (such as requesting, commanding), in comparison with this only essential element, as accidental. An unbiased linguistic analysis cannot follow such a procedure; it must, rather, reproach Heidegger for an ontological hypostatizing of a determinate characteristic trait into the essence of language. In the discussion between linguistic analysis and Heidegger we again encounter an objection that was seriously raised in the discussion between philosophical anthropology and existential analysis. Heidegger's thought, instead of keeping itself open for the vast domain of the empirical, one-sidedly accentuates something quite determinate and hypostatizes this into the "essence"; for instance, he one-sidedly searches for the "essence" of moodness (*Stimmung*) by using the "depressed" mood of anxiety as his starting point.

What does Heidegger really do? Stated more carefully,, what

is interesting in his way of proceeding? Since Aristotle's time philosophical speech has been one-sidedly determined from apophantic assertion, not from request, question, and command, also. In this way the pragmatic dimension of language is expelled from philosophical speech in favor of the semantic dimension and is relinquished to rhetoric, for instance. Heidegger, however, is of the opinion that "asking questions" is the "devoutness" of thought, in which case he wishes questioning to be understood from the listening to what has been addressed to it. This philosophical speech must not be characterized exclusively from assertion and its apophantic achievement meaning. By understanding philosophical speech not exclusively from *apophansis,* Heidegger wishes to break one of the basic prejudices of the tradition. This is precisely why he determines the "essence" of language in a critical following of the tradition as a "pointing" and "letting be seen" which consists not only in the traditional *apophansis* but also, and at the same time, in the giving of full play to a concealing. From such a conception of the "essence" of language, question and request can then be equally understood as concrete forms of this essence. However, Heidegger does not carry out this return to the individual concrete forms.

In lieu of this return, Heidegger seems to decide arbitrarily about individual concrete forms. Does he not found the apophantic acts in hermeneutic acts, the informative acts in performative acts? Is it not true that for him—in contrast to what is found in the tradition and in Husserl and Austin—that the "hermeneutic," or the "practical," aspect is definitely the primary one? Indeed, beginning with *Being and Time* he repeatedly polemicizes against the fact that one dresses up one fundamental layer of what is present-at-hand as thing, by adding value qualities to it, into something ready-to-hand or into "goods," letting the concernful acts be founded in those which are merely re-presenting.[33] It seems that Heidegger wishes to invert the customary foundation. In reality, however, he argues that there can be no question of a one-sided foundation, and for this reason he also speaks of the fact that the different acts can be equiprimordial. It is true that in this case he leaves open the way in which the relationship between these "equiprimordial aspects" is precisely to be thought of. There is no doubt that the later Heidegger is no longer able

33. Cf. SZ 97–99, 138–39.

to conceive of what is called in *Being and Time* the genealogy, or the derivation, of the different modes of Being and the acts that correspond to them, in terms of a one-sided "foundation."

It is certainly unsatisfactory that Heidegger speaks of "language" and "thought" without showing in detail how this thought comprises a thinking in a narrow sense, and then a feeling, a willing, and so on. It is therefore also difficult to determine whether or not Heidegger admits a nonlinguistic, prelinguistic, or extralinguistic experience. A few assertions from *Holzwege* make it quite clear that, for Heidegger, language is real not only in the words and sentences that we speak and write. Architecture, for example, is also a language, since its essence, like the essence of all art, is to be found in the "poetic" (*Dichterisches*), namely, the bringing to the fore of "truth." [34] Heidegger does not explicitly make the necessary distinction between language in a narrow sense and language in a broad sense.

It has often been stated, and Professor Rosen has stressed it again, that Heidegger's conquest of metaphysics does not do justice to metaphysics, specifically not to Plato. [35] The fact that Heidegger not only misunderstands the historical Plato but also is unable to bring out the genuine meaning of the Platonic doctrine of the Ideas has been shown in the clearest way, to my knowledge, by Oskar Becker. [36] However, I do not believe that one can say that Heidegger, in the wake of irrationalism, tries to substitute a poetic thought for the theory of the tradition and a "keeping silent" for language. Gnosticism has said that *sige*, not *logos*, signifies God's essence, but Heidegger does not argue along these lines. He does not substitute *sige* for *logos*. This becomes clear from the fact that he not only introduces sigetics as the law(fulness) of his thought but at the same time states that this lawfulness develops from *logos*. The keeping silent, or concealing, which Heidegger has in mind is eloquent; conversely, *sige* belongs to the essence of *logos*. Furthermore, it is not an irrational element but rather the critical or metacritical character in Heidegger's thought which forces him to this "concealing." For instance, we should relate our speaking of the essence of art to reflection on that coming to pass in which art becomes art, in which art is found, for instance, in its Greek or contemporary

34. Cf. HW 60–61 (694–95).
35. For Stanley A. Rosen's remarks, see pp. 267–70 below.
36. See note 9 above.

epochal essence. Since this coming to pass is obviously incomplete and unfinishable and cannot be unraveled in its facticity, its genuine source and origin cannot be grasped or said and thus can only be "concealed." Such a concealment delimits what is said in a critical way. The talk is exclusively about the contemporary, epochal "essence" of art that affects only us and thus is historical; the question of how art will be in another epoch should not be decided in advance. The question of whether or not Hölderlin was the one who founded the future "essence" of art that affects us is a secondary question; in answering it one need not necessarily simply follow Heidegger's conjectures.

The title "topology," like the title "sigetics," is merely an auxiliary concept for a provisional understanding. "Topology," or exposition (*Erörterung* [*Ort, topos*]), not only means *expositio* (as in Kant)—thus, "the clear, although not necessarily detailed, representation of something that belongs to a concept." This definition from the *Critique of Pure Reason* is further developed by Johann Fichte, who says in the third section of his essay on method, *Über den Begriff der Wissenschaftslehre*, "that one clarifies [*erörtern*] a concept scientifically when one indicates its place within the system of man's science as such, that is to say, when one shows which concept determines its place or position [*Stelle*] and for which other concept this place is determined by it." Fichte also draws attention to the fact that the concept of the doctrine of science cannot have a place in the system, for it determines the place of all scientific concepts (and, thus, of the system as a whole). But in Fichte this difficulty does not yet really lead beyond a systematic determination of the meaning of clarification (*Erörterung*). In the nineteenth century there was an attempt to relate in a relativistic and historical way the systems and fragments of systems to "points of view." Professor Langan has clearly pointed out that in the case of Heidegger's topology the issue is not one of relating thought to arbitrary "standpoints." In so doing he has also indicated the task of further distinguishing the "places" of topology, or exposition, from the spatio-temporal, earthly historical concretion of the coming to pass of meaning and understanding.

The way in which Heidegger incidentally employs the word *topology* cannot be decisive. When Heidegger says in *From the Experience of Thinking* that topology "indicates [*sage*] to Being the place [*Ortschaft*] of its abiding [*Wesen*]," *place* may still be understood as simply the preordinated domain and thus the "fundament" of fundamental ontology. Heidegger's letter to Ernst Jünger which distinguishes between topography and topology evokes from the word *topology* the signification "historical place determination." The word is used elsewhere in this sense. Erich Auerbach, for instance, states that the highest task of his linguistic work is to deliver a topology, that is, a place determination, of Western literature. In *Der Satz vom Grund* Heidegger distinguishes his procedure from the method used in his earlier essay *The Essence of Reasons,* further characterizing the latter by concepts such as "place," "road," "field," "exposition" (*Erörterung*).

Sigetics and topology, however, do not claim that they would like to replace logic with another kind of "logic" (in the sense that Hegel, in a way, has claimed this through his dialectics). As topology of *Being,* this topology indeed takes the Being question as its leading question; but in so doing it does not claim that cultures different from the Indo-European cultures—for example, the Japanese culture—should take the Being question as their guiding question in the same way. Whether or not the topologic or the hermeneutic could adequately be defined with words from the Hebraic tradition is a very difficult question. Theologians have recently attempted to consider the history of man's salvation as found in the Old Testament (*Heilsgeschichte*) together with Heidegger's "lighting's history" (*Lichtungsgeschichte*), just as they tried earlier to consider the existential analysis of *Being and Time* together with the Christian conception of life. However, like the young Hegel and like Nietzsche, Heidegger sees an unbridgeable cleft between his thought and the tradition of the Old Testament. Whether this view is correct or incorrect is a question about which we have been able to learn something from Emmanuel Levinas, who (following Cohen, Rosenzweig, and Buber) has tried to mediate the starting point of philosophy with the help of Hebraic tradition.

5 / Thinking and Poetizing in Heidegger

Henri Birault

THE JOINING of *thinking* (*Denken*) and *poetizing* (*Dichten*) may give rise to a question. Because authentic questioning in itself is not its own beginning, this question, if it is to be adequate and complete, transforms itself in turn into an experience of thought. This thinking experience, in which the questioning finds its principle and its measure, takes on determinations that are more and more profound and, furthermore, more closely interconnected.

First of all, this experience is the one that only thought can make of the dialogue between thinkers and poets. Put another way, it is the experience, begun early and continuously pursued, that a certain thinker makes of the essential proximity of his thought to what is poetic in some poets. In addition, it is through this very dialogue that the experience of that double implication in which both the initially thinking essence of poetizing and the "poetic character," or, more accurately, the "poietic character," of thought ("der Dichtungscharakter des Denkens," as Heidegger says in *From the Experience of Thinking*) become manifest together. Finally, this is the experience, more advanced today but by no means less puzzling, of the nontechnical, noninstrumental, nonrepresentative, nonexpressive, and, if you wish, nonsignificative essence of the first language (*parole*), grasped in its speaking and still bare force.* This language is without density and

* Because the English language, like the German, does not have an equivalent expression for the French word *parole*, I have translated *parole* either as "language" or "word." In so doing I have used the Heidegger

without voice, inconsistent and sovereign; it has nothing behind it because everything is still in front of it; it shows without proving, gives without regulating, solicits without commanding, signifies without indicating. It is the language of Being, of Essence, of the "There is," always already heard and always only surmised, which sometimes gathers itself together in order to be said in that noteworthy and originally divergent saying of the thinkers and the poets: "Pride of men, O holy language!"

In its questioning, thought which interrogates itself—starting with the experience of what is yet to come—asks and wonders how it stands with (1) thought in its relationship to poetry, (2) thought in its relationship to thought, and (3) the element or the space in which these relationships are established and dissolved.

I

THESE RELATIONSHIPS may be ones of identity or affinity, difference or intolerance, affiliation or derivation, inherence or inference, inclusion or exclusion; but in the final analysis, no matter how complex the maze of these still disentangled relationships may be, it is certain that the field where they become established can be none other than that of language and speech. Man is that being who speaks and who does not cease speaking—when he is awake and when he is asleep, when he speaks and when he keeps silent. The essence of man is eloquence. The world of language (*parole*) is *his* world, the World. Man is the word (*parole*) made man. It is on the mortals that the burden of language rests. It is on the poets and thinkers that the formidable and preposterous privilege falls, the privilege of speaking and

---

texts to which Birault refers as a guideline, translating *Sprache* as "language" and *Wort* as "word." *Mot* is translated as "word," as is *Verbe* ("Word"). Since *langage* and *langue* are also to be translated as "language," I have indicated in parentheses the corresponding French word in all instances where this seemed to be desirable. Finally, it is important to keep in mind, particularly in reading this essay, that the German word *Sprache* means (1) the act of speaking, (2) the faculty of speech, (3) the ability to speak, (4) language in a broad sense (*langage*), and (5) language in a narrow sense (*langue*). On the other hand, the English word *language* means, in addition to the two possibilities mentioned in (4) and (5), the faculty of speech (*Sprachfähigkeit*), the ability to speak (*Sprechfähigkeit*), and the manner, or mode, of speaking.

only speaking, of giving voice to language itself, of letting it say itself. Thinking and poetizing, Heidegger says, represent two modes of saying (*zwei Weisen des Sagens*). They represent not just two modes among others but the only two modes that remain at the source of what Heidegger—indifferently, it seems—calls *Sprache* or *Wort*. Actually, neither term taken by itself can be used without hesitation or correction.[1] Thus one must conceive of the necessary gap between the saying of the thinkers and that of the poets as a valley hollowed out by the original flood of speech itself. The dialogue alluded to here is to be found in the element of language (*parole*). This language, however, is monologue. It is with itself, speaks only to itself, occupies itself only with itself, and is a means for no other thing but itself. It remains in the solitude that characterizes it, even when it becomes infatuated with the essence of man "since a dialogue we are" (Hölderlin). Thus there is a double saying resulting from one and the same saying. There are two banks or sides, equally precipitous and of equal dignity, truth, or nobility—a double slope equally brightened by the sun. On one side there is the "enthusiastic" and illustrious language of the poet's song; on the other, the more perplexing and remote language of the most profound thinkers.

The experience with language is not just one experience among others, an experience that thought carries out one day in regard to a particular "object." It is the experience of thought with itself and against itself, the experience of what touches thought as intimately as possible. One must develop an "ontological" conception of language and a "logical" conception of Being that are foreign to each other in view of all that we customarily call ontology and logic. One must learn to conceive of Being as language and language as Being, as if they were in a common abode. One

---

1. The German word *Sprache* means, in French, *parole* as well as *langage* or *langue* (*die deutsche Sprache* = "the German language"). The German term *Wort* means *mot* ("word") as well as *parole* or *Verbe* ("Word"). "Der Psycholog nimmt das Wort" ("Le psychologue prend la parole" ["The Psychologist Starts to Speak"]) is the title of one of the chapters of the Nietzsche anthology *Nietzsche contra Wagner*. Heidegger's conjunction of *Sprache* and *Wort* avoids a "phonetic" or "semantic," "lingual" or "linguistic," conception of language. It also shakes off the yoke of the verb as copula of the proposition. In this way the word (*mot*), freed from every other relation except that with itself, recovers the splendor of its independence; and language (*parole*), equally unchained, recovers the original nonverbal and noncategorical force of its apophantic, monstrative, or de-clarative, power.

must learn to find once again "the calm force" of the Possible in the omnipotent irreality of language. Finally, one must practice thinking the difference between language and Thing in the perspective and wake of the ontico-ontological difference, for language is actually the difference as such. It is in this that the dialogue between thought and the poets can help us, and in a way that is sometimes irreplaceable. The following passage from Heidegger indicates the ultimate finality of this dialogue.

> The genuine dialogue with the poem of a poet is only the poetizing dialogue: the poetic conversation between poets. However, a dialogue between *thought* and poetizing is equally possible and at times even necessary, precisely because a privileged—although in each case different—relationship with language is characteristic of both.
>
> The conversation of thought with poetry tends to evoke the *essence* of language in order that the mortals learn again to dwell in language.[2]

The poetizing dialogue (*die dichtende Zwiesprache*) with poetry develops in the form of a poetic conversation among the poets (*das dichterische Gespräch zwischen Dichtern*). This is how the poetizing (*das Dichtende*) becomes the poetic (*das Dichterische*). This dialogue, or this conversation, is the only authentic one, because it maintains itself in the unique and yet ambiguous order of poetry (*Dichtung*). The difference between *dichtend* and *dichterisch* refers in fact to the double meaning of the verb *dichten*. In the original and broadest sense *dichten* means "to build," "to produce," "to accomplish," "to bring to being," or "to bring to light." In the habitual and derivative sense *dichten* refers to poetry and the poems of those people who call themselves poets. The second meaning is infinitely more restricted, and yet, in a way that is certainly not fortuitous, this meaning has long since been the customary one. If the grammatical and heavily metaphysical categories were still usable, one could say that the poetic conversation among the poets, taken in

---

2. "Die eigentliche Zwiesprache mit dem Gedicht eines Dichters ist allein die dichtende: das dichterische Gespräch zwischen Dichtern. Möglich ist aber auch und zuzeiten sogar nötig eine Zwiesprache des *Denkens* mit dem Dichten, und zwar deshalb, weil beiden ein ausgezeichnetes, wenngleich je verschiedenes Verhältnis zur Sprache eignet.

"Das Gespräch des Denkens mit dem Dichten geht darauf, das *Wesen* der Sprache hervorzurufen, damit die Sterblichen wieder lernen, in der Sprache zu wohnen" (*US* 38).

the sense alluded to here, is the only one that is faithful in "form" and in "matter" to the entire essence of *Dichtung*. This is the way in which Hölderlin "poetizes," or "poematizes," poetically his poetic relation with what is poetic in Sophocles. The scission in the dialogue is effective and very real; the essence of *Dichtung* that is at stake in the dialogue is a historical and epochal essence, always and necessarily shared; the distance separating Hölderlin from Sophocles is, for Hölderlin, a distance that can never be overcome. This dialogue without emanation is, nonetheless, the only authentic dialogue; its complete submission and its perfect correspondence to the essence and the exigencies of the poetic language, which is eternally solitary and historically foundation-giving, are the signs of its authenticity.

Of a completely different nature is the dialogue, no longer poetizing and poetic but, if one may say so, thinking and "noetic," of a thinker with the poem of such and such a poet. This dialogue does not belong to either literary criticism or philological investigation. Foreign to all "literature" and all "science," to all "aesthetics" and all "poetry," this dialogue is a dialogue of thought, a thinking conversation ("das denkende Gespräch," or "die Zwiesprache des *Denkens* mit dem Dichten," according to Heidegger). The poetic dialogue takes place within poetry; it originates in poetry and is to the benefit of poetry. The "noetic" dialogue, on the other hand, originates in thought and is to the benefit of thought, and thus remains within the confines of thought. This dialogue is not without advantage or benefit, if not for the poetic work itself, at least for understanding the poem— an understanding which is a listening as well as a reading understanding. According to Claudel:

> *Intelligere* (to understand) is to read in (*inlire*). "To read" is to assimilate oneself and the meaning to the meaning. "To comprehend" is to grasp at the same time, to join together through one's grasp. Just as one says that something catches fire [*prend*], that cement begins to harden [*prend*], that a lake freezes [*se prend*] in the winter, or that an idea catches [*prend*] the public, so is it that things take themselves together [*se comprennent*] and we comprehend [*comprenons*] them.[3]

Heidegger affirms that this uncertain and perilous dialogue, which seems to want to make thought disappear into poetry or

3. Paul Claudel, "Art poétique," *Mercure de France* (1907), p. 133.

poetry into thought, is possible and sometimes (but when?) even necessary. One guesses that this possibility is not a simple eventuality, and that this necessity is not a simple necessity of fact. The necessity is a necessity of essence, or an "ideal" necessity, "historic" and "eidetic" at the same time. It is requested at certain turning points of a universal history of thought by the very essence of the thing that is the ultimate object of this dialogue—namely, Language (*Parole*), the essence of Language as the Language of Essence, the relationship of man taken in his essence to the essence of language, a certain conversation, a certain turning over of this relationship itself. This time in this dialogue, which, just as before, has only one interlocutor, the thinker alone takes the initiative. Taken as quest for the essence, the effectively thinking thought, which is subject only to the exigencies of thought, now meets, for a better determination of what is to be called thought, the poetic saying of a certain poem and sometimes, through this saying, the very essence of poetry (*das Wesen der Dichtung*). It is in this way, solely in the mode of thought, that Heidegger thinks the essence of poetry that was poematized by Hölderlin. One will notice here the redoubtable privilege of thought and the nonreciprocity of the relationship between poets and thinkers. The poet, as the poet of poets, poematizes the essence of poetry and, if you wish, the poetic condition of poets. Although he thinks *about* the one and the other (for there is thought in each poet and in all poetry), he thinks neither the one nor the other—and he ought not to do so. Even less must he as poet be concerned about thought as thought or about the relationship between poets and thinkers. Only the thinker can think the essence of thought, the essence of poetry, the essence of the relationship between thought and poetizing. The dialogue of the thinkers and the poets is not reversible; there is thought about the essence of poetry, but there is no poem on the essence of thought. It is advisable not to forget this necessary dissymmetry, which also gives umbrage to the sovereignty of poetic language.

How can thought that interrogates itself about the essence of poetry avoid subtracting poetry from the poetic domain in order to bring poetry unduly over into a domain that is not its own? Even if the intention of thought is to affirm the supremacy of poetic saying over all other language, how can it ever deny that this affirmation is *its* affirmation, or *its* fact? Let me add that this affirmation is the judgment of a form of thought, always dominant, which never ceases being the judge—the supreme judge—of its own limits and of the grounds of its very relative humility. Therefore, the history of the relationship between philosophy and poetry is the long history of the explicit or occult pre-eminence of philosophy over poetry.

It is precisely here that the profound peculiarity of Heidegger's thought manifests itself once again. In Heidegger, the mediative experience of the language (*parole*) of the poets escapes—or would like to escape—from the fatality that we shall call the fatality of the mediation. Heidegger's emphasis on the fact that this dialogue is a dialogue of thought is not without danger for poetry; it could lead one to believe that the language of the poets is "salvaged" by another language, that of the thinkers. The attention given to poetry would then paradoxically turn against poetry. In this case poetics (*la poétique*), or the "poetic element" (le *poétique*) of poetic speech, would be replaced by a "content of thought," which poetry as such, having no "content" other than its own form, always wishes to ignore. Poetic language is the language that speaks by itself and in order to say nothing other than the saying of Language itself. Poetic language may say what it wishes. It wants to say nothing; it says itself to itself. How could it not be profaned by the devotion of this blasphemous commentary, which always transgresses poetic language in order to ask it what it wants to say? The following aphorism from Nietzsche, on the price one has to pay in order to be an artist, bears witness to this formalism of poetic language: "One is artist if one experiences as *content,* as the 'thing itself,' that which all nonartists call 'form.' In so doing one belongs without a doubt to a crazy world: for from now on all content appears as purely formal—our lives included." [4]

4. "Man is um den Preis Künstler, das man *das,* was alle Nichtkünstler 'Form' nennen, als *Inhalt,* als 'Sache selbst' empfindet. Damit gehört man freilich in eine verkehrte Welt: denn nunmehr wird einem der Inhalt zu etwas bloss Formalen—unser Leben eingerechnet" (Nietzsche, *Der Wille zur Macht* [Stuttgart: Kröner, 1964], sec. 818, p. 552). Heidegger, in quoting and commenting on this text (*N I* 141–42), shows two things definitively. The first is that, for Nietzsche, the form never exclusively means something formal that requires an antecedent or a complementary content in regard to which the form would represent merely an external limit, a borderline for the antecedent's powerlessness. The limit understood in this way does not limit; it is merely the product of a simple cessation, a border or edge. It is not what first and foremost gives consistency and subsistence to a content, which by this very fact disappears as

II

Even if the thought that converses with poetry is as vigilant as possible, it always takes the risk of suppressing the form of saying that is the whole of poetic language. If poetic language is finally to end up being what it is, if it is to be authentically speaking, if the risk of all suppression (*Aufhebung*) is to be warded off, and if the poetic language, even when it is philosophically recognized and consecrated as the word of God— the true word of the true God—is to be something other than a mode or a provisional moment, still inadequate and even dead today, in the absolute Discourse of the Absolute (or, formulated differently, in the Soliloquy of the revealed Word, who speaks to Himself in addressing Himself to us), it is necessary for thought, approaching the poetic language, finally to succeed in withdrawing or making way for the pure presence of the poem. Only in the space left by this retreat can the poetic language in effect finally start to speak as language that is unheard of and yet always already heard, eternally young in the eternal repetition of its first morning, and beautiful just as beauty is beautiful, just as the day that breaks is beautiful.

"content" while the form dominates it, through and through, in order to give it stature and stability. The second is that this dionysian and apollonian conception of form, even when it seems to convert the ancient metaphysical distinction of form and matter, never constitutes itself in the perspective of the essence of the work and the form of the work (*das Wesen des Werkes und die Werkform*). There is here no more form in itself than matter in itself, beauty itself. Nietzsche has a "logical," "arithmetical," "geometrical" conception of form and of the legality of the law (*Formgesetzlichkeit*). We might say that his conception—a logical and categorical, axiological and mathematical, commanding and imperative conception—is more "formalist" than formal. It is in this sense that Nietzsche speaks of "aesthetic evaluations," which are constitutive of the judgment about beauty, and of beauty itself, which is here frankly reduced to a simple value. Nietzsche also says that these "logical feelings" constitute the basis (*Grundstock*) of our aesthetic evaluations, which make up the entire beauty of things that are "found" by us to be "beautiful," and decreed by us to be *eternally* beautiful.

From this follows the ultimately metaphysical, modern, rationalist, and calculative character of this "metaphysics of artists" (*Künstlermetaphysik*), which is more Kantian than Nietzsche believed it to be and is still completely subordinated to the will to power understood as will to mastery and domination. From this follows, also, the abyss that separates Nietzsche's formalism from what we have called here (not without afterthoughts) the formalism of the poetic language (*parole*).

However—and it is here that the antinomy of any commentary constitutes itself—it seems now, indeed, that the integrity of poetic language can be safeguarded only at the price of a certain depreciation of noetic language. "The conversation of a thinker with a poet," as Heidegger says, certainly develops only in the domain of thought. But the question remains as to which is the beginning and which is the end, which is the motor, or the motif, of this development? The commentary here is so moderate, the conversation so modest, that it seems as if the language of the thinker never sets out except to proceed toward a silence in which one can see the suppression or the autosuppression of the effectively thinking thought. The conjuration of the mediation requires the sacrifice of the mediator. Paradox after paradox! In this dialogue involving only one person, there is always one who finally ends up by keeping silent. A short while ago it was the philosopher who understood the poet better than the latter could understand himself. Now the one who best understands the poet is the thinker, apparently mastered by a language which at first said nothing but which now speaks too forcefully in order not to make another language trivial, a language that is more talkative and longs only to keep silent. It is the language of the thinker that one must call the language of the commentator.

These difficulties are so intense and these contradictions so flagrant that they seem to ruin the very possibility or essence of the simple project of a dialogue of thought with poetry, a dialogue that would like to be equally respectful of the truth found in the poetic language and that found in the noetic language. Everything happens as if thought were unable to know poetry except by suppressing it, unable to respect it except by ignoring it. Everything happens as if the language of the poets—a mystery in plain light—must in turn ask for the groping elucidation of the thinkers, only and exclusively to finally object to such elucidation from the height of its invincible solitude. This approach of thought, which in conformity with its dearest hope dashes itself against a rival language, is a strange one. For the sake of what is poematized in the poem, the commentary, however necessary it may be, must make itself superfluous; however, it must not make itself useless or arbitrary, for the superfluous is necessary here. Here we are confronted with a point of return, a point of reversal, where the language of the thinkers hands the word over to the language of the poets; with uncertainty of the noeticopoetic dialogue, which finally ends up in a monologue; with ultimate disavowal. Here we have a double parody. There is nothing that conforms with thought as much as this disavowal of thought; a short while ago there was nothing that conformed with the essence of poetry as much as a certain disavowal of the poetic form. The goal, or the finality, of the commentary is thus always ambivalent. Consecration has a double sense: in order to bring the poetic text to speculation, it absorbs the text; and in order to efface itself before the text, it lets the text remain in its own stature. Each time a certain desire comes into being, and this desire is one of superabundance and of death: the sacrifice of poetry and the sacrifice of thought.

According to Heidegger there are, it seems, only two types of dialogue: the dialogue of the poets and that of the thinkers. But now there is a third, one that is possible—sometimes even necessary—and thus cannot be inauthentic. It is the dialogue of a thinker with a poet, the thinking experience of a certain proximity between thought and the poetic song. Everything takes place here in the one and only domain of thought, and this domain (*Bereich*), as Heidegger assures us as early as 1944, speaking of his first commentaries on Hölderlin, is the same as that found in his "philosophical" writings which appeared during the same period, "On the Essence of Truth" and "What Is Metaphysics?" Without this identity how could one explain that the joint meditation of the questions (*das Mitdenken der Fragen*), which constitutes the motif of the philosophical texts, makes more accessible to us (*zugänglicher*) the domain in which the thinking quest (*das Nachdenken*) of the commentaries on Hölderlin maintains itself? [5]

In the sole domain of thought, and in the site of one single problematic, these very same commentaries appear sometimes to have no goal other than a better and more respectful understanding of this poetic language, which, without such commentaries, would not be what it is: marvelously sufficient, belatedly autonomous, without density but still veiled. It is then, once the poem is clarified by thought, that it becomes illuminating for other poems. It is then that the poem speaks of itself and for itself. It is then that it seems to have always already spoken that way.

5. This is a reference to Hölderlin's poem: "Von wegen geringer Dinge / Verstimmt wie von Schnee war / Die Glocke, womit / Man läutet / Zum Abendessen" (*HD* 7).

Let us quote here the very impressive preface to Heidegger's commentaries on Hölderlin:

Perhaps all elucidation of these poems is but "a snowfall on the bell." Whatever may be the power or lack of power of the elucidation, one thing nevertheless always remains valid: if what is purely poematized in the poem is to assert itself with a little greater clarity, the elucidating discourse must each time shatter itself and its own effort. For the sake of what is poematized, the elucidation of the poem must tend to make itself superfluous. The last step, but also the most difficult one of all exegesis, consists in its disappearing, with all its elucidations, before the pure presence of the poem. It is then that the poem, embodied in its own law, immediately brings light to the other poems. That explains why in rereading the poems we think that we have always already understood them in that way. It is a good thing to believe so.[6]

One will notice here the bittersweetness of this commentary, which precisely wishes to "add" nothing to the text but, on the contrary, wants to restore the purity or luster of a presence that one may properly call monumental—the perfection of a certain absence, the virtue of a certain silence, the project of renunciation. If the word *interpretation* could be authorized (but it cannot be, for there is no question of interposing oneself in order to decide on the value or the price), one would say that the final goal of the interpretation consists in its disappearing, along with the interpreter, in favor of the work itself, in order to appear retrospectively as useless in favor of an appearance that is simultaneously illusory and salutary. The interpretation is from now on forever inscribed and, as it were, at work in the project of the "interpretation" that does not wish to interpret but, on the contrary, to let be, to let appear, and to let speak the language from which it, in the end, remains prohibited.

6. "Vielleicht ist jede Erläuterung dieser Gedichte ein Schneefall auf die Glocke. Was immer auch eine Erläuterung vermag und was sie nicht vermag, von ihr gilt stets dieses: damit das im Gedicht rein Gedichtete um einiges klarer dastehe, muss die erläuternde Rede sich und ihr Versuchtes jedesmal zerbrechen. Um des Gedichteten willen muss die Erläuterung des Gedichtes darnach trachten, sich selbst überflüssig zu machen. Der letzte, aber auch schwerste Schritt jeder Auslegung besteht darin, mit ihren Erläuterungen vor dem reinen Dastehen des Gedichtes zu verschwinden. Das denn im eigenen Gesetz stehende Gedicht bringt selbst unmittelbar ein Licht in die andere Gedichte. Daher meinen wir beim wiederholenden Lesen, wir hätten die Gedichte schon immer so verstanden. Es ist gut, wenn wir das meinen" (*HD* 7–8).

Such is the price that thought must pay when it is effectively respectful of the poetic saying. Such is the hard exigency of an approach that is not surreptitiously mediating the language of the poets. Here, as in many other areas, the distance between Heidegger and Hegel is infinite. It is not just by chance that Heidegger evokes the most famous formulas of Hegel, found at the beginning of the *Lectures on Aesthetics:*

> The beautiful days of Greek art as well as the golden era of the Middle Ages have passed. . . . We no longer have an absolute need to bring to light a content in the form of Art. In all its relationships, and as far as supreme destination is concerned, Art is and remains for us something of the past. It is in this way that its truth and authentic vitality are equally lost for us.[7]

Where must we situate this goal of Art, this strictly "aesthetic" transhumance which makes Art pass from the world of reality and necessity to the more inconsistent world of the contingent representation, of the emotion, of feeling and pleasure? It certainly cannot be located in symbolic art, and certainly not in the classical art, in which Art, on the contrary, reaches its highest summit. Nothing can be and nothing ever will be more beautiful, says Hegel, than classical art; its deficiency is that it is nothing but art, art without qualification and nothing more. Thus we are to find this goal of Art in romantic art, which turns its back on this summit of beauty in which the beauty, consummated by the flame of the infinite and spiritual subjectivity in itself, becomes paradoxically something secondary. In this way romantic art finds itself propelled by itself beyond itself.

Which of the romantic forms of art is then the supreme one? It is poetry. The romantic forms of art originate from the rupture between idea and reality. They work for the advent of an art without beauty and a new aesthetics that will be the aesthetics of ugliness. Poetry already stretches out its hand to prose, while

---

7. "Die schönen Tagen der griechischen Kunst wie die goldene Zeit des späteren Mittelalters sind vorüber. . . . Aber wir haben kein absolutes Bedürfnis mehr, einem Gehalt in der Form der Kunst zur Darstellung zu bringen. In allen diesen Beziehungen ist und bleibt die Kunst nach der Seite ihrer höchsten Bestimmung für uns ein Vergangenes. Damit hat sie für uns auch die echte Wahrheit und Lebendigkeit verloren" (Hegel, "Vorlesungen über die Ästhetik," in *Werke,* ed. G. Lasson and J. Hoffmeister [Hamburg: F. Meiner, 1949], X, sec. 1, 16).

repudiating as much as it can this sensible or sensual materiality without which, however, beauty would not be beauty. The gods have flown, and from this, says Hegel, a pantheon of dethroned gods has resulted. With poetry, beauty dies in beauty. Art has lost its original truth and its first vitality; it certainly can flower again, but it never will have more than marginal reality. According to the eternal essence and historical destiny of poetry, poets are today what they should be—poets in a time of distress, the distress of poetry itself.

Because old age, which is weakness in the eyes of Nature, is maturity for the Spirit, one will not be amazed that here Art experiences a double perfection, a double completion. There is the classical perfection of sculpture, which alone is genuinely beautiful, and the romantic perfection of poetry, which is more sublime than beautiful—sublime, perhaps, because it is ugly. There are two peaks: one high point of Art in its abstract and immediate naturalness, and another high point which is later, more concrete but nonetheless alone in conformance with the Idea of Art and with the becoming of this Idea. The first high point is that of pagan Greece; the second, that of German Christianity. The first is the meridional, or Mediterranean, peak of a certain apogee of life to that degree of consciousness which is "the degree of abstraction" as well as "the degree of beauty" (*die Stufe der Schönheit*). The second is the occidental, or twilight, peak of a certain apotheosis of beauty, which expires in the face of another Eden— the Eden without grace, characteristic of the basically prosaic modernity. There is the outburst of the Spirit in the one case; the first return, or first coming back, in the other. Thus, we have here the Hegelian and Nietzschean duplication and reduplication of the point of culmination: the high point according to the time of the historic representation, and the high point—the Great High Point—according to the eternity of the philosophical speculation. This eternity is always radiant, but in a double sense, because it is joyous or serious. There is a double elimination of time in favor of a matutinal or vesperal eternity, which is exultant or resultant. Here we encounter the great zenith of life and the second youth which is better than the first: "O zenith of life's day! O second youth!" Here we find the Sunday of the Spirit at the evening of life: peace glowing with reality when the Spirit returns home. This suggests a Hegelian parody of the Nietzschean parody,

"Once you were young, now—be young again! [Warst einst du jung, jetzt—bist du besser jung!]" [8]—Once you were old, now— be old again! [Warst einst du alt, jetzt—bist du besser alt!].

Because Art does not cease being related to life or to something that is experienced of life, to the will and to that original affective form with which will is identical, Nietzsche's theory of art, in conformance with the modernity of our times, is and remains an aesthetics. Aesthetics is not *the* theory of Art or of Beauty; it is *one* theory of Art and Beauty. The word *aisthēsis* taken in the broadest sense designates sense perception. Aesthetics as a theory of Art and Beauty prejudges the essential nature of the work of art and of beauty in general. What is beautiful is aesthetic only when the beautiful is that which pleases. The work of art belongs to aesthetics only when it is related to some kind of enjoyment, either of the creator or of the lover. In aesthetics, beauty no longer belongs first to the things themselves. It has abandoned the world in order to emigrate to the subjectivity of the intellectual and sensible subject; soon it will be no more than a value.

Nietzsche can give a "metaphysical" dimension to art by interpreting and justifying the world as an aesthetic phenomenon. He can denounce the romantic and musical dissolution of art by celebrating the classical type and by summoning at will a music that in the end will not be repugnant to the "great style." He can, as he writes to Erwin Rohde, "take one more step beyond the Laokoon of Lessing," "the second legislator of the arts—in particular, poetry—after Aristotle," according to Dilthey. Nietzsche can oppose the Hegelian idea of the poetic generality by formulating in various ways—which are, undoubtedly, irreconcilable—the idea of an essential bipartition of all the arts and of a double source of each art in particular. He can be more "classical" than Hegel, even when he sees in music, or in the spirit of music, the genuine origin of tragedy and, with it, the origin of all the arts. None of this changes the basically metaphysical character of this metaphysics, which Nietzsche calls a "metaphysics of artists." Thus, in its own manner and, as it were, in spite of itself, this "gospel of the artists" carries the presence of a certain decay of beauty, of a certain death of Art.

8. Nietzsche, "Aus hohen Bergen," in *Jenseits von Gut und Böse* (Stuttgart: Kröner, 1964), p. 235.

III

To DEVELOP A NONAESTHETIC CONCEPTION of the work of art and to elaborate a new rule for the dialogue between thinkers and poets is the double task that Heidegger undertakes in the first essay of *Holzwege,* "The Origin of the Work of Art," and in the commentaries on Hölderlin's poetry. Heidegger shows that, while the artist is the origin of the work of art, the origin of the artist must be sought in the work of art itself. How do we escape from this circle if not by searching for an origin common to the work of art and the artist in their reciprocal relationships? This origin of the work of art and the artist must be found in a third term, which actually is the first and at the center of this vicious circle—namely, Art. To build jointly a new set of rules for the relationships between poets and thinkers, rules capable of escaping the fatality of the mediation, and to remove the antinomy of the commentary has been the meaning of Heidegger's reflections in his numberless commentaries on poets which have appeared over a thirty-year period, particularly on the poet of poets, Hölderlin.

Within the framework of an investigation concerning the common origin of the work of art and the artist, one must notice the predominance of art. The Greeks had no word other than *technē* to designate art. The usual translation of the Greek *poiēsis,* which certainly distorts the meaning of this term, is the Roman and Christian notion of creation. The Greek *poiēsis* must be thought of as the transgressed origin of what later was called creation. Far from first designating any arbitrary manual ability, *technē* signifies, as Plato notes, the principle of all passage from not-being to being. Heidegger comments that in this sense *phusis* is *poiēsis* in the supreme sense of the term. This, however, does not mean that the world must be conceived of as a work of art, generating itself without the presence of this preliminary phase which is the artistic. The *poiēsis,* and the *technē* which is inseparable from it, designates first and foremost a form of *alētheuein.* Therefore, *poiēsis* taken in its original sense is a bringing into play of Truth. Heidegger's criticism of the duality of form and matter, of the intelligible and the sensible—a duality within which Hegel's *Aesthetics,* nonetheless, continues to move—is particularly severe in this connection. In the work of art it is proper to substitute for this duality, which is essentially metaphysical, the ontico-ontological difference between world and thing. If Art is the common origin of the work of art and of the artist, this is because with Art there materializes what Heidegger calls the bringing into play of Truth. This expression is equivocal. It says that beauty is to be thought of in terms of Truth, not in terms of pleasure, and that beauty implies a certain dissimulation or retention of the birth of Truth in the bringing into play of Truth. Art is respectful of this dimension of hiddenness that properly belongs to Truth. Beauty is not what pleases; it is the bringing into play of a truth that hides itself. That which is splendid is beautiful, not merely that which imperfectly materializes a truth conceived of in terms of a pure revelation. Art conforms to the complete essence of Truth more than does the philosophical truth itself. In the expression "the bringing into play of Truth" one must comprehend that Art brings into play the coming to pass of Truth. The issue here is not about the transcription of a truth that is more or less perfect; the issue is about the salvaging of the "operative" character of Truth itself. "In the work of art," Heidegger writes, "Truth is at work in the working of Truth itself." [9] The work of art, far from referring to a "lived" datum, whatever it may be, returns to what is most characteristic of Truth as such. In this sense it refers only to Truth, to the work, to the experience of Truth. In the same way that genuine language brings to word language as such, the work of art sets to work the coming to pass of Truth. In this sense the poetic is not nature in this or that of nature's productions, but the very naturalness of nature, the protecting dawn of the very birth of this nature, the difficulty of Truth.

The work of art reminds one of the complete essence of Truth. What we have called the operative character of Truth is what Heidegger calls "der Werkungscharakter der Wahrheit." There is a working of Truth that is constitutive of Truth itself. In its own way the philosophical tradition witnesses this, from Aristotle's notion of the Greek *energeia* to the *Wirklichkeit* of absolute German idealism. From this point of view one will note the difference between Heidegger's criticism of the ancient metaphysical duality of form and matter—a distinction within which

9. HW 59.

the entire *Aesthetics* of Hegel still moves—and Heidegger's duality of world and thing, a duality of which the work of art, in its own way, is reminiscent. In this sense the work of art is finally more instructive for the thing character of the thing than a certain metaphysical determination of the essence of the thing could be for the work of art.

Poetry understood in the broad sense, in Nietzsche as well as in Hegel, in Heidegger as well as in Plato, represents the very essence of Art. The work of art recalls this dimension of hiddenness, which is inherent in the complete essence of Truth. The splendor of the work of art is a harrowing splendor that properly belongs to the integral and irreparably divided essence of Truth and Untruth.

To challenge the privilege of poetry taken as particular literary art *and* as art in general is not sufficient to make us leave behind the traditional paths of metaphysics. The work of Schopenhauer and, to a certain extent, that of Nietzsche bear witness to this impotence. Inversely, to maintain the privilege of poetry as the art of the word is not sufficient evidence of the fundamentally metaphysical character of a certain conception of art; the nonmetaphysical thought of art as we find it in the first essay of *Holzwege* is a sign of this. In this essay the work of art is thought of poetically in the temple of language; but it is not thought of "aesthetically" or "metaphysically."

When Heidegger affirms that the origin of the work of art (and of the artist) must be sought in Art, one must understand that Truth would not be Truth without the work, the pain, and the suffering of Truth. In the expression "the bringing into play of Truth," the word *Truth* is simultaneously subject and object of the proposition. There is in the very essence of Truth something that is always already at work. The experience of thought, which has already begun but is always not yet completed and always initial and original, responds and corresponds to the "working" of Truth. Art is the origin of the work of art because the advent of Truth itself is basically always original.

From this we gain some light in regard to the new statute of the dialogue between thinkers and poets. In the postscript of "What Is Metaphysics?" Heidegger writes: "Assuredly, we know much about the things that are related to the relationship between philosophy and poetry. On the other hand, we know nothing about the dialogue between thinkers and poets who live close to one another on mountains farthest apart." [10] Let us reflect for a moment on these two propositions. First, we find here an insurmountable difference between the redundancy of acts of knowledge and the poverty, not to mention the nullity, of a certain knowing. The essential knowing of the essence is not the sum of all acts of knowledge. Second, the relationship (*Verhältnis*) is determined as *Zwiesprache;* the relationship between thought and poetry is a dialogue. The German word *Zwiesprache* refers to language (*Sprache*). This dialogue does not unfold with respect to language in the broad sense (*langage*) but develops in favor and for the benefit of language (*parole*). The language of man brings to word the wordless language (*parole*) of Being. Language lets or makes language speak. Language brings language into the element of language. Language lets language be. The letting be of language or word is the letting be of Being.

On the other hand, Heidegger establishes here a twofold difference: the difference between philosophy and the thinkers and the difference between poesy and poetry. Philosophy is not thought as such; philosophy is a mode of thought, its metaphysical and occidental, universal and planetary, mode. The human sciences, not to mention the other sciences, are no longer recognizable by-products of philosophy as such. Similarly, the difference between poesy and poetry permits us to comprehend that poesy taken as literary genre is merely a particular and privileged form of a *Dichtung* ("poetry") or *Stiftung* ("originating") that is more essential—perhaps absolutely essential—to the very essence of man. In this sense there is in the Being of man, understood as thinking being, something basically poetic: "It is poetically," says Hölderlin, "that men (all men, not only the poets) dwell on this earth (and not between heaven and earth, in the clouds of poetic fancy or imagination.)" [11]

Finally, this phrase from the postscript permits us to comprehend the essential proximity of and the insurmountable difference between thinkers and poets. This proximity is the proximity in the Selfsame, which is the element of the Difference. Thought

10. "Man kennt wohl manches über das Verhältnis der Philosophie und der Poesie. Wir wessen aber nichts von der Zwiesprache der Dichter und Denker, die nahe wohnen auf getrenntesten Bergen" (*WM* 51 [360]).
11. Johann Hölderlin, *Sämtliche Werke*, ed. N. V. Hellingrath (Munich: Müller, 1923), VI, 25.

and poetry originate equally in Being and accede to its Truth. On the other hand, this "separation" excludes all possible transition from thought to poetry—at least as long as thought and poetry are not distorted and dispirited, as long as they maintain their positions.

The repudiation of the mediation, or the antinomy, about which we have spoken often thus far, is founded here in the original difference between saying taken as the saying of the poetic song, and saying as the saying of the language of the thinkers. Heidegger says: "The thinker says Being. The poet names or hails the Holy." The saying of thought, however, is in its own way an evocation or a nomination. The hailing or the appellation by the poets, in turn, is still a form of saying. Yet the evocation of the Holy in the song of the poets must be distinguished from the effectively thinking thought of the essence of the Holy from the viewpoint of the Truth of Being. The thought of the essence of the Holy cannot be likened to the poetic incantation of the Holy. There is a commemoration of the initially thinking thought in the poets; inversely, there is a poetic character of thought itself. This initially poetic character of thought remains hidden and creates the appearance of an understanding that is semipoetic. Everyone who has experienced the essence of language as the language of essence (Being [*Sein*]) has at the same time experienced the duality of the insurmountable twofoldness of the thinking language and the poetic language; thinkers and poets, in a way that is characteristic of both, preserve language, "spare" it, bring it to completion.

By 1944 Heidegger affirmed that his commentaries on Hölderlin originated "from a necessity of thought." Far from breaking himself on the essence of poetic language in order to indulge in the delights of poetry, Heidegger returns from the thinking dialogue of the poets with the thinkers to the very essence of thought. The very moment that the dialogue of thought and poetry sanctions the dignity of the poetic language, it remains under the protection of thought alone. The dialogue establishes and annihilates itself before the pure presence of the poem and, to the contrary, lives on and becomes deepened in the thinking commemoration of what is called thinking. It is in this sense that Heidegger speaks of the "good and, by that very fact, salutary danger" that the proximity of the poetic song represents for thought. "Good and salutary danger" seems to be a contradictory expression. "Danger" is what thought must encounter in the progress which belongs to it (*Erfahren, fahren, Gefahr*). Why is this danger "good" and, correlatively, "salutary"? Good need not be understood in a moral sense. Good is what safeguards, that is to say, what keeps the essence of a thing safe and sound. The danger in the poetic song marks the limits of thought, a threat that thought must try to ward off. From this vigilance and from the memento of another language, the experience of thought maintains itself in its proper truth. Finally, only that which of itself is holy (*heilig*) can be salutary (*heilsam*); the poet sings the Holy. The Holy is the "What is safe which saves." The Holy is not the Divine. The poet is not the man of the gods; he is simply the melancholic watchman of a certain trace of the deity. The poets are the mortals who keep themselves in the wide-open openness of heaven and earth; they are the messengers, not the witnesses, of the deity of god. All poetry is "sacred," but it is not "divine"; the poet is the man who is "touched," but not "entranced," by the gods. There is no poetic enthusiasm.

And yet, in the postscript of "What Is Metaphysics?" and in the booklet *From the Experience of Thinking* the idea of a common source of the poetic song and the language of the thinkers breaks through in an apparently divergent manner. In the postscript, after clearly distinguishing between the saying of Being and the naming of the Holy, Heidegger writes:

> The question of how poetizing, thanking, and thinking, understood from the essence of Being, keep referring to one another although they remain distinct must here be left unanswered. One may presume that thanking and poetizing emerge in different modes from initial thought, an initial thought of which they make use without themselves being able to be thinking.[12]

Heidegger distinguishes here the initial thinking, which in a certain way is dormant in poetizing itself, and the thought of the thinkers. Thus, there is thought in poetizing. The poet thinks without being a thinker.

In *From the Experience of Thinking* Heidegger says, "Singing

---

12. "Wie freilich, aus dem Wesen des Seins gedacht, das Dichten und das Danken und das Denken zueinander verwiesen und zugleich geschieden sind, muss hier offenbleiben. Vermutlich entspringen Danken und Dichten in verschiedener Weise dem anfänglichen Denken, das sie brauchen, ohne doch für sich ein Denken sein zu können" (*WM* 51).

and thinking are the neighboring trunks of poetizing." [13] Here the common source is no longer on the side of thinking but on the side of poetizing in the sense of the original poetry. Thought poetizes without being poetic. There is no contradiction at all in these two texts, which merely recall what we have called the originally "noetic" essence of poetizing and the fundamentally poetic, or "poietic," character of thought.

If man as that being who is capable of thinking "poietizes" insofar as he thinks authentically, this depends first not on himself but on the essence of Being in its essential relationship to man's essence. Before he "poietizes," man is the outline of a poem, the poem started by Being. The poem in man precedes the poet in man. There is a "poematico-poetic" essence of man.

Heidegger's affirmation that Hölderlin is the poet of poets does not have the signification that Hegel could give to it. It does not evoke the belated character of poetry, its fatal extenuation, or the exaggeration of a certain narcissism (*übersteigerte Selbstbespiegelung*). On the contrary, it refers to the plenitude or overflowing thrust of a world still to come. Heidegger says, "We come too late for the gods and too early for Being." [14] He sees Hölderlin as the poet of a certain distress of poetry. However, poetry does not reach out its hand to the prose of a scientific representation any more than to the nonprosaic prose of speculative thought. The distress is certainly a lack, which is a negation, a double negation: the negation of the "no longer" of the gods who fled *and* the negation of the "not yet" of the god who comes.

Why call a thought "poetic" and "mystic" which interrogates itself today about a particular and universal form of thought, the thought of calculating thinking? Why deny the name "strictly meditative thought" to a thought that interrogates itself about the origin and destiny of our entire history?

Thought (*Denken*) is recollection (*Andenken*), the recollection of the Unthought as the original element of thought itself. The Unthought is not the unknowable object of thought; neither is it merely the unthought which a more vigilant thought would be capable of recovering. The Unthought does not stand in front of or far away from thought. It is not a provisional and merely

---

13. "Singen und Denken sind die nachbarlichen Stämme des Dichtens" (*ED* 25).
14. *ED* 7.

human lacuna of thought. The Unthought is at the very heart of thought as that which affects it as intimately as possible.

"Thought acts insofar as it thinks." This action of thought is neither "practical" nor "creative"; it is "poetic" in the sense of something that could hide itself but was not experienced in the Greek word *poiēsis*.

What for the poets is the needy time (*die dürftige Zeit*) is for the thinkers the time to be thought of mostly (*die bedenklichste Zeit*)—distress of poetry, perplexity of thought; no exhaustion of poetry, no exhaustion of thought. There is a parallel, foreboding a certain dawn: "Whereas Hölderlin builds the essence of poetry," writes Heidegger, "he also determines a new time—the time of the gods who have fled and of the god who comes." [15] In the same sense, the perplexity of our time is one of a certain absence and a certain imminence of thought.

The last lines of Heidegger's commentary on one of Hölderlin's poems entitled "Recollection [*Andenken*]" express the following: "Poetizing is recollecting. Recollecting is originating [*Stiften*]. The originating dwelling of the poet designates and consecrates the ground for the poetic dwelling of the sons of the earth. Something that is to abide comes to abide. There is recollection. The northeast wind blows." [16]

15. *HD* 44 (209).
16. "Dichten ist Andenken. Andenken is Stiftung. Das stiftende Wohnen des Dichters weist und weiht dem dichterischen Wohnen der Erdensöhne den Grund. Ein Bleibendes kommt ins Bleiben. Andenken ist. Der Nordost wehet" (*ED* 143).

6 / Hermeneutic and Personal Structure of Language

Heinrich Ott

MAN LIVES in language, as language. He is a dialogue. Heidegger quotes the following lines from Hölderlin:

> Man has experienced many things
> And many of the heavenly ones has he named
> Since the time we are a dialogue
> And able to hear from one another.[1]

This is meant as an ontological determination of man's Being. We shall use this conception as a point of departure and thus place ourselves in opposition to other conceptions of language and of man's Being.

In a short essay that was recently published, Heidegger correctly outlines the two extreme poles of thought's struggle concerning language and man's Being:

> These same questions, developed in a more or less clear and adequate fashion, constitute at the same time the as yet hidden center of those endeavors at which contemporary "philosophy" aims for its extreme counterpositions (Carnap, Heidegger). Today these positions are called the technological scientist view of language and the speculative hermeneutic experience of language. Both positions are determined by unfathomably diverse tasks. The first position wants to bring all thinking and speaking, even that of

---

1. "Viel hat erfahren der Mensch / Der Himmlischen viele genannt, / Seit ein Gespräch wir sind / Und hören können voneinander" (Johann Hölderlin, *Sämtliche Werke,* ed. N. V. Hellingrath [Munich: Müller, 1923), IV, 343 [editor's translation]).

philosophy, within the jurisdiction of a system of signs that can be construed as a technical-logical system—to restrict all thinking and saying to being instruments of science. The second position has grown from the question of what is to be experienced as the subject matter of philosophy's thinking and how this subject matter (Being as Being) is to be expressed. In neither position is there a question of a separate sphere of a philosophy of language (analogous to that of a philosophy of nature or of art); language is recognized as the realm within which every thinking of philosophy and every mode of thinking and saying dwell and move. To the extent that the Being of man is determined by Western tradition in such a way that man is that animal who "has language" (*zōion logon echon*)—even man as acting being is such only as the one who "has language"—nothing less is at stake in the dispute between the two positions than the question of man and his destiny.[2]

Man lives in language. Language is not just one of many abilities at his disposal. He dwells in language. Everything that he is and does comes to pass in the realm of language. Heidegger's statement regarding this decisive state of affairs is to the point: ". . . even man as acting being is such only as the one who 'has language. . . .'" Man can act, but he can decide only insofar as the possibilities about which he can decide are already disclosed to him as existential possibilities through language, through communication with his fellow men. The technical scientistic conception of language—which, taking its significative function as a starting point, interprets language as an instrument, as a means toward an end, as a means for providing technically useful information—forgets or fails to notice that these possibilities are disclosed through language. This conception overlooks the fact that this goal, in regard to which this means could be a means, is a goal only by means of language. This is inherently false reasoning. Language cannot be adequately interpreted as a means, as an instrumental "ability" of man. (Although it is not impossible to conceive of language as a means, in such an interpretation the essence of language, that which makes language language, is not touched upon.) It is impossible to understand adequately the goal of this means without appealing to "language" as fact. If it were possible, one would have to conceive of human beings as beings who at first are solitary, speech-

2. PT 39–40.

less, and unable to communicate, who have their value scales and so on, and who later begin to communicate by means of the instrument "language." This is an absurd conception. On the other hand it is very well possible, for example, to conceive the ability of the *homo faber*—namely, the ability to produce useful equipment for the satisfaction of all possible needs—as a genuinely instrumental ability of man, as a means to a goal. Seen historically, this is certainly an ability that man has always already materialized. The goal, however, the for-what of all human doing, is actual only within the horizon of language.

Sometimes it seems as if man has at his disposal still other abilities and possibilities—for example, the possibility of creativity in music and the pictorial arts—which fall completely outside the horizon of language and which, therefore, show that the ontological interpretation of man's being as "dialogue" is too narrow a frame of reference. This is a common objection to the universalism of the linguistic conception of man. Indeed, what is characteristic of a symphony or a painting can no longer be said in words; and yet these spheres of man's Being, too, remain embedded in the encompassing horizon of language. It is only in language that one can lay hold of the fact that what is characteristic of the work of art affects us in a way that can no longer be said in words. How art affects us and how it brings us together in experiencing its works can even be discussed again; or, rather, the way in which it affects us comes to pass in the realm of language. When we see or listen to works of art, the experience of art does not lead us into a desert, into ivory towers, into pure solitude; it brings us to communication with our fellow men who share the experience and, thus, to language—although what is then asserted is incapable of reaching the work of art itself. Moreover, insofar as pictorial art is representative, it lets come to light the world that earlier was constituted as meaningful environment (*Umwelt*) for man through the medium of language. Finally, music, although it says what is unsayable, is related to language, too, in a kind of underground relationship. What would human speech be without rhythm? Without rhythm, language would no longer be what as language it precisely is; it would be reduced to an instrument for information. (In a cable and in the so-called cable style, which aims at nothing but the briefest information, the rhythm of the words is indeed a matter of indifference.) The proximity of language and music comes to light and becomes experienceable in a privileged—so to speak, ontologically paradigmatic—musical genre, the song.

THE HERMENEUTIC STRUCTURE OF LANGUAGE

IN ORDER TO CATCH SIGHT of the hermeneutic structure of language we shall use Gerhard Ebeling's short essay *Gott und Wort* as a point of departure. This work has shown in a particularly lucid way the insufficiency of a linguistico-scientistic interpretation of the essence of language in the realm of theology. According to Ebeling, human language is without a doubt used as a means for securing information. This is one of its frequent modes of appearance, and it is perfectly legitimate to consider language in this function. But language is not exhausted herewith; its essence is not to be found here. Ebeling writes:

> The dominant conception of language is oriented toward its significative function. The word counts merely as a sign . . . for a certain thing. . . . The word, thus, is consistently reduced to a cipher and the relationship between the words in a sentence to the realm of the calculus. In this traditional conception of language as well as in its consequent mathematization, there is without a doubt something right, which cannot be abandoned. Its successful application—since ancient times in the dictionary and in grammar, and recently with computers and in cybernetics—cannot be denied. This aspect of the matter and all the possibilities contained in it do not give us the key to the essence of language. One is dealing here with an abstraction of the typically human aspect of language, an abstraction which, to a certain extent, is justified and even necessary.[3]

It is precisely this specifically human aspect which cannot be sufficiently explained on the basis of the significative function of language. The word creates for man a space to exist in; speaking, it grants him freedom and future—a space, a freedom, and a future which he cannot provide himself, which he cannot take and organize, but which can only be addressed to him.

3. Gerhard Ebeling, *Gott und Wort* (Tübingen: Mohr, 1966), pp. 36–37.

In all of this I can follow Ebeling's train of thought and agree with it. A particularly striking proof of his argument is found, for instance, in the event of the remission of guilt—taken here as occurring between individuals and not in a religious sense. An absolution (*Frei-spruch*) takes place which man is not able to obtain for himself; what he receives is not merely "signalized" but also addressed to him. It becomes event and is established by being spoken between men. (It is obviously conceivable that a mute person, for instance forgives guilt with a gesture. This is an absolution without words. But this case does not show that the remission can occur through means other than language alone. It shows, rather, that the concept of language is to include more than the acoustically expressed word.)

Ebeling is a convincing witness for the fact that, as soon as one seriously considers those linguistic phenomena in which the theologian is interested, one is unable to manage the situation with the significative conception of language, however much this conception seems at first sight to be quite self-evident. However, it seems to me that Ebeling, in stressing the "word situation" in opposition to the significative functions, does not yet express what I would like to call the hermeneutic structure of language— namely, the fact that language establishes the space of intimacy, the space for possible common preoccupations, within which something like absolution, for instance, first becomes possible at all. I call this space the world. (It is clear that Heidegger uses the term in this way, in contradistinction to *world* as cosmos and totality.) *Language establishes world.* The word taken as absolution (*Freispruch*), for instance (just to stay with this privileged paradigm), is *founded* in the Being of the world. Guilt and remission presuppose that men have common preoccupations in a space of commonly understood, meaningful relationships. For this reason language as foundation of world is more original than, for instance, language as absolution.

By considering "moral phenomena," Ebeling comes to the insight that the significative interpretation of language is insufficient. By studying other, equally compelling phenomena, Heidegger reaches a similar insight. But, by considering the phenomenon of the "lyric" poem, he succeeds at the same time in unfolding the hermeneutic structure of language. While I am in complete agreement with what Ebeling, because of his theological interest, has unfolded with respect to our philosophical understanding of

language, I would like to take a step beyond Ebeling, as Heidegger
has done, in the direction of a description of the essence of
language.

In his essay "Language," [4] Heidegger searches for the "abiding
Being" of language (*Wesen* taken in the verbal sense) in what
has been said. This method appears to be the most promising and
is perhaps the only adequate one. Heidegger's train of thought
takes its orientation from "A Winter Evening," a poem by Georg
Trakl, the first stanza of which reads:

> When the snow falls outside the window,
> The eveningbell peals for a long time,
> The table is prepared for many,
> And the house is well provided.[5]

Heidegger searches for the function of the words of the poem.
What do they intend, and what do they achieve?

> Both the third and fourth lines make assertions, speak as if they
> were establishing facts present-at-hand. The definite *is* sounds so.
> And yet it speaks summoning. . . .
>   What is it that the first verse summons? It summons things,
> tells them to come. Toward what? Not as present things among
> present things, not the table which is mentioned in the poem, over
> here between the rows of seats which you occupy. The destination
> which is co-summoned in this call is a being present which is
> hidden in its absence. By naming them, the call tells them to come
> to such an arrival. This telling is an invitation. It invites things
> as things to concern human beings. . . . In this naming, the
> things that are named are called to be and act as things [*in ihr
> Dingen*]. By being and acting as things, they unfold a world within
> which the things then abide, and in this way they are the con-
> tinuously abiding ones. . . .
>   The first verse calls the things to be and act as things, tells
> them to come. This telling, which summons the things, calls them
> over there, invites them and calls them at the same time to be and
> act as things, recommends them to the world from which they ap-
> pear. That is why the first verse not only names things but, at the
> same time, names the world. . . .
>   For world and things do not exist alongside one another. They

4. *US* 11–33.
5. "Wenn der Schnee ans Fenster fällt, / Lang die Abendglocke
läutet, / Vielen ist der Tisch bereitet / Und das Haus ist wohlbestellt"
(*US* 17 [editor's translation]).

permeate one another. Here these two traverse a center. In this center they are united. As two that are so united, they are close [*innig*]. The center of the two is the proximity. What is in the middle of two things is in our language called the "in between" [*das Zwischen*]. . . . The proximity is not a fusion. Proximity holds sway only where what is close, namely, world and things, clearly part and remain separated.[6]

The decisive discovery of the hermeneutic structure of language is enclosed in this concept of "proximity" of world and things, a proximity of dif-ference (*Unter-Schied*)[7] in which Heidegger's "ontological difference" reverberates. Inherent in the essence of language is the fact that language brings to the fore both "world" and "things"—that is, being and the horizon within which such a meaningful being is of concern to man and can be discussed by him. Language "brings" both to the "fore" (*zum Vorschein*), not in the sense of producing them, but as that which they are: the things as things and the world as world, beings as beings and the horizon of beings as horizon. Man who speaks does not primarily behave as one who produces, as one who is master of his abilities, but as one who receives—a state of affairs expressed in Heidegger's famous saying "Language speaks."

Certainly intrinsic to the structure of language is the fact that man, speaking language, is a receiver. This is not to say that language is a being before man, a something that exists somewhere for itself. Man's receiving occurs in such a way that he is not a being before language, either, but that he is completely determined in his Being by language. However, that which we wish to call here the hermeneutic structure of language, over and above this state of affairs, is the following (which in fact is connected with the conception just mentioned): When man speaks, he does not only name individual things for the purpose of the exchange of information about them. This would have been the state of affairs if man had been the master of language, if language had been indebted to man and man had not, at the same time, been indebted to language. In reality, however, while man names individual things and discusses them, he simultaneously lets appear the horizon within which these individual things appear to him and affect him. Both of these, however, things and world, are not produced by man; he receives them. Insofar as

6. *US* 21–22, 24.
7. Cf. *US* 24.

things affect man, they are already in a world, and the world in the things. Speech merely brings to the fore their being in one another.

Consider, for instance, walking with a friend in the country-side. The country has its mood and its individual aspects. We call one another's attention to individual things: "Look at that tree there with its peculiar shape. I saw such trees in Italy." "Look at that old house there. It seems to be vacant." In these particulars there is always contained the whole of the country's mood which cannot be expressed in words but which determines our speaking as well as our silent walking. Without the unsayable whole, there would be no particulars for us. While we talk about the particulars, the unsayable whole, the horizon of the particulars within only which the particulars are for us, co-appears. In this way language brings to the fore the "in one another-ness" of things and world. Only because this is so is poetry possible.

The example mentioned seems to be one-sided, taken from the realm of aesthetic experiences; but in the other realms of man's Being and experience the situation is similar. When I plan a political action with other people, for instance, we discuss only particulars; but, in the discussion of a particular situation, the whole referential context is present, too, albeit not as a closed system of possibilities. The particular possibilities are as such still undetermined, undefined; we must first discuss them. What is there, while we are speaking about particular possibilities, is the "world," the open horizon within which action becomes possible. It is only within this horizon that the possibilities manifest themselves as such and become discussable. Perhaps the "principles" of the respective horizon can be indicated in the following way: "What really is at stake for us here, and on the basis of what?" Perhaps, however, one will never reach an unequivocal end in trying to indicate these principles. This is the task of the historian, who much too often stands on shaky ground when he attempts this. Not everyone who takes action is his own historian; and even one who is, is perhaps one-sided, captured in his own judgment, and unable to describe legitimately his own horizon, although—or, perhaps, because—he is very close to it. Nonetheless, the horizon is there; for in its living presence it is not dependent on the determination or determinability of its principles and of the human objectives that constitute its foundation. The principles are not of primordial importance; they are not that to which the horizon can then be "reduced." Rather, the respective horizon is primordial, and all principles that can, in all cases, later be crystallized from it constitute a subsequent abstraction.

Thus, the "proximity of world and things" taken as linguistic structure means that language is not merely a vehicle of information in a pregiven world; but, while particulars are discussed in it, language at the same time brings with it the horizon of meaningfulness of the particulars and founds this for man. This is what we call the hermeneutic structure of language. Hermeneutics has to do with the understanding of something, together with the understanding of one another in relation to something. It is precisely this dual understanding that presupposes a horizon of understanding constituted by language. In other words, language does not accidentally constitute this horizon; it does so by virtue of its own essence.

THE PERSONAL STRUCTURE OF LANGUAGE

WE MUST TRY once more to go a step beyond Ebeling by using the same linguistico-philosophical reflection that he uses in connection with a theological problematic as our point of departure; this time our move will be in another direction. Ebeling says:

> It is possible, of course, to offer future and freedom in a provisional sense through certain measures—for instance, by saving someone who is drowning or by freeing a prisoner. In this connection, too, the cybernetic usage of language definitely has an important function for the purpose of establishing certain conditions of living. . . . However, one does not yet offer future and freedom by establishing certain conditions of living. . . . It is true that one can, to a certain extent, annihilate freedom by constraint; but one can never create freedom in that way. Freedom can only be *called forth* by literally absolving [*freisprechen*] a man, that is, by speaking to him in such a way that, as it were, freedom is played into his hands so that he may engage in the leeway of freedom that is offered him.[8]

A perspective is to be added here so that the envisaged event of language may be genuinely understood. When a man is ac-

8. Ebeling, *Gott und Wort,* pp. 44, 49.

quitted, this means something not only to him but also to the one who absolves him. The word accomplishes something not only in the one who is addressed, but equally, and at the same time, in the one who speaks; and what it accomplishes can be materialized only through the word. In the foregoing we chose guilt and absolution as a paradigm for the word event that Ebeling had in mind. But what would absolution be, what would forgiveness of guilt be, if the one who forgives was not also affected in his existence, if he did not really mean what he said and was not involved in what he was saying? In such a case the word would be a lapsing mechanism, and it would not accomplish precisely what the task of the word is—namely, to bring about freedom. The word is therefore necessarily something *between* persons which, when pronounced, lays claim to and engages at least two persons and in a certain sense changes both of them in their being. This is a consequence of the dominating personal category of the "in between." Without this personality and interpersonality, the word event that Ebeling has in mind would be impossible.

It was Martin Buber who took it upon himself to interpret language as such from this interpersonality, not only in regard to the essence but also in regard to the genesis of the word. He writes:

> A precommunicative phase of language cannot be devised. Man never stood before his fellow man before he had lived in his regard, had lived toward him—in other words, before he had dealt with him. Before there was addressing speech, there was no language; it became monologue only after the dialogue broke off or broke down. The speaker at the dawn of history was not surrounded by objects that he had to cover with names; nor did events intrude upon him which he enticed away with names. Only in partnership did world and destiny become for him a subject matter of speech. . . .
>
> I wish to clarify what is meant with the help of an ethnological reference—namely, with the help of those remarkable word structures that our thought can understand adequately only as a residue of an earlier linguistic level, those that have maintained themselves in the languages of several relatively isolated societies, especially those of the Eskimos and the Algonquian Indians. In these so-called polysynthetic, or holophrastic, languages the constitutive sentence unit is not the word but the sentence-word.[9]

9. Martin Buber, "Das Wort, das gesprochen wird" (1960), in *Werke* (Munich: Kösel, 1962–63), I, *Schriften zur Philosophie* (1962), 442 ff.

Buber recalls Hamann's "bold statement," namely, that the first human word was "neither a noun nor a verb but at least a whole sentence." Starting from here, he attempts (with reservations) to reconstruct the genesis of language as such from the insight into the fundamental dialogical character of language, deeply aware of the fact that "the mystery of language's genesis and that of man's genesis are the same." [10] The sentence, not the word, is to be thought of as primary, since precisely for man it is not the individual and isolated thing but a whole situation that is primary. The situation is always a social one. In this way Buber conceives of the primary event of language as "the communicating and receiving of knowledge about an actual situation between two or more people . . . who are connected with one another because they depend on one another in a special way." [11] This occurs, for example, on a job where there is division of labor and where one person draws the attention of another to a new situation, for example, a sudden danger.

Thus, from the very start Buber demarcates his position from an obvious misunderstanding: namely, that this primary "situation word" is similar to the "improvised" cry of distress and the recurrent signal that are found in animals, too, and is therefore a kind of further development of these primitive beginnings. This demarcation seems to me to be Buber's essential point. In opposition to this, the human word has its own characteristic origin:

> We cannot derive it from either one of these two, for this undifferentiated primordial situation word, precisely as word, must also have made already resonant that abrupt and discovering freedom which is alien to any animal and in which the one man addresses himself to the other in order to inform him about being or event.[12]

With the expression "abrupt and discovering freedom" Buber, in his language and within his context, looks at the same situation that Heidegger calls the "clearing of the 'Da,'" which constitutes the Being of man as "Da-sein." The stress, however, is different: Heidegger stresses that which clears up for man; Buber, on the other hand, stresses that which man's discovering freedom accomplishes. Both of these, however, occur abruptly, for they are the same. For Heidegger, too, man's comportment in regard to

10. *Ibid.*, p. 449.
11. *Ibid.*, p. 448.
12. *Ibid.*, p. 449.

the clearing of the "Da" is not a mere passivity, a mere hearing and receiving, but a doing in the freedom that is appropriate in each case, an active re-sponding (*Ent-Sprechen*). Thought occurs "abruptly." "That there is a thought always and abruptly: whose wonder could be able to fathom this?" [13]

This dialogical interpretation of the essence of language and the reconstruction of the genesis of language as a dialogical event illuminate one another. The latter is a mere function and illustration of the former and, apart from the former, has no independent truth; thus it is not an independent assertion of natural history or history of the mind. According to the interpretation of language that has been illustrated this way by the (presumable) beginnings of language, Buber wishes also to understand the phenomena that are characteristic of contemporary language— namely, dialogue and poetry. According to him the poem too— and even specifically—is something that is spoken out dialogically:

> For, unlike a cry or a signal, speech, even taken as it was at the dawn of history, does not have its end in itself; it places the word from itself into Being, and the word endures (*besteht*). Speech is "*endurance*" (*Bestand*). And, as continuously enduring, speech receives its life always anew in the veritable relation, in the spoken-ness of the word. The genuine dialogue as well as the poem bear witness to this. For the poem, too, is spoken-ness, spoken-ness in regard to a thou, wherever its partner may be.[14]

Consequently, language—particularly in what Heidegger calls "that which is purely spoken," namely, the poem—is spoken-ness between persons, between I and thou, between persons who "intend" (*meinen*) one another, who address themselves to one another. The very core of language can be thought of adequately neither as being spoken out nor as being addressed to, for language is both, and both equiprimordially, in the reciprocal relatedness of the "in between." This is what is called here the personal structure of language: namely, that language has its characteristic place in the "in between" between persons and nowhere else. Anyone who says "something," who gives "something" to be understood, says it *for someone* whom he "intends" with it and by whom he lets himself be affected while he "intends" him

13. ED 21.
14. Buber, "Wort," pp. 449 f.

and speaks to him. The solitary speaker is an abstraction, a privative abstraction, even when he occurs in reality.

Here the connection between the hermeneutic and personal structures of language begins to dawn. The fact that language "gives something to be understood" is a function of its hermeneutic structure; but, according to what has been said, this is possible only by virtue of its personal structure.

Before reflecting further on this connection, let us ask how this personal structure of language can be verified. A simple and obvious proof is, without a doubt, the fact that a child learns the language in dialogical relationship with father, mother, brothers, and sisters. A proof is also found in the fact that in discussions we seldom argue exclusively *ad rem* but first and foremost *ad hominem*. Even where one argues exclusively *ad rem*, a certain attitude and orientation toward the interlocutor is at the root of the argument—for instance, respect or confidence or both: respect and the fear that the other will see through each argument *ad hominem;* confidence in one's own objectivity, which needs no argument *ad hominem.*

The most important proof for the personal structure of language is found in the fact that one must take great pains to find the phenomenon of a solitary speaker. If solitary speech were the normal way of language and its ontological structure, and if dialogical speech were merely an accidental supplement, the ontic testimony for this ontological datum should easily be found. In fact, however, the monologue is to be determined from the dialogue, as Buber rightly does. Even when man seemingly becomes monological, when, like the drunken vagabond, he holds soliloquies, even then is he dialogical; he does not want to be alone and thus speaks to a partner whom he does not have. He speaks, but nobody listens. Perhaps nobody is there to listen to him. However, the same thing often happens as well where people seemingly speak with one another. The monologue is a defect not in speech but primarily in our listening. When a man in company delivers soliloquies, it is because he is not willing to listen. He does not realize the moment of listening, which, nonetheless, belongs to speech in the full sense. In this respect his speech is defective. In this sense the monologue is in fact an "abstraction," a deficient mode of what speech properly is.

In comparison, the monologue of poetry is of another kind. It is a stylistic means of expressing a man's inner event which at first is hidden from his fellow men, an event in which someone takes or changes a stand. Such a position-finding or change, however, is dialogically related to the intrahuman situation within which the relevant man finds himself. In this way I can at first monologically within myself address myself to another and tell him what I will later tell him in reality, or I can try out for myself different possibilities of speech in order to determine my definitive standpoint in his regard.[15]

The Connection between the Two Language Structures

It is therefore not difficult to understand the personal structure of language by looking at its mode of appearing. The next problem is to relate this structure to the hermeneutic. If both structures are equally fundamental to the essence of language, they must belong together.

In the course of our present reflection, our attention must have been drawn to the fact that the "in between," which in Buber expresses the personal relation and makes it possible to think this relation with the help of an adequate category, emerges in Heidegger also, albeit with another meaning: as the "in between of the "proximity" of world and things. Things and world, the particular being and its horizon, "penetrate one another" and remain, nonetheless, two entities, unmixed. This is their "in between," their "dif-ference" (*Unter-Schied*).[16] In the same way the personal spheres of I and thou "penetrate" one another in the encounter, in our Being-with, and yet I and thou remain unmixed. They remain two beings. The "in between" keeps them, so to

15. Walter Biemel made the following remarks: "On the one hand, I am very impressed with the way in which Professor Ott succeeds in assuming Heidegger's view toward his own problematic, as it were, to make this view his own and to let himself be stimulated by it; on the other hand, I should like to raise the question, somewhat in the nature of a cautious objection, as to whether his reflections on language do not remain too much on the level of *Being and Time*. In this connection I have a second remark. It seems to me that Buber's approach remains too anthropological and as such cannot correspond to Heidegger's view. On the other hand, I must admit that Professor Ott attempts to take Buber beyond this narrowness."

16. Heidegger relates the "in between" to the Latin *inter* and the German *unter* (cf. *US* 24).

speak, separated and thereby enables a personal relationship, prevents an apersonal, mystical union. Herein a *formal* relationship between both conceptual meanings is found, at least so far. Is there, in addition to this, an underground, real relationship between these two? We wish to speak here of the hermeneutic "in between" and the personal "in between," corresponding to the hermeneutic and personal structures of language, both of which consist precisely in the respective "in between."

Do the personal "in between" of I and thou and the hermeneutic "in between" of things and world make one another mutually possible? The following idea suggests itself here: when persons mutually "intend" one another, when they mutually affect one another, they are able to make one another understand something; they are able to understand *one another* in regard to something and for that reason are able to understand *this something*. The primordial connection between "meaning" (*Sinn*) and "personhood," the basic datum of man's Being as such, makes itself understood here. However, it is not something simple, one particular something, which the one makes the other understand. Something like that would be a simple significative occurrence between subjects who at first are worldless—between subjects who in their worldlessness at first are solitary and thus not yet I and thou within the relationship of the personal "in between."

In reality, however, the particular something which persons understand and make one another understand and in regard to which they understand one another—for example, the old vacant house in a lonely countryside as a spectacle in regard to whose specific content two friends "understand one another" in their experiences—is indeed already in its world, in its horizon within which it becomes meaningful and understandable. This world, however, is not the world of this thing as such (the thing as present-at-hand does not have any world, for only Dasein is "Being-in-the-world"), but the world of this thing as something *which can be understood*. This means that the world in which the thing is and by which it is "penetrated" in the "proximity" is at the same time a world for the persons who have understood one another and will understand one another, who understand one another now in regard to this thing, this particular something (the lonely house, the political action, and so on). The "world" encompasses, so to speak, the "things" that belong to it and at the same time the persons who understand one another in regard to these things.

"World" taken in the sense indicated here is found only where there are persons who understand one another. To understand one another is to understand one another in regard to something, and, conversely, to understand something implies that persons understand one another. Wittgenstein's definition, "To understand a sentence means to know what the case is, to know when the sentence is true," [17] seems at first sight only to be concerned with the understanding of a sentence by a solitary subject. In reality, however, the issue in this definition is whether one understands a sentence that another pronounces. When I know what the case is, when the sentence is true, then I share the world with the other person, participate with him in the same world in which something like that can be the case. According to its own self-understanding, however, this definition is valid only for statements in the strict sense. On the other hand, a poem, for instance (if we follow Heidegger herein), is not concerned with statements. Yet here too is found an understanding of something as an understanding of one another. People thus can understand one another with regard to Trakl's poem "A Winter Evening" (but this is a way of understanding that cannot be captured in Wittgenstein's definition). This means, however, that those who understand one another, and therein understand the poem, take part in the world from which, for example, the things mentioned in the first stanza appear: the snow that falls outside the window, the evening bell that peals for a long time, the house, and the table. This world cannot be defined or described in the way in which one can name something particular; yet the world is there as that which is not said, enabling the understanding of something and of one another with regard to something. For someone who does not understand this world and is unable to take part in it however often he reads the poem, the individual lines of the poem in the final analysis are word structures without connection; that is to say, he understands the words, yet he does not understand the poem. (Obviously, this can never mean that he does not know what the case is, assuming that the poem is true.)

The world "from which" things appear and with regard to

17. Ludwig Wittgenstein, *Tractatus Logico-Philosophicus* (London: Routledge & Kegan Paul, 1922), proposition 4.024.

which they become understandable thus encompasses things and persons. This world, or the "in between" between world and things, is made possible by the "in between" of the persons who mutually understand one another. The expression "is made possible," however, does not mean that the hermeneutic "in between" is finally founded in the personal "in between." Rather, this relationship goes equally in the other direction: there would be no personal "in between" without the hermeneutic "in between." How can men encounter one another and be affected by one another if they do not associate with one another in regard to something and understand one another in a world in which they both participate? A worldless personal "in between" is inconceivable. Both structures belong together, equally originally and equally constitutively.

We must stress the fact that our understanding of something as understanding of one another in a world from which things appear does not merely mean a "neutral" common participation of some kind in a world of the same sort. It is to be understood in the sense of the personal "in between" and thus in the sense of a reciprocal being affected by one another. The poetizing poet's understanding of his own poem takes place with regard to the fact that the one who hears the poem (while understanding it) will be affected by it, and the fact that the poet therefore finds himself with the one who hears the poem in the realm of a personal "in between" that bridges time and space. The understanding of the poem by those who perceive it together—by two friends, for instance, who read it together—modifies their personal "in between": they communicate in the understanding of the poem and in this communication are mutually affected by one another. Their understanding participation in the world that speaks to them from the poem is a personal "participation" in one another. This is true not only for the poem but for all mutual understanding. Two people who tell one another about what happened to a third person and herein understand one another modify their personal "in between." In this way the two modes of the "in between" are connected with one another.[18]

18. Theodore J. Kisiel made the following comments: "It seems to me that Professor Ott's attempt to relate the hermeneutic structure to the interpersonal structure of language is fundamentally more amenable to Gadamer's conception of the hermeneutic than to Heidegger's. Gadamer restricts his hermeneutic field to the horizon of the familiar language of

If it is true that anything that is somehow understandable in such a manner—and this means anything that is real for man—has its aura, its world, around itself from which it appears, from which it is of concern for man, and if it is also true that this world, in turn, is constitutively related to the aura between persons in such a way that the one "in between" could not possibly be without the other, then obviously any existential phenomenon, and even any phenomenon of reality as such, acquires its dimension in the personal "in between." This does not occur in just a secondary way but as an ontological and constitutive moment. When we reflect ontologically upon the reality of the real, a characteristic shows itself which cannot be thought of as not being there or, rather, which can be unthought only by abstraction. (One must make himself expressly aware of this abstraction as an abstraction from the fullness of phenomenal reality.) This characteristic is that all that is real as such abides in the personal "in between." Anything real acquires thereby a characteristic openness that cannot be further determined here. Whether, and in what sense, it is openness toward God will be decided in the decision of faith.

---

the world and its things, the home (*Heimat*) of man; Heidegger always orients himself beyond this horizon, to the language of the domicile (*Geheimnis*) that lies 'under the between' (*Unter-Schied*) of world and things, where the unsaid opens onto an abyss of the unsayable. By extending the meaning of *symbol* to include all the words of a language, one can apply Ricoeur's aphorism, 'The symbol gives rise to thought,' to Gadamer's hermeneutic; Heidegger, in strikingly similar terms, asserts that it is withdrawal that gives rise to thought by continually drawing it on. Just as the symbol is charged with a surplus of sense, so withdrawal is not an empty indeterminate but the superabundant and inexhaustible source of possibilities of meanings to be said out of an ineffability that can never be said. While Gadamer is satisfied with the paradigm of a 'dialogue' with the tradition, Heidegger points to the rare discourse of the solitary thinker which takes its course beyond human control and which can bring about a new epoch that abruptly breaks with the tradition. It is here that Heidegger's intentions, it seems to me, breach the particular possibilities of the interpersonal in favor of the radical possibilities of the solitary man facing the mystery of Being—for example, the possibility of impossibility that Heidegger finds in the aloneness of death. This formulation of radical authenticity (*Eigentlichkeit*) in the early Heidegger is later paralleled by Heidegger's talk of an *Er-eignis*, where, after the turn, the *possibility* of impossibility becomes the inexhaustible possibility of saying within the unsayable, through the lone thinker's plunge into the abyss of Being."

Discussion

WILLIAM J. RICHARDSON: At issue is the ontological structure of language, and Professor Ott's interest is ultimately theological. Working in a Heideggerian context that sees language as "essencing" (*Wesen*) in such fashion that it is more accurately conceived as possessing man than as being possessed by him, Professor Ott engages in a dialogue with Gerhard Ebeling on the one hand and Martin Buber on the other in order to translate the Heideggerian context into terms more congenial to the theologian.

Professor Ott begins by adopting Ebeling's argument that, even though language may be used as a means of communication, it is not this instrumental character that identifies it as specifically human. What identifies language as human is the fact that the word is essentially a gift to man, bringing him space, freedom, and future. Man receives the gift of the word, just as he receives the gift of forgiveness, from someone else. Professor Ott goes beyond Ebeling, however, by arguing that language thus conceived establishes, or founds (*stiftet*), a space, or domain (*Raum*), of manifold meaningfulness within which men encounter and speak to one another of their common concerns. In Heideggerian fashion, he calls this domain the world. With the help of Heidegger's analysis (apropos of Trakl's "A Winter Evening") of the interpenetration (*Ineinander*) of world and things, where the "in between" (*das Zwischen*) in this case names the ontological difference, Professor Ott maintains that it is of the essence of language to bring forth both world and things, that is, to help them appear as what they are: world as world and things as things. To help them appear is obviously not to fabricate them but to accept them as gifts. This relationship between man on the one hand and the correlation of world and things (the ontological difference) on the other is what Professor Ott calls the hermeneutic structure of language.

Within the horizon of the world thus illuminated by language, men encounter one another. In fact, quoting Martin Buber, Ott maintains that language first emerges through the "communicating and receiving of knowledge about an actual situation between two or more people." In other words, language in its deepest origin is interpersonal. Witness, for example, the way a child learns to speak from his parents. The fact that the essential place of language is in the "in between" that both separates and unites persons—that is, in Dasein as *Mitdasein,* precisely in terms of the *Mit*—is what Professor Ott calls the personal structure of language.

How are we to conceive the relationship between these two structures? Obviously there is a formal similarity, for essential to each is an "in between." In the hermeneutic structure the "in between" divides world and things; it names the ontological difference. In the personal structure the "in between" names the *Mit* of *Mitdasein,* the *inter-* aspect of the interpersonal dimension of man. But there is more than a merely formal similarity. By reason of the "in between" in the personal structure of language, one makes another understand something about a thing (*Ding*) within the world. But Dasein thus conceived as *Mitdasein* is already an in-the-world-being for whom the ontological difference —the "between" dividing world and thing—has already come to pass. Hence, "both structures belong together, equally original and equally constitutive."

There are many things to be admired in this paper, not the least of which are the competence, the care, and the courage with which Professor Ott goes beyond the merely textual Heidegger and the merely textual Buber. His effort to thematize, in terms of the problem of language, the interpersonal character of Dasein is also admirable. Although Heidegger never fully develops this important aspect of his thought, it is vitally important that it be developed if one is to fill out the skeleton for an anthropology suggested in *Being and Time* and, furthermore, if one is to elaborate Heidegger's experience of language into a full-fledged hermeneutic. Professor Ott's paper calls our attention to this need and makes an auspicious start toward meeting it.

To be sure, one is inclined to have some reservations. I feel a little uneasy about the way Professor Ott makes the partners in his dialogue serve his purpose. I am not sure that Ebeling, Buber, Heidegger, and Ott can be put together in the same box without a bit of squeezing. Buber in particular—especially in the light of his own explicit criticism of Heidegger—would be surprised to learn, I think, that all that differentiates his radically dialogical conception of man from Heidegger's radically ontological conception of Dasein is a question of accent. But these are minor matters and, alongside the great positive value of Professor Ott's paper, perhaps picayune.

There is a more important issue, however, that is worth an explicit question. It seeks simply a clarification. When Professor Ott says that language establishes, or founds, a world, we infer that language in this case is the language of man. This reminds us of the early Heidegger, who attempts to think the Being question by taking Dasein as his starting point. On the other hand, when Professor Ott insists, with Ebeling, that the word is essentially something received as a gift, this suggests the later Heidegger, who attempts to think the Being question by taking Being as giving itself to man as the starting point. I would like Professor Ott to elaborate further his understanding of founding as acceptance and, in doing so, to clarify his conception of the relationship between the early and the later Heidegger that permits him (apparently) to think them both together.

A second question follows the first. If the word is a gift, who or what is the giver of the gift? Professor Ott takes the position of Ebeling but articulates it in the language of Heidegger. The giver in each case is surely not the same. For Heidegger in the *Letter on Humanism,* for example, the giver is Being: "Language is the language of Being, as clouds are the clouds of the sky." [19] More recently, even Being itself is a gift, given by the *Es* of *Es gibt*—that is, issuing from *Ereignis,* so that the *Es* is the giver and *Ereignis* the giving of the gift.[20] But *Ereignis* in turn is "the One that is not at all something new but the most ancient of ancients in Western thought: the primal Ancient that hides itself in the name *Alētheia.*" [21] I wonder if Professor Ott will go this far with Heidegger? If so, I wonder if he shares Professor Marx's uneasiness about the "new beginning" to be hoped for if we must rely on the poets to bring men salvation simply by helping them to correspond with another to the *Ereignis of Alētheia* through "dwelling poetically upon the earth"?

A final question would seek to explore the same problem, perhaps, but in an entirely different context. This question is suggested by Professor Ott's closing remark, in which he tells us that,

19. *HB* 119 (302).
20. *SD* 19–25.
21. "Dieses Selbe [das] nicht einmal etwas Neues ist, sondern das Älteste des Alten im abendländischen Denken: das Uralte, das sich in dem Namen *A-lētheia* verbirgt" (*SD* 25).

since our experience of everything actual within the world is conditioned by the personal structure of language, this may have ramifications for man's relation to God, but that such a matter is to be resolved by the decision of faith. This reminds us that Professor Ott is, first of all, a theologian dialoguing with Ebeling and Buber, who are also theologians, in what is clearly a theological enterprise. Yet in his reflection he seems to accept a Heideggerian context, which, in the special sense that Heidegger gives the term *God* in *Identity and Difference*, is conscientiously and doggedly a-theistic. I would like Professor Ott to tell us how he conceives of the relationship between God on the one hand and the Heideggerian framework on the other, where the ultimate Source of what is, is the *Es* of *Ereignis*. I would like him to explain the relationship between the world as "founded" by man and as "created" by God.

OTT: First of all may I say that it is a great honor to have a Heidegger interpreter of William Richardson's stature comment on my small attempt, and I am grateful for his fundamental questions. I am particularly pleased with our agreement on one point: namely, that the interpersonal reality dimension should be incorporated. As far as this dimension is concerned I should point out that, although it is not altogether lacking in Heidegger, it does not extend far enough in his thought. This does not mean, however, that it is completely excluded, as has been too readily claimed by certain critics. Heidegger has pointed to this dimension, and it can be developed and incorporated.

Heidegger is aware of this inadequacy, just as he generally shows himself to be deeply aware of the "relativity" of his thought. He once told me that there are three equiprimordial dimensions of thought: the relationship of man to himself, the relationship of man to his fellow men, and the relationship of man to the world. He added, "My own thought moves along the third road."

In my view this undeniable one-sidedness is particularly noticeable in *Being and Time*, where the being-there with others (*Mit-Dasein*) appears within the horizon of the "they" (*das Man*). Within the realm of the "they," that is, within the realm of what proximally and for the most part is, those who are there with others are disclosed in connection with the world of tools. However, where Dasein ek-sists authentically as himself, man is separated from the "they," and the individual is radically isolated.

I am convinced that in this connection one should stress the fact that precisely where Dasein ek-sists authentically there is implied a deep and genuine solidarity with his fellow men. "Mineness" (*Jemeinigkeit*) and solidarity taken in their deepest ground belong together.[22] One may call such a conception a correction of Heidegger; but perhaps it is, in fact, only a development and an integration.

In my attempt to deal with the phenomenon of language, the step (perhaps a step beyond Heidegger) was an easy one because it seemed to me that the thing-world structure discovered by Heidegger and the I-thou relation shown by Buber inherently and even unavoidably belong together.

Let us now turn to the individual issues. In comparison with Heidegger and Buber, Ebeling, who was in fact influenced by Heidegger's criticism of the scientistic-significative conception of language, plays a relatively subordinate role in my attempt. In Ebeling's approach the hermeneutic structure of language does not come to full development; I use his work merely as a point of departure. I am aware that Heidegger and Buber differ substantially in many aspects, and I try to live with this fact. However, their differences do not necessarily prevent their agreeing with one another on an important discovery in regard to language.

I should like to refrain from any attempt to blend the early Heidegger with the later by means of some theory or other. However, it seems to me that they are not so far apart. It seems to me, also, that the later Heidegger's ways of thought should be translatable into the terminology of *Being and Time*, if not completely, at least into its diction and strict phenomenological method.

There still remains the basic question (*die* Sach*frage*) which Professor Richardson raises and which I shall try to answer less from Heidegger's position than from the experience of language. What is the relationship between the "establishment of world" through language and the "acceptance of world" that equally comes about through language? When we speak, we let the world (in Heidegger's sense of the term, not in the sense of "cosmos" or "totality of being") light up. With every statement or word, a

22. Cf. Heinrich Ott, "Mitsein und Eigentlichkeit," in *Wirklichkeit und Glaube* (Göttingen: Vandenhoeck & Ruprecht, 1969), Vol. II, *Der persönliche Gott*, sec. 14.

"world" is called for (one should examine the extent to which this takes place in poetic speech as well as in everyday speech, and so on). This is possible only because "world" is already given, pregiven to the one who speaks, and thus because "world" speaks its own silent language.

In this way the speaking of each individual who speaks is simultaneously receptive and creative; by means of speech, the individual modifies the pregiven world and establishes it equally in a new way. His speaking is simultaneously receptive and establishing. This would have to be verified concretely, first of all in regard to what is spoken in the pure sense, that is, in the poem of the poet. Also, whenever language makes itself heard (*im Vollzug ihres Verlauten*), it receives and establishes world. This is its essence as language. In other words, I might consciously try to comprehend Heidegger's thought completely within the perspective of the understanding of the experienced and experienceable individual phenomenon, of the individual linguistic phenomenon. It seems to me that Heidegger's insights are relevant within this horizon and that here, also, we can refrain from mythicizing him and somehow hypostatizing "Being," "language which speaks of itself," the "dif-ference," the "e-vent," and the very ancient "there is."

I admire Professor Kockelmans' decided attempt to avoid such hypostatizations, his attempt not to remain within Heidegger's terminology but rather "to do something with Heidegger." I have attempted to do the same thing, but not in a "totalizing" glance at the "Total Meaningfulness," which addresses itself to man as a silent voice of Being so that man can then speak for himself. I have attempted a trans-lation into the concrete. (Perhaps better formulated, I have attempted to keep an eye on the concrete, to keep the phenomenal ground firmly beneath my feet, to adhere to the individual phenomenon [*Being and Time!*].) In the final analysis this is an analogous concern.

From this point I can very briefly answer Professor Richardson's second and third questions. Viewed from the horizon of understanding, which is characteristic of the "phenomenology of the individual case," I must definitely refrain from answering any question with respect to a "giver of the gift." It is still not clear to me to what degree I understand Heidegger in this regard. If my misunderstanding goes beyond the usual, I hope this great man will pardon me.

From this point of view it also becomes clear immediately that one must be extremely cautious in applying Heidegger to theology. At the end of my paper I spoke of a personal aura of everything that is real, which for the "eyes of faith" may be found in the "in between" between God and man. It is obvious that, as far as this last step is concerned, under no circumstances would I appeal at this point to Heidegger, but rather to the Bible (and in this I hope that I am in complete agreement with Heidegger).

On the same ground, I am also very reluctant to try to hear a doctrine of salvation in Heidegger (although I grant that such a tone co-vibrates in Heidegger's thought). The fact that the poets rescue mankind and help mankind to make a new start in the direction of salvation may be one element; but the aspect of the interpersonal humanness, which has not yet been worked out by Heidegger in his conception of poetry, will be the more essential element, because the issue involves accounting for the future of mankind from the present. What Heidegger can contribute to this is perhaps to be found in the question concerning new forms of social—that is to say, human—dwelling on earth.

7 / Ontological Difference, Hermeneutics, and Language

Joseph J. Kockelmans

IN A MORE THAN REMARKABLE ESSAY, "M. Heidegger's 'Ontological Difference' and Language," Johannes Lohmann attempts to determine precisely how the hermeneutic structure of thought is related to the ontological difference and how we are to understand the relationship between them in regard to language, particularly in regard to the subject-predicate relation characteristic of the grammar and logic of the Indo-European languages.[1] In formulating this question, Lohmann takes a quotation from Heidegger's *The Essence of Reasons* as his point of departure. I shall briefly summarize the argument presented in this quotation, mentioning only those passages which are especially relevant to my topic.[2]

The Essence of Reasons begins with a reference to Aristotle.[3] According to Heidegger, the problem of ground arose for Aristotle in two different but somehow connected forms—namely, as *archē* and as *aition*. Aristotle understands *archē* as that by which a being *is* (ground of the whatness of a being), that by which a thing *becomes* (ground of its thatness), or that by which a thing *is known* (ground of its truth). In the realm of *aition,* on the other hand, there are four types of ground. Heidegger claims that, in Aristotle, the relationship between these two different types of ground is obscure and that the common denominator of all these types of ground taken as one is more obscure yet. Generally

1. See pp. 303–63 below.
2. See WG 10–16 (15–29).
3. WG 7 (5–6).

speaking, however, one may say that, for Aristotle, ground is that which enables us to answer the question "Why is a thing the way it is?" [4]

The problem of ground is taken up later by Leibniz, in his investigations concerning the meaning and function of the "principle of ground." It is Leibniz' reflections that Heidegger uses as a point of departure for his own investigation.[5] Heidegger first formulates the problem of ground, showing that the problem is fundamentally one of truth; since truth is found primarily in Dasein's transcendence, the question is one of transcendence.[6] In the second part of the essay Heidegger explains precisely what transcendence is, particularly what is to be understood by "world" taken as that whereunto Dasein transcends beings.[7] In the final part of the essay Heidegger tries to analyze ground in terms of transcendence.[8]

Heidegger argues first that we have access to Being's meaning only in a being whose nature it is to transcend beings toward Being. The bridge between the problem of ground and Dasein's transcendence consists in the ek-sistential notion of truth. Heidegger justifies this reduction of the problem of ground to the problem of truth by referring to Leibniz' conviction that the principle of ground is based on the nature of propositional truth, and by subjecting this conception to criticism. Heidegger states that the conception of propositional truth as conformity presupposes another conception of truth. Truth as conformity presupposes that the being to be judged is already manifest on the basis of a preceding manifestation; thus, propositional truth presupposes ontic truth. Ontic truth, in turn, manifests itself only within the realm of Dasein's ontic comportment with other beings. In order for beings to manifest themselves for what they are in ontic comportment with man, Dasein must have an antecedent comprehension of their Being, thus, of the Being of their beings. Therefore, it is the unveiledness of Being in Dasein's comprehension which first makes possible the manifestation of

4. William J. Richardson, *Heidegger: Through Phenomenology to Thought* (The Hague: Nijhoff, 1963), p. 162.

5. WG 7–9 (7–11).
6. WG 8–18 (11–33).
7. WG 18–42 (35–99).
8. WG 42–54 (101–31).

beings. This unveiledness of Being is the truth of Being, onto-logical truth.[9]

The most basic form of man's comprehension of Being, namely, that which from the outset guides every way of his be-having toward beings, is neither an explicit grasping of Being as such nor a conceptual comprehension of that which is grasped. Heidegger calls this kind of understanding of Being "preonto-logical." In order to conceptually comprehend Being, man's un-derstanding must make this preontological comprehension of Being its problem and theme of inquiry. This is the task of on-tology. Between the preontological understanding of Being and the explicit ontological comprehension of Being there are many stages. These stages as well as the varieties of ontological truth which correspond to them reveal the richness of what, as pri-mordial truth, is at the root of all ontical truth. Since there lies in the unveiledness of being a prior unveiledness of its Being, and since ontical as well as ontological truth concerns beings in their Being and the Being of beings, ontical and ontological truth belong together essentially because of their relationship to the *difference between Being and being* (the ontological difference). Thus, the essence of truth as well as the essential distinction be-tween ontical and ontological truth is only possible given this dif-ference. Yet, if it is characteristic of man to behave toward beings by understanding their Being, then the ability to differentiate being and Being must have the roots of its own possibility in the ground of Dasein's essence. Heidegger calls this ground of the ontological difference the *transcendence* of Dasein.[10]

In his comment on this passage Lohmann first briefly re-capitulates the distinctions pertaining to the truth concept which Heidegger introduces and then relates them to one another as well as to man's transcendence. He says that in Heidegger's view "ontic" truth is materialized first on the level of man's "moodlike" concernful dealing with beings, whereas the ontic rendering manifest which becomes predicatively interpreted in language is only one special case of our moodlike concernful dealing with things. Ontic truth, now, regardless of whether it is prepredica-tive or predicatively interpreting, comes to pass in all cases in

9. *WG* 9–13 (15–25); Richardson, *Heidegger*, pp. 163–64.
10. *WG* 13–16 (23–29).

the *as* structure, which is characteristic of the letting something become manifest, of the addressing of something as something. In other words, ontic truth comes to pass in the *as* structure, either in the apophantic *as* of our predicative interpretation in sentences or in the hermeneutic *as* of our concernful dealing with things. The latter of these two *as* structures is basic. Furthermore, the comprehension of Being which becomes manifest in ontic truth and which illuminates and guides all comportment in regard to beings, precedingly as well as concomitantly, is the point of departure for the comprehension of Being as such and for the understanding of that which is so comprehended.[11] That which is now understood in understanding, interpreted in interpretation, and asserted in assertion as such is the meaning (*Sinn*), which in understanding was predelineated as that which can be articulated, in interpretation appears as that which has been articulated, and as "meaningful articulation" becomes conceptually determined in man's speech.[12]

After this brief recapitulation of some of the ideas from Heidegger's *The Essence of Reasons* as well as certain relevant themes from *Being and Time*, Lohmann asks the following questions: What is the basic element of the "articulation of meaning" characteristic of the ontico-ontological rendering manifest as found in understanding, interpretation, and assertion? According to Heidegger's text this is on the one hand the hermeneutic and apophantic *as* structure but on the other hand the ontological difference, which is founded in Dasein's transcendence. How, then, are the *as* structure and the ontological difference related to one another, and how must this relationship be understood in connection with the subject-predicate relation of our grammar and logic? [13]

In trying to answer these questions, Lohmann first establishes the fact that Leibniz' conception of the subject-predicate relation as *inesse* of predicate in subject and this, in turn, as *idem esse* articulates the logical form of the assertion as found in the grammatical structure of the Indo-European proposition; for the logical inherence of the predicate concept in the subject concept is expressed there as objective identification. However, this structure of the assertion is necessary only if one uses a linguistic

11. SZ 148–60.
12. SZ 151.
13. See pp. 308–9 below.

form in which supposition plays an essential part. Since each word of a sentence that makes use of supposition explicitly signifies the Being of a being, or a being in its Being, we may also say that the subject-predicate relation necessarily presupposes the ontological difference.

In the ancient Indo-European languages this "ontological differentiation" is explicitly expressed in the grammatical form of the word. The nouns as well as the verbs, according to their elementary morphological structures, are composed of "root," or "stem," and "ending." The root, or stem, stands for the "conceptual expression," whereas the ending stands for the expression of the relation between the concept and an "object," or thing, which is given in and by the context of the sentence.

In order to prevent misunderstanding, Lohmann carefully explains that the concept of supposition referred to in this context should not be identified with the nominalist conception of it found in the late Middle Ages. "Supposition" was originally conceived of as a function of the individual word, which (taken as subject of the sentence) in the normal case "lays" its "significations" (instead of the meant object, or thing) "under" the predicate of the proposition. The original doctrine was more differentiated than the nominalist conception suggested by Ockham, for instance. Originally, the doctrine of supposition tried to connect the subject-predicate relation within the proposition to the relationship between "concept" and "thing," thus, to the relationship between Being and being. Furthermore, the original conception implied an explicit distinction between the logical function, which is given in the grammatical form of the word (*suppositio in habitu*), and the logical operation of the actual judgment proposition (*suppositio in actu*). For both of these it is true that the supposition, which is just one of the many properties of a word found within a proposition, is attributed to the word taken as action, so that the word in a certain sense makes the ontological difference appear.

Insofar as all language taken as speech is a speaking by means of "concepts," whereas, nonetheless, the thing itself is meant, one can say that all languages taken as speech must make use of supposition and thus must contain the ontological difference as structural moment. All speech comes to pass as "understanding interpretation" in the *as* structure of intentionality, that is, in the explicit structure of understanding something as something, or in the structure of understanding something *under* something (*sup-positio*). However, in addition to this *suppositio in actu* there is the *suppositio in habitu,* and here the different languages separate from one another. In the *suppositio in habitu* the "ontological difference" becomes explicit in the form of language, and it is only then that onto-logy comes to pass.

In other words, all languages must somehow linguistically express the hermeneutic *as* structure and thus must imply *some kind of* "apophantic" *as* structure—that is, an articulated structure of understanding something as something. Therefore, they must make use of supposition and also must contain the onto-logical difference as structural moment. There are, however, many languages that do not make the ontological difference *explicit* in their linguistic structures. These languages develop in "ontological indifference." They lack a *suppositio in habitu,* do not contain the apophantic *as* structure, which is characteristic of the Indo-European languages, and thus do not make use of the subject-predicate relation.[14]

In connection with these considerations I should like to formulate the following questions, which I shall try to answer in the balance of this paper. (1) How does Lohmann conceive of the relationship between the ontological difference and the hermeneutic and apophantic *as* structures on the one hand and of their mutual relation to the subject-predicate relation characteristic of the Indo-European languages on the other? (2) How is Lohmann's description of the ontological difference related to Heidegger's conception of it? (3) How does Heidegger conceive of the relationships among ontological difference, the hermeneutic structure of thought, and language?

In formulating these questions it is not my intention to express any critical judgment in regard to the value of Lohmann's essay or to suggest any shortcomings in his explanation. I am convinced that Lohmann is dealing with a very important aspect of Heidegger's philosophy, that he understands Heidegger correctly, and that, in applying these insights to the various linguistic structures that we find in this world, he has opened up a great number of unexpected and important perspectives. My aim in asking these questions is merely to come to a better understanding of Heidegger's thought in its gradual development and to

14. See pp. 309–11 below.

clarify a few issues that, I believe, could easily lead to some misunderstanding.

I

As FAR AS THE FIRST QUESTION is concerned I shall limit myself to the following brief remarks. Lohmann's first thesis is that the apophantic *as* structure (regardless of the concrete linguistic form in which it manifests itself) necessarily presupposes a more fundamental hermeneutic *as*, which is characteristic of our concernful dealing with things; each linguistic letting something be seen *as* something necessarily presupposes man's understanding of something *as* something, and this understanding is found primarily in his concernful dealing with intramundane things.[15] Lohmann's second thesis is that both the linguistic and the hermeneutic *as* structures presuppose, as a condition of their possibility, the ontological difference.[16]

To these two theses, taken from Heidegger's philosophy, Lohmann adds several others by comparing the different language structures as these are found on earth. I shall now point out those views of his which are immediately relevant to my topic.

First, in the Indo-European languages, as opposed to Chinese, for instance, the ontological difference is made explicit in the linguistic structures belonging to this language family. This is done in different ways in the different language groups.[17]

Second, in all cases the necessary condition for making the ontological difference explicit is found in the supposition, which all of these languages use in some sense. *Supposition* is to be understood here as the transformation of the merely conceptual meaning of a word (for instance, "mortal") into a meaning that is objectively founded ("a mortal [man]," "the mortal [man]"). Such a transformation presupposes a continual ontological differentiation, since each word in the sentence explicitly signifies the Being of a being, or a being in its Being. This ontological differentiation is expressed in the ancient Indo-European languages in the grammatical form of the word. *Nomen* as well as

15. *SZ* 148–60.
16. *WG* 12–16 (16–29).
17. See pp. 309–11, 317–22, 330–43 below.

verbum are composed of "root" and "ending," the root expressing the conceptual content and the ending expressing the relation of the concept to a thing that is somehow given in and by the context of the sentence. In these languages, therefore, each nominal and verbal form as such contains the expression of the relation of a Being (Being mortal, for instance) to a being (a determinate mortal being) and thus allows the ontological difference to appear. It is the bifurcation of the word form which immediately reflects the ontological difference, that is, the logico-ontological difference between Being and being.[18]

Third, the particular way in which the supposition is materialized in the Indo-European languages (as opposed to the Semitic and the Bantu languages) is the necessary condition for the subject-predicate relation, which is characteristic of these languages. In the Indo-European languages the nominal sentence (that is, the propositional structure according to the principle of "congruence" which follows from the supposition) and the verbal sentence are built into one another. The nominal sentence (using the verb *is* as copula) in a sense assumes verbal character, whereas the verbal sentence adapts itself in its structure to the nominal sentence. In these languages, therefore, the supposition connects the subject-predicate relation, found in the proposition, with the relationship between "concept" and "thing" (which falls under the concept and is expressed by it); and it is necessary to make an explicit distinction between the logical *function*, given by the grammatical form of the word, and the logical *operation* of the actual judgment proposition. The approximation of nominal and verbal sentences makes it understandable, furthermore, that in these languages the subject of the sentence is identified with an *agens*, or ego, and that the term *subjective* in the sense of "belonging to the subject of the sentence" has come to mean "being related to an ego." [19]

Fourth, when Leibniz conceives of the *verum esse* of the subject-predicate relation as *inesse* of predicate in subject and this, in turn, as *idem esse*, he merely renders explicit the logical form of the assertion as found in the grammatical structure of the Indo-European proposition. The logical inherence of the

18. See pp. 309–11, 317–22 below.
19. See pp. 310–12, 316–17, 324 below.

predicate in the subject (the fact that "mortality" is contained in "humanity") is expressed as objective identification (*omnes homines = mortales*). One could perhaps say, also, that such a truth conception is a rendering explicit of the grammatical congruence which serves as a principle for the structure of the sentence (congruence, correspondence). If this is true, it becomes understandable at once that the Chinese truth concept, for instance, differs radically from that promulgated by Aristotle and Leibniz.[20]

Fifth, on the basis of this paradigmatic case, we can formulate a general rule—namely, that the "logic" of a language is expressly contained in its "morphology," in that the morphological form co-determines the *syntaxis* of that language. This explains why Chinese logic, for instance, differs radically from Western logic, and why an onto-logy could originate in the Western world but not in the realm of those languages that do not make use of supposition.[21] Finally, it explains how people in the Western world came to forget the genuine meaning of the ontological difference; the forgottenness of the ontological difference is caused by the ambiguity of certain basic ontological expressions, which in turn is caused by taking a linguistic structure to be a universal law of thought.

Sixth, and finally, the function of the copula, which is found in most Indo-European languages, is to bridge the gap brought about by the explicit expression of the ontological difference in the various linguistic structures. Since the copula *is* comprises all modes of Being, the basic unity of the Indo-European Being concept becomes immediately understandable. On the one hand the unity of the Being concept and on the other hand the fact that the copula basically expresses congruence and thus agreement and therefore does not have temporal meaning explain why, in traditional onto-logy since the time of Plato, Being is generally understood as something that is continuously present, why this continuously Being present is conceived of as Beingness (*ousia* [*Seiendheit*]), which can then be taken as *to koinotaton*, as highest *genus*. Finally, this explains why a distinction is to be made between the "that" of the being present (*energeia* [*existentia* (*Wirklichkeit*)]) and the differentiating "what," the way of look-

20. See pp. 309, 311–14, 329–42 below.
21. See pp. 313, 330–34, 338–40 below.

ing at that which is present (*Idea* [*essentia* (*Aussehen, Sicht-samkeit*)]).[22]

II

I WISH TO POSE THE SECOND QUESTION mainly to avoid misunderstandings. Lohmann's essay seems at first sight to misconstrue Heidegger's conception of the ontological difference. First of all, it is not completely clear precisely what the expression stands for, and, secondly, it seems as if Lohmann is trying to explain and even to justify the forgottenness of the ontological difference much more than to show us the way to transcend traditional metaphysics. For example, when speaking of the ontological difference, Lohmann regularly uses the expressions "the Being of a being" and "a being in its Being." In explaining the difference between supposition and predication, he makes the following remarks: "The supposition changes the universality of the conceptual 'Being' into a 'being,' lets a 'being' appear in its 'Being,' in contradistinction to the predication, which is supposed to express 'the Being of a being.'" "In the verb *es-ti* the Indo-European languages unite the significations of the existence (the 'that it is') and of the 'being true' with those of the predication of the (essential) 'quiddity' and the (accidental) 'being such.' . . ." [This verb] bridges the cleft of the 'ontological difference,' which was torn open in the 'supposition' structure of the Indo-European word form." [23] From these and similar statements one might easily conclude that Lohmann intends to suggest that Heidegger's ontological difference is to be understood as the opposition of a being as ontic reality and its mode of Being—eventually, even as the opposition of the medieval *existentia* and *essentia*.

A more attentive reading of the text, however, shows that Lohmann limits himself to quoting *The Essence of Reasons* when referring to Heidegger's conception of the ontological difference, "the difference between Being and being, which is founded in Dasein's transcendence." [24] Although he does not explicitly elab-

22. See pp. 310–11, 329, 340–41 below. Cf. N II 203–23, 237, 411–12.
23. See pp. 309, 324, 329–30 below.
24. WG 15 (27).

orate on the way in which Heidegger wishes to understand this expression in his attempt to overcome traditional metaphysics, it is certainly not Lohmann's intention to reduce the vast problematic to which Heidegger refers as the "ontological difference" to merely linguistic, or even morphological, considerations. Lohmann wishes to limit himself to showing how the ontological difference is made explicit in the linguistic structures used by those languages that make use of supposition, and the consequences to which this rendering explicit leads insofar as logic and onto-logy are concerned.

III

IF THIS INTERPRETATION of Lohmann's intention is correct, it becomes clear why we must formulate our final question: What is Heidegger's understanding of the relationships among the ontological difference, the hermeneutic structure of thought, and language? Before attempting to answer the question, I wish to explain briefly how Heidegger came to the problem, and why I believe he was originally unable to link the ontological difference and language.

Heidegger has said repeatedly that "the forgottenness of Being is the forgottenness of the difference between Being and beings." [25] The difference between Being and beings was forgotten because of an ambiguity intrinsic in the expression commonly used in referring to beings as the subject matter of metaphysics: *to on hēi on.* The expression is ambiguous in more than one sense. The expression "being as being" referred to the whole ensemble of beings considered in terms of what makes them be, their "Beingness." The Beingness of the ensemble of beings can mean the common denominator of all beings, "Being in general," or it can mean the ultimate ground which lets the ensemble of beings be. Therefore, metaphysics as the study of beings as beings has from the very beginning been conceived either as the study of Being in general or as the study of a supreme, or divine, Being.[26] The ambiguity of the expression *to on hēi on* is connected with an equally fundamental ambiguity of the word *on.* Gram-

25. HW 336; KM 212.
26. WM 19.

matically, this word is a participle that may be used as either a noun or an adjective with a verbal meaning. Thus, it either means that which is, a being, or designates that by which a being "is," namely, its Being. Heidegger wishes to transcend classical metaphysics by thinking Being as a process through which this ambiguity and ambivalence can be overcome.[27] In so doing he gradually became aware of the necessity of thinking Being neither as Being in general nor as supreme Being, but as the process of unveilment.[28] When Heidegger uses the term "ontological difference" in this context to refer to the basic theme for thought, it is not his intention to refer to the ambivalence that has been the source of confusion in metaphysics for so many centuries. He intends, rather, to refer to a more fundamental difference between Being taken as the original process of unconcealment and beings taken as things that have their proper modes of Being and, thus, their meaning. The proposal to ground metaphysics by examining the meaning of Being as the process of unconcealment through which the ontological difference between Being and beings *taken in the sense just indicated* comes about has been Heidegger's concern from the very first page of *Being and Time*. To ground metaphysics in this way necessarily means to transcend it, to pass beyond it; classical metaphysics, by reason of its forgottenness of the genuine meaning of the ontological difference and, thus, because of the ambiguity connected with it, is unable to meditate the Being process, which is the ground.[29]

The expression "ontological difference" appears for the first time in *The Essence of Reasons*, although it was alluded to earlier in *Kant and the Problem of Metaphysics*.[30] A few words must be said about *Being and Time*, since both of these works remain within the general perspective of its problematic.

Heidegger's main concern in *Being and Time* is to lay the groundwork for metaphysics by trying to bring to light that ontological structure in man which is the source of his natural tendency to become involved in metaphysical speculation. Since metaphysics, historically seen, is concerned with Being, whereas man in all his aspects is finite, the main problem is how to explain the relationship between Being and finitude. Heidegger's in-

27. HW 161–62, 317–18; WM 8; WD 175.
28. Notably in WG and WM.
29. Richardson, *Heidegger*, pp. 10–15.
30. WG 15 (27); KM 212.

vestigations show that Being and finitude are related to one another in man's comprehension of Being, which is intrinsically finite. That is why first of all the ultimate meaning of the finite comprehension of Being must be phenomenologically revealed. In this process of revelation it becomes clear that man's finite comprehension of Being materializes itself in the transcendence of beings toward Being, that is, in man's openness toward Being taken as a process that comes to pass in man. From a phenomenological point of view, the process of transcendence is man's Being-in-the-world, where *world* stands for the horizon projected by Dasein and within which Dasein dwells and encounters other beings, and *Being-in* means that in which this world becomes luminous insofar as Dasein, by virtue of its comprehending ek-sistence, makes manifest the Being of beings. So intimate is this correlation between world, or Being, and Dasein, which is its illumination, that only insofar as Dasein is "is there" Being.[31]

"The difference between Being and beings" as an expression referring to the fundamental problem of metaphysics appears for the first time in *Kant and the Problem of Metaphysics*, but the over-all context is still that of *Being and Time*. With regard to the starting point and the course of development of fundamental ontology, Heidegger says that the existential analytic intends to show how all concern for beings presupposes the transcendence of Dasein, that is to say, its Being-in-the-world. With this transcendence is achieved the projection of the Being of beings in general, which is hidden and, for the most part, indeterminate also. By means of this project the Being of beings indeed becomes manifest, but the difference between Being and beings remains concealed.[32] Heidegger goes on to say that the primary task of the existential analytic is to illuminate this projection as finite through reference to Dasein's thrownness, concern, anxiety, and temporality.

We have already said several times that the term *ontological difference* is explicitly used for the first time in *The Essence of Reasons*, namely, in the first part of the essay, where Heidegger tries to situate the problem of ground as formulated by Aristotle and Leibniz within the general perspective of his own thought. In order to avoid repetition, I shall limit myself to recapitulating Heidegger's view by quoting only the pertinent passage:

31. Richardson, *Heidegger,* pp. 103–4; *SZ* 212.
32. *KM* 212.

Each after its own fashion, ontical and ontological truth concern *being* in its Being and the *Being of* being. They belong together essentially, by reason of their relationship to the *difference between Being and being* (the Ontological Difference). The essence of truth, which is and must be bifurcated ontically and ontologically, is only possible given this difference. Yet if what is distinctive about Dasein is that it behaves toward being by understanding Being, then *the* ability to differentiate the two (in which the Ontological Difference becomes factical) must have struck the roots of its own possibility in the ground of the essence of Dasein. To anticipate, we name this ground of the Ontological Difference the *transcendence* of Dasein.[33]

All of these elements taken together would seem to suggest the following statements, which express Heidegger's conception of the meaning of the ontological difference: (1) The Being question of *Being and Time* is formulated in *Kant and the Problem of Metaphysics* and *The Essence of Reasons* in terms of the ontological difference. The identity of Being and Truth as a process of unveilment is maintained. (2) The ontological difference comes about only by reason of Dasein's power to differentiate between Being and beings; this power is identical to Dasein's transcendence. (3) The final term toward which Dasein transcends being is not the beingness of being but rather Being taken as the emergence of the difference between Being and beings, that is, the emergence of the ontological difference. (4) It is possible that Heidegger was already aware of the need to admit that the ontological difference has a certain primacy over Dasein.[34]

33. WG 15–16 (27–29).
34. Richardson, *Heidegger,* pp. 174–75. Walter Biemel commented: "In my view, too much stress is placed here on the ontological difference. The dimension in which Heidegger's questioning moves is first opened up through the discovery of the ontological difference. But the further he proceeds along his own way of thinking, the clearer he is able to describe the context, so that he no longer needs to take his point of departure in traditional philosophy—which is precisely what takes place in the onto-logical difference. There is connected to this, also, the fact that the con-cept of transcendence, which still occupies such an important place in *Kant and the Problem of Metaphysics,* is later given up. This change in conceptualization, which means at the same time this change of his thought in the sense of the unfolding toward 'that which is proper,' can be demonstrated very precisely (see Heidegger's *Letter on Humanism,* and note the change that has taken place in the meaning of a series of basic concepts originally used in *Being and Time*)."
Professor Kockelmans responded: "This remark is a fundamental one.

At first sight it is amazing that in dealing with the ontological difference Heidegger does not mention language, especially considering that in *Being and Time* he pointed to the intrinsic relationship between the apophantic *as* structure of the Indo-European assertion and the hermeneutic *as* characteristic of man's understanding as found in his concernful dealing with intramundane beings. This relationship, as Lohmann correctly shows, intermediates between the ontological difference and the apophantic *as* structure of the assertion.[35] Upon closer consideration, however, it becomes quite clear why Heidegger does not succeed at this point in making the necessary link. Although he has already concluded that Being must be conceived of as identical with Truth taken as a process of unveilment and that the ontological difference comes about only by reason of man's transcendence, at this time Heidegger does not yet understand how that toward which man transcends, namely, the world, can be brought into contact with Being taken as Truth. Furthermore,

---

Generally speaking, I must say that I agree wholeheartedly with it. It is certainly correct to stress that in *Letter on Humanism* the term *transcendence* no longer appears, and that in *Zur Sache des Denkens,* for instance, Heidegger explicitly states that he wishes to think about Being without any reference to beings. All of this does not mean, however, that the question hidden in the ontological difference characteristic of Western thought no longer exists. Furthermore, in many of Heidegger's publications that have appeared since 1947 the term is used continually; although in these cases the term no longer refers to Heidegger's original conception, it still refers to the basic problem that Heidegger tried to solve in *Being and Time.* It is precisely because of this complication that I stated that Lohmann's interpretation of the ontological difference asks for further investigation and clarification.

"It seems to me that the following quotation clearly indicates Heidegger's final view on the issue: '[The expression "to think Being without beings"]—like the expression "without any reference of Being from beings," which was used on page 25 [of "Time and Being"]—is the short expression for "to think Being without any reference to a foundation of Being from beings." "To think Being without beings" thus does *not* mean that the relationship of Being to beings is unessential, and that one can leave this relationship out of consideration; it says, rather, that Being must not be conceived of in the way this has been done in metaphysics.' I should like to paraphrase this passage in the following manner: Thinking about the ontological difference can be done in two different ways. In the first way one keeps referring to the manner in which this has been done in classical metaphysics (*Being and Time, The Essence of Reasons*); the second way is the one typical of Heidegger's later publications. What Heidegger later rejects is not the issue hidden in the ontological difference but merely 'the metaphysical characterization of the ontological difference' (SD 35–36)."

35. SZ 157–58.

there can be no doubt that the analysis given in *Being and Time* of *logos* as an existential of Dasein and as the ontological foundation of language is completely inadequate in giving a justified answer to the question concerning the relationships among the ontological difference, the hermeneutic structure of thought, and language.[36] There are no texts establishing these relationships, and, furthermore, Heidegger admits the impossibility of answering these questions on the basis of the language conception found in *Being and Time*. "I know only this one thing: it is precisely because the reflection on language and Being has determined the course of my thought that the explanation of them has remained as far as possible in the background. Perhaps the basic weakness of my book *Being and Time* is that I dared too early to go too far ahead." [37] So many serious problems concerning the relationships between Being and world, Being and time, Being and thought, and Being and language are involved here that even in 1954 Heidegger was still convinced that the "adequate word" concerning the relationship of language to Being was still lacking.[38]

36. Richardson, *Heidegger*, p. 171.
37. *US* 93.
38. *US* 93. John Rudoff commented: "The linguistic analysts seem to assert that this entire line of questioning rests on one or another of several misunderstandings of the effects of words. They would assert that the whole line of questioning about the ontological difference is caused by the use of the term *is* in Indo-European languages. For this reason they would think that the fact of our *articulation* causes our notion that there is such a phenomenon as the ontological difference. Heidegger, on the other hand, emphatically asserts two things: first, that Dasein's 'transcendence' is ontologically prior to the ontological difference, and, second, that this ontological difference itself is the ontological condition of both the hermeneutic and the apophantic *as* structures. In short, we would in some sense feel that the ontological difference precedes the 'talking about it.' There is a need to explore fully exactly what happens to the world when it 'gets articulated.' This is the problematic in Heraclitus and in Parmenides; and, although their opinions are apparently opposite, the problem binds them together. It serves as a departure point for the thought of the later Heidegger—and for our own thought as well."
Professor Kockelmans responded: "It has been my impression that most linguistic analysts remain within the traditional interpretation of the ontological difference; and it is precisely this traditional interpretation, which Heidegger refers to with the term *metaphysics*, that he attempts to overcome. For this reason it is extremely difficult to compare Heidegger's thought with any traditional conception of philosophy. If Professor Rudoff's description of what a linguistic analyst might say about Heidegger's attempt is correct, then I certainly agree with him that here, too, we have two completely opposing views. For Heidegger, the difference as such is a presupposition for man's concrete articulation. Heidegger's reference to man's transcendence is found in *The Essence of Reasons*. He

IV

KEEPING THIS ADMONITION in mind, we must now proceed to the question of how Heidegger finally comes to conceive of the relationships among ontological difference, the hermeneutic structure of thought, and language. Heidegger reaches his final, but still provisional, point of view after going through various intermediate phases. For our purposes, these phases can be marked by the following publications: "On the Essence of Truth" (1930), *An Introduction to Metaphysics* (1935), "The Origin of the Work of Art" (1936), "Hölderlin and the Essence of Poetry" (1936), the *Logos* lecture (1944), and *Letter on Humanism* (1946). As evidenced in these publications, Heidegger gradually becomes aware of the fact that the privileged position in the process of unveilment is occupied not by man but by Being. Being, however, can then no longer be taken as "beings as such in the totality," or as "Being of beings"; it must be understood as the process of unconcealment and as the coming to pass of the ontological difference. This conception of Being is then linked with what was originally called "world" and finally, through an elaboration of the original *logos* concept,[39] identified with *Logos* taken as that which gathers all beings into Being on the one hand and as saying or aboriginal utterance on the other. Finally, particularly in his *Letter on Humanism* Heidegger more precisely specifies Dasein's function in regard to Being (taken as "mittence" [*Geschick*]) as well as in regard to language.[40] I shall return to some of the issues raised here at a later time in this paper.

does not maintain this manner of speaking in his later works. In other words, the assertions that Professor Rudoff cites do not pertain to Heidegger's final view. It is obvious that, according to Heidegger, the ontological differentiation precedes all articulated speech. I would not say that the world is to be articulated; the term *world* can be used legitimately in several senses; it is, rather, Being that is to be articulated. Furthermore, I do not think Heidegger believes that Being is to be articulated by philosophy. It is philosophy's task to reflect on an articulation which has always already taken place and which, as concrete articulation, partly shows but also partly hides Being. It is this latter element which Heraclitus, for instance, and Heidegger have wanted us to understand: namely, that Being is an intrinsically finite and historical process."

39. VA 207–29.
40. HB 70, 78, 79, 116, 119; 65, 77, 82, 86, 87, 88, 118.

I wish to use the last part of Heidegger's lecture on language delivered in 1950 as a point of departure for the balance of this paper.[41] But first a few general remarks should be made with respect to Heidegger's later approach to the language problem. These remarks are based on the first part of the above-mentioned lecture and on the series of lectures held in 1957, entitled "The Essence of Language." [42]

In the first lecture Heidegger takes Georg Trakl's poem "A Winter Evening" as an occasion to elucidate his own view on the relationship between Being (taken as simultaneously including Fourfold, world, and *Logos*) and language (taken as the original stillness in which all things find rest).[43] Heidegger wants to establish that the "Being" (*Wesen*) of original language has want of man's language and, by reason of this want, ap-propriates to man what is proper to himself in order to ap-propriate man to itself in the process of its own "coming to pass." This means that man's language must be understood as his hailing response to the hail of aboriginal language as it abidingly comes to pass (*west*).[44]

When a man speaks, he takes up a language that is already constituted; in his speech, he listens to what this language has to say. To say something means to point something out, to show it. The very essence of language, then, is to be found in the fact that language says something, shows something, lets something appear. Man must listen to language in such a way that he lets its saying speak itself out to him. In his own speaking, which essentially implies his listening to language, man must "say after" what he has heard before.

But if man's own speaking essentially implies his listening to language, then his speaking can come about only insofar as his being was already open to language's saying. Man hears language's saying only to the degree that he belongs within the domain which language discloses to him. Only to those who "belong" to language does language grant the possibility of listening to it and, therefore, the possibility of speaking.[45]

As we have seen, saying, properly speaking, means to point

41. *US* 9–33.
42. *US* 157–216.
43. *US* 28–30; Richardson, *Heidegger*, p. 577.
44. *US* 30–33; Richardson, *Heidegger*, pp. 577–78.
45. *US* 11–15, 145–49, 199–202, 252–55.

out, to show, to let appear, to offer, to hand down, to render free in a revealing and concealing way. What is shown and handed down by language's saying is, in the final analysis, the world. The mode of Being characteristic of this saying is to render free the world in a revealing and, at the same time, concealing way.[46] The saying of language lets what is present appear and conceals what is absent. It renders free what is present in the direction of a permanently being present, just as it fetters what is absent in its permanently being absent. The saying thus "joints" the openness of the "clearing" for which each appearing looks and from which each concealing flees. The saying is the gathering together (*logos*) of a manifold pointing that joints together all that appears and lets what was shown sojourn everywhere by itself.[47]

What is called to the fore by the saying of language is not present in space in the same way that tables and chairs, for example, are present in a room. Even the place which is co-summoned in the saying's calling and to which, therefore, what is summoned is called has a mode of being present that remains stored in its remaining absent. In the final analysis, this place is the world. It is to the world that the saying calls the things that are summoned; it invites them as things to "concern" man. The things so summoned gather together around themselves the world. The saying summons the thing and lets it be what it is; but the thing is what it is only as a thing that "bears," so to speak, the world in which it then sojourns as this thing that it is and in which it can appear as meaningful.

Just as the saying of language summons things, so does it also summon a world. It entrusts a world to the things and, at the same time, "stows" the things in "the luster of a world." This world grants things their proper modes of Being, whereas things "bear" their own world. Language's saying thus makes things come to a world and a world to things. But since world and things can never be independent of one another, these two ways of "making something come" cannot be separated. They penetrate each other, and in so doing they cross, as it were, a middle point in which they belong together. In the saying of language the ontological difference opens up of and in itself a middle, a center, through and toward which world and things are united with one another. This saying makes the things be things and

46. *US* 20–22, 198–202. Cf. *PW* 69–80.
47. *US* 256–58.

the world be world, and thus carries them toward one another. What the saying summons first is the difference between world and things in their essential correlatedness.[48]

In this way the saying makes world and things be what they are. It makes what is present and what is absent come to their characteristic modes of Being from which they can manifest themselves as what they are and sojourn according to their own characters. Precisely what this ap-propriation that comes about through the saying of language is cannot be explained by comparing it to the action of a cause; nor can it be described as a certain occurrence or event. The only thing that we can say of this ap-propriation is that it ap-propriates; it lets things be what, properly speaking, they are, makes the world come to the fore in its proper character, and grants to man his sojourn in his own proper mode of Being so that he can manifest himself as speaking. The only thing that man can do in his own speaking is to listen to the primordial ap-propriation that comes about in language's saying and to try to respond to it in his own speech.[49]

Let us now turn to a brief commentary on the last part of Heidegger's lecture on language. In reading the following, it is most important to keep in mind two things. (1) What is said about language in the last part of this lecture was to be repeated almost verbatim by Heidegger in 1957 in connection with the Ge-stell characteristic for everything that is technical.[50] (2)

48. US 20–28.

49. US 258–60; ID 28–32. Cf. Chapter 1 above. Walter Biemel commented: "The translation of Ereignis as appropriation seems to be dangerous. In appropriation we find the nuance of taking possession of, which contradicts the meaning of Ereignis. The latter should be thought of, rather, in connection with the letting be."

Professor Kockelmans responded: "Heidegger's term Ereignis is very difficult to translate into English; for Heidegger, the word has many connotations, which, taken together, are not found in any English word with which I am familiar. Many attempts have been made to translate it (cf. Z. Adamczewski, 'Martin Heidegger and Man's Way to Be,' Man and World, I [1968], 363–79). I have used various translations, depending on the context and the element which I felt was mainly stressed. I have never used appropriation in isolation; the term was used only in connection with event. The danger Professor Biemel points to certainly exists; I have tried to avoid it by hyphenating the word (ap-propriation) and explaining that its meaning is not 'taking possession of' but rather that process which brings something into that which it, properly speaking, is. I should like to point to one passage at least in which Heidegger does not hesitate to use the term Eigentum in this connection (cf. SD 22)."

50. ID 26–30.

Nonetheless, Heidegger points out here that, among all "cultural" phenomena having a similar function, language occupies a privileged position. The reason for this will occupy us in what follows shortly.

As we have just seen, in Heidegger's view man's language is a response to the saying of aboriginal language (*Logos*). Originally it is language that summons (hails [*Geheiss*]) things and world, beings and Being. Language summons things to give a bearing to world, and the world is summoned to "yield" things in their thing-ing. By summoning them in this way, language sets world and things, Being and beings, apart without separating them and thereby brings about the ontological difference. This must be understood, however, in the proper way. It is not the case that, before language's summoning, both Being and beings are separate or even distinct. The ontological difference that comes to pass in language must be understood as a process that language itself brings about. The difference as process refers to a *dif-ferre*, a "bearing of each other out," as if both Being and beings shared a common center that remains interior to both, a common measure that serves as the single dimension of both, a primal unity by reason of which each adheres to the other and out of which both "issue forth." The ontological difference is a scission (*Schied*) between (*Unter*) Being and beings that refers them to each other by the very fact that it cleaves them in two.[51]

In other words what is summoned in the coming to pass of language as *Logos* is the correlation of Being and beings, and both are summoned toward the unifying scission of the difference that prevails between them. "In the hailing that summons things and world (beings and Being), what, properly speaking, is hailed is their scission."[52] Finally, that which does the hailing is again the scission: "It is the scission which hails." Elaborating on the latter, Heidegger says: "The unifying scission gathers together the two differentiated elements out of itself, insofar as it hails them into the fissure which it itself is."[53] In other words the difference is at the same time unity and "two-ness," hailing and hailed, differentiating and differentiated, and the scission as

51. *US* 21–22, 24, 25; Richardson, *Heidegger*, pp. 578–79.
52. *US* 26.
53. "Der Unter-Schied ist das Heissende. . . . Der Unter-Schied versammelt aus sich die Zwei, indem er sie in den Riss ruft, der er selber ist" (*US* 29).

such is nothing but the tension and mutual adhesion of unity and duality.[54]

Language, originally seen, is this scission, as the coming to pass of the ontological dif-ference out of original *Logos*. Language comes to presence as the scission that takes place between world and thing, Being and being, totality of meaning and concrete meaning structure.[55] Language wants to show and does show a unity by taking this unity apart in mutually opposite elements. But, Heidegger argues, in order for *Logos* as scission to come about, there is need for man; the differentiating cannot give issue to the differentiated except in and through and for that being whose nature is to be open to *Logos* as scission. It is the dynamic tension between differentiating and differentiated which constitutes the need for man, which hails him to be himself. This ek-static openness to aboriginal *Logos* is the emerging of man's language, which therefore has its source both in language and in man himself.[56]

The ek-static openness, however, is not just a structural relationship between man and language but also the bringing of this relationship to fully authentic functioning. Authenticity in the use of language is achieved at the moment of man's free response to the hail addressed to him when the scission takes place, that is, when the differentiating utters its need of man in order that it may give issue to the differentiated. By responding, man gives voice to the differentiated, that is, to world as well as things and, thus, to Being and beings in their difference, which is nonetheless equally a belonging together. This responding hail comports, first of all, a docile attend-ing that pays attention to the hail of address coming to man out of the *Logos* as scission, of which man is by nature an attendant. In order that the attend-ing be docile, man must remain unobtrusive without being passive. He must advance, though with reticence, toward the hail as it comes to him. "This advancing with reticence characterizes the manner in which mortal man responds to the hail of *Logos* as scission. In this fashion mortal man dwells authentically in aboriginal language." [57]

Summarizing these ideas, one might perhaps say that Hei-

54. *US* 29–30.
55. *US* 30.
56. *US* 31–32.
57. *US* 32.

degger conceives of Being in terms of *Logos*. Inasmuch as *Logos* is truth, the coming to pass of that scission is what gives rise to the ontological difference; insofar as *Logos* is utterance, is it the coming to pass of language. In either case man's task is to respond to the hail addressed to him out of the need of *Logos* for a "Da" in order that the differentiating may give rise (issue) to the differentiated. The adequate response to this hail is the coming to pass of man's language in complete authenticity.[58]

V

IF WE COMPARE Heidegger's later view on the relationship between ontological difference and language with his earlier one, it will be clear that in his first period he describes the ontological difference in terms of man's thought concerning Being. In this process the initiative is originally taken by man. Being is already understood as the coming to pass of Truth (*alētheia*), as the process of unconcealment. However, that which sets Being apart from beings in the coming to pass of the ontological difference is man's thought. The setting apart takes place effectively in man's transcendence.

In his later works Heidegger conceives of the "thought of Being" as a process in which Being plays a predominantly active part. Being's thinking in regard to man is the main issue of the discussion. Heidegger says that the coming to pass of the ontological difference takes place in language's saying; it is only in the saying of language that Being addresses itself to man. Thus, it is in language's saying that Being "thinks" and "speaks." Being is

---

58. Richardson, *Heidegger*, pp. 578–81. Bernard P. Dauenhauer raised the following questions: "Man's response to the truth of Being can conceal the truth of Being in several different modes. Among these are: (1) irresponsible and erroneous misrepresentation, (2) error arising in the course of earnest endeavor, and (3) the concealing consequent to any unconcealing. Are all these modes of concealing fundamentally rendered possible by the concealing involved in Being's self-disclosure? Or are some of these modes derivatives of others and thus perhaps different in structure?"

Professor Kockelmans answered: "Because of the historicity and finitude of Being, the truth of Being includes a positive and a negative element. This "datum" seems to be at the root of the third alternative. The other modes of concealment certainly presuppose the finitude, historicity, and even the possibility of inauthenticity in man himself (taken concretely)."

now no longer merely the coming to pass of Truth as unconcealment; it is now equally *Logos* in the full sense of the term.

The second approach obviously does not exclude the first but is merely a logical development of the first within the realm of the hermeneutic circle. There is certainly an important shift in approach to the issues, and a certain further development is undeniable; but the shift is perfectly consistent with the intentions of the earlier works and is in a genuine sense borne out of fidelity to them.[59] In this connection it is important to realize that from beginning to end there are three indispensable poles in the process that Heidegger wishes to describe: Being, man, and things. At the first stage of thought's interpretation, man seems to occupy the privileged position in the process. On a higher level, however, it becomes clear that Being taken as world and at the same time as *Logos,* where *Logos* in turn is taken as *alētheia* and as saying, has a primacy over man's transcendence in that Being is the necessary condition of the possibility of man's transcendence.

I should like to submit a few theses for discussion. First, Heidegger understands ontological difference to mean that "process" in which Being (taken as equiprimordially comprising Truth as process of unveilment, world as Total Meaningfulness, and saying as aboriginal utterance) and beings (taken as concrete ontic things or as the whole realm of things) become differentiated.[60]

Second, this process comes about primarily in thought and is to be taken as coming to pass in language. It is to be noted here that thought is equiprimordially the thought of Being and the thought of man. Therefore, the question of the ontological difference can be approached either from the viewpoint of the concrete

59. Richardson, *Heidegger,* pp. 578–81.
60. Heinrich Ott raised the following question: "Once Being is interpreted as Total Meaningfulness, how can the character of "mittence" be integrated into this interpretation?" Professor Kockelmans answered: "In speaking of Being, I have sometimes used expressions that are intended to clarify what Heidegger means by this term. One of these expressions is 'Total Meaningfulness.' Isolated from other expressions meant to clarify the meaning of Being, this expression gives an erroneous impression of what Heidegger really means. It does not manifest the historicity of Being, a subject which becomes an issue of major concern in Heidegger's later works. Following Richardson, I have attempted a more complete description of what Heidegger understands by Being (see pp. 211, 217–18 above). From this fuller description it becomes clear how the different 'mittences' of Being can and must be distinguished."

projects of man's transcendence or from the saying of Being's language in regard to man. It is understood that in the final analysis Being's thinking is found nowhere but in Being's language as this is listened to by man.

Third, the ontological difference is the necessary condition of the possibility of the hermeneutic *as* structure of thought as well as of the apophantic *as* structure of man's language.

Fourth, the hermeneutic *as* structure of thought means mainly the fact that thought lets something appear *as* something. We may add that the hermeneutic aspect of thought also includes the fact that all understanding implies "fore-having," "fore-sight," and "fore-conception," and that this "hermeneutic situation" characteristic of all human thought is essentially connected with the "hermeneutic circle." Not only does this explain how the question of the ontological difference can be approached from two points of view; it also explains why the question must be approached from two sides, and why Heidegger had to take man's relation toward Being and beings as his starting point.

Fifth, whereas the hermeneutic *as* structure of thought and the apophantic *as* structure of language are necessary consequences of the coming to pass of the ontological difference, the apophantic *as* structure as materialized in the Indo-European languages rests on certain *not necessary* linguistic assumptions. This remark is important in that it points to the basic difficulty with which Heidegger has struggled from the very beginning. If one approaches the whole cluster of problems contained in the expressions "ontological difference," "hermeneutics," and "language" from man's point of view, that is, from the concrete projects in which man materializes his transcendence, one is unable to indicate a *necessary* relationship between the first two poles and the third. The simple reason for this is that in the Indo-European languages the residue of the ontological difference and the hermeneutic structure of thought as found in the apophantic *as* structure of those languages appears to contain contingent elements. However, by approaching the same cluster of problems from the viewpoint of Being's thinking as found in language, one can avoid this complication; in this way one shows that Being's thought is found nowhere except in language, regardless of the concrete linguistic structures language may assume.

Sixth, as far as the last remark is concerned (namely, that Being's thought is found nowhere except in language), I understand Heidegger's position to be the following. In a given epoch of Being's "mittence" the ontological difference comes to pass effectively in all realms of meaning characteristic of that epoch (man's concernful dealing with things, science, technology, art, religion, and so on). All of these realms of meaning, which correspond to different forms of man's experience, are articulated in the various languages which people use in that epoch. The expression "the saying of Being's language" refers to the whole of meaning that comes to light in that epoch. That is to say, it refers not only to the meaning found in an explicitly articulated form characteristic of the various concrete languages but also (and even predominantly) to the meaning that shows itself in the way people live, concernfully deal with things, care for one another, actively involve themselves in science and technology, create works of art, and dedicate themselves to their God. It is in this saying, which thus comprises all of this, that the totality of meaning as such—that is to say, Being—partly shows and partly hides itself. "Thought receives the materials and tools for this self-vibrating structure from language. For language is the most delicate, but also the most susceptible, all-encompassing vibration in the vibrating structure of the ap-propriation. We dwell in the ap-propriation inasmuch as our Being is given over to the ap-propriating event." [61]

Discussion

James M. Edie: I do not want my comments on Professor Kockelmans' extremely interesting and provocative paper to place me exclusively in the role of devil's advocate. I have no doubt that the problems with which he, Lohmann, and Heidegger are wrestling are of the most serious philosophical moment. I am posing questions concerning not the truth or falseness of Heidegger's philosophy of language but rather the meaning of some of the theses that he asserts or seems to assert. Perhaps Heidegger's thought will be mapped out one day, by persons as yet

61. "Das Bauzeug zu diesem in sich schwebenden Bau empfängt das Denken aus der Sprache. Denn die Sprache ist die zarteste, aber auch die anfälligste, alles verhaltende Schwingung im schwebenden Bau des Ereignisses. Insofern unser Wesen in die Sprache vereignet ist, wohnen wir im Ereignis" (ID 30).

unknown to me, in sufficient clarity of detail and argument to furnish us with a basis on which to make a properly motivated judgment as to its truth or falseness. Before any argument or conclusion can be accepted (and I freely admit that conclusions can sometimes be legitimately accepted, even though some or all of the arguments advanced in their support at any given time are rejected), one must first come to some clarity as to what the argument or conclusion means. In saying this I am, of course, approaching Heidegger from without. The distinction of meaning from truth and the priority of meaning over truth are, I take it, already well established at the present time, both in phenomenology and analytic philosophy. It is from this double framework of criticism that I approach Heidegger for purposes of discussion and clarification.

I do not want to belabor points that have already been suggested concerning Heidegger's own language. That a compatriot of Frege, Husserl, and even Wittgenstein should indulge in the kind of linguistic obfuscation of which Heidegger is guilty is, it seems to me, a kind of *laesa majestas* with respect to the German language—a topic that in itself is worthy of the reflection of those philosophers concerned with his philosophy of language. The science of linguistics has shown us that, of the three to four thousand natural languages presently known to mankind, none is privileged. Each language, for all purposes of human expression, is the equivalent of every other, and there is nothing that can be said in one language that cannot be said equally well in any other. Anyone familiar with contemporary linguistics is not likely to challenge this conclusion. However, one may begin to doubt this after encountering such Heideggerian sentences as "This responding hail comports, first of all, a docile attend-ing that pays attention to the hail of address coming to man out of the *Logos* as scission, of which man is by nature an attendant" or "Saying is the gathering together (*Logos*) of a manifold pointing; it joints together all appearing and lets what was shown sojourn everywhere by itself." No doubt Heidegger and his interpreters have something definite in mind when they write in this manner, but it is ironic that a native speaker of the English language, even one of relatively sophisticated linguistic competence who has been trained in technical philosophy, cannot tell immediately upon reading these phrases whether or not they are meaningful utterances in his natural language.

I remark on this fact only to bring to reflexive consciousness the kind of oddity that may escape the attention of those so learned in the exquisite nuances of Heidegger's thought as to forget that his romantic metaphors and self-indulgent etymologies are in need of philosophical explication, not only as to their explanation (*Auslegung*) but also as to their interpretation (*Deutung*). Is it anything less than a gross anthropomorphism to speak of being as hailing man or to endow Being with the attributes of consciousness? If one chooses to call "the hail of being" "aboriginal language," one must not totally neglect the ontological relationships that obtain among (1) men who "hail" by speaking, (2) the "Being" of language, which is a historical being in process of becoming, similar to but certainly distinct from the process of Being, and (3) the scission between Being and beings. It is the first that "speaks" in the strict sense of the term; and "Being," or "scission," can be held to speak only in a transposed or metaphorical sense, which may indeed be unique but nevertheless must be made clear in some disciplined manner.

It seems to me that one reason Heidegger confuses the linguistic process (which, I fully grant, is something much greater than the individual speaker or any given linguistic community, the latter being in some sense an "objective spirit" within which and thanks to which individuals can speak) with the very process of Being may be his failure to understand or take note of the distinction between *parole* and *langue*, which has been elaborated in structural linguistics. In the primary sense all language is *parole* since *langue*, until it is spoken, exists only as a system of structural possibilities for speech. Of course, once *parole* is instituted, *langue* is there, whole and entire, as an infinite range of possibilities, only a few of which can ever be instantiated and all of which are implicated in this one given act of speech. The relation of *langue* to *parole* is that of an ideal structure to its own factual and always partial instantiations. Without the ideal system of phonological, morphological, and syntactical rules that defines a given speech system, there would be no language, only noises. This speech system (*langue*), which underlies and is partially instantiated in any given act of speaking, provides a given speaker with an indefinite range of possibilities at any given moment. *Langue* is, as the romantics liked to say, the infinite in finite form. Precisely because *langue* is "generative" in this way and provides the abstract structural possibilities for a great and endless variety and profusion of new sentences, it can give the illusion that it—language—precedes the speaker, that it has a higher ontological value, and that "language" speaks *in* man rather than the inverse. But can this confused metaphor give us a true appreciation of the relationships that obtain between fact and essence, between real instances and their ideal structures? That there is no fact without essence, no *parole* without *langue*, is not sufficient to give the ontological primacy to the ideal over the real. To say that "language speaks in man" is to say—if by *language* one means *langue*, the structural system of diacritical oppositions necessary and sufficient for a system of sounds to constitute a language—that the ideal and the possible have ontological priority over the real and the factual. This is to fall into a Platonism which the later qualification of language as the "language of Being" hardly redeems. But, if by *language* one means *parole*, that is, all the actual instances of speech that take place within a synchronously defined period, one is clearly making language ontologically dependent on the community of individuals speaking it. In any strict sense, therefore, one must say not that languages speak but that men speak languages, or speak by means of languages.

However, I am almost embarrassed to present such simple-minded reflections and will—presuming, *dato non concesso,* that the validity of Heidegger's style can be independently justified—turn to more weighty matters. In what follows I would like to raise two questions which, if they can be answered will help to clarify the import and limits of the theses advanced in Professor Kockelmans' paper with regard to their meaning.

First, I find Johannes Lohmann's contention that there is a "grammar and logic" of the Indo-European languages that is the sufficient condition and unique source of the traditional doctrine of propositional truth (as this was formulated by Aristotle and Leibniz, for instance) most disconcerting. I am also surprised to find that this doctrine, based on the supposed subject-predicate structure of the Indo-European languages (a privileged but by no means coercive structure, either of syntax or morphology), involves an explicit linguistic expression of what Heidegger calls the "ontological difference," which at once unites and separates beings and Being.

Let me take up the first point very briefly. When Lohmann goes so far as to speak of the "logic" of the Indo-European languages as being distinct from the "logic" of the Bantu, the Chinese, and the Semitic languages and even states that "it becomes understandable at once [on the basis of grammatical differences] that the Chinese truth concept, for instance, differs radically from that promulgated by Aristotle and Leibniz," I find him at least implicitly guilty of the kind of psychologism on the grammatical level from which Frege and Husserl freed us on the level of logic. If by *logic* one means formal logic, I do not think the thesis even merits refutation; if by *logic* one means the formal conditions of meaningfulness, noncontradiction, and validity, there are not several logics but only one, and it is as coercive for the Chinese and the Hebrews as for the Greeks. Lohmann cannot mean to identify logic with grammar; as far as I am aware, the last scientific linguist of repute to suggest such a theory was Benjamin Whorf (if even he held this, which is doubtful), and most linguists today are well schooled in distinguishing logic from grammar. According to a recent study:

> Propositions are defined, classified, and analyzed by their logical form and content, which are matters for logicians; sentences are defined, classified, and analyzed by their grammatical (and secondarily by their phonological) structures, which are matters for the linguist to determine. In all languages in which logical enquiries have been systematically undertaken, there are certain general, though not universal, correlations between sentence types and proposition types; and in all languages there are similar correlations between sentence forms and types of meaning or situational functions (command, enquiry, statement, and the like).[62]

What Lohmann must mean to say is that the grammatical manner in which, for example, affirmative, negative, universal, particular, hypothetical, causal, conjunctive, and disjunctive statements are formed in Chinese is, on the level of "surface" structure, quite different from the manner in which such forms occur in Semitic, Indo-European, and other languages. We are completely safe, however, in asserting that there is no language known to man that does not have the means of making the logical and semantic distinctions designated by these and similar forms. Even within the Indo-European languages, for instance, we find

62. R. H. Robins, *General Linguistics* (Bloomington: Indiana Univ. Press, 1964), p. 192.

that the Greek expresses in its morphology a distinction between the optative and the subjunctive for which there are no corresponding morphological forms in Latin. This is not to say that it was impossible for the native speaker of Latin to make the necessary semantic distinctions between the optative and the subjunctive moods; these distinctions were made in a nonmorphological manner within his language. In the same way one can say that, though the Chinese language and many others are devoid of the particular morphological devices through which the ordinary attributive proposition is formed in the Indo-European languages, this semantic necessity and possibility of human speech is achieved in a different manner. There is within the science of linguistics a growing branch called transformational generative grammar (which Noam Chomsky has done much to popularize in recent years), the concern of which is to lay out with clarity and precision the purely formal grammatical rules according to which the "surface grammatical structures" of a given empirical language are related to the universal "deep logical structures" underlying every natural language. In transformational grammar this is a question of empirical research. In philosophy the recognition of this distinction between "surface" and "deep" structures is most explicitly made by Wittgenstein and some of his followers; but Husserl, also, in the first chapters of *Formal and Transcendental Logic* (though he had no knowledge of contemporary linguistics), makes essentially the same distinction:

> It is . . . not without reason that people often say that formal logic has let itself be guided by grammar. In the case of the theory of forms, however, this is not a reproach but a necessity—provided that, for "guided by grammar" (a word intended to bring to mind *de facto* historical languages and their grammatical description), "guidance by *the grammatical itself*" be substituted. . . .
> Nothing else has so greatly confused the discussion of the question of the correct relationship between logic and grammar as the continual confounding of the two logical spheres that we have distinguished sharply as the lower and the upper.[63]

63. Edmund Husserl, *Formale und transzendentale Logik: Versuch einer Kritik der logischen Vernunft* (Halle a.d.S.: Niemeyer, 1929), p. 18 (English translation by Dorion Cairns, *Formal and Transcendental Logic* [The Hague: Nijhoff, 1969]).

In short, if there is an essential difference between the Chinese and the Indo-European languages, it occurs not on the deep level of the formal logical structures necessary for the expression of propositional meaning but on the surface level of the phonological and grammatical structures in which the underlying formal possibilities are realized. When Professor Kockelmans, following Lohmann, says that "the 'logic' of a language is expressly contained in its 'morphology,' " and that a difference in morphology and syntax explain "why the Chinese logic . . . differs radically from Western logic," he flies in the face of the most important discoveries of contemporary linguistics.

Even if we were to accept Lohmann's point, I seriously doubt that his contention involves the explicit linguistic formulation of what Heidegger calls the "ontological difference." As far as I can see, Lohmann's examination of the simple attributive proposition (S is P) in the light of the medieval doctrine of supposition leads only to a grammatical explanation of how it is possible and necessary (in some cases) to subsume a given factual instance under a general type. A subject or a predicate can stand for (supposit) a thing, a quality, or a general type. When we say that Socrates is a man, that man is mortal, and that Socrates is mortal, we involve ourselves in a complex play of suppositions of terms which presupposes, as Lohmann says, a continual "ontological differentiation" as each word in the sentence comes to signify the "Being of a being or a being in its Being." This recognition that every fact is experienced, thought, and expressed (when it is expressed) as being the instantiation of a type, and that every type is experienced, thought, and expressed (when it is expressed) as the essence or type of a possible individual instance that would fall under it—is this Heidegger's ultimate definition of the ontological difference? If it is, the doctrine suddenly becomes crystal clear; but at the same time it becomes so thoroughly demythicized that I doubt many Heideggerians would admit that this is just what the Master of the Black Forest really means to say. This hardly seems an advance over Boethius!

The second question I want to pose concerns Heidegger's notion of truth. It seems to me that, in his attempt to identify Being and truth in an ontological as opposed to a linguistic sense as the process of unveilment, his new sense of truth requires that we abandon the hard earned phenomenological distinction between meaning and truth. What presents itself, whether pre-linguistically (in a perceptual situation) or linguistically (when the meaning of an experience is thematized in judgment) is a meaning structure that has a certain priority over and independence of its own truth (or being). Language is, above all, the means we have to fix and hold before us, in our cultural space, the meanings with which we endow our experience of Being. As Heidegger says, it is to language, and especially to the word, that we can attribute our ability to distinguish one thing from another and to keep all things interrelated with one another in the coherent structure which is the experienced world. The word, or language, does not merely refer to something outside itself, to a nonlinguistic reality and situation, but also and primarily enables us to maintain and fix (to articulate) the sense of the world and of all beings in the world. For this reason Heidegger says that language is not essentially and exclusively *for* communication, that it has a more important function within the tissue of experience. It is because man speaks that he has a world, and so on. But is this experience of meaningfulness and the ability to distinguish meaning within the flow of experience *truth*? Is unveilment *truth*? Is all truth absorbed into *Lichtung*? On the basis of Heidegger's explicit repetitions, it is difficult to permit him to say otherwise; but if we say this, we make error, lying, and untruth unintelligible. There would be, for Heidegger, only successful cognitions, no unsuccessful ones. The experience of truth, however, requires such a distinction. This is what Aristotle and Leibniz and Husserl saw. Truth always and necessarily involves us in a movement of verification that goes outside of and beyond meaning (certainly beyond linguistic meaning), a breaking through the apophantic and hermeneutic circles of meaning toward the things themselves. In other words, if Being is the process of unveilment, and if truth is the experience of Being, we have an identification of truth and meaning to which human experience is totally incidental. If truth is the unveiling of Being, what is the relation of truth to meaning? Phenomenologically we know that they are not identical. The phenomenology of truth must follow the phenomenology of meaning; in order to know if something is *true*, we must know what it *means*. Heidegger seems to subvert this order; indeed, he seems to abandon the phenomenology of reason altogether and to subsume it under something else—*Lichtung*—which escapes all rational argument. For this reason we say that he is arbitrarily replacing clarity with obscurity and is working not for *logos* but against it. The ultimate reason that he should not do this is that, when all is said and done, we can and must still ask if what he is saying is *true*. And we must ask this in the very sense of truth that he attempts to subvert.

KOCKELMANS: Professor Edie's comments range over such a number of important problems that they would seem in their richness to constitute a separate paper rather than a commentary on my own. Consequently, I shall not be able to deal with all of the issues he introduces. Within this limited space, however, I shall offer those remarks which, in my opinion, are vital to a proper understanding of Heidegger's position as a whole as it pertains to other possible philosophical perspectives. In making these remarks I shall try to be as clear as possible, even if this entails having to repeat myself occasionally.

Professor Edie begins with the hope that one day someone will succeed in explaining Heidegger's thought "in sufficient clarity of detail and argument to furnish us with a basis on which to make a properly motivated judgment as to its truth or falseness." I agree that Heidegger's thought is indeed difficult, and inherently so; his later publications in particular remain far away from life wisdom and world wisdom, to use an expression from one of his most recent publications.[64] However, I also believe that anyone who talks about Heidegger's "philosophy" with greater clarity and precision than Heidegger, misunderstands the genuine meaning of Heidegger's thought and misleads his audience. One will never understand the real message of Heidegger's thought if he is unwilling (for whatever reason) to carefully study the works with an open, unprejudiced mind. That this undertaking requires a number of years is quite true; but, in my view, the enterprise is more than worthwhile. Furthermore, does the same not hold true for all great philosophers—Aristotle, Spinoza, Kant, Hegel, Nietzsche, Bergson, and many others?

Professor Edie says that meaning's distinction from and priority over truth is established in phenomenology as well as in analytic philosophy. Although I shall return to this statement in another context, I wish here to make one general observation. It is well known that Husserl maintained the classical conception of

64. *SD* 1.

truth throughout his entire life, and that the same conception of truth is found in analytic philosophy. This truth conception goes back to Aristotle, although in many cases it is taken in the Leibnizian interpretation. Heidegger has never referred to this conception as being wrong, nor has he ever explicitly criticized the view. His claim, however, is that still another conception of truth is more primordial than this current (and correct) one. This more basic conception of truth as the process of unconcealment is described from the viewpoint of Dasein in *Being and Time* and in other of Heidegger's works of the same period, whereas it is studied from Being's point of view in all of his later works, beginning with "On the Essence of Truth." It is obviously beyond the scope of this rejoinder to attempt to explain this conception from each of these perspectives.

A somewhat similar remark could be made here in regard to Heidegger's use of the term *meaning* (*Sinn*) and its distinction from other related terms, notably, *signification* (*Bedeutung*). Speaking of *meaning*, Heidegger says:

> When beings which are found in the world are discovered along with the Being of Dasein—that is, when they have come to be understood—we say that they have *meaning*. But that which is understood, taken strictly, is not the meaning but the being, or, alternatively, Being. Meaning is that wherein the intelligibility of something maintains itself. That which can be articulated in a disclosure by which we understand, we call "meaning."

Only when this meaning becomes articulated is there a question of significations.[65] From this text it becomes clear that Heidegger's use of the term *meaning* (differences in terminology notwithstanding) is typically phenomenological. However, his use of the term is quite different from that generally found in analytic philosophy; for Heidegger refers to all articulated, particularly all linguistically articulated, meaning with the term *signification*.

In these cases I am not arguing that Heidegger's usage is the preferable one; I am merely pointing to the vast differences that undeniably exist. Furthermore, I wish to state that, although Heidegger's usage may not be the preferable one, it is, nonetheless, legitimate and well founded. Given these basic differences, it is obviously very difficult to translate Heidegger's statements about truth and meaning into a language commonly used

65. *SZ* 151 ff. Cf. pp. 21, 49–52 above.

by other philosophers. In any event, when one talks about meaning's distinction from and priority over truth, the statement makes sense only if *truth* is taken in its common meaning; if the term *truth* is taken in Heidegger's sense, such a distinction would seem to be meaningless.

Professor Edie states that Heidegger indulges in linguistic obfuscation and commits treason with regard to the German language. Is this really true? It must be admitted that Heidegger's language is "peculiar," and in many instances his use of language is quite different from our everyday way of speaking, particularly different from the ordinary use of English. Similar observations could be made, however, about other great philosophers; furthermore, this "peculiar" use of language is, as it were, dictated by the equally "peculiar" subject matter of Heidegger's thought. The question of the extent to which this use of language is an obfuscation and commits treason in regard to the German language is one that must be decided by linguists, provided they have sufficient understanding of Heidegger's thought. Some linguists who certainly fulfill this condition have examined this question and concluded that, with one exception, Heidegger never violates the rules of the German language.[66]

I think that the question of whether or not there are "privileged" languages is irrelevant as long as we take this statement as a generality. However, in many instances one language simply finds itself in a privileged position with regard to another language. It is a well-known fact that translators in such cases encounter great difficulties. I am thinking here not only of a translation of Aristotle into one of the Polynesian languages, for instance, but also of a translation of Hegel's *Phenomenology of Mind* into English. Furthermore, I believe that, for every "cryptic" passage from Heidegger (in many cases the translation is even more cryptic than the original), one could easily quote an equally "cryptic" passage from Aristotle, Scotus, Kant, Hegel, Fichte, and so on. Is it correct, therefore, to require that a statement show itself to be a meaningful utterance in a natural language upon immediate reading?

Professor Edie takes Heidegger to task for using romantic metaphors and self-indulgent etymologies. I must refer here to Erasmus Schöfer's book, in which this common objection is ex-

66. For further discussion of this subject, see pp. 34–44 above, pp. 281–301 below.

tensively dealt with and easily refuted.[67] From past experience I can say that, whenever I have examined one of Heidegger's famous "etymologies," I have always found his view to be reasonable, very well possible, and shared by at least some of the great authorities in the field. That Heidegger does not always choose the most obvious etymology is understandable from the general perspective of his philosophy as a whole; without "destructive retrieval" we shall never get to the core of the problems.

Professor Edie's distinction between *Auslegung* and *Deutung* is not very clear to me. As far as Heidegger's conception of this difference is concerned, I would refer to *Being and Time*. In addition, Professor Biemel made some remarks on this topic in his comments on Versényi's criticism of Heidegger.[68]

Professor Edie's reference to the term *anthropomorphism* leads to a very delicate and important topic. If the term is taken in a pejorative sense, it is not found in Heidegger's thought. However, if this term is meant to refer to a distinction between objective (*sachliche*), or thinglike, categories and human, or ek-sistential, categories, then Heidegger indeed has a great preference for the latter. In my opinion this is understandable in view of his attempt to overcome objectivism and scientism. In other words, in the latter case the term *anthropomorphism* refers to a perfectly legitimate approach to the world.

The distinction between *langue* and *parole* is certainly not denied or overlooked by Heidegger. In *Being and Time* as well as in *On the Way to Language* Heidegger shows that he is acquainted with the "traditional" conceptions of language and speech. Although he evaluates these conceptions in a positive way, he explicitly stipulates that his own thought moves not on the level of these reflections but rather on a more elementary, if you wish, a deeper, level. What Professor Edie calls "objective spirit" certainly has a similarity to what Heidegger has in mind when he says "Die Sprache spricht." However, we must remember that an expression such as "objective spirit" presupposes a Hegelian perspective that is substantially different from the one adopted by Heidegger. When talking about language, Heidegger never refers to a "structural system of diacritical oppositions necessary and sufficient for a system of sounds to constitute a language." In avoiding this use of the term, he is not manifesting

67. See pp. 281–301 below.
68. Cf. *SZ* 182–210; pp. 99–100 above.

any criticism of reflections in which expressions like this are used; he is merely claiming that his thought develops on a level where this way of speaking is not (yet) helpful.

Before going on to the more substantial questions and objections Professor Edie raises in his commentary, I should like to make one general remark in regard to the first half, in which he touches on a great number of important problems, most of which are not explicitly dealt with in Heidegger's works. If Professor Edie concludes from this that the importance of Heidegger's thought is to be in any way minimized, I certainly cannot agree with him. In my view Heidegger is one of the most influential "philosophers" of our era. What Professor Edie says about Heidegger's use of language does contain a great deal of truth, but I feel, however, that one should try to evaluate on inherent grounds the reasons and motives that have brought Heidegger to his particular way of using language. When one does so, it quickly becomes clear that, however "strange" his use of language may seem at first sight, it is never arbitrary, and it always serves an important cause.

I find I can go along with most of the ideas in Professor Edie's first major remark without having to abandon Lohmann's position or my own. In formulating Lohmann's position (to which I subscribe) by stating "there is a 'grammar and logic' of the Indo-European languages that is the sufficient condition and unique source of the traditional doctrine of propositional truth," Professor Edie is misrepresenting the view that both Lohmann and I have tried to defend. We do indeed maintain that the fact that Aristotle and Leibniz define truth in the way they have factually done is *intrinsically* connected with the fact that they spoke Indo-European languages. If they had expressed themselves in the Chinese language, for instance, they would never have come to conceive of truth in the way they factually did. The reason for this is that the Chinese language, in contrast to the Indo-European languages, does not make an explicit use of supposition and thus lacks the "classical" conception of the ontological difference, which is essential to that truth conception.

However, in adopting this view we are not forced to reject the distinction between logic and grammar or the distinction between surface and deep structures. As far as these distinctions are concerned, I should like to point out two things: (1) The remarks made on page 200 of my essay were explicitly meant to leave room for these kinds of distinctions. In a certain sense it is true that all languages must make use of "supposition" and thus must at least contain, if they do not express it explicitly, the ontological difference as structural moment. (2) It is certainly not my position to suggest that what can be said in one language cannot be said in another. I admit that Aristotle can be translated into Chinese and Lao-tzu into English. The question is merely whether or not the Chinese language suggests, in its own linguistic structure, Leibniz' conception of truth, as most of the Indo-European languages indeed do.

After these remarks Professor Edie suggests that, even if Lohmann's point were correctly taken, it is doubtful that this involves the explicit linguistic formulation of what Heidegger calls the "ontological difference." In the explanation of why this is in question, there are several things that ask for rectification. Supposition is a logical property of the subject term of a statement, not of its predicate term. The consequence of this is not that each word of the proposition comes to signify the "Being of a being"; merely the predicate term comes to do so. This distinction entails the recognition that every fact (provided that it is experienced, thought, and expressed) is not only the instantiation of a type but also much more than that. A simple reduction of the predication to a class-membership relation does not justify all that is the consequence of supposition. Finally, this recognition certainly does not constitute what Heidegger calls the "ontological difference." The distinction between subject and predicate as found in the Indo-European predicative statement necessarily presupposes a distinction between a thing and its Being, which is the ontological difference. The *classical interpretation* of this distinction has led to quasi problems in metaphysics, and *it is these quasi problems* which Heidegger tries to overcome by reflecting more carefully on the ontological difference.

Professor Edie's second question is a very complex one for two reasons. First of all, he describes Heidegger's view in typically non-Heideggerian language. I doubt if this description does justice to what Heidegger means. For instance, the statement that "what presents itself . . . is a meaning structure that has a certain priority over and independence of its own truth (or being)" is not understandable from a Heideggerian point of view. Second, in his objection, Professor Edie uses the terms *truth, meaning,* and *Being* in a different sense than Heidegger does. If these "terminological" difficulties were clarified, it would become clear that "truth" as unconcealment must be attributed to Being, not to man. The process of unveilment implies both a positive and a negative aspect, and thus on that level there is certainly room for "untruth." Furthermore, there is certainly room for untruth if we take truth in the common sense of the term, in which case we can refer to true or untrue statements pronounced by man. But here, that is, on this level, there is no essential difference between Heidegger and Husserl, for instance.[69]

Professor Edie further states that, "if Being is the process of unveilment and if truth is the experience of Being, we have an identification of truth and meaning to which human experience is totally incidental." We must note first that, for Heidegger, "truth" is not the experience of Being; furthermore, although the process of unveilment is independent of my individual Dasein, it nonetheless remains true that without man there would be no Being. In other words, the fact that Being shows itself and partly hides itself in this era in the Western world, for instance, is obviously independent of me the moment I first become aware of it; on the other hand it is also obvious that this is not independent of Western man in his historical development. What Husserl calls "the meaning of the things themselves" necessarily presupposes, in Heidegger's view, "the truth of Being." Finally, I feel that I must object to Professor Edie's statement that Heidegger is "subverting" the very sense of truth. With regard to what Professor Edie calls "truth," Heidegger has always and repeatedly said that it represents a correct view, but not a fundamental one.

69. Cf. *WW.*

The World in Another Beginning:
Poetic Dwelling and the Role
of the Poet

Werner Marx

THE CONCERN of all of Heidegger's later works is the
preparation of the possibility of another beginning of creative
human Being—"another" beginning as compared with the one
which was brought about by the poetic philosophizing of the
pre-Socratics. The necessity of such a new beginning follows for
Heidegger from his insight into the "highest danger," which lies
in the essence ruling in technology. This ruling essence threatens
to bring about a state of affairs in which man merely labors to
produce "materials" [1] in a totally uncreative way and conceives of
himself as nothing but material. The arrival of "another" beginning would be, in Hölderlin's words, the arrival of "*das
Rettende*"—that which would bring about a saving. "*Das Rettende*" would consist in creative dwelling which, again in
Hölderlin's words, would be a "poetic" dwelling: man would
"dwell poetically on this earth."

Whatever the precise meaning of such poetic dwelling may
be, Heidegger sees in it the possibility for man's life on this planet
to be "primordial," (*ursprünglich*), "genuine" (*echt*), and "salutary," (*heil*), and his thinking is guided by the will to help prepare the way for it to come about. In the recent history of
thought, and especially in the history of philosophy, there are, of

---

1. The word *materials* is only an approximation of the phrase
"Seiendes von der Seinsart des Bestandes," which refers to the mode of
Being of the entities produced: they are not poetic; they do not reflect the
"Fourfold."

course, numerous examples of efforts directed at saving humanity by bringing about a primordial, genuine, and salutary state of affairs. However, we become aware of that which is unique to Heidegger's efforts precisely when we try to fit his later works into the general tendencies of our time. For Heidegger, as we have noted, this primordial, genuine, and salutary state of affairs is to have the form of a "poetic" dwelling of man. But what does Heidegger mean by "poetic"? It is certainly correct to infer from this qualification that, for Heidegger, poets and their poetizing play a decisive role in bringing about the other beginning, however the task of the philosopher or the thinker in relation to poets and poetizing may then be conceived.

The purpose of this essay is, in the first place, to clarify the "conditions of thought" under which it was possible for Heidegger to arrive at the notion that the poet and his poetizing play this extraordinary, uncanny role. In the second place, we shall ask whether it is at all thinkable that the poet's assumption and realization of this role could lead to a "poetic dwelling" of the man who is not a poet, or, more exactly, of humanity—and, if so, how this is to be thought of concretely.

We are fully aware that this attempt to direct a question to Heidegger—phrased in terms of his "efforts" toward "goals" and of the role of the poet which, when assumed and realized, should "lead to something"—is open to the following objections: In the first place, it may seem that this attempt does not take into account the fact that, for Heidegger, the arrival of the "other beginning" occurs "suddenly" (*jäh*)—hence, in such a way that there can be no "goal" whose attainment could be the object of his "efforts." In the second place, it may be pointed out that this way of questioning is entirely contrary both to Heidegger's way of thinking and to the significance of the basic tenets he has developed.

Our reply to the first objection is that in the following we deal only with the conditions which must already be fulfilled before the other beginning can suddenly arrive; this is in fact precisely the way in which Heidegger proceeds. The second objection is one that we must abide with. In this inquiry we do want our criticism to proceed immanently, but this entails evaluating the "total conception" by asking whether the thoughts are consistent and whether they have been thought through to the end. Thus, we feel jusified in employing an approach which seems to be the only one appropriate for this purpose.[2]

I

WHILE WE DO NOT INTEND to present the development of Heidegger's thought here, we must briefly characterize the transformation his thought had to undergo before it arrived in the dimension in which it perceived the task of determining the "possibility" which could lead to another beginning consisting in "poetic dwelling." This dimension represents for us the first of the "conditions of thought" under which Heidegger was able to attribute this special role to the poet.

First of all, Heidegger had to have realized that his early characterization of the fundamental structure of Dasein—his characterization of transcendence understood as Being-in-the-world—was inappropriate because of the direction he had ascribed to its movement. He had conceived of transcendence as the opening up to the totality of relations (*Bezugsganze*) of meaning, to the world; "being in the whole" was thought of as transcended toward the world as the "whereto." [3] Heidegger had also conceived of the "understanding of Being" as moving in the same direction: Dasein was thought to project itself—though "thrown"—toward the meaning of Being and toward the ways in which entities are: for example, toward readiness-to-hand and presence-at-hand. In contrast, Heidegger had to realize that it is first and foremost world and Being which "give" and "grant" to

2. The subject of this paper was first treated in a lecture entitled "The Meaning and Task of Philosophy in Another Beginning," delivered by Werner Marx in 1954 before the Graduate Faculty of the New School for Social Research, New York. The lecture was subsequently published under the title, "Heidegger's New Conception of Philosophy: The Second Phase of 'Existentialism,'" in *Social Research*, XXII (1955), 451–74. The introductory character of this lecture was necessitated by the level of understanding of Heidegger then prevailing in the United States. A more thorough discussion of the same topic can be found in Marx, *Heidegger und die Tradition* (Stuttgart: Kohlhammer, 1961) (English translation by Theodore Kisiel and Murray Greene, *Heidegger and the Tradition* (Evanston, Ill.: Northwestern Univ. Press, 1971).

3. WG 20, 21; SZ 87.

Dasein the fact that, and the way in which, entities appear as present in the light of their presence. This changed sense of direction is now indicated for him especially by the fundamental determinant *"Ereignis,"* or *"ereignen,"* which brings to word the "giving" and "granting" that sends everything into its "own."

Second, Heidegger had to expand the insight into the historicity of Dasein which he had gained in *Being and Time* into what he now calls "mittence" (*Geschick*), which denotes the gathering of a sending (*Versammlung eines Schickens*) that has sent itself to Dasein and commissioned it in ever differing ways in the history of Western thought. He had to conceive of the establishment of the "first" beginning by the Pre-socratics as such a "mittence"; otherwise the possibility of the "mittence" of "another" beginning would not have been thinkable.

Third, Heidegger's conception of *alētheia* had to have developed already into a "basic trait of Being," or of "essence."[4] *In Being and Time,* the references to the Greek *alētheuein* and *alētheia* served only to characterize how Dasein dis-covers entities as "true ones" by forcefully tearing from concealedness (*lēthē*) the truth in the form of "discoveredness" (*Entdecktheit*). There Dasein was shown to be able to do this by virtue of the fact that its *Sein* is constitutionally "disclosed" (*erschlossen*)—lit up (*gelichtet*)—in and on its *Da;* accordingly, Dasein was there conceived to be a "clearing" (*Lichtung*).

If *alētheia* is conceived as a basic trait of Being, then clearing is intrinsic to Being itself as a dimension of overtness in which unconcealedness—*"Ent-borgenheit,"* *"Un-verborgenheit"*—occurs: for the presence of being as such and in the whole, as well as for the experience of it. However, since *lēthē* is part and parcel of *alētheia,* this dimension must be conceived simultaneously as one which is permeated by the self-concealing of concealedness, by "mystery" (*Geheimnis*), and by dissimulation resulting from the reign of error (*Irre*).[5] Concealedness as mystery and error permeates the clearing.[6] The term *unconcealedness* is meant to demonstrate that all that is overt originates in concealedness and re-

4. Cf. WW 24 ff.
5. The characterizations of "mystery" and "error," which are considerably different in "On the Essence of Truth" and "The Origin of the Work of Art," are brought together here for the sake of simplicity; similarly, the fact that the clearing of presence can also conceal itself is not considered.
6. WW 19 ff.

mains tied to it as the sphere which holds "unto itself," in the mode of withdrawal (*Entzug*), that which may always remain hidden from Dasein as well as that which may eventually arrive in unconcealedness for Dasein. This "relationship" of concealedness and unconcealedness indicates more exactly how the "mittence" commissions (*schickt*) Dasein to various ways of "unconcealing." Today, Dasein is commissioned to that noncreative mode of unconcealing which brings to the fore (*hervorbringt*) nothing but materials; this is the "mittence" which Heidegger has called *Ge-stell*.

Yet the insight that Dasein can unconceal through bringing to the fore indicates that "mittence" could one day commission Dasein to bring to the fore in a creative way: in the authentic way signified in the primordial meaning of bringing to the fore (*poiēsis*). Unconcealing could become "poetic." If this were to happen, "that which saves" would arrive, and the condition for the sudden arrival of another beginning would be fulfilled. But what kind of Dasein is able to unconceal in the way of *poiēsis*? It seems reasonable to assume that this will be first of all the Dasein of a poet. We must add that, for Heidegger, the thinker can likewise unconceal in an authentic way; the reason for this privileged position of poets and thinkers, which makes them neighbors, is that both dwell in a special way in the "house of Being"—and that means in the element of language. Language thus seems to be another "condition" in Heidegger's conception of the special role played by the poet in the preparation of another beginning consisting in poetic dwelling.

II

WE NOW WISH to show that Heidegger conceives of the essence of language as belonging to *alētheia,* and that it is only by virtue of this particular conception of the essence of language that the poet is able to bring "the poetic" to the fore and thereby prepare for another beginning consisting in "poetic dwelling." It must be emphasized immediately that this determination of "the essence" of language is by no means meant as an answer to the traditional question of "what" something is.[7] When in the follow-

7. *US* 201.

ing we speak of the "structure" [8] and the "content" of language—which we do in conscious violation of Heidegger's conception of the essence of "essence"—this is only for the purpose of clarification; otherwise we remain close to the text in order to substantiate our thesis.

1. Only from the standpoint that Being, world, *alētheia*, and "mittence" "give" and "grant" the arrival of that which is present in its presence, and on the assumption that language has to do with this giving and granting, does it make sense to affirm that the layout (*Aufriss*) of language also includes a nonhuman activity: Saying (*Sage*). This saying is carefully differentiated from human speaking, even though human speaking is also included in the layout. Saying "demands" (*heisst*), "calls" (*ruft*), and collects itself into the "word," which also does not belong to the human sphere. Dasein—which belongs to Saying (*der Sage gehörend*)[9]—listens to it and its word and brings what it hears "correspondingly" into human-sounding words; specifically, the poet brings it into the words of the poetic song and "work" (*Sprachwerk*): namely, into that which arises purely out of poetical composition (*im "rein Gedichteten"*).

2. That the "layout" of language as thus conceived has the same structure which we previously noted in *alētheia* is attested to first of all by Heidegger's own characterization of Saying as "a freeing that conceals while bringing into the unconcealedness of the clearing" (*lichtend-verbergend-frei-geben*).[10] But there is also much other evidence suggesting that for him the "relationship" of concealedness to unconcealedness is carried out in Saying. Thus, he uses for Saying the image of a stream [11] in which everything which addresses itself to Dasein is embedded; this addressing is silent, it makes no sound, and yet it can be heard as a "silent form of Saying" (*Geläut der Stille*),[12] a streaming which brings everything into its own.[13] This stream of silence originates in a "place of silence" (*Ort der Stille*), which Heidegger, in his

8. Cf. D. Sinn, "Heideggers Spätphilosophie," in *Philosophische Rundschau*, XV (1967), 81 ff.
9. Here Heidegger exploits the fact that the German words *gehörend* ("belonging") and *hörend* ("hearing") are cognates; thus, in belonging to Saying, Dasein is also listening to it.
10. *US* 200.
11. *US* 255.
12. *US* 30, 215.
13. *US* 29.

most recent publications, calls "*lēthē*." [14] What does it mean to say that the stream of silence originates in *lēthē*? It means, above all, that the stream has its source (*Quelle*) in that which has not yet been said and which must remain unsaid: the "unsaid." [15] Thus, all "giving" and "granting" of that which is linguistically present comes from *lēthē*, from concealedness. The stream flows from *lēthē*; even when it flows in unconcealedness, it remains permeated by concealedness, mystery, and the "unsaid"; *lēthē* holds (*hält*) and relates (*ver-hält*) everything that is overt in Saying; thus, the "unsaid" remains a contributory determinant of Saying. Therefore, the entire process of Saying has "*alētheia* structure," and this structure forms the basis of the giving and granting which Saying performs as a nonhuman activity. This interpretation is not contradicted by the fact that, for Heidegger, the essence of Saying consists in "pointing to" (*Zeige*), and that the "giving" and "granting" of Saying thus results from this pointing to. The "giving" and "granting" of Saying occurs only in the "free and open of the clearing" (*Freie der Lichtung*), "to which every essence, be it pre-sence or ab-sence, must point." [16] In the unconcealedness of the clearing, pointing to (*das Zeigen*) grants the nearness of a pre-sence for the arrival of whatever entities are present; for ab-sence, deriving from farness, the nearness remains concealed in the arrival. [17]

Saying's manifold pointing to extends—as we read [18]—"into all regions of pre-sence." What are these regions (*Gegenden*)? We referred to Heidegger's characterization of Saying—as a freeing that conceals while bringing into the unconcealedness of the clearing—in order to characterize the *alētheia* structure of the movement of Saying. But we have not yet mentioned that this movement has a definite "content." What is freed is "world." Heidegger writes, "Saying [*sagen*] means freeing while concealing and bringing into the unconcealedness of the clearing *as* proffering [*dar-reichen*] of that which we call world." This proffering of the world is "the ruling essence in Saying" (*das Wesende im Sagen*). [19]

Heidegger attempted to conceive of the proffering of the

14. *SD* 78.
15. Cf. *US*.
16. *US* 257.
17. *US* 21, 22.
18. *US* 255.
19. *US* 255.

world in a few steps [20] as the occurrence of "nearness" (*Nähe, Nahnis*) bringing the "against one another over" (*Gegeneinander-über*) of "World regions" (the same regions just referred to as regions of pre-sence) into a "neighboring nearness," the world regions of the Fourfold of earth, heaven, divine, and mortal. Since this same occurrence also brings about Saying, nearness and Saying are for Heidegger "the selfsame" (*das Selbe*).[21] Saying is "nearness" (*Nahnis*) of the World regions, and for this reason it also manifests the proximity (*Nachbarschaft*) by virtue of which—through their characteristic ways of Saying —the poet and the thinker are neighbors.[22]

Saying thus not only is a movement which has *alētheia* structure. Saying also "permeates and structures" *alētheia*,[23] in that it nears the World regions—as the very regions of presence from which present entities appear and disappear in each case. In this sense we speak—cautiously—of a "content"; but, since this content belongs to the dimension of granting, we do not thereby mean anything like the content of that which is granted by Saying, for example, the content of a poem.

We conjecture that for Heidegger the dimension of the world so conceived is nothing other than "the poetic," especially since, as he says, the proximity of poet and thinker gave the "hint" (*Wink*) for this particular conception of the essence of language.[24] "The poetic" would thus be the ruling essence in Saying (*das Wesende im Sagen—das "Wesen der Sprache"*) and thereby simultaneously "the language of the essence" (*die Sprache des Wesens*).[25] It would be these two, both as the proffering of the world and as the "*Bedingnis*" discussed in the same context, through which the nonhuman world calls the "thinging" of things into Being.[26]

How can this conjecture be reconciled with the obvious fact that today the poetic by no means constitutes the "content" of that Saying which speaks to Dasein under the reign of the *Ge-stell*? When one bears in mind that here also Heidegger conceives the essence of language as belonging to *alētheia*, it becomes clear

20. Cf. esp. *US* 202, 214 ff.
21. Cf. *US* 202, 214.
22. Cf. *US* 202.
23. *US* 257.
24. Cf. *US* 198 ff., 208 f.
25. Cf. *US* 200 ff.
26. Cf. *US* 216, 232 f.

that there is no contradiction. This denial of the poetic is brought about by the *lēthē* belonging to *alētheia*—which of course means that *lēthē*, too, belongs to the essence of language, when language is completely understood.[27]

If one were to assume, however, that the "mittence" of *alētheia* liberates the inherent "content" of Saying—the poetic— and that it also does the granting, then the next question would be: What role is left for poets and poetry? Is the characterization of the essence of language given up to this point actually in harmony with Heidegger's concept of the poet and poetry?

III

HEIDEGGER CONSIDERS THE POET—and the thinker—to be "used" (*gebraucht*). What he means by this first becomes clear in light of the above determination of the essence of language. The poet is "used" to bring the poetic into human word, whereby the poetic is the actual content of "Saying." The poet is supposed to "cor-respond" (*entsprechen*) to this content, that is, he is supposed to hearken and respond to it, to what the stream of Saying silently says to him. For this reason Heidegger called the poets *"die Entsprechenden."* They cor-respond not only to the "content," however, but also to the *alētheia* structure of Saying. For this reason Heidegger conceives of their human naming as an unconcealing. They must bring what they hear into the dimension of human language. The specific conception of the essence of language as Saying is the decisive condition of thought leading to the extraordinary and important role Heidegger attributes to the poet in the preparation of another beginning consisting in poetic dwelling.[28]

If this is the role of the poet, however, we must ask: Has Heidegger shown in any greater detail how the poet assumes and realizes it? Has Heidegger shown how a proper realization of this

27. Cf. *US* 186.
28. Erling W. Eng raised the following questions: "Is Heidegger's conception of the poet, like Hölderlin's, not a prophetic one that has more in common with the position of the ancient Hebrew prophets and psalmists than with the Greek poets? Furthermore, is this not in accord with Heidegger's effort to replace the metaphysics of light, so very Greek in character, with an 'archaeology' of the word?"

role can result in a primordial, genuine, and salutary "poetic dwelling" for the man who is not a poet, or for all of humanity?

To begin with, how does the poet assume his role, and how does he realize it? An interpretation of Hölderlin's words, "Whatever remains, however, is instituted and brought about by the poets," [29] has led Heidegger to the notion that the poet is the one who sets the "measures," the basic "standards" for the historical world of Dasein. "Poetry is the act of instituting Being verbally." [30] The poetic work maintains the standard in that it contains "that which remains" within time that tears everything away (*reissender Zeit*).[31] Thus, the poet can be said to take on his role only if he works in such a way that he sets the standard. Again Heidegger conceives of this standard-setting or measure-taking in terms of *alētheia*. The measure can be taken only by a mortal poet, and one understands this process (*die "Mass-Nahme"*) adequately only when one conceives of it as an unconcealing. This unconcealing must prepare for the "poetic dwelling" of humanity. It is the "fundamental act" [32] of "initial building." [33] It "builds" "for the dwelling of man" [34] and is therefore "the primordial letting-dwell." [35] It is here that we find most clearly delineated the role which the poet has to take on and realize, for we read, "The authentic building occurs insofar as there are poets who take the measure for the architectonic, for the blueprint (*Baugefüge*), of dwelling." [36]

From where does the poet take the measure, and who gives it to him? He takes it from "sights of the heavens" (*Anblicke des Himmels*); the "images" appear to him in the heavenly "light" (*Helle*). The heavenly light is, however—quite in accordance with the "relationship quality" (*Verhältnishaftigkeit*) of *alētheia* —permeated by "darkness." "But the heavens are not pure light." [37] The "authentic image," from which all the others are derived,[38] contains not only the familiar but also "inclusions of

---

29. "Was bleibt aber, stiften die Dichter" (cf. *HD* 31 ff.).
30. *HD* 38.
31. *HD* 37.
32. Cf. ". . . dichterisch wohnet der Mensch . . . ," *VA* 196.
33. *VA* 202.
34. *VA* 198.
35. *VA* 202.
36. *VA* 202.
37. *VA* 201.
38. *VA* 200.

the foreign." [39] It harbors "the concealed in its self-concealing." [40] The one who conceals himself is the unknown God, who appears as the "unknown" through the overtness of the heavens.[41] Thus, the measure is given to the poet ultimately by God through heavenly signs. For Heidegger, this fundamental act of building measure-taking is poetizing in the most authentic sense. He writes, "The essence of the poetic is seen by Hölderlin in measure-taking, through which the measuring of the human essence is accomplished." [42] If the essence of the poetic lies in measure-taking, then we may well conclude that the measure also allows that content which we have previously called "the poetic." [43]

Has Heidegger shown, however, how the measure *taken* by the poet and how the poetic work corresponding to the poetic comprising the ruling essence in Saying could lead to another beginning consisting in "poetic dwelling" for humanity? In order to be able to answer this question, we must obtain a better, more detailed answer to the question: In what does "poetic dwelling" consist?

IV

IN THE ESSAYS "Das Ding" and "Bauen, Wohnen, Denken," Heidegger "thought forward to" how man would dwell if and when another beginning were suddenly to arrive. His characterizations in these essays must be taken to represent his conception of a primordial, genuine, and salutary human state of affairs. Although he considers dwelling to be "the basic trait of Being, according to which mortals are" they have "yet to learn" it.[44] Man must learn to cease conceiving of himself as an *animal rationale* wanting to substantiate; he must learn to "die." He must also learn to dwell on the earth under the heavens and in the

---

39. *VA* 201.
40. *VA* 197.
41. *VA* 197.
42. *VA* 196.
43. As far as we know, Heidegger never answered the question of how the relationship between the measure and the poetic element of Saying is to be characterized.
44. *VA* 162.

sight of the gods. He must learn to experience the "nearness" of the World regions, to dwell "in" the Fourfold (*Geviert*), and to manifest and preserve its truth (*verwahren*) "in" the things.[45] This is to occur in that "the mortals foster and care for growing things and that they take it upon themselves to erect the things which do not grow," [46] so that "the thinging" of the things will be a "nearing" which really "concerns" man.[47]

In the context of this paper we do not need to take up individually the characterizations which constitute such a primordial, genuine, and salutary dwelling. Heidegger exemplifies them by showing how a "mortal" experiences the arrival of the Fourfold in the "thinging" of a jug and a bridge. But is this dwelling a "poetic" dwelling? Although in these two essays Heidegger does not designate it as such, we would answer in the affirmative, for the four regions which are experienced in "dwelling" are the same ones which nonhuman Saying points to, and the same ones which are unconcealed by the human naming of the poet and contained in the poetic work. It is also true that the "thinging" which the dwelling man experiences is the same as that which the nonhuman word as *"Bedingnis"* [48] lets occur. That this dwelling is a "poetic" dwelling is also confirmed by the fact that in his remarks on ". . . *dichterisch wohnet der Mensch* . . . ," Heidegger demands of the mortal who is not a poet that he carry out a "measuring," and he specifically calls this "measuring" "poetizing." [49] The mortal must "measure" the "dimension" of the "in between" of heaven and earth by looking up to the divinities, thereby measuring himself with the heavenly measure.[50] As we noted above, this is the measure which the poet has already taken for him.

Therefore we can now reformulate our question as follows: What actually induces the mortal who is not a poet to take up the measure which the poet has already taken for him and embodied in a poetic work? How does Heidegger actually conceive of the interconnection between the role taken up and realized by the poet and "poetic dwelling"? In searching for an answer, we find only the statement that the measure must be "spoken to man

45. *VA* 151.
46. *VA* 152, 173.
47. *VA* 179.
48. *US* 233.
49. *VA* 199 ff., 203.
50. *VA* 195.

and communicated to him through the measure-taking of poetiz-ing." [51] How is this "communicating" to be understood concretely?

If we were to take this statement literally, we would expect that the poetic works would have to be communicated to man directly, or that "esoteric" works would have to become "exoteric," if the other, "sudden," beginning were to occur for all of human-ity. But according to Heidegger there are only very few in our "needy time" who are able to perceive the lack of the salutary (*das Heillose*) in it, and only "single individuals" (*Einzelne*) are still following the traces and going after the vestiges of the holy to the extent that they "venture it with language" (*mit der Sprache wagen*).[52] How shall the "singing" of these "single indi-vidual" poets [53] find a direct way to the masses of our industrial society which—in Heidegger's own characterization—no longer hear anything but the claim of the *Ge-stell* and cor-respond to it in the language of information.

If it does not seem possible today that the measure embodied in poetic works could be communicated to mankind directly, what about the possibility of communicating it *indirectly* by making use of the fact that every man dwells in the very element in which poetizing is carried out: the language? Up to this point we have brought out only the fact that poets and thinkers dwell in a privileged way in the house of language; but doesn't it belong to the essence of every man to dwell in this house? Isn't the "authentic abode" (*eigentlicher Aufenthalt*)[54] of every man's Dasein the language? And wouldn't language "say its essence to" each individual? [55] In his various discussions of the essence of language, Heidegger did in fact consider the possibility that man might attain to a proper relationship to the true essence of lan-guage if he were prepared to engage in a "contemplative thinking experience" (*sinnend denkende Erfahrung*) with the language. Heidegger also discussed the way in which thinking might attain to the "region" (*Gegend*) in which it would experience the "prox-imity" of poetizing and be thereby transformed.[56] But it is not our present task to examine this way. In this essay we want to take

51. "Dem Menschen zugesprochen und durch die Mass-Nahme des Dichtens mitgeteilt" (*VA* 198).
52. Cf. *HW* 293 f., 250 f.
53. *HW* 251.
54. *US* 159.
55. *US* 12.
56. Cf. *US* 159.

seriously the "role" which Heidegger attributed to poets; for the poets, together with other thinkers who share the trait of being "more venturesome," are the ones who are to realize the "turn-about" (*Umkehr*).[57] As Heidegger explicitly explains, this turn-about can be realized only in the "sphere" of language.[58] It is thus clear that the "indirect communication" of the poetic work to every man is also possible only in the element of language. However, considering that for Heidegger—as we have brought out—the essence of language lies in *alētheia*, and that today Saying, as *lēthē*, withdraws totally, with the result that the poetic content withdraws as well, the "indirect communication" would have to be conceived as transforming this withdrawal of Saying into a "bringing to the fore" and "pointing to" the poetical, which in turn would have to be such that every man could hearken to it and cor-respond to it through "poetic dwelling."

If we pursue this thought further—which, in our opinion, does lie in Heidegger's characterization of the "role" of the poet—we find ourselves immediately in an *aporia*, which is perhaps inherent in Heidegger's "layout": in the essence of language as conceived by him. If the works of the poets find access to Saying —that is, to Saying in the form it has in withdrawal—and if they are to transform it into an essence of Saying which can be called "the poetic," then the power of affecting the granting nonhuman sphere would be attributed to the human sphere of the poem after all, which was itself granted as such by Saying: the power of affecting the "granting" sphere would be attributed to the "granted" sphere.

Heidegger has never discussed this *aporia*; moreover, he has never attempted to conceive concretely how single poetic works could totally transform Saying, in the form it has in withdrawal, into the poetic, even though the transformation of our own dwelling, which keeps becoming less and less poetic, into a poetic dwelling and the sudden arrival of the new beginning could not possibly occur before this condition had been fulfilled.

As a final fundamental consideration, suppose that this "indirect communication" is conceivable, and that a point has been reached at which Saying no longer withdraws its poetic content. Would this not mean that the kind of speaking we require for

57. *HW* 286.
58. *HW* 286.

everyday life and for scientific work would disappear? In the place of unequivocal, transparent statements, there would remain only Saying permeated by mystery, by *lēthē,* and the ambiguous human naming cor-responding to this Saying. It is just when one considers that the beginning of "poetic dwelling" must be preceded by a total transformation of Saying and human speaking into "the poetic," and that poetic dwelling would be conceivable only in the element of a language universally changed in this manner, that such a "goal" of Heidegger's later thinking would become a problem.

The "poetic" character of the kind of life for man on this planet to which Heidegger "thought forward" suggests a question which could just as well be directed at other attempts which strive to overcome the plight of our time and attain to a genuine and salutary state of affairs: namely, the question of whether attempts to "save" man's "creative" possibilities to be (*Seins-möglichkeiten*) from the ever increasing tendency of our time away from creativity necessitate renouncing other possibilities to be which apparently belong to man just as essentially. In particular the question is whether such attempts necessitate renouncing the possibilities lying in man's capacity for understanding and substantiating which, in the Western world, have brought him onto the road of science. Is it really unavoidable that the essence of man be determined *either* on the basis of reason *or* on the basis of mortality? Does Being in its immeasurable wealth really demand of us an either-or—such as is basic to all tendencies which recognize only one single state of affairs as "genuine"? Does the task not consist, rather, in conceiving of the essence of man and his life on this planet in a way which allows all of his possibilities to unfold?

In our "transitional" time, in which the old measures (*Maßstäbe*) totter and the new have not yet appeared, we must be thankful and open for every attempt which gives us the possibility to reflect on the arrival of new measures. But at the same time we are confronted with the task of exposing the "conditions of thought" behind each such attempt; for we must always continue to question these conditions, and we must keep the thought in flux. Particularly when the thought concerns nothing less than a radical change of being and of the essence of man, it is necessary for us to investigate thoroughly whether it has been conceived consistently and whether it has been thought out to the end.[59] The result of this investigation is: If the concern of all of Heidegger's later works is to bring about another beginning consisting in poetic dwelling, and if this entails attributing a decisive role to the poets, then it seems to us that the total conception is incomplete in the very respect which is decisive for this concern —in the treatment of the possibility of realizing the interconnection between the "role of the poet" and "poetic dwelling."

Discussion

CALVIN O. SCHRAG: Professor Marx's thesis is not only well formulated but also, in my opinion, fundamentally correct. Heidegger's overcoming of metaphysics, according to Professor Marx, is essentially the result of his development of a new "fundamental structure." This fundamental structure is presented as the structure of *alētheia* in such a way that it opens up a new approach to the meaning of truth. In this new structure *Nous* and *Logos* are dethroned as absolute monarchs—they no longer reign in an exclusive way, says Professor Marx—and mystery (*Geheimnis*) is given a much more privileged role to play. When

59. Wolfgang Zucker made the following comments: "Professor Marx raises the problem of what actual significance the prophetic poet might have in and for a world which, in the age of the *Gestell*, has reached the groundless bottom (*Bodenlosigkeit*) of the forgottenness of Being. It may be suggested that Heidegger points to a possible answer, without spelling it out, in the increased emphasis on the *Sage*. Is it correct to understand the double meaning of the German term in the sense that every stage in which thinking by its utterance (*sagen*) both manifests and conceals Being is also a stage in the mythic fate (*Geschick*) of Being itself and therefore the true word of the Saga? Must not the age of the *Gestell* therefore be understood as just a new and probably an ultimate phase of that history of Being which began with Plato's metaphysics and reached its termination in Nietzsche's devaluation of all values? If this interpretation is correct, would not the appearance of the poet announce the beginning of a new chapter in the Saga, a new beginning of both thinking and Being?"

Professor Marx responded: "I would be inclined to doubt that the term *Sage* has for Heidegger the connotation of what in German is called '*die Sage*' (*US* 253). It seems, rather, to denote the significance of a *Sagen*, which is not an *Aus-sagen* (a *Sagen* that, according to Hegel, brings whatever is thought to a total manifestation). *Sage* is, for Heidegger, the nonhuman, silent Saying, integrally belonging to *alētheia*, emanating from *lēthē* (concealment [*Geheimnis*]), and permeating all Saying. I find Professor Zucker's contribution very meaningful, though it seems to me to transcend the connotations which Heidegger associates with *Sage*" (cf. *US* 200, 252).

truth is approached in terms of mystery, an inevitable concealment accompanies it. For Heidegger, then, the meaning of truth and the sense of Being have their origin in concealment. This, says Professor Marx, is Heidegger's decisive weapon against the tradition.

The role of language in the latter-day Heidegger, continues Professor Marx, is conceived in terms of the articulation of this new fundamental structure. The most impressive instance of the articulation of this structure of *alētheia* is the thinking and speaking of poetic existence. Poetic indwelling provides a new beginning for the articulation of the fundamental structure. Professor Marx then proceeds to work out the connection between language and the structure of *alētheia* and shows how mystery in the mode of concealment is correspondent to the "unsaid."

I find myself in basic agreement with what I consider to be the central thrust of Professor Marx's "creative" interpretation of Heidegger. There are, however, three specific issues in this interpretation on which I would like to focus.

The first issue has to do with what may well be a miniscule semantical point that has little bearing on the larger design of Professor Marx's interpretation. Nevertheless, it is an issue that, if clarified, would contribute to a further understanding of Heidegger's approach to language. Professor Marx says that language as conceived by the latter-day Heidegger is the "articulation" of the structure of *alētheia*. I wonder if this characterization of language in terms of "articulation" is a proper one, particularly when the latter-day Heidegger is under discussion. This characterization is used by Heidegger in *Being and Time,* where language is discussed as that constitutive structure through which Dasein's being-in-the-world is articulated. However, Heidegger's project in *Being and Time* finds its touchstone in the method of transcendental philosophy. In the latter-day Heidegger there is a movement beyond this method and design. As a result, language assumes a much closer proximity to Being itself; it becomes the "house of Being." It would thus seem that language is rethought in such a manner that it becomes the concrete presence of Being rather than an articulation of transcendental structures. The term *articulation* unavoidably suggests that language is a "vehicle" or "instrument" or even an "external sign" for some kind of recessed meaning. This may falsify what would appear to be a much closer connection between thinking and speaking, language and meaning, in the philosophy of the latter-day Heidegger. In any case, I wonder if Professor Marx might address himself to this issue, elaborate on the propriety of the use of *articulation*, and possibly explicate the difference between the early and the latter-day Heidegger with regard to the status of language.

The second point that I wish to raise is solely a matter of clarification. The new fundamental structure of *alētheia* involves, according to Professor Marx, a kind of double movement of concealment and unconcealment. At one point Professor Marx states that concealment permeates the sphere of unconcealment. I suspect, but am not certain, that the converse is also true, that unconcealment permeates concealment. It is not clear from the context what status the "sphere of unconcealment" has and what occasions its connection with concealment. Is the sphere of concealment the sphere of an irreducible mystery, or is it simply the not yet unconcealed? Are the significations of "concealment" and "unconcealment" somehow dialectically borne by each other, or is a priority (either logical or ontological) to be granted to one over the other? Perhaps Professor Marx might further elucidate this somewhat puzzling issue.

The third issue that I wish to raise in a sense goes beyond the designs of Professor Marx's paper, yet it strikes me as being singularly important for an understanding of the philosophy of the latter-day Heidegger. How does one square Heidegger's new beginning through poetic indwelling with his insistence on the importance of historicity (*Geschichtlichkeit*)? Heidegger has urged us to take history, in its fundamental meaning, seriously. Indeed, in the end Being becomes historicized, enabling us to speak of the "historicity of Being." At the same time, however, we are urged to consider the perspectives of poetic thought. As Professor Marx is quick to point out, Heidegger is not the first philosopher to appeal to poetic thinking and indwelling. Professor Marx alludes to Schelling, who saw the task of philosophy as that of bringing mankind to a state of paradise in which he could live in harmony with his own natural powers. Similar allusions, it would seem to me, could have been made to Schopenhauer's appeal to aesthetic contemplation and Nietzsche's claim that only in the aesthetic phenomenon is life justified.

What seems to characterize these traditional "aesthetic" approaches, however, is that they are, in the end, a-historical. Apparently this is not the case with Heidegger—or is it? For all that Heidegger has to say about the historical as a determination of Being, might it be that in the end he retires from concrete historical thinking and comes to rest in a poetico-mystical vision? Admittedly, the state of affairs is somewhat more complex than this. There can be for Heidegger no simple return to the aesthetically oriented approaches which have intermittently appeared in the tradition; for aesthetics itself is "trans-valued" in a fundamental way. Yet, it does appear that, on the issue of historical thinking, Heidegger is able to offer us at most only a metahistorical scheme in which the concrete experience of the historical is placed in jeopardy. A metahistorical approach seems destined to conceal the concrete solicitations of meaning within the mundane lifeworld of historical dialogue and action and, to this extent, remains impoverished.[60] I wonder if Professor Marx, in conclusion, might address himself to this implicit criticism of the project of the latter-day Heidegger.

MARX: Professor Schrag is entirely justified in criticizing my use of the word *articulation*. In the original version of my paper I did say that language as conceived by the latter-day Heidegger is the *articulation* of this structure of *alētheia*. I lost sight of the fact that in *Being and Time* Heidegger had called *Rede* "the articulation of intelligibility." [61] He thus had used the word *articulation* as a specific term to denote the structure of language as he conceived it at that time. I certainly did not want to confuse his early conception of language with that of his later writings, to which I addressed myself exclusively. Moreover, if the English word *articulation* suggests, as Professor Schrag points out, that language is a " 'vehicle' or 'instrument' or even an 'external sign' for some

60. In response to Professor Schrag's remarks, Walter Biemel made the following comments: "Heidegger is not looking for a mythical solution, nor for a standstill of history. He wishes, rather, to place historicity in Being itself. The fact that we are unable to predict this history by no means signifies that we are unable to overcome it. Heidegger is not a Platonist. History comes to pass in the dialogue between Being and Dasein, a dialogue which is conceived of in terms of address and response. Heidegger does not praise a utopian final phase, although he occasionally makes suggestions which could give rise to such a misunderstanding; these suggestions prepare for history as the history of Being. This is the sense in which Being must be conceived of as e-vent. Thus, I should like to object to Professor Schrag's assertion that Heidegger does not take history as seriously as he did at first."

61. SZ 161.

kind of recessed meaning," then for that reason also it was wrong of me to use the word *articulation*.

First, to follow Professor Schrag's suggestion that I briefly characterize the difference existing between Heidegger's early conception of language and his later one, I might point out that, for the early Heidegger, *logos* (*Rede*) and language (*Sprache*) belonged to the existential structure of Dasein.[62] *Reden* is the way that Dasein, because of its constitutional factor of "disclosedness," "signifies" (*bedeutet*)—that is, moves in an interpreting way within the meaningful whole, articulating that which makes up whatever it has in an "attuned" (*befindlichen*) way understood in its "sense" [63]—and is, as articulated *Rede*, spoken out. The meaningful whole—and the specific meanings constituting it—are in turn founded in significance (*Bedeutsamkeit*), which denotes for Heidegger the structure of everyday world.[64]

Since meanings in turn found the Being of word and language,[65] one might argue that already, in *Being and Time*, language and word emanate from the world. However, world was at that time still the "whither" (*das Woraufhin*) of transcendence, as I remarked in my paper. Accordingly, Heidegger could not very well have conceived of *Rede* and *Sprache* as being "given" and "granted" by world. Such a conception became possible only after he did away with the notion of transcendence precisely because its direction of movement was held to be wrong. As I tried to show in my paper, only at that time did it become feasible for him to conceive of the granting of meanings as a nonhuman occurrence brought about as one way of "*Ereignen*," which brings everything into its own. Only then could this nonhuman occurrence become the silent way of Saying, which grants and gives to Dasein meanings that Dasein can listen to silently and then respond to by bringing whatever is "*zugesagt*" to humansounding word and human speech. World is then no longer the environmental world in which Dasein lives in its everyday ways; rather, world is the Fourfold of the four "neighborhoods." Nor is *Sage* founded in meanings which, in turn, are founded in the meaningful whole and in significance (*Bedeutsamkeit*). It is perhaps doubtful whether one can, within the context of the philos-

62. *SZ* 161.
63. *SZ* 151.
64. *SZ* 87.
65. *SZ* 87.

ophy of the latter-day Heidegger, legitimately speak of "meanings" and of "sense." However, in order to illustrate the difference between Heidegger's early conception of language and his later one, one might say that *Sage*, as the *Sage* of world, Being, and *Ereignen*, lets meanings arrive; this is in contrast to word and speech being founded in meanings, as was the case earlier, or as Heidegger put it at that time, "To significations, words accrue." [66]

Second, I have tried to show in my paper how Heidegger's latter-day conception of *alētheia* changed from that in *Being and Time*. I might explicitly add here that this later conception has undergone various changes, though Heidegger never marked these changes himself. I do not believe, however, that he has at any time held that "unconcealment permeates concealment" within the overt dimension which *alētheia* represents for him. Unconcealment originates in concealment; this origin stays with that which it has originated and therefore keeps permeating unconcealment. For that reason, a dialectic of concealment and unconcealment cannot exist. Heidegger's conception of concealment as the "source" of unconcealment can clearly be seen, as I contend in my paper, from the way he has conceived of Saying —as a "stream" which originates in that era of silence and mystery. Whatever nonhuman Saying says originates in concealment, and whatever is unconcealed remains permeated by it. I have quoted in my paper Heidegger's view that this sphere of mystery contains that which will always remain mystery as well as that which has not yet been un-concealed.

Third, I would not want to characterize Heidegger's present position as a "poetico-mystical" one, as Professor Schrag does. I would agree that the "mittence" (*Geschick*) of the essence ruling in technology seems to be the last one which commits man (*schickt ihn*) within a whole series of such "mittences" which, in its entirety, Heidegger has called the "*Seins-Geschick* of metaphysics." They all are "epochs of error." Once metaphysics has been overcome, a "*Seins-Geschick*" for Dasein no longer seems to exist. If world should suddenly occur, Dasein would no longer be committed and yet would respond "poetically" to that which poetic Saying says, either through creative thought or creative poetry, or simply through poetic dwelling. It seems that at that time Dasein could no longer be characterized as "historical" (*ge-*

66. SZ 161; cf. also SZ 87.

schichtlich), nor would it experience anything "historical" in any sense remotely reminiscent of the significance which we ascribe to the world's historicity and history. But the open dimension of *alētheia* as well as all the movement of concealment and unconcealment would remain, granting presence and absence; and Dasein would remain as the one which is in a unique way able to "understand" such presence and absence in a poetic way. Since one would assume that these occurrences would not remain the "same," a "term" should be found to express the possibility of change even in those times. Heidegger has, however, not provided such a "term" within his total conception of the "other beginning." I surmise that it is ultimately this lack which Professor Schrag has noted and which has prompted his question.

LASZLO VERSÉNYI: Professor Marx seems to imply that the relationship between *Gestell* and *Geviert* is a disjunctive one historically—that in a given age the world is disclosed either in terms of the one or the other but not both—and that disclosure of the world in terms of the *Gestell* is an exclusively modern phenomenon. I would like to question both of these statements.

If *Gestell* is Heidegger's term for the type of approach to the world that subjects all things as items of production (*Her-stellen*) to man's might [67] rather than letting them be—that is, letting them "gather the Fourfold" [68] into an essential disclosure—then I wonder whether both of these modes of disclosure have not been present at the same time throughout history. Could not people— and quite possibly the majority of people—have approached a Greek temple, in the fifth century B.C., for example, in terms of the *Gestell* and viewed it as an expression of the wealth, accomplishments, and consummate productive might and power of contemporary Athens? Cannot people still view a work of architecture in terms of the *Geviert*—as the focal point of disclosure which gathers together heaven and earth, mortals and immortals, and opens up all that is essential in the world? If the essential trait of modern technology is, for Heidegger, that it is directed at world mastery through calculative thinking, has not such an attack on the world been present to some extent at every stage of world history? For example, was it not present in the ancient

67. "Jenen herausfordernden Anspruch, der den Menschen dahin versammelt, das Sichentbergende als Bestand zu bestellen" (VA 27).
68. VA 146.

Sophists' claim of universal *technē* and *polymathēma,* which made man the self-assured and self-certain contriver and measurer of all things? It seems, if one defines essential and unessential thought as Heidegger does, that neither is a modern phenomenon but both have coexisted at all times.

MARX: Professor Versényi poses his question with specific reference to the two passages in Heidegger's volume *Vorträge und Aufsätze* which define *Ge-stell* and *Geviert,* respectively. My answer will refer only to what I consider to be Heidegger's conceptions in these paragraphs and how he would, in my view, have to answer this question.

Ge-stell is the name for the specific "mittence" of Being which occurs as the total withdrawal (*lēthē*) of "the poetic" (*das Dichterische*), and this opens world (*Geviert*). Such withdrawal "commissions" Dasein to unconceal being as mere material (*Bestand*). Since *Ge-stell* indicates the universal way in which this "mittence" (*Seins-Geschick*) occurs today, it does not seem legitimate to characterize any period in the course of "*Seinsgeschichte*" other than the present one as *Ge-stell.* Similarly, it does not seem legitimate to characterize the comportment in which people might have "viewed" Being as an expression of the world's accomplishments and consummate might and power.

The world (*Geviert*) would appear for Heidegger only if and when "another beginning" of "poetic dwelling" were to suddenly (*jäh*) come about. That arrival must be prepared by the poetizing of a few poets and by the thinkers, whose thinking has already undergone the "turn" (*Kehre*). The "turn" in the thoughts of the thinker and the "turn" of the *Seinsgeschick* are not the same, though the former is necessary for the latter to happen. Such preparatory thinking of world can take place only after the withdrawal (*lēthē*) of world has been experienced and thought as *Seinsgeschick.* Once this is done, thinking can conceive that world had once before appeared, namely, in the experiences of the pre-Socratics, and might appear once again. Though world (*Geviert*) might have been experienced in one way or the other during the rule of metaphysics, it did not appear as a *Seinsgeschick;* and this is why Heidegger considers metaphysics as an "epoch of error" denoting the "rule of error." Today, the withdrawal of world is complete, and it can reappear only if and when "another beginning" should come about.

Professor Versényi, therefore, understood me quite correctly when I considered *Ge-stell* and *Geviert* to be "exclusive" of each other. I would, however, not wish to use the term *disjunctive* to characterize the specific way that the one "excludes" the other; for *Seinsgeschick* is an occurrence of *alētheia* and therefore is today "present" in the very form of withdrawal (*lēthē*) that *Ge-stell* represents.

THEODORE J. KISIEL: I would like to corroborate certain echoes which I heard in Professor Birault's talk and which became stronger in some of Professor Marx's comments. They relate to just how the "measuring of man's poetic dwelling" may be brought about in an age of technology, that is, to the possible transposition of *Gestell* to *Geviert*. The first of these echoes was sounded when Professor Birault indicated that philosophers are thinkers, but that thinkers are not necessarily philosophers. I ask myself, "Who else?" I would suggest the scientist.

Such an assertion immediately comes up against the seemingly antiscientific thrust of Heidegger's "backtrack," epitomized in the frequently quoted sentence "Science itself does not think." But this intentionally provocative remark does not mean that scientists do not think and are not concerned with the issues of thinking. Heidegger indicates that revolutionary innovators of science, men like Bohr and Heisenberg, move beyond the calculative methods of their science and on to various levels of thinking in its essential sense when they are led to make decisions with regard to the fundamental concepts of their science, thereby creating new ways of posing questions and seeking answers.[69]

If scientists are thinkers in the Heideggerian sense, in their way they also dwell in close proximity to the poet. Scientists point to a certain poetic emotion that guides them in their discoveries, which ultimately evoke such criteria, or "measures," for a scien-

69. Walter Biemel made the following comments: "In Heidegger's view it is in philosophy that a basic project of Being comes to pass; science establishes itself on this ground. The modern philosophical projection of world makes modern science possible. The understanding of being as a whole changes here; this is the decisive moment. Being (*Seiendes*) becomes object. Here we find already the characteristic trait which later comes to the fore so clearly in modern technique. We can make a distinction between the opening up of a domain and its occupation. According to Heidegger, the opening up of a domain comes to pass in philosophy's projection of being. Anyone who questions his own science and comes to a new project of being is, in Heidegger's view, a philosopher."

tific theory as simplicity, symmetry, and elegance, criteria which are as much aesthetic as logical. Einstein goes so far as to call his experience of the cosmic harmonies a numinous experience, a religious emotion, an experience of the holy.

Poets in the proper sense, in dialogue with such thinkers, have responded in kind. Could it be, then, that "abstract" art, such as that inspired by relativity theory, and technological sculpture and perhaps even cybernetic music contain the seeds for the transposition of the "prelude" (*Gestell*) to the "event" (*Geviert*)? If so, a jet aircraft stands on the runway not simply as available stock but also as a thing of beauty. "Das Flugzeug fliegt": this might well be an example of a thinging thing that gathers the world of the Fourfold, as Saint-Exupéry's novels illustrate. The scientific metric understood in this sense would then contribute directly to the poetic measures of man's dwelling in a technological world.

MARX: My answer is limited to restating what I take to be Heidegger's own thinking. I agree with Professor Kisiel that the projects (*Entwürfe*) of a number of scientists, those projects that are fundamentally concerned with the "essence" of all that is, are philosophical ones in their own right. However, they cannot be considered as responses to the "silent Saying," which in our times, the reign of the *Ge-stell*, withdraws "the poetic" (*das Dichterische*). They are certainly not attempts to respond to the projects' nonhuman silent Saying, which points to "the poetic," that is, to the Fourfold, and which, through the nonhuman word, lets the "thinging" of things (*Bedingnis*) be. They are responses to the way language withdraws "the poetic" in its *lēthē* and commits Dasein to answer through the "language of information."

The dialogue between contemporary poets and philosophizing scientists is taking place under the rule of the *Ge-stell*. Heidegger refers to *Ge-stell* as a "prelude" only because a recognition of this "essence" implies the awareness that man is the only entity that can respond to whatever "mittence" might commission him. Once man has become aware of his "role," he may also respond to demands of a "mittence" which shows (*zeigt*) "the poetic."

9 / Panel Discussion

Laszlo Versényi: The preceding papers have dealt with the new beginning that Heidegger wants to initiate in his latest writings on language, and I want to raise, very briefly, a question concerning our need for such a new beginning for thought. Perhaps the best way to articulate this question is to compare this new beginning with an old beginning, the historical beginning of philosophy in Western thought. This old beginning was above all a critical beginning. Philosophy emancipated itself from poetry by ceasing to be an unquestioning acceptance and transmission of a more or less inspired tradition. No longer satisfied with merely pronouncing, chanting, and incanting, philosophy became, instead, a raising of questions, an asking for reasons and justification, a reflecting, measuring, and judging. Heidegger's new beginning is in many respects a reversal of the old. The two languages, philosophy and poetry, that the old beginning separated are now to be brought together again. Critical, dialectical thinking and the language of reasons must be overcome, and a more essential type of thought, a more essential type of language, must be brought into its own.

I share Professor Marx's uneasiness concerning the responsibility of this new mode of thought that is responsible not to itself but to something wholly other, to whose call it is a response. However, the only question I want to raise at this point is: Why is this new beginning necessary? As Heidegger answers this question frequently and in many different contexts, I will arbitrarily choose one formulation of his answer namely, that which appears

[261]

in *Die Frage nach dem Ding* and *Der Satz vom Grund*. In these works Heidegger indicates why, in his view, the new beginning is necessary by appraising the nature and outcome of Kant's *Critique of Pure Reason*. Heidegger asks, What happens in Kant's *Critique of Pure Reason*? His answer is that a critique is a rational inquiry that aims at clarifying the structure, determining the scope, and ascertaining the power of what is inquired into. Therefore, when a critique is turned upon reason, its aim is "the self-knowledge of reason, confronted with and left to itself. A critique is thus the execution of the innermost rationality of reason." It is self-directed thought whose sole dimension is "the I-ness of the I, the subjectivity of the subject." [1]

Such a critique of pure reason is a critique of the "faculty of fundamental principles," where *faculty* means power, the ground in which something originates, and *fundamental* means whatever underlies something as its ground. Thus, a critique of pure reason as the faculty of fundamental principles is a critique of reason as the "founding foundation" and "ground-laying ground" of all.[2] It is an inquiry that establishes reason, that is, human subjectivity, as the measure of all that can be. A critique is self-grounding thought in a double sense; it finds its own foundations and grasps its own ground, and, at the same time, it lays itself down as the measure and ground of all.

A critique as self-grounding thought is a radicalization of the principle of sufficient reason. The principle that nothing *is* without reason or ground means that nothing *can be* unless it is supported by reasons and rests on grounds; and these reasons and grounds, in order to be sufficient, must be sufficient to reason itself, must be reasons given within the framework projected by reason in its demand for reasons. This being so, the principle of sufficient reason is not only demanded by and grounded in human reason as its foundation; it also makes human reason, the subjectivity of the subject, the ultimate ground and foundation of all truth and Being.

Heidegger's objection to this subjectivization and humanization of Being and truth is straightforward. It results not in essential disclosure but in concealment, and leads to the oblivion of the Being that has been characteristic of Western philosophy from Plato to Nietzsche. The rule of reason as the rule of sub-

1. *FD* 96; *SG* 132.
2. *SG* 131.

jectivity is an attack on the world that does not allow the world to reveal itself as it is in itself but rather subjects and subordinates the world to man's will to power for the sake of establishing man's "absolute rule over the earth." [3] When man becomes the pre-eminent subject, everything in the world becomes subject to his aim-directed calculations, and all is subjected to his might. Man's "relation to beings is the mastering advance into world conquest and world rule." [4] Thus, the final result of the rational project, of humanistic-subjectivistic metaphysics qua world projection for world conquest, is the rise of modern technology, this attempt at a mastery of all things that forces all that is to reveal itself in the manner most serviceable to our insatiable will to power.

Now, clearly, if Heidegger is right in his genealogy of technology as the ultimate offspring of Platonic-Cartesian-Kantian rationality, which is essentially nothing but the will to power whose ceaseless clamor we cannot resist, even though it makes us forgetful of Being and truth, then the time has come for a new beginning, for an abandoning of critical reason and an initiating of a new, more essential type of thought. But I doubt that Heidegger's genealogy is right. In his critique of critical reason he conveniently disregards one essential aspect of Kant's *Critique*, namely, that it was a critique of reason in the sense of setting limits for reason and curbing reason's unreasonable demands for reasons.

If Kant had forgotten or ignored the fact that the reasons reason gives to reason can never be totally sufficient to reason because they are grounded in reason and as such cannot serve as its grounding ground, and that therefore rational thought can never of itself overcome its ultimate groundlessness and find an unshakable foundation on which to rest, then Heidegger could indeed accuse critical reason—at least as far as it is alive in Kant's *Critique*—of being ultimately uncritical and, in its thoughtlessness, of laying a groundless foundation for our attempts at world mastery. But it seems to me that this is not the case. Indeed, the greatest accomplishment of the *Critique* is that in it, for all its demand for reasons, reason clearly recognizes that ultimate reasons and unconditional grounds are not within

3. *N II* 166.
4. *N II* 171.

its domain; that even its own demand for the unconditional ground of all that is conditioned is not an unconditional demand but one conditioned and demanded by the nature of reason itself. Recognizing this, reason curbs itself (in the *Critique*); it imposes limits on its own unsatisfiable and, therefore, unreasonable demand. In this way the critique of reason culminates in the self-criticism of reason, which leads not to its overextension but to its proper restraint. In other words, far from being bent on the universal mastery of all through technology, critical reason recognizes its own powerlessness to ever attain an absolute ground —in itself or anywhere else—and thereby masters itself. This is its greatest virtue: not world mastery, but self-mastery.

I do not want to overemphasize this particular example of a Heideggerian interpretation that does not quite do justice to what is interpreted; it is merely an illustration of the questionable nature of Heidegger's approach to much of Western thought. What I want to emphasize is that, if Heidegger's account of the birth of technology out of reason by the will to power is questionable, then, quite possibly, so is his call for a new beginning; and the thinking of the new beginning—no longer being critical—is incapable to decide whether this call for a new beginning is questionable or not. It seems that, from the point of view of the new beginning, the literal truth of what Heidegger says about the history of thought is almost beside the point. The story Heidegger tells us is so striking, has such persuasive power, that, even if all its particular points should be false, the story might still be regarded as true in a larger sense—namely, as revealing in the manner of a magnificent metaphor more than any true but pedestrian account ever could. This would mean, however, that in the new beginning we are already taking Heidegger's account poetically, as poetic rather than philosophical truth, and have thus already succumbed to that from which philosophy in its patient and critical reflection tends to protect us.

We have already succumbed, therefore, to one tyranny, the tyranny of poetic thought, which, to my mind, seems every bit as dangerous for man as the tyranny of thoughtless technology. To be safe from both of these, to master ourselves rather than to be mastered and overwhelmed by either poetic or technological thinking, we need precisely that which Heidegger wants to overcome: critical, reflective, dialectical thought and language.

JAMES M. EDIE: My comments will be directed primarily to Joseph J. Kockelmans and Otto Pöggeler, since their papers deal with those aspects of the philosophy of language of which I have some knowledge and in which I am primarily interested.

What most impresses the philosopher of language who approaches Heidegger's thought on this subject from without—let us say, from the viewpoint of phenomenology on the one hand (Husserl) and from the viewpoint of contemporary analytic philosophy on the other (Wittgenstein)—is not the great richness of this thought but rather its seeming poverty. In saying this I am thinking primarily of Heidegger's repeated definition of the essence of language as "pointing out," "showing," "letting appear," "handing down," "rendering free," "offering," and the like. These various expressions all serve to bring out only one of language's fundamental aspects. Speaking, Heidegger says, shows what is present and conceals what is absent; it brings what was unsaid out into the light and lets what has been said recede; it makes things be things and the world be world. Though he may occasionally allude to other aspects of linguistic usage, this is apparently, for him, language's "essence," whereas all the rest is accidental. But language is used not only for pointing out and for showing (even when we take these terms in their full Heideggerian import). It is also used to sigh, to command, to request, to pray, to enquire, *to lie*, to express wishes, conditions, and counterfactual conditions, simply to avoid silence, and for many other purposes. Heidegger seems not only to emphasize the illocutionary usages of words to the exclusion of everything else but even to ignore altogether the existence of such other perlocutionary functions and forms of sentences and words.

It may be objected that Heidegger is not just a philosopher of language and is not concerned with providing a complete account of the many diverse and complex uses of language, that he is concerned primarily with an attempt to "think Being," and that his remarks on language are only incidental to his project of rescuing Being from the oblivion into which it has fallen in Western thought. However, we cannot simply accept his claim that he is the first philosopher in history to have understood the "ontological difference" at its face value. Marshall McLuhan also claims that he is above and beyond the critical evaluation of his thought by those who remain caught in "linear" language. In the case of Heidegger, his "thinking of Being" also involves, at least incidentally, a philosophy of language. We must, then, judge what he is saying, at least in part, in the light of what other philosophers have said and are saying on this subject. He is not the only or the first philosopher to have put the phenomenon of language at the center of his preoccupations. Leaving Husserl and Wittgenstein aside, think only of Vico! Heidegger is a solitary thinker, seated above the clouds, alone, on a mountain in the Black Forest. He is the ideal opposite of the kind of philosopher one encounters in Oxford or Cambridge, who continually tests his own insights, assertions, and arguments against the critical acumen of his colleagues' judgments and thus always seems to philosophize publicly and, so to speak, in committee. This is not to judge the one or the other but to distinguish them. Each attitude carries with it its own dangers and tyrannies. Heidegger certainly has the right to pursue his philosophical career as he best sees fit, but can we say the same of his disciples and expositors—at least of those who wish to make his thought available to others? Do they not have some philosophical obligation to confront other currents of thought, particularly those dealing with the same problems and sometimes even arguing similar positions? If Heidegger has genuine insights into the problems of the philosophy of language, should these not be explicitly related to what the rest of the world is doing and thinking? It is, at least, to provoke this kind of response from the commentators that I am formulating this brief remark.

My final point can be made very briefly. Throughout the papers presented on Heidegger's philosophy of language we have heard again and again the term *thought* (*Denken*). We have not heard much about perception, imagination, or the other forms of intentionality. We have heard mainly about hermeneutic thought, apophantic thought, poetic thought, the thought of being, and so on. It seems impossible to deny that "thought" is a category of almost mystical importance in Heidegger's philosophy. He takes thought in a seemingly very global, vague, and loose sense to cover all the possible forms of intentionality, to be synonymous with consciousness itself. Like Descartes (to whom he is not often compared), Heidegger seems to take thought to include thinking, feeling, imagining, willing, and remembering, and even to include sensing and affectivity. My warning is that the philosopher who ignores the hard earned phenomenological distinctions operative among the various structures of consciousness (such as thinking, perceiving, imagining, evaluating, and so on) is ultimately going to have to relearn them. Thinking also has a narrow and precise sense which is eidetically fixed and distinct from other forms of intentionality. Heidegger does not turn his back on the work which phenomenology has accomplished in distinguishing the levels of intentionality; he simply ignores it. For this I reproach him. I think that one of the reasons his notion of the hermeneutic is so hopelessly vague—nobody here has been able to clarify it—is in part that Heidegger has no phenomenology of perception. The prereflexive, the prepredicative, the fully thematic, are all conflated into one "thought." This becomes even more serious if *thought* is to be replaced by language (*Sprache*) without distinction and qualification. It will not do simply to say that "*Logos . . .* has its source both in language and in man himself." These two sources are not coordinate; one is ontologically subordinate to the other. Language and consciousness are not coordinate sources of experience; it is only Homo sapiens who speaks, and the experience of speaking cannot be arbitrarily inflated to include all other levels and kinds of experience without distinction.

Again, it is not a question of Heidegger against Husserl or of Heidegger against Wittgenstein, but rather a question of the patient and sometimes humble philosophical effort to test the one by the other.

STANLEY A. ROSEN: Although it is not necessary for me to praise Heidegger in the context of this work, in this brief commentary I am limited to alluding to what I consider to be the main features of the fundamental problem in his treatment of language. The essence of my criticism is as follows: First, I believe that Heidegger's account of Western metaphysics is mistaken at crucial points, particularly where he presents an interpretation of Plato. Second, I believe that his own overcoming of Western metaphysics is, in fact, a radical exaggeration of tendencies long visible in the history of Western metaphysics—most clearly, although by no means exclusively, in the post-Hegelian attacks on reason, culminating in Nietzsche's celebration of art. Third, I believe that we take nothing away from Heidegger's genius by saying that his teaching, once expressed by him, can be restated in the language of the tradition with no greater strain than that required for assimilating the teaching of any other major thinker. Fourth, and last, I believe that Heidegger's thought, when considered in its entirety, terminates in the most radical of all aporiae, one that may be regarded as implicit either simply in human thought or, if you prefer, in an excessively daring, excessively hubristic effort to replace language with silence.

The question of Heidegger's interpretation of his predecessors is an important one. He has insisted on such an interpretation, and his insistence and persuasiveness have had an influence on others. In my view, Heidegger has failed to provide us with an adequate interpretation of Plato and, therefore, of the difference between Plato and Aristotle. For this reason, if for no other, his account of the subsequent progress of Western thought is one-dimensional and therefore more forceful than persuasive. For our present purposes, we need not linger over this particular issue.

Generally speaking, Heidegger's reading of Greek philosophy strikes me as Gothic rather than Mediterranean. He exaggerates the *lachrymae rerum,* and, despite his reverence for Heraclitus, he has forgotten at least half of the implication of the *pais paizōn.* Heidegger has not done justice to the irony or playfulness of Eros, and so he dehumanizes or silences Eros by transforming it into agriculture or viniculture. With all respect for the *The Will to Power,* one cannot philosophize with a hammer when studying Plato. The most important consequence of Heidegger's hammer is not radically different from the consequences of Ockham's razor. Like the contemporary ordinary linguistic analysts, Heidegger interprets the Platonic *on* and *ousia* as a forgetting of the temporality of presence. He reinforces this temporalization of *on, ousia,* and finally *idea* by releasing *poiēsis* from its subordination to *physis,* or, differently stated, by historicizing *physis.* In ordinary English, the emancipation of time and poetry from the timeless order of *logos,* or theoretical discourse, results not simply in the replacement of *theōria* by poetic thinking but in the replacement of thinking by listening, of speech by silence. As I have suggested, this result is implicit in Western thought, metaphysical or otherwise.

Instead of offering a historical pedigree, let me state the problem itself. All language, whether of Being or beings, is finite, determinate, and hence negative as well as affirmative. This insight goes back at least to Plato, but I mention only the modern formulation, *omnis determinatio est negatio*. My own hermeneutic of this principle is as follows: Every manifestation of Being, whether a thing, a mood, or a speech, to give three examples, conceals, and in that sense negates, the manifestation of Being as free from negative determinations. At the same time, there can be no apprehension of thing, mood, or speech (to retain my three examples) except *as* (*als*) thing, mood, or speech. Therefore, the manifestation of Being is apprehended as what it is, or as not anything else, which in turn points not merely to its own formal structure but away from that structure toward the *as* as such, if I may use the expression, toward difference as difference. This, I believe, is the main point of Heidegger's Being interpretation; I add, parenthetically, Wittgenstein's remark: What I am seeking is the grammatical difference.

The dual function of the negative aspect of determination is to provide us with things and the non-thingly manifestation of things; and this is as evident to metaphysicians as it is to Heideggerian postmetaphysicians. But the non-thingly manifestation of things is itself accessible only in and through the determinations of languages: words and their relations, *logos*, or dianoetic discursiveness. It is not accessible in, through, or as silence. Although one may grant that things and words, to say nothing of difference as difference, are silent, it is senseless to maintain that they say to us, precisely in their silence, their significance, which we then incorporate into speech. One stretch of silence is exactly as silent, and hence as nonsignificative, as another, prior to speech. I believe it is a very radical misapprehension of the truth to speak of a "language of silence"—one that finally makes the distinction between speech and silence impossible. Silence signifies, thanks to the articulateness of language. This language may well be poetic rather than theoretico-logical. I would add, however, that it must be good and beautiful, rather than bad and ugly, poetry. In any case, every speech about, or every bespeaking of, difference as difference is different from difference as difference by virtue of its own determinate, indeed, reified (in the broadest sense), nature. The differences among speeches about difference as difference become visible thanks to the adequacy of the articulateness of the speech, or its ontic structure, subtlety, and density. The ontological adequacy of language is a function of its ontic adequacy and therefore of its ontic nature. In other words, we cannot talk about Being except by talking about beings, and we ought not to try. The result is too often not new, but very old, and very bad, poetry. It is the ontic determinations of language and experience that bring us before things, differences, and difference as difference, permitting us to say what is the difference between one speech and another. If these determinations are temporalized, and reconstituted as perspectives, projections, poems, and "mittences," they disintegrate into differences. Difference as difference is no longer visible; one speech becomes as good as another, or indistinguishable from silence; and the result is nihilism.

I am very much distressed by the failure of Heidegger's students to appreciate that there must be a difference between good and bad speech, a difference that is essentially connected to the difference between good and bad actions. I deplore the radical neglect by "fundamental ontologists" of the political implications—in the human, historical, and hence ontic sense—of their ontological pursuit of or subordination to the "mittences" of Being. The result is very much like the mathematical ontology which they ostensibly reject or wish to supplement. Must we be content with a passive "responsibility" to a silent, discontinuous, and hence incoherent Being, which entails an active irresponsibility to human conditions for the possibility of all speech?

THOMAS LANGAN: In the course of our discussions two tendencies in the interpretation of Heidegger's philosophy have been calling to one another from mountains which are farthest apart. The one tendency we may call that of the Heideggerians of the radical new beginning; the other, that of the topologists of Being. Two responsible interpretations have come about because of an ambiguity in Heidegger's thought which has been reigning there from his analysis in *Being and Time* of the hermeneutic circle of interpretation to his call in "Time and Being" to think Being directly, without the mediation of the beings (*Seienden*)—in other words, to go beyond metaphysics definitively. How can Heidegger ask us to do that when he has said in *Holzwege*, "Being never comes to be without the beings"?

We can perhaps get at this problem by reflecting for a moment on the paradox of finite creativity as it manifests itself in language. An original poetic utterance manifests the language speaking. Language can only speak when Dasein understands. If an original utterance is in total discontinuity with what has been said before, no one can understand it. If, however, an utterance is only a repetition of what has been said before, it is small talk (*Gerede*), or in the region of merely calculative thinking.

These reflections on that originative poetic utterance in which Being manifests itself while dissimilating itself are situated at the heart of the paradox of finite creativity. Hegel assured the intelligibility of history by robbing it precisely of this essential element of creativity. The forward steps in the becoming of the absolute Idea involve no creating; the movement is a coming back to itself, an *Er-Innerung,* an interiorizing return of the absolute principle from the exteriorization of itself that occurred when it op-posed itself in order to know itself. The Heideggerian *Ereignis* is no negation of the negation; it is the manifestation of a new aspect of Being, which, because it is only one, obscures the other aspects.

If each "mittence" (*Geschick*) of Being were in every respect radically discontinuous with the earlier epochs of Being's history, there could be no *Nach-denken* of the *Irre.* Yet is not this *Nach-denken* a necessary condition for Dasein's openness to the future gifts of Being? Is it not the way we are to hold open the place (*Ort*) of its *Er-eignen?* Although Being takes possession of Dasein, the waiting thinker, as Heidegger tells us in *From the Experience of Thinking,* must know when and where to risk the step backward (*Schritt zurück*). The topology of Being cannot cause an *Ereignis,* which is a gift; but it does fulfill, it seems to me, two functions essential to Dasein: (1) Such a *Nachdenken* is the highest preparation for the dawn of the new beginning. (2) It is how the shepherds of Being ontically dwell in authenticity—by gathering up all the sense they can from the lights and shadows of Being's past illumination and concealment. My question is whether this sketch holds promise for those who would try to bring the interpreters emphasizing the radicalism of the new beginning together with those affirming the continuing importance of historicity and topology.

WALTER BIEMEL: I should like to discuss two points in Professor Versényi's criticism which, in my view, seem to be unjust with respect to Heidegger. First, Professor Versényi describes Heidegger's position as if it were a relapse into a prephilosophical period in which poetry occupied the place of thought. In this relapse the gains, that is, the progress reached with the rise of philosophy, were given up. If such were the case, we would have to protect ourselves from Heidegger as from the greatest danger; for to concern oneself with him and to have dealings with him would mean, basically, to abandon the efforts of thought and to fall back into a poetic "playing."

It is important, it seems to me, to try to come to grips with this point. Although Heidegger says a great deal about poetry, this by no means signifies a relapse into a prephilosophical dimension. Plato, whom Professor Versényi likes to quote, also speaks very poetically. This does not mean that he abandons philosophy; his poetic speaking is meant precisely to bring people to philosophy.

When Heidegger talks about poetry, he speaks not as a poet but as one who wishes to understand what comes to pass in poetry. He regains for poetry its truth dimension, in which its genuine justification is to be found. This process begins in Kant and can be followed through Schelling and Hegel to Nietzsche. The issue here is not one of changing philosophy into poetry but one of understanding art as such, uncovering its truth function. I think that this is one of the most exciting questions facing us.[5] I wish to conclude this point by stating that Heidegger's investigations concerning poetry try to do justice to poetry from the side of thought and are by no means intended to let philosophy lapse into a playful, artistic fantasy.

The second point is connected with the first and is related to Professor Versényi's thesis that Heidegger's interpretation of metaphysics is a poem in the sense of a mere fantasy, which lacks all critical spirit. I must vehemently object to this view. I am not acquainted with any thinker who reads and interprets the philosophers with as critical a spirit as Heidegger does. Nowhere have I found such a sharpness of interpretation and manner of dealing with the works of the philosophers.

His interpretation of metaphysics as a whole takes place in the light of the thought of Being. This can evoke criticism. But what Heidegger is mainly concerned with is the termination and overcoming of the state of metaphysics which Kant so deeply deplores. Kant, in his *Critique of Pure Reason*, calls metaphysics

---

5. It is in this sense that I have tried to show in my art analyses the truth which comes to the fore in Kafka's works. Cf. Walter Biemel, *Philosophische Analysen zur Kunst der Gegenwart* (The Hague: Nijhoff, 1968).

"the battlefield . . . of endless quarrels." The history of metaphysics changes, in Heidegger's interpretation of Kant, from a "battlefield . . . of endless quarrels" into a meaningfully comprehensible and reasonable movement. In the light of Heidegger's interpretation we suddenly discover that the history of metaphysics is not simply a matter of the clashing of arbitrary and conflicting opinions; one can find in this history a process of development that can be traced step by step. One may wish to interpret many philosophers in different ways, and this is very well possible. (Heidegger has always encouraged his students not to accept what he says, not to cling only to what he says, but to make new interpretations, to reveal new things.) However, and here I must repeat myself, by means of his guiding clues Heidegger changes what seems to be chaotic into a meaningful connection. One who fails to notice this does not understand what really matters, and is working at cross-purposes with Heidegger.

It would be important if we could read together one of Heidegger's interpretive works, for instance, "The Time of World as Picture," in order to examine and explain the question of whether what comes to pass at the beginning of modern time is obscured in this essay or clarified. Do we experience in it something decisive about the transition from the Middle Ages to the modern era, or is this essay just a "poetic" fantasy?

In this connection I must also expressly object to the view that Heidegger wishes to tyrannize through his thought. He repeatedly points to the fact that we should not try to cling to the results but should follow the road he takes in his attempt. He wishes only to show us the direction and then to let us find our own way.

One danger certainly present consists in the fact that we often jump to the last, most difficult phase of Heidegger's thought and cling to concepts there without having carried out the work of reasoning (*Denkarbeit*), which in Heidegger's own case precedes these concepts and constitutes their foundation. (For this reason a discussion of his work is very fruitful.) In this sense Professor Edie's remark—namely, that Heidegger's students have a great task to accomplish, not just to reproduce what Heidegger has shown but to make it their own—is justified.

JOSEPH J. KOCKELMANS: A dialogue concerning Heidegger's philosophy can move on two levels. The participants may presuppose that everyone involved in the dialogue is familiar with Heidegger's philosophy in general; in this case the purpose of the dialogue is to test the validity of the various interpretations and to achieve greater insight into certain details. Alternatively, the participants in the dialogue may presuppose that at least some of them have no knowledge of Heidegger's thought. In this case the goal of the dialogue is to explain Heidegger's basic views to people who are not familiar, or sufficiently familiar, with his thinking. The papers presented clearly represent a dialogue of the first type. If I were asked to talk about Heidegger's conception of language to people completely unfamiliar with Heidegger's thought, I most certainly would have done so differently from the way in which I have proceeded. In writing my paper I had in mind those who know Heidegger well, those who are sufficiently open to his thought; my interpretation was not concerned with attempts to justify his view as "the truth."

It seems to me that Professor Edie's remarks concerning Heidegger's conception of language immediately force Heidegger into a certain direction. Professor Edie argues that Heidegger talks either about speech or about language taken as a diacritical totality, and so on. I am certain that Heidegger has never said anything about language as Professor Edie understands it, and I very much doubt that he has ever said anything about speech as Professor Edie conceives of it. On a few occasions Heidegger touches on the traditional conception of language and speech. He believes that the views on these subjects which have developed since the time of Plato and Aristotle contain a core of truth and that contemporary conceptions of them are correct, but that this does not constitute the content of his own reflections on language and speech.

Heidegger uses the term *language* in a very broad sense. When he talks about language, he does not think exclusively of Greek, German, or any other diacritical system. However, one must realize three things here. (1) It is perfectly legitimate to use the term *language* in a very broad sense so as to include everything by means of which mankind brings meaning to light in an articulated way, regardless of whether this is done concretely, by means of language in the narrow sense of the term, or through works of art, for instance. (2) Heidegger makes it perfectly clear that he uses the term *language* in a very broad sense. (3) That which linguists call a language is only one element of what Heidegger has in mind when he uses the term. However, language in the narrow sense is certainly the most important component of language in the broad sense; without it, the articulation of meaning would be practically impossible.

I agree that Heidegger's thought does not possess a great "richness," in that it does not deal with a great number of issues from a great variety of approaches. Its seeming "poverty" is obvious, in that it deals with only one basic question, which is most often approached from quite similar, if not identical, points of departure. This is particularly true of Heidegger's later publications; and this is true, also, of his conception of language. But this fact notwithstanding, it seems to me somehow unfair to criticize Heidegger for not having dealt with a great number of linguistic phenomena and problems. Heidegger's concern is not with man's use of language but with the "language" of Being, which is "addressed" to man and asks for a "response."

As far as Professor Edie's reference to the ontological difference is concerned, I must point out again that Heidegger has never claimed to be the first philosopher in history to have understood the ontological difference *at its face value.* This difference underlies almost all philosophy between that of Plato and that of Nietzsche and has led to a great number of misconceptions and quasi problems. Heidegger wants to overcome these misconceptions (which in some cases are tangibly suggested in our Indo-European propositions) by trying to bring to light the genuine meaning of the difference.

When Professor Edie says that Heidegger's thinking of Being involves a "philosophy of language," he is again using a non-Heideggerian expression. In Heidegger's view there is no room for a "philosophy of. . . ." This remark does not mean to suggest that from his basic philosophical perspective these "philosophies of . . . " could not be developed as regional ontologies, for instance. Heidegger has never objected to this; but one does not find such ontologies in his publications. Thus, one looks there in vain for them, as well as for answers to problems with which Heidegger has never dealt up to the present time.

I do not think it is correct to judge Heidegger's conception of "language" in the light of what other philosophers have said and are saying on the subject. What Heidegger calls language is very seldom dealt with by other philosophers; and, when it is, it very rarely appears under the general heading "language." In other

words, since Professor Edie uses the word *language* in his statement in two quite different senses, his approach seems to be
invalid.

The question of whether or not Heidegger's commentators
should confront his thought with other currents of thought, particularly those that are concerned with similar problems, is again
an ambiguous one, and for the reasons just cited. If there were
philosophers dealing with similar, even remotely similar, problems, this would certainly be very helpful. However, since almost
all philosophers are dealing with problems other than those in
which Heidegger is mainly interested, the situation becomes
more complex. I grant, however, that those who wish to make
Heidegger's thought available to others should at least explicitly
warn of the obvious misunderstandings that can arise from the
seeming similarity in conceptualization and terminology between
Heidegger and other philosophers.

All of Professor Edie's remarks on thought versus perception,
for example, rest precisely on this very understandable miscon-
ception. For Heidegger, the term *thought* has a meaning that
comes very close to what others call *philosophy*. The different
modes of thought (taken in the Cartesian sense of the term) are
found in Heidegger (mainly in *Being and Time*) as different
forms of man's orientation toward the world (ek-sistence), but,
indeed, they are not found there under their usual labels. Heidegger avoids words such as *perception, imagination, thinking*
(taken in the narrow sense), *willing, remembering,* and so on,
for two reasons. First, he avoids these terms in order to avoid
perpetual misconceptions. By using terms coined by the tradition, one takes up views from the tradition which are different,
from those which one wishes to defend. Second, nowhere does
Heidegger adopt an analytic attitude comparable in any way to
that adopted by Hume and Mill. It obviously is not Heidegger's
intention to claim that a philosopher cannot deal with the problems hidden under these quite common labels, but he has never
done so explicitly. He wishes to do other—and, in his view, more
important—work first. I do not think it is right to criticize a
philosopher for attempting to find a way to philosophy's basic
problem.

Finally, I feel that Professor Edie exaggerates Heidegger's
view in saying that he replaces thought with *Sprache;* and Professor Edie is certainly mistaken in interpreting thought in terms

of consciousness and *Sprache* in terms of language, in the sense of analytic philosophy. In order to avoid misunderstanding, may I make it clear once more that I am not claiming that what Professor Edie intends to say is meaningless; I claim only that Heidegger never talks about the problems that Professor Edie has in mind.

PART III

Heidegger's Language:
Metalogical Forms of Thought
and Grammatical Specialties

Erasmus Schöfer

THE CIRCLE

The Circle as Form of Thinking. Up until now we have
dealt with the simple opposition between two members [namely,
with the paradox].[1] We have seen different attempts which Heidegger has made to combine elements which logically contradict
one another. In addition to darting from one antinomic member
to another by means of an either and an or, this can be done by
combining the elements in a circular form of thought. Such
thought, which likewise renounces inference, syllogism, and de-
duction, has been forbidden in traditional logic since ancient
times as *vitiosus* and is also, normally speaking, held to be un-
productive. Heidegger has emphasized repeatedly and *expressis
verbis* that he does not share this evaluation of the circle. There
are various indications in his language that this evaluation is not

1. In *Die Sprache Heideggers* (Pfullingen: Neske, 1962), Erasmus
Schöfer has made a careful study of Heidegger's language, mainly from a
linguistic point of view. The book consists of two parts. In the first part
the author reflects on Heidegger's idiom and critically examines the way
in which Heidegger creates new words and gives existing words new
meanings. The second part of the book is devoted to an analysis of
Heidegger's syntax and style. In the first chapter of the second part
Schöfer discusses four types of thought and grammatical specialties often
used in Heidegger's works. This essay is the translation of Schöfer's discussion of two of these types, namely, the circle and the tautology as
figura etymologica. These two metalogical forms of thought as well as the
linguistic specialties to which they lead in particular have been misunderstood by Heidegger's critics.

merely a theory; it has also been effectively materialized in his thought. Therefore, the linguistic particularities of such a movement of thought (*Denkbewegung*) are to be considered in connection with the explanation of metalogical modes of expression.

Leisegang gives a great number of examples of the "logical circle." I shall quote two here which are particularly illustrative. "Athanatoi thnētoi, thnētoi athanatoi, xōntes ton ekeinōn thanaton, ton de ekeinōn bion tethneōntes: Immortal [beings are] mortal, mortal [beings are] immortal, living their death, but dying their life." "Certainly when we evaluate it properly, we will see that destruction is nothing but production, and production nothing but destruction. In the final analysis, love is hatred, and hatred a kind of love." [2]

In this Heraclitean saying and in Giordano Bruno's idea, the particularities of the supersession of antinomic oppositions and those of the circular form of thought show themselves to be united with one another as, in fact, is often the case. Perhaps Leisegang does not distinguish sharply enough between these two moments. If opposites are identified with one another in a certain way, this combination can generally be seen from the viewpoint of one member as well as from that of the other, and circular propositions similar to those just mentioned emerge. However, the circular way of thinking does not have to be employed exclusively for an inner unification of heteronomous elements; it can determine the mode of the view which combines (*Zusammenschau*) disparate elements or can even be a general hermeneutic principle. The *coincidentia oppositorum* which is thought here, and which is particularly noticeable in the two examples given, is an additional logical moment within the logical circle, which Leisegang further describes (as have others) as a particularly mystical form of thought and speech: "The form which is characteristic of mystical thinking constitutes a circular movement of thought, which takes its point of departure from one concept, adds others, and returns to the first concept." [3]

The Hermeneutic Circle as a Basis for Understanding. When Heidegger speaks of the circle of our understanding, it seems at first as if he has exactly the same phenomenon in mind as does Leisegang. As an example of circular inference, he mentions the

---

2. Hans Leisegang, *Denkformen* (Berlin: de Gruyter, 1951), II, 62, 66.
3. *Ibid.*, p. 73.

procedure in which he gives a derivation of the concept of "Being": "It is said that we have 'presupposed' the idea of existence and of Being in general, and that Dasein gets interpreted 'accordingly,' so that the idea of Being may be obtained from it." [4] Thus, just as in Leisegang, a "concept" is taken as point of departure, another is added to it, and one returns again to the starting point. There is still to be added to this formal similarity the contrast between the circular inference and the inferential procedures of logic, which are clearly seen by both Heidegger and Leisegang as opposite to the inferential procedure of the circle.

Nonetheless, Heidegger and Leisegang comprehend the logical circle in fundamentally different ways. For Leisegang it is a possibility of combining opposite elements in one train of thought whose effective development, as far as its essence is concerned, is determined from the model of organic life, growing from seed, via blossom and fruit, back to seed. For Heidegger, the circle is a structural element of each human act of understanding as such. It is the "hermeneutic" circle: understanding, the (interpretive) explanation of a phenomenon, is possible only insofar as the one who understands brings with him (*heranbringen*) from his point of departure a certain preunderstanding in regard to this phenomenon. He cannot understand it "neutrally," "in itself." Retroacting in a circular way, the understanding of the newly added phenomenon will change his starting point also.[5]

Taken in the sense of Leisegang, the circle is just one form of thought—and in fact a determinate one, to be attributed to contents of mystical thought. Taken in the sense of Heidegger, it is the basic structure of all of man's understanding of states of affairs; the circle is unavoidable. From this it becomes clear that the circle as Heidegger sees it will certainly not always expressly

---

4. *SZ* 314.
5. Heidegger has explicitly and extensively commented on these questions at several places in *Being and Time* (cf. *SZ* 7, 152–53, 314–16). Schleiermacher was the first to consider the "hermeneutic circle," namely, in connection with the question concerning the conditions of text interpretation. It was also explained in this sense by Emil Staiger (*Die Kunst der Interpretation* [Zurich: Atlantis, 1955], pp. 9 ff.) and extended generally to the question concerning the possibility of historical objectivity by Hans-Georg Gadamer ("Vom Zirkel des Verstehens," in *Martin Heidegger zum siebzigsten Geburtstag, Festschrift,* ed. Günther Neske [Pfullingen: Neske, 1959]). Going beyond the realm of aesthetics and history, Gadamer has described the hermeneutic circle as a universal aspect of philosophy, particularly in his book *Wahrheit und Methode* (Tübingen: Mohr, 1960).

manifest itself in a conspicuous linguistic form; it is related, rather, to the sequence of thoughts and sentences that can be contained in a series of completely "normal" propositions. The value of bringing in a sharp separation here is certainly doubtful. This "normal" sequence of sentences obviously is also possible; in fact, it is found in connection with the circle taken as a form of thought according to Leisegang's conception. However, if we focus on the praxis of the explicitly formulated examples, circular thought taken in Leisegang's sense obviously comes more quickly to explicit consciousness of its own structure in order to make that structure manifest in the explicitly circular formulation of one or more sentences. Perhaps one can conceive of Leisegang's logical circle (*Gedankenkreis*) as the hermeneutic circle which has been made explicit and in this way understand both these phenomena in their relationship and interdependence.

In any case, because of Heidegger's various references to the circle in *Being and Time,* because of statements about "the turning forth" (*herausdrehen*) of a question or of an analysis from a starting point that has been handed down,[6] and because of his rejection of the referential procedures of traditional logic, we are expressly bound to pay careful attention to a possible reflection of the circle in Heidegger's language in connection with our investigation of linguistic sediments of metalogical thought. Our looking for it is unfruitful, however, as far as Heidegger's early works are concerned; but this is not the case in his later works. As we have said, the circular process of understanding comes about in a linguistic form that is normal in this regard. Although one could certainly find impressive things by analyzing greater sentential periods, this will not be done here.[7] It is only at a later date that the circle of understanding as a form of thought (taken in the sense just discussed, as an explicit representation of the hermeneutic circle) comes to the fore in a much clearer way.

Examples of Circular Thought. In order to characterize the Scholastic understanding of the nature of God, Heidegger formulates a sentence that is typical of Leisegang's typology: "He is the Absolute [*das Absolute*] which is existence, which exists in its essence and continuously abides in its existence."[8] Later, in

6. SZ 197, 201.
7. Cf. Schöfer, *Die Sprache Heideggers,* pp. 192–93. Some examples which are dealt with as "paradoxical" are appropriate here also.
8. KB 75.

"On the Essence of Truth," he writes: "The essence [*Wesen*] of truth is the truth of the continuously abiding Being [*Wesen*]." [9] With this he does not intend to formulate a dialectical statement or one taken "in the sense of an interpretive expression [*Aussage*]," but rather the "saying of a turn [*Kehre*]" within the history of Being. It may also be that this sentence, which Heidegger formulates after it has first been explained, is formed in this hermetic way explicitly to make it impossible for our understanding to imagine itself being in a safe harbor with the result of this procedure, merely on the basis of a definition that was hastily put together and in itself provisional in character, before our understanding had any grasp of the inner difficulty of the matters involved.

This motivation is not decisive, however. Let us consider an analogous sentence and Heidegger's explanation of it:

> The principle of the ground—the ground of the principle [*Satz*]. Let us stop for a moment, supposing that we are permitted to do so: the principle of the ground—the ground of the principle. Here something turns around in itself. Here something curls itself up in itself without, however, closing itself, but rather unlocking itself at the same time. Here is a ring, a living ring, something like a snake. Something catches itself with its own tail. Here there is a beginning which is already completion.[10]

What is meant here is that both sides of this construction belong together; in fact they are, and also say, essentially the same thing, without, however, being so emptily identical as $2 = 2$. They are the two parts of a circle. Each can be taken out of the circle, yet each can exist as half of the circle only when they both exist at the same time, when the whole circle exists.

A manifestly totally different kind of thought that remains within the realm of the circle and has left very clear marks on language is contained in the following paragraph:

> *Homo est animal rationale. Animal* does not mean just any living thing; plants, too, have life; yet we cannot call man a rational vegetable. *Animal* means "the animal" (beast), and *animaliter* means (in Augustine, for instance) "like an animal." Man is a rational animal. Reason is the becoming aware of what is, and this

9. WW 25–26.
10. SG 31.

always means, at the same time, what can be and ought to be. To become aware of implies, stepwise, to take up [*aufnehmen*], to receive [*entgegennehmen*], to undertake [*vor-nehmen*], to go through [*durchnehmen*]—and this, in turn, means to talk over [*durchsprechen*]. The Latin for talking over is *reor;* the Greek *rheō* (as in rhetoric) is the ability to take something up and before one [*vor-nehmen*] and to go through it [*durchnehmen*]; *reri* is *ratio;* *animal rationale* is the animal that lives insofar as it becomes aware of [*vernehmen*] in the manner described. The becoming aware of, which governs reason, produces and adduces goals [*Ziele*], establishes rules, provides means, and tunes in on these modes of doing [*her-zu-stellen, auf-stellen, bei-stellen, ein-stellen-auf*]. Reason's becoming aware of unfolds itself as this manifold positing [*stellen*] that everywhere, and first and foremost, is proposing [*vor-stellen*]. Thus, one might also say *Homo est animal rationale:* Man is the pro-posing animal.[11]

This paragraph takes a determinate conception of the sentence *Homo est animal rationale* as its point of departure and returns to the same statement. At this point, however, it is understood differently—understood, if you wish, dialectically, on a higher level. Paths take us over linguistico-etymological analyses which, like the whole chain of thought, are oriented toward the goal by means of the hermeneutic preunderstanding of that goal.

While reading particular sequences of sentences, one sometimes has the impression that the reflection swings up (*sich aufschaukeln*) in a certain sense, somehow similar to a chain reaction or to the electromagnetic event that takes place when one starts an induction motor. Consider the following, for example: "It can be ascertained only in thought, evaluated as what is to be thought in its questionableness, and preserved as what has been thought in memory [*Gedächtnis*]."[12]

This is particularly clear in the following paragraph dealing with "proximity" (*die Nähe*). My italics are meant to emphasize how a word that is posited as a goal in one sentence appears as a starting point in the next, until what first initiated the questioning closes the circle as the last element.

What is proximity? In order to find the essence of proximity, we considered the pitcher nearby. We were looking for the essence

11. WD 27 (61).
12. VA 114.

of proximity and found the essence of the pitcher as a *thing*. But with this discovery we become aware of the essence of proximity at the same time. The *thing* "*things*" [*dingt* = "*engages*"]. It *dwells engaging* heaven and earth, the divine and mortal beings; *dwelling*, the thing brings the four in their distances *close* to one another. This *bringing close to one another* is a closing in [*nähern*]. *Closing in* is the essence of *proximity*.[13]

TAUTOLOGY AS *Figura Etymologica*

Tautology. Another of our modes of thinking and speaking that is "pathological" in the view of traditional logic is the so-called tautology. In the "logical circle" tautologies (in addition to paradoxes) appear in many places, namely, wherever two members are identified with one another "chiastically," as in the two quotations from Heraclitus and Bruno ($A = B, B = A$). Of course a tautology is very seldom experienced in the same way as a paradox. Whereas the latter affects normal thought in a stimulating and challenging way, it is characteristic of the former to leave reason cold and at most to elicit a mental "shrug." The impression is created that nothing is really said in a tautological "expression," that everything remains as it was before.

Even when a tautological way of speaking claims to be meaningful, the *mens communis* is still inclined to turn down this claim, although it is likely to accept a similar one made by paradoxical speech. The thing to do, therefore, is to clarify those elements of Heidegger's language that show traits of tautological thought.

Heidegger speaks in a pejorative sense of a "meaningless tautology"[14] and later defines this term in a neutral way: "When someone continually says the same thing—for instance, the plant is a plant—he speaks in tautologies."[15] The second quotation is found in his explanation of the identity principle, in the course of which he points to the fact that the current formulation of this principle, $A = A$, does not let the real meaning come to the fore—the expression of the identity of an A with itself, the tauto-logy

13. VA 176.
14. WG 22.
15. ID 14.

(*to auto*). "The identity principle is better formulated as follows: *A* is *A*. Each *A* is the same with itself. It is in the selfsameness that the relation of the 'with' is found, thus a mediation, a combination, a synthesis: the unification into a unity." [16] General conclusions can be drawn from this situation—which has been deliberated since the time of German idealism—regarding the possible content of tautological expressions: the identity as such *and* in its structure is indicated in these expressions. It remains to be shown how important this is for thought.

Heidegger's Neologisms. In the essay "What Is Metaphysics?" Heidegger writes, "Nothing nihilates of itself." In *The Essence of Reasons* one finds, "World never is; rather, it 'worlds' [*weltet*]." [17] In a lecture given in 1950 entitled "The Thing" the following appears: "But how does the thing continuously abide? The thing things [*dingt*]." "World abides insofar as it worlds [*weltet*]." [18]

The fact that Heidegger forms new verbs expressly to be able to write these sentences is a sign that he has a special goal in mind. At first sight these sentences look like somewhat unusual tautologies, like references to the fact that something does (*tut*) itself. Such an expression seems as eccentric as it is meaningless. But let us first consider some other instances before we attempt an interpretation of the characteristic neologisms.

"The very *asking* of this *question* . . . is determined by . . . " is a form that, with some modification, is found in almost all of Heidegger's works.[19] Other examples are: "That in the face of which *anxiety* is *anxious* and . . . that in the face of which *fear* is *afraid*." [20] "[*Temporality*] is not, but it *temporalizes* itself. . . . *Temporality temporalizes*, and indeed it *temporalizes* possible modes of itself." [21] "Resoluteness . . . is . . . that authenticity which, in *care*, is the object of *care*, and which is possible as *care*." [22] "This *unity unifies*." [23] "This '*possibility*' which makes this 'if *possible*' first and foremost *possible*." [24] "The modes according to which these *representations represent*." "Something

16. *ID* 15.
17. *WM* 34; *WG* 44.
18. *VA* 172, 178.
19. Cf. *SZ* 7.
20. *SZ* 186.
21. *SZ* 328. This formulation occurs most frequently in *Being and Time* but is also found elsewhere. Cf. *KM* 170; *WG* 46.
22. *SZ* 301.
23. *KM* 59; cf. *WG* 16. This expression occurs in other works as well.
24. *KM* 109. Similar expressions occur in *Being and Time*.

like a *ruling rule.*" [25] "Das *Wesen west* [the essence continuously abides]." [26]

Grammatical Considerations of the Figura Etymologica. Linguistics and rhetoric very early introduced the term *figura etymologica* for constructions pertaining to the etymological relationships between the words which depend upon one another in the sentence. With this term they characterized mainly a stylistic figure of ancient rhetoric. In German the combined usage of a noun and verb which show a clear etymological relationship is believed to be awkward and is usually avoided; in high school papers it is corrected with the marginal note "*WdA.*"

The erlking can promise to play a very beautiful play with the child, and one can sleep the sleep of the just. According to the popular tongue twister, Fischer's Fritz fished fresh fish. The singer, too, sings, the angler angles, and the caller up calls up; but today no one plays a play, one rarely walks a walk, and who, in normal speech, says that the rain rains? [27] In German one finds the syntactically different types of the *figura etymologica* only in a child's language, where they are used for very special, mostly stylistic reasons, and in cases where evasive words are lacking. The accusative of the "inner object" is most often the source of such constructions in poetry and in ordinary language.[28]

This typical accusative, which occurs relatively seldom in comparison with the accusative of the "outer object," is certainly found in all Indo-European languages, just as is the *figura etymologica,* which is usually attached to it.[29] An object already essentially contained in the verb is then attributed to an action expressed by a transitive or intransitive verb: I live, my life; he fights, a fight. This is found also without etymological iteration: I cry, tears. The tautological moment is obvious in such combinations. It is precisely because of the fact that its mental achievement is obviously nothing that this grammatical possibility of

25. *KM* 130, 141.
26. Cf. *WW* and other works.
27. Heinrich Böll has certainly achieved poetically a specifically intensive description: "When the storms blow for weeks at a time, the rain rains" (*Irisches Tagebuch* [Munich: Deutscher Taschenbuch 1961], I, 101).
28. Cf. Konrad Duden, ed., *Der Grosse Duden* (Manheim: Bibliographisches Institut, 1959), Vol. IV, sec. 1018.
29. K. Brugmann and B. Delbrück, *Grundriss der vergleichenden Grammatik der indogermanischen Sprachen* (Strasbourg: Trübner, 1897–1916), II, 620 ff.

expression was neglected and superseded in the Indo-European languages.[30]

The classical philologist knows quite well that this so-called *figura etymologica* in the accusative of the inner object occurs in classical Greek, not only in a great number of fixed phrases, but also in the free creations of prose and oration. According to Schwytzer the accusative of the content serves "as a facultative enforcement of the verbal concept or as a formal support of an adjectival or (seldom) genitive attribute necessary for the meaning." The following sentences may serve as examples: "Machēn emachonto [They battled the battle]," and "Aischron gar aprēkton polemon polemixein [It is objectionable to fight a meaningless war]."

> The content accusative comes very close to the result accusative insofar as the substance of both comes about only through the verbal action; however, in the case of a "resultative" accusative a largely visible and constant result occurs, whereas in the case of an "inner object" an imperceptible result (or one that is perceptible only in its effects) is brought about, one that disappears when the verbal action is completed.[31]

In the Greek sentences of the type just cited it seems that the verb governs, that it carries the sentence. Schwytzer's interpretation underlines this impression in that he defines the accusative object as being "the facultative enforcement" or "formal support." This may be the case in many examples of classical Greek, although the question of the objective validity of the composition attributed to it at the time has not even arisen yet in such a

---

30. As a means of intensifying the expression, the tautology is still current only in the Balto-Slavic languages (cf. E. Hofmann, *Ausdruckverstärkung* [Göttingen: Vandenhoeck & Ruprecht, 1930], pp. 96 ff.). Likewise, from the viewpoint of the accumulation which is full of emotion, J. B. Hofmann mentions some cases of the *figura etymologica* in the everyday Latin language (*Lateinische Umgangssprache* [Heidelberg: Winter, 1936], p. 95). Without giving any further explanation, in his essay "Die mittelalterliche Mystik und die deutsche Sprache," Herman Kunisch points to the fact that many examples of the *figura etymologica* can be found in Seuse and the later minnesingers. He adds as commentary: "And here the Latin parallel in the horologium shows that there is a question of a peculiarity which realized itself only in German" (*Deutsche Kultur im Leben der Völker*, XV [1940]).

31. Eduard Schwytzer, *Griechische Grammatik* (Munich: Beck, 1950), II, 74.

characterization. If one realizes, on the basis of a superficial investigation, (an expert is undoubtedly necessary here), that in most cases of such a *figura* the noun is the etymologically older component, whereas the verb is a denominative (or at least seems to be so), the supposition suggests itself that in the formation of this *figura* the noun was found in the middle of the sentence and a verbal action was then coordinated with it. This, however, had to be—and this consideration is decisive—an action that was essentially equal to the substantival thing, completely corresponding to it, identical with it. This is why the verbalized noun was posited once again, why a verb was formed with the same etymon.

Even the assumption that stylistic motives dominated in the constitution of the *figura etymologica formalis* is unsatisfactory. The possible objective achievement of this grammatical structure from early times could no longer be experienced; it had been lost. It is very likely that in the formation of this structure the expressive need, which follows from the fact that thing and action, either from the viewpoint of the noun or of the verb, appear to be also inherently inseparable, was decisive.

Be this as it may—and it should be difficult to reach clarity here for the Indo-European languages with only the help of linguistic investigations—for our inquiry into Heidegger's language we must maintain that this practice of directly combining a noun and a verb of the same etymon was customary in classical Greek. It is almost certain that Heidegger became aware of the particularity of the *figura etymologica* in his intensive work with Greek texts and then developed it, undoubtedly in a changed syntactic form, for his thought on the German language in a way that, one may assume, it was originally used in the Indo-European languages. This is another case in which there is a noticeable influence of certain characteristics of the Greek language on Heidegger's language.

The Efficiency of Heidegger's Neologisms. Let us consider once again the examples of Heidegger's neologisms that were mentioned earlier. It immediately becomes clear that they do not exactly correspond to the accusative of the inner object. Their syntactic structure is one of a subject-predicate statement. The verbs are intransitive, but are used transitively in special cases.

In the concept *"natura naturans,"* which was used by the Scholastics and by Eckhart and later became the "definition" of

God's essence in Bruno's and Spinoza's pantheism, we find a noun-verb combination which is built up in a similar way. It is characteristic that this formula was used to signify divine nature, which renews itself from itself, circles in itself, and remains identical with itself, and whose activity was thought to consist in the fact that it had to create and perform for itself: *naturam.* "Per naturam naturantem nobis intelligendam est id quod in se est et per se concipitur." [32]

The question questions, the possibility makes possible, the rule rules—if the mental objects evoked in the nouns are in any way able to display an activity, they do in the verb exactly what they already are; they effect themselves. The thing is active in the strictest sense; nothing can be inserted between it and its doing; there is no difference. Anyone who has the least linguistic flair will experience how intensive, how dense, these constructions are. As a result, the three examples just given are comparatively peripheral; other verbs can be substituted for those found in the examples without any loss as far as our understanding of the sentences is concerned: the question tries to fathom, the possibility allows us, the rule regulates.

However, a sharper, comparative view shows at once that the substitution is possible only if "synonymous" verbs are used—that is to say, only by deconcretizing the verb content, by functionalizing it, something that often occurs in abstract, conceptual ways of speaking as well as elsewhere. On the other hand, if one pays attention to the content of the verb and attaches great importance to it, the verb's substitution is connected with an experienceable change in content; in the constructions considered here, the substitution is connected with a change in the insistence with which the activity of a mental object is understood from itself.

In the most important instances of Heidegger's *figura etymologica*—namely, in cases such as "care cares," "temporality temporalizes," "the essence essences," "nothingness nihilates," "the world worlds"—we are dealing precisely with this strict attention to the verb content. Heidegger says: "World essences in that it worlds. This means the world's worlding can be neither explained by something else nor fathomed from something else." (It would have been clearer if Heidegger had said, and I presume

32. Spinoza *Ethica* I.

he must have meant, "The world's essence is . . .."). The similarity to the *per se concipitur* of Spinoza's definition is obvious here. Heidegger's further explanations, too, make it clear that he wishes to express this identity of thing and achievement, the world that brings itself about. "Man's desire to explain, after all, does not reach to the simpleness of the simplicity of this world-ing." [33]

This linguistic phenomenon can be equally clearly grasped in the following neologisms, referred to above. Temporality "temporalizes itself"; it temporalizes "possible modes *of itself*." "Nothingness nihilates of *itself*"; "the essence of this nothingness is: the nihilation." Concerning temporality, nothingness, and the like, basically no statement can be made other than that they effect their own essence in the mode of an *entelecheia*, that they are their own activities. *To world, to nihilate*, and *to temporalize* are integral verbs with respect to "world," "nothingness," and "temporality"; other verbs fall short of the object grasped in the subject and thus entail an intensity degradation. We thus witness here an exciting spectacle, namely, how a state of affairs is encircled, mentally and linguistically expanded, and developed in manifold determinations of the kind we have brought in here as subsequent explanations; how the train of thought is then pulled together in a syntactic form, which is shaped with a language-creating intuition, and culminates in a hermetically closed sentence; and how this state of affairs is suddenly raised for the German language into the bright light of explicit verbalization, made available to language and thought.

Returning to the starting point of our reflections concerning tautology, we are now able to say that the essential linguistic effect of the *figura etymologica* taken as Heidegger has coined it factually consists in a tautology in which "object" and "activity" are expressed as identical. The subject of the sentence, "this fatal grammatical category," [34] is incorporated in the other grammatical category, the predicate, and vice versa. Yet it is obviously not an "empty" tautology but the intended expression of the unity of the two elements. Here the unity of what is one with itself is quite different from the case in the principle of identity ($A = A$); this unity is formally made visible and conceivable in a

33. VA 178.
34. WM 26.

sentence, a decomposition, but not *as* a statement insofar as the content of the unity is concerned. The performance of the thing and the performance of language coincide here.

Is Predication, Identity, and Forms of Thought. With this ascertainment we touch on another question that affects linguistics as strongly as it does Heidegger. To what extent does the subject-predicate structure of the Indo-European sentence determine the mode of Western thought? How narrow or how wide are the boundaries of a thought set by the essence of linguistic predication? The principle of identity makes clear the detour by which thought is only in a position to grasp a thing as itself. This principle reveals how thought, which aspires to comprehend and say the thing precisely as itself in its identity, is continuously forced by the structure of the sentence to say something *about* the thing, namely, to represent the thing as if it were, in a certain sense, standing opposite to itself and then being mediated.

We are not thinking here of the fact that all human, and therefore all linguistic, understanding always grasps something *as* something because of its naming—thus, not of that *as* structure, that hermeneutic *as*, with which Heidegger deals in *Being and Time* [35]—a fact which has precipitated in our linguistic knowledge from the "intermediate world of language" between man and "the things themselves." Here the question is concerned with the structure of the proposition and of propositional truth, of the apophantic *as* about which Heidegger speaks in *The Essence of Reasons*.[36] This *as* and our saying *is* are the same. The *is* underlies each proposition. Johannes Lohmann examines, for different languages and language types, the extent to which this difference between subject and predicate caused by the *is* becomes linguistically explicit through formal reference, the extent to which it becomes mentally manifest. Lohmann has shown that there are different degrees of clarity in this difference, from its clear and continuing designation in the western European languages to its concealment, or, more exactly, its nonexistence, in Chinese.[37]

From these facts alone Walter Bröcker should have realized that Heidegger, in his attack on Western logic and propositional truth, does not overlook what Bröcker blames him for—namely,

35. *SZ* 148–53, 158–60, 359–60.
36. *WG* 10 ff.
37. See pp. 303–63 below.

that logic thinks it deals with the *general* structure of propositions. When Bröcker writes, "The *as* (the *is*) is that which is primordially logical," he is standing on the ground of Husserl's general, ideal logic, which has already been refuted in this form by the results of linguistics alone.[38] Heidegger wants to bring to light precisely this claim of logic, which Husserl has naïvely abstracted from the structures of the Greek proposition and then has generalized in order to distill from this claim a corresponding concept of truth; Heidegger does this by referring to the heterogeneity of the *as* in "our concernful dealing with tools" on the one hand, and in our theoretical consideration of things on the other. Compare here, too, Heidegger's explanation of the Greek *aisthēsis:* the "simple sensory perception" as the primary meaning of *alētheia.*[39] One must thoroughly oppose Bröcker when he writes: "The logical structure *S is P* is the same, regardless of whether *S* is a thing or a tool, and regardless of whether *P* is a property or a functional state of affairs [*Bewandtnis*]. And the *as* (the *is*) has in both cases the same function of subsuming objects under concepts." [40] Here the very essence of "circumspection" (*Umsicht*) and of "concernful dealing with" as described in *Being and Time* is already watered down. Bröcker again comes to a proposition ("If I circumspectively concernfully deal with equipment and say, or silently think, this pair of tongs here is completely unfit . . .")[41] and then formal-logically analyzes it.

---

38. Cf. Leo Weisgerber, "Sprachwissenschaft und Philosophie zum Bedeutungsproblem," *Blätter für deutsche Philosophie*, IV (1930–31), esp. 33 ff. For linguistics, the categories "subject" and "predicate" must, on the whole, already be understood differently for each native language. One would therefore be arguing on the basis of unclarified presuppositions if one were to assume that these logical categories are generally accepted in the domain of the Indo-European languages and even beyond this realm. Even within the realm of one language the subject, for instance, already has different values, depending on whether it is found in a sentence with two or three clauses. The considerations and investigations in this regard are still in a state of flux and cannot be pursued further here. We must keep in mind Heidegger's first attempt in this regard. For the linguistic view, we may refer to the reflections of Weisgerber and Lohmann, who go more deeply into the question (Leo Weisgerber, *Vom Weltbild der deutschen Sprache* [Düsseldorf: Schwann, 1953–54], I, 233 ff., esp. 242–44; II, 163 ff., esp. 178–82; Johannes Lohmann, "Vom ursprünglichen Sinn der aristotelischen Syllogistik," *Lexis*, II [1949], 205 ff.). Cf. W. Bröcker, "Heidegger und die Logik," *Philosophische Rundschau*, I (1953–54).
39. *SZ* 33.
40. Bröcker, "Heidegger und die Logik," p. 54.
41. *Ibid.*

Dasein, however, according to Heidegger, does not formulate such a proposition; it simply puts the pair of tongs aside.

Only later does it become completely clear that Heidegger gives a deeper foundation (*untergreift*) to the position of formal logic, that the question concerning the *is* is a question about the form of truth, a question that is answered in Heidegger's conception of truth as unconcealment. This becomes evident especially in various linguistic indications: Heidegger's refusal to formulate definitions; his use of metaphors to express what is essential to a thing; his turn toward the word, toward the essential "name"; his use of different verbs of the group "to abide" (*wesen*), "to govern" (*walten*), "to last continuously" (*währen*); his thinking in the form of questions and negations. All of these are ways to avoid the normal predication and its implications and, nonetheless, to say something.

In the preceding statements explaining Heidegger's *figura etymologica*—and this is the reason we are dealing with these things—we have one of the most important attempts to name (by means of the proposition) the intended thing in a yet undivided manner, in its full intensity, in its dynamic immanence, and without an "*is* predication." It seems to me that, considering the possibilities of language, Heidegger has been eminently successful with this very old form, now opened up for the German language.

It is basically from these facts that one must understand Heidegger's later orientation toward poetic language. Seeing the poet's possibility *to name*, Heidegger searches for a corresponding possibility *to say*.[42] "That which is difficult here is found in the

---

42. In his "Präliminarien zu einer Theorie der Literatur," Albrecht Fabri notes the fact that in the history of thought particular sentences have appeared repeatedly, withdrawing themselves from an immediately grasping understanding and yet, at the same time, continuously and repeatedly provoking and challenging thought's endeavors. In these sentences a saying thought manifestly succeeds, in a completely unparalleled and excellent way, in bringing to verbal expression something essential. Following are some of Fabri's ideas: "What does this sentence say? As long as one can ask and answer this question, one is dealing with an imperfect sentence. The more perfect a sentence is, the darker it is. The perfect sentence is a pure sentence form. It does not say [anything]; it remains silent. Therefore, in regard to the perfect sentence, our understanding of it presents itself in the form of its exact reproduction; in regard to the imperfect sentence, our understanding of it presents itself in the form of a substitution by one or more other sentences. The perfect sentence is pure

language" and in the question "of whether the essence of Western languages is formed merely metaphysically by the onto-theology in itself, and for that reason definitively, or whether these languages allow for other possibilities of saying and thus, at the same time, of a saying not-saying (*sagendes Nichtsagen*)." [43] It may be said here that it has seldom become so clear how justified the demand for a consideration of a language explicitly related to action really is. If our inquiry into language is to recognize its object in all of its modes of appearing, this inquiry must concomitantly consider the influence of language on man's action and thought. In the form of his own thought Heidegger senses the inexorable working of the linguistic form which is at his disposal and yet not at his command. Heidegger's interest (which becomes ever more manifest) in Eastern thought as a thought that is effected in a completely different linguistic form can therefore also be clarified from this perspective.

Albrecht Fabri has connected some aphorisms with a quotation from Gertrude Stein which has since become famous, namely, "Rose is a rose is a rose is a rose." These aphorisms of his throw some light on this context:

> However, is the rose in Gertrude Stein's poem not more beautiful than if one calls it *beautiful*? Insofar as to understand means to understand something *as something else*, to understand the rose *as rose* means precisely not to understand it. And that is what the tautology accomplishes through its emphatic refusal to formulate definitions. That which is defined is submerged in the definition; definition is always somehow synonymous with murder. [44]

The Effect of the Paronomasia. Heidegger's propositional periods can be considered as a kind of *figura etymologica*, or, taken in a broader sense, as a kind of paronomasia, as a string-

---

resistance. One can indeed think *it*, but one cannot think something *in addition to it*" (*Variationen* [Wiesbaden: Limes, 1959], p. 21).

In connection with these aphorisms, I would like to say by way of restriction that the perfect sentence as such, thus thought in the same intensity, does not allow for a modification. If one is willing to put up with a decrease in intensity, one can think something in addition to it, connect thoughts with it. It is with the help of these thoughts that thought keeps itself moving; philosophical works are filled with them. "Perfect" sentences are culminating points, peaks as hard as diamonds, in which language and thought arrive at a final unity, an *atomon*.

43. ID 72.
44. Fabri, **Variationen, p. 76.**

ing of words of different word types which, however, belong to the same word stem.[45] The variation of an intellectual object, of a phenomenon, is manifested when one looks at the different positions of the words with regard to their linguistic content. In view of this, Heidegger is able specifically to illuminate the structures found within the phenomenon in question—for example, the question (*die Frage*), the questioning (*das Fragen*), what is asked in a question (*das Gefragte*), the putting a question to (*das Anfragen*), that which is questioned about what is asked in the question (*das Befragte*), the questioner (*der Frager*).[46] What manifested itself as the variation of a phenomenon appears now in yet another perspective.

We have seen that the etymological iteration accomplishes a repeated focusing on the "thing" that has been grasped in the basic word. In the paronomasia, however, this does not occur with the same strength of identity as in the formations of the type "the world worlds"; it occurs in the modification which that "thing" experiences conceptually and linguistically through the different perspectives one has on it. Thus, when a determinate central phenomenon is analyzed and articulated in its constitutive moments, the one, basic, varied stem word keeps continuously maintaining that phenomenon from which the point of departure was taken almost "visible" in the middle of the structural totality and, at the same time, in the middle of the explanation.

Certainly the words that are formed from a stem word with the help of derivative syllables are, on the basis of the historical development of the languages, quite often no longer determined from the meaning of the two composing elements as far as content is concerned; they signify something completely different. This is why one may no longer grasp the "thing" expressed in the stem word in the individual members of such etymological iterations. This is indeed at times the case in Heidegger's later works; one with a naïve understanding of language is not sufficiently prepared for this. In the later works other motives—neologisms, etymological regression, and others—are operative, also, making our understanding difficult. Since such complicated passages are not found in his early writings, we do not encounter these diffi-

45. See Schöfer, *Die Sprache Heideggers*, pp. 147, 154, where examples of Heidegger's propositional periods are given and explained.
46. SZ 5–6.

culties there. A passage from one of Heidegger's later works, *What Is Called Thinking?*, illustrates how, in connection with the two words *zeigen* and *ziehen*, the different mental entities (*geistigen Sachen*) formed from this pointing and drawing (*Zeigen und Ziehen*) find their verbal expression in the derivations from both of these verbs:

> Once we are drawn into the withdrawal, we are drawing toward what draws, what attracts us by its withdrawal. And once we, being so attracted, are drawing toward what draws us, our essential nature already bears the stamp of "drawing toward." As we are drawing toward what withdraws, we ourselves are pointers pointing toward it. We are who we are by pointing in that direction—not like an incidental adjunct, but as follows: this "drawing toward" is in itself an essential and therefore constant pointing toward what withdraws. To say "drawing toward" is to say "pointing toward what withdraws."
>
> To the extent that man *is* drawing that way, he *points* toward what withdraws. As he is pointing that way, man *is* the pointer. Man here is not first of all man, and then also occasionally someone who points. No: drawn into what withdraws, drawing toward it and thus pointing into the withdrawal, man first *is* man. His essential nature lies in being such a pointer. Something which in itself, by its essential nature, is pointing we call a sign. As he draws toward what withdraws, man is a sign.[47]

I have chosen this example not because I think it is a particularly clear one. But Wandruszka gives precisely this example as chief evidence for his condemnation of Heidegger's etymologies. He asks "whether perhaps the seductive ease of the etymological motivation in German is not responsible for the fact that in Heidegger the progress of thought is determined to a great extent by the *figura etymologica* (or *pseudo etymologica*), whose verbal magic becomes all the more inescapable the more consistently it is applied." [48] However, if one gets an impression of "verbal magic" and even of "inescapable influence" from the example given in the text, he must not have tried very seriously to

47. WD 5–6 (9).
48. Cf. Mario Wandruszka, "Etymologie und Philosophie," *Der deutsch Unterricht*, Vol. X (1958). The differences between Wandruszka's quotation and the text of *What Is Called Thinking?* can, I believe, be explained by the fact that Wandruszka quotes another edition. For the sake of objectivity, I have quoted his version.

understand the text or to reflect on the linguistic achievement of the *figura etymologica* employed there.[49]

Just as in each linguistic procedure whose effectiveness has been recognized by an author who has consciously employed it, there is obviously here, too, the danger that what was described is being applied at the wrong place or in an exaggerated form. It can deteriorate into a mania, into a merely stylistic means, and thus loose its value. But this can be properly evaluated only after one has gained a clear idea of the intentions of the author and his method.

It is clear at once that the possible different forms of the paronomasia will often hurt the naïve language experience of a German-speaking person.[50] A style that is as varied as possible and determined by a continuous change in expression is commonly accepted as ideal. The concatenation of words of the same stem almost always contradicts this ideal. A mind trained in drawing conclusions deductively from one thing to another and accustomed to distinctions will be particularly annoyed by the impression that he is confronted with tautologies, with that circling around the object, an impression which a thought that

49. Sometimes passages of texts in Heidegger's later works give the impression of a certain tough softness, a kind of viscosity. Our linguistic understanding does not encounter the usual opposition in regard to the known word content and is furthermore unable to grasp the reinterpretation of individual elements from the context, since this, in turn, consists for the greater part of reinterpreted or even new elements. Our linguistic understanding starts to flounder. Even one accustomed to reading these texts is subject to this danger. Yet these texts have an exceptional force as far as their content is concerned. It manifests itself (if our concentration holds) by taking a common linguistic interpretation of a passage as its point of departure, reflecting on Heidegger's new creations in regard to linguistic content as well as in regard to linguistic form, and continuously keeping them in mind. What is required here is certainly strong, intellectual force and the willingness to follow the spiral movement into this unfamiliar linguistic plane. One can read such a text, in contradistinction to many others, only by penetrating into it step by step, starting from the very beginning. This explains, also, the lack of seriousness on the part of all polemics that attempt to show the "meaninglessness" of Heidegger's language on the basis of an isolated passage from such a text.

50. There are kinds of paronomasia available that are grammatically to be classified differently: "die in der *Sorge gesorgte* . . . Eigentlichkeit" (*SZ* 301); "die . . . Bewegtheit des *erstreckten Sicherstreckens*" (*SZ* 375); "die *furchtsam* die *Furcht befürchtet*" (*SZ* 345); "die *allgemeinste Allgemein-heit*" (*SZ* 9); "die Entschlossenheit *erschliesst*" (*SZ* passim; partial iteration). A classical example of multiple paronomasia is the Byzantine emperor's title BBBB, *basileus basileōn basileuōn basileusi*, King of Kings Governing (literally, "Kinging") over Kings.

employs the *figura etymologica* easily evokes. That may also be the reason that one hears the reproach of "verbal magic," "obscurantism," and the like in this connection.

The objection based on stylistic grounds cannot be pushed aside with a shrug of the shoulders. But an ideal of linguistic beauty and balance, whatever kind or form it may be, is always in conflict with that other demand according to which the linguistic "means" should be appropriate, as far as content is concerned, to the "thing" of thought (*die Sache des Denkens*). It is only from this point of view that it can be justified to run counter to the codex of a language and to change it. The location of the middle ground on which this conflict can and must be settled is perhaps not yet recognizable in the case of Heidegger's language.

11 / M. Heidegger's "Ontological Difference" and Language

Johannes Lohmann

HEIDEGGER, QUOTING LEIBNIZ, writes the following in *The Essence of Reasons:*

"Thus, a predicate, or consequent, is always contained in a subject, or antecedent; and in this fact consists the universal nature of truth, or the connection between the terms of the assertion, as Aristotle has also observed. This connection and inclusion of the predicate in the subject is explicit in relations of identity. In all other relations it is implicit and is to be revealed through an analysis of notions, upon which a priori demonstration is based.

"The above holds true for every affirmative true assertion, whether universal or singular, necessary or contingent, as well as for both intrinsic and extrinsic denomination. This wondrous secret goes unnoticed, this secret which reveals the nature of contingency, or the essential distinction between necessary and contingent truths, and which even removes the difficulty regarding the inevitable necessity of free beings.

"From these things, which have not been adequately considered due to their great simplicity, there follow many other things of great importance. Indeed, from them there at once arises the familiar axiom: 'Nothing is without reason,' or 'there is no effect without a cause.' If the axiom did not hold, there might be a truth which could not be proved a priori, i.e., which could not be resolved into relations of identity; and this is contrary to the nature of truth, which is always identical, whether explicitly or implicitly." [1]

1. L. Couturat, ed., *Opuscules et fragments inédits de Leibniz* (Paris: Alcan, 1903), pp. 518–19.

Here, bound up with his characterization of "*first* truths," Leibniz characteristically gives a definition of what truth is *firstly* and in general. He hopes thereby to demonstrate that the *principium rationis* is "born" in and from the *nature veritatis*. For the success of his demonstration, he thinks it is necessary to point out that the apparent self-evidence of such concepts as "truth" and "identity" hinders the kind of clarification of them that would adequately set forth the origin of the *principium rationis* and the other axioms. But what now stands in question is not the derivation of the *principium rationis* but the explanation of the problem of the ground. To what extent does the passage quoted above offer us some clue in this analysis?

The *principium rationis* exists because, if it did not, there would be beings which would necessarily be without reason. For Leibniz, this means that there would be truths which resisted resolution into relations of identity; there would be truths, that is, which would necessarily run counter to the "nature" of truth in general. Because this is impossible, because there is such a thing as truth, there is also such a thing as the *principium rationis*. For the principle arises from the essence of truth. But, the argument continues, the essence of truth lies in the connexio (*symplokē*) of subject and predicate. Thus, with explicit though unjustified reference to Aristotle, Leibniz begins by construing truth as truth of the assertion (proposition). He then defines the nexus of subject and predicate as the *"inesse"* of the predicate in the subject, but he goes on to define this *"inesse"* as *"idem esse."* Here "identity," as the essence of propositional truth, obviously does not mean any empty sameness of something with itself but "unity" in the sense of the original oneness of that which belongs together. Truth, then, means consonance. And consonance is only "consonance" as correspondence with that which announces itself as "at one" or "alike" in the identity. By their very nature, "truths," i.e., true assertions, refer to something *by reason of which* they can be consonant. The dividing connecting in every truth is what it is only "by reason of . . . ," i.e., as a connecting that "founds" itself. Thus an essential relationship to something like "reasons" dwells at the very heart of *truth*. The problem of truth now enters the "neighborhood" of the problem of ground. The more originally we seize upon the problem of the essence of truth, therefore, the more persistent must the problem of ground become.

Can we add something more original, something that goes beyond the definition of the essence of truth as a character of the assertion? Nothing less than the insight that this definition, however construed, is, though unavoidable, nonetheless derivative. The correspondence of the nexus *with* being and its resulting consonance do not *as such* render being immediately accessible. Rather, as the possible "subject" of a predicative definition, being must already be manifest both *prior to* and *for* our predications. Predication, to become possible, must be able to establish itself in the sort of manifesting which does *not* have a *predicative* character. Propositional truth is rooted in a *more primordial* truth (unconcealedness); it is rooted in that prepredicative manifestness *of being* which we call *ontical truth*. The character of its manifestness, and of the pertinent kinds of explanatory defining, varies with the many kinds and realms of being. Thus, for example, *discoveredness,* or the truth of that which is present-at-hand (e.g., of material things), is uniquely different from the *disclosedness* of existing Dasein, or the truth of the kind of being which we ourselves are. As numerous as the differences of these two kinds of ontic truth may be, all prepredicative manifestness is such that, at a *primary* level, manifesting never has the character of a mere rendering present as intuition, not even in "aesthetic" contemplation. We will be inclined to characterize prepredicative truth as intuiting *only if* ontic, and presumably authentic, truth is defined as propositional truth, i.e., as a presentational connection. For the next most simple thing to a presentational connection is, indeed, a plain presentation (one free from combination). The proper function of presentation is to *objectivize* being—which itself must then always be already manifest. Ontical manifesting, however, takes place in our situating ourselves in the midst of being, through our moods and drives, as well as in the conative and volitional kinds of behavior toward being that are grounded in the way we find ourselves situated. Yet even such behavior—whether displayed in a prepredicative or a predicative manner—could not make beings accessible in themselves were their manifesting not already guided and clarified by an understanding of the Being (the constitution of Being, implying what something is and how it is) of beings. *The disclosedness of Being alone makes possible the manifestness of being.* As the truth about Being, this disclosedness is called *ontological truth*. The terms *ontology* and *ontological* have so many meanings that they conceal the proper problem of an ontology. The *logos* of *on* means the addressing (*legein*) of beings as beings. But it also means that to *which* beings are addressed (*legomenon*). To address something *as* something does not necessarily mean to *grasp* that which is addressed *in its essence*. The *understanding* of Being (*logos* in a very broad sense), which from the outset clarifies and guides every way of behaving toward being, is neither a grasping of Being as such nor even a comprehending of that which is grasped (*logos* in the narrowest sense = "ontological" concept). The sort of understanding of Being that has not yet been conceptualized we call "preontological" or "ontological in the broader sense." In order to comprehend Being, the understanding of Being must have developed of its own accord and have made Being (which is understood, generally projected, and somehow disclosed in it) its problem and theme of inquiry. There are many stages between the preontological understanding of Being and the explicit problematic involved in conceptualizing Being. One characteristic stage is the project of the constitution of the Being of being whereby a determinate field of being (perhaps nature or history) is, at the same time, marked off as an area that can be objectivized through scientific knowledge. The preliminary definition of the Being (understood here as what something is and how it is) of nature is established in the "basic concepts" of natural science. Although space, locus, time, movement, mass, force, and velocity are defined in these concepts, the essence of time, movement, etc., does not become a problem in its own right. The understanding of the Being of what is present-at-hand is expressed conceptually here, but the application and scope of the conceptual definition of time, locus, etc., are wholly determined by the basic inquiry to which being is submitted in natural *science*. The basic concepts of modern science do not include "authentic" ontological concepts of the Being of the being it treats, nor can the latter be obtained simply through a "suitable" extension of the former. Original ontological concepts must instead be obtained *prior* to any scientific definition of "basic concepts," so that only by proceeding from them will we be in a position to evaluate the manner in which the basic concepts of the sciences apply to Being as graspable in purely ontological concepts. The manner in which ontological concepts apply to Being will always be limited to and circumscribed by a definite point of view. The "fact" of the sciences, i.e., the factical constituent of the understanding of Being that is necessarily included in them as in every way of behaving toward being, is neither a tribunal for founding the a priori nor the source of our knowledge of the a priori but merely a possible clue to the primordial constitution of the Being of, for example, history or nature. It is a clue which must itself be constantly subjected to the sort of criticism that has already gotten its bearings in the fundamental problematic of all inquiry about the Being of being.

The several possible levels and varieties of ontological truth in the broader sense reveal the richness of that which, as primordial truth, lies at the basis of all ontical truth. The unconcealedness of Being is the truth of the Being *of* being, whether or not the latter is real. In the unconcealedness of being, on the other hand, lies a prior unconcealedness of its Being. Each after its own fashion, ontical and ontological truth concern *being in* its Being and the *Being of* being. They belong together essentially, by reason of their relationship to the *difference between Being and being* (the Ontological Difference). The essence of truth, which is and must be bifurcated ontically and ontologically, is only possible given this difference. Yet if what is distinctive about Dasein is that it behaves toward being by understanding Being, then *the* ability to differentiate the two (in which the Ontological Difference becomes factical) must have struck the roots of its own possibility in the ground of the essence of Dasein. To anticipate, we name this ground of the Ontological Difference the *transcendence* of Dasein.

If one characterizes every *way of behaving* toward being as intentional, then intentionality is possible only *on the basis of transcendence*. It is neither identical with transcendence nor that which makes transcendence possible.[2]

In the interpretation which further develops and "unfolds" the implicit meaning of this idea, Heidegger explains Leibniz' interpretation of the propositional truth taken as identity as "original agreement of what belongs together." In the sentence this truth manifests itself as the consonance of the nexus between the subject and the predicate concepts, which is such only as the cor-respondence of this nexus with being. As this consonance of subject and predicate is merely a reflection of the correspondence of what is asserted, taken as a whole with being, this "truth" of what has been asserted is thus grounded in a more original truth ("unconcealment," "manifestness") which does not have a predicative character and which is called here "the ontic truth."

The ontic truth, which is to be divided into the discoveredness of what is present-at-hand and the disclosedness of Dasein, finds its expression in a moodlike and instinctive finding oneself in the midst of beings and the conative and volitional relations with being which are co-founded therein. The ontic rendering manifest which predicatively becomes interpreted in language is only a special case of this. The "prepredicative," as well as the "predicatively interpreting," ontic making manifest and becoming manifest, come to pass in the *as* structure, which is characteristic of the letting something become manifest or the addressing of something as something. The comprehension of Being which becomes expressed herein and which illuminates and guides all

2. *WG* 10–11 (15–29).

comportment in regard to being, both precedingly and concomitantly—that is, the preontological comprehension of Being,
or the ontological comprehension taken in the broad sense—is
the first step and starting point for the comprehension of Being
as such and for the understanding of what is so comprehended—
that is, the ontological problematic expressly understood as such,
the "ontological" concept.

It follows then that the "ontological" comprehension of Being
taken in the broad sense and the ontological truth taken in a
corresponding way constitute the ground of all ontic truth and
manifestness and are presupposed by this. However, one becomes
fully and consciously aware of this only in the "philosophical"
problematic of a Dasein which makes itself a theme of investigation.

According to the name, onto-logy is the "science of being as
such" (on hēi on). Such an onto-logy—that is to say, such an
"addressing" of being as being and thus an addressing of being
in the direction of its Being—comes to pass implicitly before
every "science," on the basis of Dasein's transcendence, as intentionality (to use the medieval expression for the habitus of
this psychic experience, which Brentano renewed and extended
beyond the realm of the "intellectual").

The as structure of what is comprehended in the "intentionality," the "understanding" of "something as something," constitutes the "interpretation," of which the assertion constitutes a
derivative form.[3] That which is understood in the understanding,
interpreted in the interpretation, and asserted in the assertion as
such is the meaning (Sinn). In the understanding this meaning
is predelineated as that which can be articulated. In the interpretation it appears as that which has been articulated as such.[4]
Finally, as "meaningful differentiation," "articulation" is the
conceptual definition of man's speech since the time of Aristotle,
of its "phonic" as well as its "logical" aspects.

What is the basic element of the "articulation of meaning"
characteristic of the ontico-ontological rendering manifest which
comes about in assertion, interpretation, and understanding? According to Heidegger's text this would be on the one hand the as
structure (of the addressing of something as something), but on

3. SZ, 195–96.
4. SZ, 195–96.

the other hand the ontological difference, the difference between Being and being, which is founded in Dasein's transcendence and which necessarily comes to light with the ontico-ontological bifurcation of the essence of "truth as such." How then are the *as* structure and the "ontological difference" related to one another, and how must the relationship between them be understood in regard to the subject-predicate relation of our grammar and logic?

Leibniz conceives of the *"verum esse"* of the subject-predicate relation as *"inesse"* of predicate in subject, and this in turn as *"idem esse."* This is the logical form of the assertion found in grammatical structure of the Indo-European proposition. The logical inherence of the predicate concept in the subject concept (the fact that "mortality" is contained in "humanity") is expressed as objective identification (*omnes homines = mortales*).[5] However, this structure of the expression is certainly not a logical necessity. It presupposes a continuous "supposition," [6] the transformation of the merely conceptual meaning of words (for instance, "mortal") into a meaning that is objectively founded ("a mortal [man]," "the mortal [man]"). We can now also say that it presupposes the continuous "ontological differentiation," as each word in a sentence (insofar as the word is not merely an *"outil grammatical,"* to quote A. Meillet) explicitly signifies the Being of a being, or a being in its Being.

In the older Indo-European languages this continuous "ontological differentiation" is expressed in the grammatical form of the word: *nomen* as well as *verbum,* according to their elementary morphological structures, are composed of "stem" and "ending," the stem (for instance, the Latin *equ-* ["horse"] or *alb-* ["white"]) as "conceptual expression" and the ending (in this case the "case endings" *-us, -ī, -ō, -um, -e, -ōrum, -īs, -ōs, -a, -ae, -am, -ā, -ārum, -ās*) as expressions of the relation of the concept in regard to an "object" which is given in the context of the sentence. Each ancient Indo-European nominal or verbal form as such therefore contains an expression of the relation of a "Being" (the "Being horse" or the "Being white") to a "being" (a determinate "horse" or "white thing," or determinate "horses" or "white things"). Indo-European speech thus, from the beginning,

---

5. Cf. W. Bröcker, "Die Sprache und das Sein," *Lexis,* I (1948), 46.
6. Cf. *ibid.,* pp. 45–46.

moves exclusively within the realm of the "absolute ontological difference."

This is neither self-evident nor unimportant; it is, rather, a fundamental, specific characteristic of the Indo-European language structure, a characteristic which determines in a very fundamental way not only the position of the Indo-European languages within the totality of the types of language structures which are either factically available or apriorically possible, but also the Indo-European language taken in and for itself. The Indo-European language is primarily a language that makes use of supposition (*supponierende Sprache*).[7] This way of speaking, although borrowed from the medieval manner of speaking, nonetheless is not in complete correspondence with it.

In the Scholastic formulation the *suppositio* is conceived of as a function of the individual word (*proprietas termini*) which, taken as "subject" (*suppositum*), normally "lays" its "signification" (instead of the really meant "object") "under" the predicate of the proposition: "*dictio supponit suum significatum pro re.*" This basic formula which appears in the oldest of the known forms of "suppositional logic," namely, that of William of Shyreswood (d. ca. 1267),[8] is then reduced to "*dictio* [or *terminus*] *supponit pro re*" in that typical "Ockhamism" which, as nominalism, dominated the late medieval university and which, in this doctrine of the *proprietates termini*, had found the logical fundament of the Ockhamists' philosophico-theological world view. The expression "*terminus supponit pro re,*" meant, for Ockham, simply that the word (the concept) stands (*stat*) for the meant "object."[9]

In the form of the doctrine of the *proprietas termini*, which was adopted by Ockham, only the fact of the difference between the mere signification of the word and the "thing itself" remained. Taking this as its point of departure, nominalism founded and carried through its devaluation of the universal, of

---

7. I used this term in my review of Carl Meinhof's *Die Entstehung flektierender Sprachen* (Berlin: Reimer, 1936), which appeared in *Gnomon*, XVII (1941), 385–98.

8. See M. Grabmann, ed., *Die "Introductiones in logicam" des Wilhelm von Shyreswood (nach 1267)* (Munich: Verlag der Bayerischen Akademie der Wissenschaften, 1937).

9. Cf. the texts quoted in Carl von Prantl, *Geschichte der Logik im Abendlande*, 3 vols. (Leipzig: Hirzel, 1855–70), III, 333 ff. *Suppositio* is explained as *pro aliis positio* (*ibid.*, p. 373, n. 876).

the Platonic *"idea,"* in favor of the *"res,"* and in so doing founded a realism in the modern sense. The original logical content of the doctrine was essentially more differentiated. It connected the subject-predicate relation within the proposition to the relationship between the "concept" and the "object" (which falls under the concept and is expressed by the concept in the proposition) and distinguished also between the logical function given by the grammatical form of the word (*suppositio in habitu*) and the logical operation of the actual proposition (*suppositio in actu*). In both cases the "supposition," which is just one among the many *proprietates termini,* is attributed to the word (of speech as well as of language) taken as action. Thus the word in a certain sense allows the "ontological difference" to appear; but, as a consequence of this, language does so, too, and can therefore equally be called "supposing" (*supponierend*), as can the one who speaks, insofar as he speaks in this form.[10]

Insofar as each speaking, seen from the viewpoint of language, is a speaking in concepts, whereas, nonetheless, the "thing itself" is meant, one can say that all languages taken as speech must be "supposing," that they must contain the "ontological difference" as structural moment. All speech comes to pass as "understanding interpretation" in the *as* structure of "intentionality," in the structure of understanding something as something or also of understanding something under something (*sup-positio*), or in the structure of meaning something with something, of which Ockham's *terminus supponens pro re* ("the concept which stands for the object") represents a "derivative mode."

In addition to the *suppositio in actu* there is the *suppositio in habitu,* as Shyreswood expresses it. Here the languages separate from one another. In the *suppositio in habitu* the "ontological difference" becomes explicit in the grammatical form of the language; that is, there onto-logy explicitly "comes to pass."

The languages which are "supposing" in this pregnant sense are those which Meinhof calls the "inflecting" languages (if one includes the African "class languages," about which Meinhof is not completely clear). The languages which "inflect" in this way correspond to the types which Finck describes in chapters

10. Cf. the observations that Bröcker makes about the "saying of Being" as "letting be seen" and the aspects of this letting be seen, in "Die Sprache und das Sein," pp. 47–48.

4, 7, and 8 of *Haupttypen des Sprachbaus*.[11] In the "genealogical classification" these languages coincide with the Bantoid, Semitic or Hamito-Semitic, and Indo-European language families. These three types, which in Finck's work do not appear as a group, either in their naming ("stringing," "root inflecting," "stem inflecting") or in their description, have in common, as I pointed out in my review of Meinhof's book, the fact that grammatical congruence (concordance, correspondence) serves as the principle for the structure of the sentence: (*hic*) *vir bonus* (*est*), (*haec*) *mulier bona* (*est*), (*hi*) *viri boni* (*sunt*), and so on.[12]

Grammatical congruence as the building principle of the sentence presupposes a "classification" of the nominal vocabulary. In comparison with the distinction between those languages that do classify and those that do not, the distinction which Meinhof has stressed so expressly is of secondary importance—namely, the distinction between "class languages" such as the Bantu languages (in Finck, for example, seventeen classes) and "genus languages" (masculine, feminine, and neuter in the Indo-European languages; masculine and feminine in the Semitic languages; if the *numerus* is taken into consideration in the classification of the Bantu languages, a higher number—up to nine—is reached here too). If "inflection" is taken in the sense of Meinhof's circumscription of the "inflecting languages," "inflection" is to be understood as the declension of the *nomina* according to "classes" (in which, however, the *numerus* is to be included, also; thus, in the Latin example used above: *equus albus, equi albi, equa alba, equae albae*).

Such a delimitation of the "inflection" would actually be adequate only in the Bantoid languages, the sentence structure of which is based solely on a class expression conceived of in this way. The possibility of translating this Bantoid concept of "inflection" into the Latin one and the fact that the concept of "inflection" which is so determined only partly coincides with the Latin and with the Indo-European "inflection" in general and perhaps does not even touch upon their essential significance show that the Indo-European "inflection" and the "supposition"

11. See Meinhof, *Die Entstehung flektierender Sprachen;* F. N. Finck, *Haupttypen des Sprachbaus* (Leipzig: Teubner, 1909).

12. The logical function of grammatical congruence and its connection with the "supposition" has been explained in Lohmann, *Gnomon*, pp. 385–98, and in Bröcker, "Die Sprache und das Sein," p. 46.

which is explicitly expressed therein are not homogeneous, that they have, as we may say anticipatively, two faces.

We can disregard here the morphological difference between "inflection" by means of "endings" and "inflection" by means of "inner *Ablaut*." In the Indo-Germanic languages the vowel gradation contributes from the very beginning and in an increasing degree much more to the conceptual modification than to the expression of the relations within the sentence. Beginning with Greek grammar, "inflection" (*klisis*) has been used as the expression of the morphological declensions whose purpose is to express the grammatical propositional relations. "Inflection" is thus the morphological correlate of the *suntax(is)*, which, as a heritage of Stoic logic, signifies the "inner," "logical" form and formation of the sentence (the "logic" of a language expresses itself in its "morphology"). The syntactical correlate of the morphological "inflection form" is the "state of affairs" (*pragma suntakton*) of Stoic logic, which, as a "defective linguistic form of signification" (*lekton ellipes*), is in need of, but also capable of, "being joined" (*suntak-ton*) or "putting together" (*suntaxis*).[13]

The *"ratio"* of this junction (of the *sun-taxis*) can be an "inner," purely log-ical *"ratio"* or an "outer," ob-jective one, founded in Kant's "forms of intuition," namely, space and time. It is in this way that the difference is founded between what is called the "nominal sentence" and the "verbal sentence" in the Semitic grammar. The building principle of the "nominal sentence" is the "congruence" between "subject"—in Arabic, *mubtada* (*a quo incipitur* [point of departure"])—and "predicate"—in Arabic, *ḥabar* ("information"). In the Semitic languages, which do not have the Indo-European copula, this congruence can appear in full purity. The congruence is the morphological form of expression of the identity, which according to Leibniz is precisely the essence of propositional truth.[14] For the nominal sentence (taken in the sense of Semitic grammar) one can use Leibniz' formula *"inesse qua idem esse"*—that is, the conceptual inherence (of *mortalitas* in *humanitas*) which is conceived of as objective identity (*omn-es homin-es = mortal-es*) —as the description of its morphological structure. However,

---

13. The sentence is a "complete and independent form of expression" (*lekton auto-teles*).

14. Cf. p. 309 above.

conceptual inherence and objective identity (conceived of as formal relations between concepts taken purely as such or also conceived of as and in regard to "objects in general") are purely logical, merely thought relations—that is, relations of Being itself and of the "ontological difference" which is given in and with it. If the nominal sentence is taken as logical form, in which case abstraction must be made from the real or alleged material "signification" of the "classes," [15] then its structure does not contain any extramental moment. It is the expression of a merely "subjective" movement and relation, a movement of thought itself but not of the object taken in and for itself.

The verbal sentence, which has its center in the *verbum*, is the expression of the "objective" movement and relation with respect to space and time, taken as forms of intuition (Kant) or taken in an objective way as forms of the world's "mundaneity." To the *verbum* belong the "factor predications," [16] which signify the relations characteristic of the sentence and which find their morphological expression partly in the personal affixes of the *verbum* (or in personal forms which are equivalent to these) and partly in the "case" forms of the *nomen* (or in the affixes which are equivalent to these). Therefore, Meinhof can include the Indo-European inflection (and, to a certain extent, the Semitic), insofar as it is "case" inflection (in the *nomen*) and "personal" inflection (in the *verbum*), under the heading "supposition." The supposition together with the "ontological difference" finds its immediate expression in the "identity structure," in the *inesse qua idem esse* of the purely nominal sentence. In the verbal sentence, on the other hand, the supposition appears to be mixed with the forms of outer intuition (space, time, and spatiotemporal movement). The supposition results from them merely in a secondary way insofar as the factor predication, for instance, taken as *agens* and as *patiens* (the relation of the doer or of the one who is affected by the action to the action: "the dog barks," "the man beats the dog")—taken as an expression of this action, expressed by these factors—attributes an objective sig-

---

15. Lohmann, *Gnomon*, p. 387.

16. *Kāraka-* ("factor") is the expression in ancient Indian grammar for the relationship of *nomen* and *verbum* as *agens* and *patiens* to the instrument (that is, the relationship of the "doer," the "object," and the instrument in regard to the activity), and so on. The label *factor predication*, signifying the case forms and "prepositions," was introduced in Lohmann, *Gnomon*, p. 392.

nification to the concepts of the sentence ("dog," "man," "bark," and "beat") only in a secondary way. But each factor predication and each "case" form at least indirectly work "supposing" (*supponierend*), whereas the nominal compound ("the dog's barking," "the battle of the nations," "world war") remains within the conceptual sphere. The examples in English are unfortunately inadequate insofar as the English article in itself has a suppositional function.

In reference to these propositional types, namely, the nominal and verbal sentences, which are expressly distinguished in the Semitic grammar, one could comparatively formulate the logical relation of the Bantoid, Semitic, and Indo-European language structures in such a way that in the Bantoid languages the type called "nominal sentence" (the propositional structure according to the principle of "congruence") is the only one found. In the Semitic languages the nominal and verbal sentences ("inner" and "outer" relations) stand side by side, whereas in the Indo-European languages these two are built into one another in a characteristic way. The nominal sentence (with the *verbum is* as copula) in a sense assumes verbal character, while the verbal sentence adapts itself in its structure to the nominal sentence. For example, compare propositional forms such as "*Socrates venenum laetus hausit*" or "*Cicero consul fit*" with "*Socrates laetus est*" or "*Cicero consul est.*" [17]

This discussion leads to a number of questions. If the Bantoid type is based merely on the "identity" structure of the nominal sentence, whereas the Semitic type and the Indo-European type, each in its own way, connect nominal and verbal sentences to one another (in a relation which one might call an "inner" and an "outer" one, respectively), then one could postulate a priori a fourth type, grounded merely on the structural principle of the verbal sentence (that is, of the "outer" relation). Is such a type to be found in the "a posteriori" classification of types of language structures brought to the fore by the investigations conducted between the time of Humboldt and that of Finck? Of the eight types given by Finck, only the "Georgic language" is suitable for this purpose (Finck was the first to include this type in the system of types).[18] The Georgic language is primarily char-

17. Cf. Bröcker's observations with regard to the German "Being" propositions in "Die Sprache und das Sein," pp. 47–48.
18. Finck, *Haupttypen des Sprachbaus*, chap. 9.

acterized through the relational expression in which the *verbum* is like the hub of a wheel and can receive up to three "factor predications." This can be illustrated with an example taken from the Gospels: *da-x-ban-n-a* ("he [-*a*] washed [-*ban*-] them [-*n*-] to him [-*x*-]"), in which "he" = Jesus, "them" = his feet, and *da*- is a "preverb" which more or less = off.

In the case of the *nomen*, too, the relational expression is here connected with the conceptual expression in a looser union and with an accumulation of functions. That is why Finck calls this language structure "group inflecting." (This expression certainly does not coincide with the "root" and "stem" inflection: the Caucasian "group" is not the "object" of the inflection, as the Semitic "root" and the Indo-European "stem" really are, but its result; therefore, in this case the basic conception of the inflection concept is given up.) Syntactically this type is characterized by a propositional construction which is connected with certain "action forms" of the *verbum* (aorist tense, perfect tense) and which, when literally translated into Indo-European languages, seems to be passive: by-father written a-letter = father wrote a letter (aorist); father (dative) written a-letter = father has written a letter (perfect).[19] Therefore, from the Indo-European point of view something is lacking insofar as the verbal form as well as the whole sentence construction is concerned—namely, the distinction of a determinate factor (in our case, the *agens*) as "subject," and herewith the approximation of the verbal sentence to the subject-predicate scheme of the nominal sentence which in our languages results from this distinction. (This Indo-European approximation, in turn, is the presupposition for the usual identification of the subject with an *agens* and an ego; this identification characterizes the modern European way of thinking, in which "subjective" immediately becomes identical with "related to an *ego*.") All of this shows that in the Georgic type we have the scheme of the purely verbal sentence as basis for sentence construction.

It is therefore possible to characterize the four types which are described by Finck [20] from the viewpoint of the Semitic grammatical concepts of "nominal sentence" and "verbal sentence," that is, from the viewpoint of the distinction between the sentence as identity structure and the sentence structure resulting

19. *Ibid.*, p. 134.
20. *Ibid.*, chaps. 4, 7, 8, 9.

from outer, "objective" relations. In this way the sentence structure in the Bantoid languages is one-sidedly governed by the identity structure, and in the Georgic, or southern Caucasian, this structure is one-sidedly determined by outer relations. The Semitic and Indo-European languages combine nominal sentence and verbal sentence; in this way these two sentence types stand side by side as syntactical structures in the Semitic languages, whereas in the Indo-European languages the subject-predicate scheme of the nominal sentence is fused with the relational scheme of the verbal sentence into a unity.

Let us now consider how the definition of the types according to a morphological point of view, the point of view which predominates in Finck, is related to this "logical," or "ontological," determination of the language structure on the basis of the "ontological difference," which in these types is either immediately or mediately operative. It is clear that Finck's concept of inflection, which in this regard is in agreement with the commonly used concept and differs from Meinhof's, determines the inflection first of all as the expression of the "outer" propositional relations—that is to say, of the verbal "factor predications"—and not as the expression of the nominal subject-predicate relation. Finck uses the term *inflecting* only for those types which exlusively, or at least predominantly, use the verbal sentence as syntactic scheme, that is to say, his last three types (Semitic, Indo-European, and Caucasian). Of these three types, the Semitic and the Indo-European, according to the explanation given above, belong to the "supposing" languages. On the basis of their morphological structure Finck calls them "root inflecting" (Semitic) and "stem inflecting" (Indo-European). The question, therefore, is how the supposition can then be expressed in this specific morphological structure.

We have already spoken about the function of the "stem" in the "supposition." The Indo-European stem is logically the expression of a concept, which is referred to the "object" that the word signifies within the context of the sentence by means of the "ending," that is to say, by means of the inflection. The Indo-European word form, which is thus divided into two parts, was described above as the reflection of the logico-ontological difference of Being and being. If the "supposition" is now the result of the "ontological differentiation" in the linguistic form as such, then we should a priori have to expect such a fundamental morphological bifurcation of the word form for all the "supposing" language types taken in the strict sense.[21]

This basic bifurcation of the word form is now in fact found in all three "supposing" types, albeit occurring factically in characteristically different ways. In the Bantoid word the "class character" is put before the "stem" of the word (*mu-untu* ["man"], *ba-ntu* ["men"]); the "class character" corresponds to the Indo-European ending and, in this way, founds the obligatory twofoldness of the word form. The Semitic word form equally is fundamentally divided into the consonantic "root" and the elements which modify it. This is why the Semitic type is called "root inflecting"; for instance, *katab* ("[someone] wrote," "[someone] has written"), *kātib* ("writing," "writer"), *kitāb* ("book"), *kutub* ("books"), *maktūb* ("letter"), *maktab* ("school"), and *kutubī* ("bookseller") are Egypto-Arabic forms of the root *k-t-b*, which vocalized as *verbum* signifies "to write."

This Semitic root is one of the great miracles of man's language. It alone made the discovery of letter-writing—at first pure consonant-writing—possible. Here language itself, by fundamentally dividing vowels and consonants in their function in the constitution of forms, already prepared the "phonological" analysis of the word body, that is to say, the presupposition for this form of writing. In the final analysis, however, the root is even more miraculous if one considers it from its conceptual side. It signifies, as Finck says, "nothing intuitively imaginable, but something purely conceptual." Locke's explanation of the essence of the "idea" of the triangle is called to mind in Finck's description of the root:

> Just as difficult as it is to imagine clearly and distinctly a triangle which is neither rectangular nor oblique-angled, neither equilateral nor nonequilateral, and at the same time is nonetheless all of this and even more, so difficult is it for an Arab to make intuitively present to himself a *k-t-b* which signifies neither the representation indicated by *kātib* nor that indicated by *kitāb*, and nonetheless implies both and even more.[22]

The Semitic "root" thus appears here as the embodiment of pure conceptuality, as "materialization of the idea," just as the per-

21. Cf. pp. 309–10 above.
22. Finck, *Haupttypen des Sprachbaus*, p. 97.

sonal God of the Semites "embodies" the "highest Idea," the *malista on* of Greek philosophy.

The "root," which in a certain sense forms the center of the Semitic word and yet at the same time encompasses it, is as such unanalyzable for our linguistic consciousness. Conversely, in Indo-European languages the other pole of the bifurcated word, namely, the ending, fulfills, in an unanalyzable unity, the function of the "supposition." Characteristic of the Indo-European ending is the fact that it unites in itself all suppositive functions in a phonetically indistinct manner—for instance, the accusative plural *equōs* as opposed to the Turkish *at-lar-ï,* in which *-lar-* signifies the plural and *-ï-* the accusative, and opposed to Semitic forms such as the Egypto-Arabic *ti-ksar* ("you [masculine] break down"), *ti-ksar-ī* ("you [feminine] break down"), *ti-ksar-ū* ("you [plural] break down"), *yi-ksar* ("he breaks down"), *yi-ksar-ū* ("they break down").[23]

From the "cumulation of functions" in the Indo-European ending it follows that the individual function as such cannot be expressed by a determinate phonetic form. An ending of the plural or of the genitive alone is impossible; there is only an ending of the genitive singular or the genitive plural. In the Indo-European languages the "form variation," as Lewy calls this phenomenon of the "signification of one and the same inner form by means of different outer forms,"[24] goes far beyond this differentiation, which is conditioned by the "cumulation of functions." The complex form, too, normally shows a multiple variation; for instance, in Latin we find genitive singular forms such as *deae, dei, regis, domūs,* and *eius,* and combinations such as (*haec*) *domus bona* (*est*) and (*hic*) *scriba bonus* (*est*), where the syntactic congruence is expressed in an incongruence of the

23. *Ibid.,* p. 101.

24. Ernst Lewy, "Heimatfrage," [*Kuhn's*] *Zeitschrift für vergleichende Sprachforschung auf dem Gebiete der indogermanischen Sprachen* (hereafter cited as *KZ*), LVIII (1931), pp. 1–15. It appears to me that, in view of the whole context, H. H. Schaeder, following Friedrich Specht, *Der Ursprung der indogermanische Deklination* (Göttingen: Vandenhoeck & Ruprecht, 1948), is incorrect in concluding that Lewy has depended upon A. Meillet's idea because of the fact that Meillet, in his *Caractères généraux des langues germaniques* (Paris: Hachette, 1937), incidentally speaks of the *variété des formes* as characteristic of the Indo-Germanic languages. Specht assured me that it has always been far from his thoughts (and, I will assume, from those of Schaeder also) to suppose a conscious borrowing with concealment of the source, as one might in reading conclude from the wording.

phonetic form. In this connection Bröcker distinguishes "materialistic" languages which "tie their grammatic significative functions to a determinate phonetic material," and "idealistic" languages in which the grammatic category, largely emancipated from a possible connection with determinate phonetic symbols, has a purely intellectual existence.[25] The Indo-European languages certainly represent an extreme instance of this "linguistic idealism." The comparison of this fact with the tendency toward "abstraction" from that which is outwardly visible and which then becomes degraded to mere "appearance," a tendency which dominates European "philosophy" and "science," is obvious.

Something further seems to be connected with the "immateriality" of the Indo-European languages. If one considers the Indo-European language family in its relationship to the other great language families of the world, those which Finck describes as "basic" types and which at the same time are all "excessive" types, extreme forms of the realization of the possibilities of the human language structure, then, historically seen, the Indo-European family strikes us specifically by the extreme lability and fragility of its outer form. Phenomena such as the Semitic trilateral root (*k-t-b* in the given example); the Bantoid class prefixes; the *agglutinatio*, that is, the loosely stringing unifying of the formative elements of the Ural-Altaic languages; the manner of form construction which Finck calls "group inflection" in the southern Caucasian languages; the monosyllabicity of the Indo-Chinese word form; and the bisyllabicity of the root word in the Malayo-Polynesian languages all adhere as a rule to these linguistic types as a possession that cannot be lost. The Indo-European stem-ending form, on the other hand, shows almost everywhere a tendency toward volatilization, becomes almost ungraspable, "spiritualizes itself" toward new structures. The new structures certainly correspond to the stem-ending form "logically" (in that, for instance, the supposition function is taken over by the article, and in addition the factor predication is taken over by "prepositions"), but they have given up the characteristic outer form of the original type. The dissolution of the phonetic materialization of the category as such, which was characteristic of the Indo-European type from the very start, therefore

---

25. W. Bröcker, "Über die Prinzipien a priori einer allgemeinen Grammatik," *Zeitschrift für romanische Philologie*, LXIII (1943), 380–81.

encroaches here also on the logico-ontological fundament of the type, of the materialization of the "ontological difference" itself.

The original Indo-European word form and the Semitic word form have the principle of bifurcation in common. In the Indo-European languages this is established through the "stem" and its "inflection"; in the Semitic languages, through the "root" and the elements which modify it. However, the designation of the Semitic type as "root inflecting," which is obviously a construction analogous to the characterization of the Indo-European languages as "stem inflecting," is to a certain extent misleading. The Semitic "root inflection" coincides neither in its material form nor in its function with the Indo-European "stem inflection." The Indo-European "inflection" is the modification of a concept (which as such is already available) according to the syntactical relations to which this concept is related in the sentence, whereas the Semitic "inflection," insofar as it is understood as "root inflection," constitutes the concrete conceptual expression (from an imaginary root which receives a concrete form only in writing). The affinity between these two is to be found in their relationship to the "ontological difference."

In both cases the bifurcation is not a simple one, as is the case in the Bantoid word, whose class prefixes have a "pronominal" character which can be compared with our "article"; thus *mu-ntu/ba-ntu* is more or less like the French *l-umm/layz-umm, lah-fahm/lay-fahm*. In both the "inflecting" types an intermediate domain inserts itself between pure "conceptuality" and pure "objectivity" as the two poles of the "ontological difference." To a certain extent this domain belongs to both types; it represents neither pure conceptuality (as does the Semitic root) nor pure objectivity (as does the Indo-European ending). In both types signification consists in the elements of the "word construction." However, in the Indo-European languages these elements are added to the "root" (*scrib-ent-[em]* or *scrip-tōr-[es]* ["the writer(s)"]), whereas in the Semitic languages, provided they are properly called "root inflecting," they must be ranked with the "inflection," because the difference between *kātib* ("writer") and *kitāb* ("book," "writing") is not fundamentally different from that between *kitāb* ("book") and *kutub* ("books"). Therefore, in the Semitic languages the specification of the conceptual expression from the relative indeterminateness of the unanalyzable "root" (*k-t-b*) into a concretely intuitable "word signification" is combined with the act of "supposition," that is, with the relating of the conceptual expression to the thing which now precisely (*hic et nunc*) is co-intended therein. In the Indo-European languages the uniform act of "supposition" (in the unanalyzable "ending") stands opposite the conceptual expression, which is completely articulated in itself.

Within the "ontological difference," therefore, we find the same possibility of shifting which Bröcker and I established for the subject-predicate relation in the sentence:

(The word names something, but the sentence says something. To name is to name something, but to say is to say something about something.) The subject of the saying, the *prōton hypokeimenon* of the sentence, is the being taken as a whole, demarcated by a determinate speech situation (to which in coherent speech the "context" belongs, also). This primordial subject is also formally made subject in the "impersonal sentence" of our language: "It rains." We have here no anomaly, no special form of the sentence, but rather the original primordial sentence.

In regard to the primordial subject of the sentence, the individual namings already appear as predicates, but the last and highest predication of the sentence as such consists in the positing act, that is to say, in the execution of the decision about the validity of what is named in the sentence in regard to that which is so named. The concrete sentence is something that, with respect to the decision function, constitutes a unity, a self-sufficient complex which exists in itself. (The sentence is constructed of "names"— the *verbum* is primarily the name of a concept, just as is the *nomen*. In the Indo-European propositional scheme a name names the subject, that about which something is to be expressed, and a second name names the predicate, that which is expressed about the former. Strictly speaking, however, each name—with the exception of the pure "proper name"—names a predicate, as it says something about the being which is named by such a name.)

Just as from the viewpoint of the primordial subject—namely, being taken as a whole—all names appear more or less as predicates, so, conversely, considered from the decision function the individual names become restricting determinations, attributes of the primordial subject, and in this way subjects within the linguistic sentence. Thus, "it-rains" = "rain-is." All complicated sentences, too, can be derived in this way from a restriction of the *it*, the undetermined primordial subject. It is from this ambiguity of the names, which are predicates as well as attributes of the *prōton hypokeimenon,* that the difficulties connected with a satisfying definition of the sentence originate. In the final analysis, however, the different possibilities of sentence construction which we find materialized in the world's language types result from this ambiguity, also.[26]

Thus, in the predication of the sentence the subject-predicate boundary moves, each time according to the logical structuring of thought, between the two poles of the indeterminate *it*. In other words, the boundary moves (according to our explanation) between the poles of the still completely unarticulated "being taken as a whole" and the pure "thesis"—the act of decision about the validity of that which has been expressed in the sentence.[27] In our explanation of the "ontological difference" in the languages of the world we find on the one hand pure Being, the "Idea of idea" (represented by the Semitic root or by its "idea"), and on the other hand the pure act of the supposition, of the individuation of the *hic et nunc*, as the two poles in which, respectively, Being and being manifest themselves in the morphological structure of language. Three things, however, are to be observed in this regard.

According to Humboldt, language is primarily *energeia* and is at first to be understood as such. However, the logical form of language as *energeia* is the sentence.[28] It is from the sentence *in actu* that the concrete "languages" originate as types of morphological configuration. The languages represent its embodiment as *ergon*. The ideal sentence contains all possibilities of linguistic formation together with the system in its totality which shows itself in the concrete languages in the individuation of its varieties. This is also why all attempts at gaining a satisfactory definition of the sentence from ready-made sentence configurations are destined to fail. Correspondingly, we find the variability of the subject-predicate relation uniformly revealed in the various logical possibilities of articulating the ideal sentence and, thus,

26. W. Bröcker and Johannes Lohmann, "Zur Wesensbestimmung des Satzes," *Forschungen und Fortschritte*, XV (1940), 356.

27. Even if the "predicate" is reduced to the "thesis," the predication maintains the *as* structure of "addressing something as something." The "as what" is in this case the quality of the thesis, the "modality" as qualification of the affirmation (possibility, actuality, and so on) or its qualification as wish, command, question, and so on.

28. The text (literary or otherwise) is obviously also *ergon* of the sentence *in actu*. In the sentence *in actu*, *langue* and *parole* are not yet separated. This, too, shows that the sentence is the basic form of language.

the variation of the "ontological difference" in the morphological word form distributed among the different linguistic types.

A characteristic inversion appears thereby in the relation of the act (predication or supposition) to that which is affected by the act (subject or the *suppositum* of the supposition), an inversion in which a basic law of linguistic formation comes to the fore. As we have formulated above: "To name is to name something, but to say is to say something about something." In the *as* structure of the supposition ("*dictio supponens pro re*"), however, this "naming of something" becomes "to name something (*res*) as something (*dictio*)" or "to designate something (*res*) through something (*dictio*)." The *as* structure is common to the "predication"—that is, to the saying something about or of something, to the letting something appear as something [29]— and to the "supposition." In the actual supposition, however, the *as* relation of the predication is inverted insofar as the supposition presupposes the actual decision of the predication as already effected (the [man:] is white) and, conversely, determines the object with the fixed predicate (the white [:man]). The supposition changes the universality of the conceptual "Being" into a "being," lets a "being" appear in its "Being," in contradistinction to the predication, which is supposed to express "the Being of a being." According to the formulation which we used above, the supposing *nomen* taken as "subject" of the sentence is an attribute of the "primordial subject," which stands outside the articulated sentence, lies before it; but the attributive relation appears as an inversion of an explicitly predicating concept relation which corresponds to it. "The good man" is a determination of "a man of goodness," but "the man is good" is the predication of "a man's goodness." This is particularly important for the propositional structure in "ontological indifference," with which we shall occupy ourselves next.

Our starting point for these considerations consisted in establishing the relation of the Semitic "root inflection" (which fills the abstract root signification with a concrete content) and of the Indo-European "stem inflection" by means of the "ending" (which is an immediate reflection of the "supposition" of the word in the actual sentence) to the "ontological difference." The Semitic "root" embodies pure Being, the "Idea of idea," whereas

29. Cf. p. 308 above.

the Indo-European "ending" embodies the act of the "supposition" and thus the "ontological differentiation" taken as act. This
gives us the guiding clue for the logico-ontological determination
of the Indo-European sentence structure in which the "ontological
difference" as act, that is, the "ontological differentiation," becomes expressly materialized in the verb *to be*. This is something
as unique as the Semitic "root." Philosophical thought has circled
around this verb since the time of the ancient Greeks. Not even
in the other "supposing" types does it have an equal. Even such
a phonetically decayed language as French has maintained this
verb in its characteristic peculiarity. The Russian language, however, has given it up. The peculiarity of this verb can be specified
in an absolute and in a relative way—absolutely, in the position
which it occupies in the Indo-Germanic languages in their morphological and syntactic system; relatively, in its relationship to
the expressive means of other types of verbs which logically can
be compared with it.

The verb *és-ti/s-énti* ("is/are") belongs to that archaic layer
of Indo-Germanic verbs which derive their forms immediately
from the "root" and thereby subject the root to a "vowel gradation" (*Ablaut*) between singular and plural (along with dual),
arranging the grammatical form construction in a specifically
irregular way. Even on the oldest linguistic levels of the Greek or
ancient Indian languages this type of verb occurs only in rem-
nants. However, the German *ist/sind* has maintained its original
form and has been only slightly modified.[30]

This type of verb, however, remarkably defective from the
very start, is in need of completion through forms of other roots
—specifically, *bhū* (the Latin *fui*, the Slavic *by-ti*, the English
to be); the Germanic *ves-* (*war, gewesen, das Wesen, abwesend*
= the Latin *ab-s-ent-*) and *vert-* (the Gothic *wairþan* is "perfective" in regard to *wisan* ["to be"]); and *stā-* ("to stand"; the Irish,
Romanic, and even Latin *existo* and, in their "perfective" aspects,
the Greek *estḗ* and the Slavic *sta-ti* ["to become"]). In the Germanic languages the root (*e*)*s-* was at first limited to the indicative and conjunctive of the present tense (in High German the
conjunctive stem *s-ī* = the Latin *s-ī-[mus]*). It later was carried
over to the imperative, infinitive, and participle (hence, *sei, sein,*

---

30. The German *sind* goes back to the unaccented ("enclitic") *senti*,
whose unstressedness, just as in Greek, must be accounted for by its
function as "copula."

seiend; in the Alamannic dialect, *g[e]si[n]* instead of *gewesen*) through a movement which originated in the southwest, in the Alamannic language, a movement from which Low German proper remained excluded.

The verb *és-ti* is thus a "root verb"; however, because it also has the durative aspect of the present-tense stem, which in the Stoic time doctrine is called the "time mode of extension" (*paratatikos chronos*), other forms of this verb do not seem to be original.[31] This durative aspect of the verb is otherwise ordinarily "materialized" by means of suffixes or infixes which enlarge the

---

31. The Stoic *tempus* system, upon which, in the final analysis, our grammatic nomenclature depends, is for the first time determined in its motivation through which it is incorporated in ancient Stoic thought as such by Hans-Erich Müller in "Die Prinzipien der stoischen Grammatik" (Ph.D. diss., Rostock, 1943). For this system a determinate kind of trichotomy is characteristic, one in which a state of indifference is added as a third element to a pair of opposites—for instance, in ethics: good, evil, and (in this regard) indifferent (*adiaphoron*). The names of our nominal genera correspond to this and are therefore characterized as Stoic conceptions: *masculinum, femininum,* and *neutrum* ("neither one of the two," that is, "neutral," in this connection). The same thing is also true for the "fundamental modes of action," as one says in modern grammar, of the Greek verb: (*chronos*) *paratatikos, syntel(est)ikos,* and, in this regard, *aoristos* ("undetermined"). The genuine, opposite poles are here *extension* (without termination) and *completion* (terminated-ness), expressed by the "extended" present-tense stem and by the "reduplicated" perfect-tense stem, respectively. Between them the aorist stem, which morphologically is the "simplest" one, stands for the "action," the operation as such, which must be characterized neither as "continuously taking place" nor as "having reached its *telos.*" Thus, the stress here is essentially different from that found, for instance, in the Slavic system of "modes of action." First and foremost, however, that which we first understand by *tempus* (namely, present, past, and future: *enestōs, parōichēmenos, mellōn*) is here seen only secondarily and in connection with these "modes of action." The grammatical *tempus* labels are abbreviations of these Stoic double names—for instance, (*paratatikos*) *enestōs = praesens, paratatikos* (*parōichēmenos*) = *imperfectum, aoristos* (*parōichēmenos*) = *aoristus,* and so on. There is also handed down a corresponding trichotomy for the "*genera verbi*": *activum, passivum,* and *neutrum.* On the other hand, the trichotomy which has become customary (*activum, passivum,* and *medium*) is Aristotelian, or Peripatetic. Aristotle also uses *metaxu* for the nominal "*neutrum.*" The Aristotelian (and Peripatetic) trichotomy which adds the *mesotēs* to the pair of opposites obviously is essentially different from the Stoic. The latter is "logical" in character, in harmony with the position of "logic" in the ancient Stoic system; Aristotle's *medium* is "actual" (*real*). The crossing of Stoic and Peripatetic influences in Greek grammar must be noticed in other cases also. For the rest, from what has been said it follows that we are moving along the paths of Stoic logic in our concept formation concerning the "ontological indifference" (in addition to a corresponding "ontological difference").

root. This phonetico-symbolically materializing function of the enlargement of the root is specifically obvious in the present-tense classes—for instance, in forms of the ancient Indian seventh class such as *bhi-ná-t-ti* ("he cleaves"), *bhi-n-d-ánti* (*"findunt,"* "they cleave"), in regard to the root *bhid-*. They are "extension forms" (*Streckformen*) according to Heinrich Schröder's interpretation of this process in his doctrine of German word construction. Compared with this the bare root taken as a verb usually shows the aorist "action mode," which, according to A. Meillet, gives expression to the action, pure and simple.

Exceptions to this can be found primarily in some very old roots of a special formation—for example, *ed-* ("to eat," taken as "to chew") with the participle *d-ent-* ("tooth"), *ei-* ("to go"), and the German root *es-*.[32] But even in this group *es-* is again characterized by the fact that it has a completely abstract meaning without any concretely intuitive background. This fact also distinguishes it from other roots which are found in the Indo-Germanic languages in the signification "to be." These roots, which complement *es-*, include *bhū-*, which according to Specht[33] means "to appear" but according to others means "to become," "to grow"; *ves-* ("to dwell"); *stā-* ("to stand"); the German *werden* ("to turn," *"verti"*); and *gene-* (*gignomai, gene-sis;* "to be brought about," "to bring about"). It can therefore be established that from time immemorial there has been a verb in the Indo-Germanic languages that, as far as we can see, has primarily had the signification of the pure predication—of the "saying of Being," of the "letting something appear in speech as something."[34]

This abstractness of the basic signification of the verb is further confirmed by the fact that the only nominal derivation of the root (*e*)*s-* which is certainly very old is a "present participle" or a form which originated from this, having the signification

<hr />

32. For this group, cf. A. Bloch, "Zur Geschichte einiger suppletiver Verba im Griechischen" (Ph.D. diss., Basel, 1940).

33. Friedrich Specht, "Beiträge zur griechischen Grammatik," *KZ*, LIX (1932), 58 ff.

34. A. Meillet's famous treatise, "La phrase nominale en indo-européen," *Mémoires de la société de linguistique de Paris*, XIV (1907), I ff., which in its general perspective was quite naturally determined by the leveling tendency of the "developmental" psychology of Darwin's era, should (seen from that point of view) be rewritten. The fundamental meaning "to exist" which he postulates for the verb *esti* certainly rests on a pure construction.

"true." This form is represented by the Anglo-Saxon *sōd*, the English *sooth*, and the Old Scandinavian *sannR* on the one hand, and by the Gothic *sunjis*, the ancient Indian *satyáh*, the Avestan *heiϑya*, and the Old Persian *hašiya* (**s-ont-*, or **s-n̥t-i̯os*) on the other. Both forms constitute the "abstract" antipole of the concrete *d-ent-*, *d-n̥t-*, *(o)dont-* ("tooth"). Thus, in the Indo-European languages "truth" was regarded as a function of the *is* predication.[35]

From what has this Indo-European conception of "truth" originated? I believe that the alleged facts represent the exact counterpart of the conception of "truth" as *alḗtheia* ("appearing"), which lives also in those forms of the root *bhū-* complementing *es-*, if Specht's interpretation of Homer's *epha(w)e* (*de chrysothronos ēós*) as the old singular of the root aorist *ephu-* (to which, then, *pha(w)os, phōs* ["light"] would belong as a resultant *nomen*) is correct.

The *as* structure of the predication (the "being such") is designated in many languages by a demonstrative or anaphoric *pronomen*:[36] in Arabic, *Zaïdun huu̯a ḡālibun* ("Zaidun he conqueror" = "Zaidun is a conqueror"); in Hebrew *I̯ahu̯ē hū hā elōhīm* ("Jahweh is the [true] God"); or, in Chinese, *shih4* ("[being] such") in *T'a1 shih4 chung1-kuo2-jen2* ("He is Chinese [a man of the Middle Empire].")[37] This is a kind of natural materialization of the predication, which can form itself time and again, and which also creeps into the "*is* sentence" of everyday language ("Charles, he is well out of it"). The *pronomen* which in the Indo-Germanic languages would be fit for just such a predica-

---

35. The fact that "truth" is first formed as a "relative adjective" is quite normal. (The ancient Indian *satýam* [Gothic *sunja*] was formed then as an "*abstractum*.") This fact belongs within the general context which I have brought to light in "Eine slavische Suffix-substitution," *Zeitschrift für slavische Philologie*, X (1933) 351–65. According to this context the concept of "middle," for instance, is originally lacking in the Indo-European languages; there is instead an adjectival expression for that which is in the middle: **medhi̯os* ("*medius*"). This is true for all relative concepts. Concerning the "contrasting" function of the suffix *-i̯os* ("so . . . and not . . ."), see Friedrich Specht, "Eine Eigentümlichkeit indogermanischer Stammbildung," *KZ*, LXII (1935), 217–18; idem, *Der Ursprung der indogermanische Deklination*, p. 124 ff.

36. For the Semitic languages, see Brockelmann, *Grundriss der vergleichenden Grammatik der semitischen Sprachen*, 2 vols. (Hildesheim: Olms, 1961), II, 103 ff.

37. Finck, *Haupttypen des Sprachbaus*, p. 13.

tion is a stem formed from the root s- (*so [masculine], *sā [feminine]; the Greek *ho, he;* the Gothic *sa, sō*). Does the verb *és-ti/ s-énti* thus constitute the verbalization of this *pronomen*[38] according to forms such as *ei-ti/i̯-énti* (in regard to the root [e]i-), and *edˀti/d-énti* (in regard to the root [e]d-)? This is an etymology which would best do justice to the characteristic signification and function of the Indo-European *esti.*

In the verb *es-ti* the Indo-European languages unite the significations of the existence (the "that it is") and of the "being true" with those of the predication of the (essential) "quiddity" and the (accidental) "being such." This Indo-European verb, which is central in every respect, encompasses the whole realm of Being, joined together as a unity, which then expressly unfolds itself in the so-called transcendental concepts that leave each specific mode of Being behind themselves, such as *ens* (*on*), *verum* (*alēthes*), *bonum* (*agathon*), and *unum* (*hen*) of classical and medieval philosophy. The concept of *ontōs on*, of the "true" and at the same time the highest being, could originate only in connection with this verb. It bridges the cleft of the "ontological difference," which was torn open in the "supposition" structure of the Indo-European word form, in that it connects with one another the propositional forms of the "nominal" and "verbal" sentences, which in themselves are fundamentally separated.

The "syn-thetic" character of the "copula," which brings the simple sentence as well as the different sentence forms together in the unity of the "thesis," clearly manifests itself specifically in the comparison of the Indo-European *is* sentence with the sentence structure of the Bantoid type, which, as we explained above, remains within the pure identity structure: [39] *Mu-ntu uzo mu-bi* ("Man, this, bad" = "This man is bad") and *Mu-ntu uzo mu-bi a-ti* ("Man, this, bad, he says" = "This bad man says"). According to the "open" sentence construction, which strings the determinations rather loosely to the "subject" of the sentence, this type has accordingly been called the "stringing" type in empirical typology since Finck.

38. The pronoun s-, as C. Bopp has already assumed, is in all likelihood hidden in the case ending of the nominative singular (*ek̯uo-s* ["horse"]).

39. Finck, *Haupttypen des Sprachbaus,* p. 63.

In those types of sentences in which the "outer relation," whether in the form of a purely "verbal sentence"[40] or in a construction which is more nominal in character, dominates the sentence construction, we find more or less clearly an existential verb or pair of verbs, instead of the identifying, positing *is,* for the affirmation and negation of existence. Here we are concerned with a fact which, to the best of my knowledge, has not yet been noticed, although the whole structure of thought of the different races of mankind is determined from this fact, as can be gathered, for instance, from Chinese philosophical speculation in relation to Greek and Western thought.[41] The form of

40. Because of our orientation toward the Indo-European Being concept, for the present let us lump together the existence verb of the "ontological indifference" and the structure of the "verbal sentence." The Chinese *wo³ yu³ ch'ien²,* the Turkish *param var,* and the Georgian *me m-a-k-'v-s p'uli* reflect, each in a characteristic way, the sentence form and thought form of their types. The Georgian "having" is an explicit "having" of "something ready-to-hand" ("for-me there is money"). That is why the "having" of a dog is signified differently than the "having" of an inanimate thing. On the basis of what will be pointed out later, it will be clear that this form of thought is to be classified between the Indo-European (ego subjective) and the Chinese (purely objective) forms of thought, a fact which is in harmony with the character of this type's verbal form, as was briefly outlined above (see pp. 316–17). A determinate relationship to time is further connected with this, but this would require a separate investigation. In my essay "Ist das indogermanische Perfectum nominalen Ursprungs?" KZ, LXIV (1937), 42–61, in which I dealt with this problem materially, I was unable to reach a solution because at that time the "horizon" for the present problematic was completely lacking for me. If one wishes to formulate the question from the viewpoint of language's "inner form," this horizon is given in the inner structure of the conceptuality of Being, which is hidden in the "uniforming synthesis" of the *is* of our language but is manifested there in manifold relations in the morphological structure of the verb as well as in the construction of the sentence. This is why this group-inflecting type is morphologically the richest and syntactically the most complicated one. By falsely attributing to this type a more or less "passivistic" conception of the verb, as has been customary since Schuchardt's important work ("Über den passiven Character des Transitivs in den kaukasischen Sprachen," *Wiener Sitzungsberichte,* I [1895]), and as I, too, have done, the inner problematic of the verb of these languages is covered up rather than explained.

41. In Chinese thought there is a typical "perspectival shift" in regard to our own way of thinking. This process was seen in principal and as a linguistic phenomenon for the first time by Ernst Lewy in such a way that the different grammatical categories in the different linguistic types have to adopt a form which is proportionally different. In my essay on the perfect tense ("Ist das indogermanische Perfectum nominalen Ursprungs?"), I applied Lewy's axiom to the reciprocal relationships between the ancient Armenian and ancient Georgian *perfectum* (the passage in *Lexis,* I (1948), 189 alludes to this), but I saw the matter un-

truth of this peculiar type of thought can perhaps be formulated by modifying Leibniz' *"inesse qua idem-esse,"* with which we dealt earlier, to *"inesse qua co-existere."*

In the classical ancient Chinese language this pair of concepts, pronounced in the modern Pekingese dialect, is yu^3/wu^2; this pair has been central to the speculation of the deepest thinkers of Chinese culture, for instance, Lao-tzu, in the same way that the concept of "Being" has been central to Greek philosophical thought since Parmenides. If one translates this pair of concepts as "Being" and "not-Being," as translators of Lao-tzu usually do, then one has established a seeming identity in which what is specifically significant submerges or is concealed. The fact that "Being" and "Nothingness" are conceived of in ancient Chinese in an equally original way, in reciprocal opposition, is

_____

clearly, at least insofar as I attributed the shifting of the expression to the "external form" in opposition to an identical "inner form" (the *"perfectum as such"*). In reality, however, it is the "inner form" as such—that is to say, first and foremost the "form of thought"—which shifts. This becomes particularly clear in the Chinese language, with its radically different form of thought.

In the place of the *"para-doxa"*—that is, the "abstraction" from the *doxa*, from the ordinary conception, an abstraction which for us is characteristic of philosophic thought (consciously and explicitly defended as such from the time of Heraclitus and Parmenides)—we find in Lao-tzu, for the expression of the higher level (the level of the *ontōs on*) which is reached by philosophical thought as well as by the action which is philosophically determined, the signification through the "negation" or the "relative privation." This occurs in such expressions as "the making in which there is found no making" (*wei² wu² wei²*), "the activity in which there is no activity" (*shih⁴ wu² shih⁴*), "the pleasure in which there is no (vulgar) pleasure" (*wei⁴ wu² wei⁴*), "the wishing of the not-wishing (as desiring)" (*yü⁴ pu² yü⁴*), "the learning of that which is not-learning (in the usual sense)" (*hsüeh² pu⁴ hsüeh²*), "the knowing of the not-knowing (in the normal sense)" (*chih¹ pu⁴ chih¹*). This doctrine is one which cannot be grasped by means of words, at least insofar as they are taken in the usual sense (*pu⁴ yen² chih¹ chiao¹* ["not reason-able doctrine"]).

The "reflection," the turning back of the mind and its function toward itself (*noēsis noēseōs*), which is the second characteristic of Western philosophical thought, is expressed as linguistic "reduplication." This is done partly in Western thought, but in Chinese thought it is connected with the negation. Thus, both the formal characteristics of Western philosophical thought are here connected into a unity (as "paradoxical reflection" or as "reflective *paradoxa*").

Chinese thought as it has developed within the realm of the "ontological indifference" is strictly "nondiaeretic"; this can be shown everywhere. What is taken apart in Western thought remains here together: theory and praxis, logical and ethical law, rational and intuitive knowledge (*ratio* and *divinatio* ["mathematics" and "mantics"]), knowledge and belief, world ("heaven") and God.

already manifestly a significant difference with respect to our concept formation: in "logic" the thesis precedes the negation, the antithesis presupposes the thesis of which it is the antithesis; in the "ontic" of "existence" nothingness precedes something.[42]

The Chinese yu^3 taken as a verb is "Being" (present-at-hand) and at the same time "having" (being-there), and wu^2 is its opposite. Let us first consider three types of sentences. (1) The sentence Wo^3 ("I") yu^3 $ch'ien^2$ ("money") taken in indifference means something like "I have money" = "For-me is money (there)." Yu^3 designates the "being-there"; that which precedes it indicates the "where" of the "being-there" (thus a sub-ject, *hypokeimenon,* taken in the sense of the outer, place relation). However, that which precedes yu^3 can also be "that for which being-there is." In this case we can make it the "subject" of the sentence ("I have money"). (2) The "subject" concept, if we wish to employ it in the Chinese manner, is to be conceived of in a broader sense than we are accustomed to doing. Consider the following example: (Sha^3n-hsi^1) $Chao^4$-$ch'eng^2$ ($hsien^4$) yu^3 yi^1-ke lao^3 $p'o^2$-tzu ("[In Shensi] in [the district town] Chaoch'eng was an old woman").[43] If one tries out the various possible combinations (each of the three place concepts which stand before yu^3, and any possible combination of them, can be made "subject"), one will become convinced of the elasticity of the "subject" function in the Chinese sentence. (3) It is also possible that all "subjects" can be left out, in which case we have the typical fairy-tale beginning: Yu^3 y^1-ke lao^3 $p'o^2$-tzu ("Once upon a time there was an old woman"). Since the Chinese "verb" taken as pure conceptual expression is temporally completely indifferent, this could equally mean "there *is* an old woman" and in the earlier example "at such and such a place there *is* . . ."

It is certainly true that the Chinese sentence lacks our subject-predicate structure, which, as we have explained above in connection with Leibniz, is a "selfsameness structure"

---

42. "Wu^4 sheng^1 yü^3 yu^3, yu^3 sheng^1 yü^2 wu^2 [Things originate from Being; Being originates from Nothingness]" (Lao-tzu, *Tao Te Ching,* chap. 40). This is true, at least if taken in and for itself; taken relatively within the system of the unity of oppositions (as this has been developed in chapter 2 of the *Tao Te Ching*), these concepts condition one another ("yu^3 wu^2 hsiang^1 sheng^1 [Being and Nothingness generate one another]").

43. The words in parentheses can be omitted without causing a change in the construction of the sentence.

(*Selbigkeits-Struktur*) although not a structure in "empty self-sameness." (In the examples just given, I = having money; the old woman = being-there.) However, if we conceive of "subject" (*hypokeimenon*) in its original meaning as the "substratum," or the "fundament," of the relationship expressed in the sentence, then the subject concept can also be applied to the Chinese sentence, in which one finds first and foremost, in addition to the I subject, the place and time determinations. (1) The "subject" wo^3 in the first sentence, "Wo^3 yu^3 $ch'ien^2$," is in this sense ambiguous; it is I subject in regard to "having" and at the same time "substratum" in regard to "being-there." This ambiguity, however, is manifest only in our translation; it does not exist in the original Chinese. (2) In the second sentence, the Chinese says in a certain sense, "Chaoch'eng has an old woman." In our language, however, it is merely "the old woman" as the one "who has this dwelling place" that can be made the subject of such a "having relation" (exactly as this takes place in the Latin *habito* ["I dwell"]). (3) The third sentence form, which begins with yu^3, represents, as the immediate relation of "being-there" to "being taken as a whole" (and seen from this perspective), the Chinese equivalent of our "impersonal sentence"—for example, "It is raining." [44] This type of sentence is the Chinese form of the sentence "without subject," in which, as we have explained above with regard to the *is* sentence, the actual subject coincides with the "primordial subject" (the *prōton hypokeimenon*), or, put another way, this primordial subject as subject is not restricted by determinations.

The Turkish pair *var/yok* corresponds to the ancient Chinese pair yu^3/wu^2. For Finck, Turkish, with Ottoman Turkish as a concrete example, represents the "subalternating" linguistic structure. [45] Chinese, which Finck calls "root isolating," [46] and Turkish correspond in that their sentence construction is above all determined through the bare concatenation of the elements of the sentence—that is, through the mere "position" of the words. In both of these types, that which determines stands in the at-

44. Cf. W. Bröcker and Johannes Lohmann, "Comment définir la phrase," *Lexis*, I (1948), 35–39.

45. Finck, *Haupttypen des Sprachbaus*, chap. 5.

46. One could say equally well "root grouping" according to the manner in which the monosyllabic unchangeable words are connected with one another in the sentence. ("Root" is obviously a metaphor; it signifies the monosyllabic unchangeable Chinese word as such.)

tributive connection before that which is determined, whereas in the predicative connection the "subject" stands before the "predicate" (in Chinese, $k'ung^1$ $t'ai^2$ ["the empty tower"], $t'ai^2$ $k'ung^1$ ["the tower is empty"]). In both types speech develops formally in the "ontological indifference," and it seems to me that this has been materialized in the most radical way in the classical ancient Chinese linguistic form. In Sanskrit (or in the Sanskrit–Indo-European languages) on the one hand and in Chinese on the other, Humboldt saw two extreme realizations of the possibilities of the human language structure standing in direct opposition to one another:

> Within the whole realm of language which is known to us, the Chinese and Sanskrit languages constitute in this way two fixed extreme poles; they are not similar to one another as far as their adequacy for mental development is concerned but are certainly similar in the consistency and perfect implementation of their systems. The Semitic languages cannot be considered as falling between them. According to their outspoken tendency toward inflection, they belong together with Sanskrit in one class. All other languages, however, can be considered as belonging between these two extreme poles, since all of them come close either to the Chinese deprivation of the words from their grammatical relations or to the intimate adjunction of the sounds which signify them.[47]

Humboldt's viewpoint in regard to "inflection" and "isolation" is purely morphological.[48] We are now able to replace this view with a more differentiated one.

47. Wilhelm von Humboldt, *Über die Verschiedenheit des menschlichen Sprachbaus* (Berlin: Schneider, 1935), p. 326.

48. Humboldt distinguishes four basic types of human language construction—namely, the grammatically "form-less" Chinese type (which "isolates" the word meaning morphologically), the "inflecting type" (which is the most perfect with respect to its adequacy in the development of the mind, even the "only right" one), the "agglutinating type" (which F. N. Finck calls "subordinating"), and the "incorporating type" (which is found in North America and which Humboldt initially represents via the language of the Mexican Indians, whereas Finck refers to the language of the Greenland Eskimos). In H. Steinthal, *Characteristik der hauptsächlichsten Typen des Sprachbaus* (1860), ed. Franz Misteli (Berlin: Dümmler, 1893), the "isolating" type is divided into the "root-isolating" (Chinese) and "stem-isolating" (Malayan) languages, and the "stringing" linguistic type is added there. Finck, who on the whole follows Misteli's systematization but tries in addition to found the system psychologically by means of a derivation from the temperaments of the human "races" (as was done before him by the Irishman James Byrne), increases Misteli's number of basic types by two. He separates the Semitic and the Indo-European languages as "root inflecting" and "stem inflecting,"

The ancient Chinese monosyllabic word is, like the Semitic "root," an unanalyzable, purely conceptual expression; but this expression is taken in "ontological indifference," so that it is not in need of a formal "objectivation" in the sentence ("supposition"). It thus stands in absolute opposition to the "word" of the three "supposing" types, particularly to the ancient Indo-European "word," which shows in its form an explicit obligatory supposition (by means of the "ending") and usually a complex articulation of the conceptual expression represented by the "stem" (or also, an articulation through "roots" and deriving elements). The Turkish "word," or the Turkish "root," in opposition to the Chinese, can to a certain extent assume deriving as well as supposing "suffixes," or "endings." Yet in a certain sense the Chinese "word" is closer to the Indo-European "word" than to the Turkish. This becomes manifest when we compare the Turkish "existential sentence" with the Chinese. "I have money" is in Chinese *Wo³ yu³ ch'ien²*, but in Turkish *Param var* ("My [-*m*] money [*para*] is on hand," or "My money's being on hand"). The Turkish sentence is one-dimensional. All Turkish sentences can be resolved into a simple series of pure namings in which the formative elements can also be logically included. What comes first in each case is a determination of what follows. The first sentence of the story which Finck uses in his *Haupttypen* to illustrate this, (*Hoca Nasreddin*) *efendi-nin bir kuzu-su var imis* ("The lord [master Nashreddin] had a lamb"), contains the following naming series: of the lord (of master Nashreddin), of a lamb, of its being on hand, past (tense). A sentence like *Bu kiz güzel dir*, which at first sight seems to be equal word for word to the Latin *Haec puella pulchra est*, means, according to its structure, "This girl, of her beauty, existence" (*dir* is not the

---

respectively, and introduces the Georgian language as "group inflecting." The "logical" derivation of the system which is given here does not exclude Finck's "psychological" derivation (*Der deutsche Sprachbau als Ausdruck der deutsche Weltanschauung* [Marburg: Elwert, 1899], and *Die Klassifikation der Sprachen* [Marburg: Elwert, 1901]) but complements it. At any rate it is completely independent from Finck's derivation; the two systems have in common only the fact that they both seem to be confirmed by the geographical location of the languages. The basic importance of linguistic geography for the interdependence of the inner formation of languages can be shown with the help of many details. A "phonologic" linguistic geography of the earth—which must correspond to the "logical" one—appears in outline form in Trubetskoy's last, posthumously published works (cf. *Lexis*, I [1948], 301–2).

copula but originated from *tur*, which means "to stand" and then also "to stand there [as something]").

Therefore, in connection with the Turkish sentence one cannot speak of a subject-predicate structure. Heinrich Winkler has reduced the sentence construction of this linguistic type to two basic laws:

> 1. The language originally has only nounlike *nomina*, of which the first always represents the *rectum* and the second one the *regens*, provided the context admits of such a relationship.
>
> 2. If this is not so, there is found a predicative relationship in which the preceding *nomen* is subject and the following, predicate.[49]

The second rule is merely a special application of the first; this becomes evident at once if one refrains from projecting our subject-predicate structure onto the Altaic sentence. The difference is not in the manner in which both concepts are connected with one another but in the different ways in which the concept combination is used, namely, as *naming* ("goodness, man" = "the good man") or as *saying* ("of the man, goodness" = "the man is good"). This is determined partly through the content of the concepts and partly through the context in which the combination is found.

The Chinese sentence transcends this one-dimensionality of a mere concatenation of concepts by placing the ruling concept of the sentence in the middle as a kind of "verb," whereas it must be placed at the end according to the law of the Altaic language structure. In comparison with the "subordinating" Ural-Altaic sentence construction, the Chinese is "centro-ordinating." The central arrangement creates a sentence in which the structure, though remaining within the "ontological indifference," comes close to the "verbal sentence" type.

This process can be compared in a certain sense to the verbalization of the nominal sentence in the Indo-European language type (by means of inserting the "copula"). In both cases a simple determining relation established as such—in Chinese the determination of the following concept through the preceding (*k'ung¹ t'ai²* ["empty tower"], *t'ai² k'ung¹* ["tower,

49. Heinrich Winkler, *Die altasische Völker- und Sprachenwelt, Schriften des Osteuropa-Instituts Breslau* (Leipzig: Tauchnitz, 1921), VI, pt. 1, 32.

emptiness = the tower (is) empty"]) and in Indo-European the determination of the object through the concepts which are related to it as something identical (*turris deserta* ["empty tower," or "the tower (is) empty"])—is changed into a relation which is predicated explicitly as such—in Chinese *t'ai² yu³ k'ung¹* ("in the tower is emptiness [there]") and in Indo-European *turris est deserta* ("the tower is [an] empty [one]"). In both cases the simple series is broken; that is, the arrangement of the concepts in "ontological indifference" as in Altaic, or in "ontological difference" as in Bantu is broken. The simple concatenation of the *relata* (*relatum* 1 : *relatum* 2 : and so on) is replaced by a differentiated connection (*relatum* 1 : relation : *relatum* 2); but the relationship between the *relata* is an "outer," "objective" one in Chinese and an "inner," "log-ical" one in the Indo-European languages.[50]

A dominating trait manifests itself here in the relationship between Chinese thought and Indo-European, or Greek and Western, thought, a trait which is manifested equally in the relationship between Chinese and European cultures. As Humboldt has pointed out for languages, this trait is unique in the relationships of languages and of cultures to one another; it can be briefly characterized as a total difference within the context of an equally total comparability. One can observe this trait in various aspects of a culture—from such formalities as the mourning color (white or black) or the place of honor (left or right) to the overall *habitus* of philosophical thought and of the conception of life and world view.[51] There is obviously not only a question of "two extreme realizations of the possibilities of man's language which are related to one another in polar opposition," [52] but a question of two realizations of human possibilities, each of

50. A sentence of the modern everyday north Chinese language such as *T'a¹ yu³ ping⁴* ("He is sick," "With him is sickness," "He has (a) disease") can in this way be logically opposed to the Aristotelian (*Sōkratēs*) *hugiainei* (*Peri Hermenēias* 16b9) as an illustration of the Chinese "ontic" inherence on the one hand and the Indo-European "logical" inherence (*methexis* according to Plato, [*nun*] *huparchein* according to Aristotle) on the other. Here, too, the Chinese "subject" is the founding *relatum* (*"referens"*) of an external "objective" relation, whereas the Indo-European subject is the *"referens"* of an inner "log-ical" (subject-predicate) relation.

51. Humboldt has given some indications and references concerning the observation of this trait in the conception of life and world view. See *Über die Verschiedenheit des menschlichen Sprachbaus*, p. 75.

52. *Ibid.*, p. 78.

which in its own way is perfect. From this the incomparable, paradigmatic value which the Chinese language as well as the Chinese culture and its history have for us becomes evident.

According to general testimony the Chinese is the most economical man on earth, achieving the highest degree of efficacy with the most restricted means. His language is equally economical; with the help of a very few modifications he has molded the monotony of the Altaic linguistic structure into a means of expression which is perfect in its kind—this in opposition to the exuberantly growing fullness of the Indo-European form construction, which first tests all possibilities in order to cast them aside later. A similar sharp opposition is found between the historical unity and uniformity of the Chinese language and culture, which has endured from the most ancient times, long before the Homeric era of the Greeks, up until the present, and the world of the Indo-Europeans, which bifurcates and dissipates itself into numerous languages and nations. Both China and Europe are historically minded to the highest degree, and yet what opposition there is between the historical attitude of the Chinese and that of the European! The Chinese has rested securely in the past of his nation and family—until the most recent shock to his historical forms of life through the explosive effect of Western technical civilization, which destroys all naturally grown life. As late as 1900, songs dealing with the battle of Mu^4-yeh^3 (about 1100 B.C.) and the kings of that time were as familiar to him as the knowledge of Bismarck or Napoleon is to Europeans. The European is oriented toward the future, and because of this he loses the present. His temporal horizon is the "subjectivity" which "transcends" objectivity as well as the "immanence" of the "innerworldliness" and that of his own thinking and which in this way makes him "consciously aware" of this immanence as opposite to the outer world. This temporal horizon first took shape in the absolute "ontological difference" of his language and manifested itself for the first time in his conception of Being, long before this horizon was thematically considered in modern European philosophy. It is much more difficult to see through the structure of the Being conception of Chinese thought precisely because of its non-unfolded simplicity, which, however, is the absolute opposite of a so-called primitivity.

In this context a few provisional indications must suffice. As far as the Chinese time concept is concerned, I wish to limit myself to quoting the grammarian and linguist George von der Gabelentz, who has specialized in the Chinese language:

> Among contemporary Asiatics the Chinese is the historian par excellence, and the ancient monuments of his literature, too, bear witness to this orientation and gift of his mind. His historiography does not adhere, as is the case in our historiography, to the *propter hoc*, but rather to the *post hoc*. As a rule it does not refer to the past, nor does it anticipate, but rather it reports things in temporal sequence; the same rule is followed in novels. Occasionally we extend our account by means of attributes and relative sentences: "The happy child brought the watch to his father, who gave it back to its owner." To a Chinese something like this would be abominable. Chinese biography obviously first makes its heroes the objects of speech: "N. N. stemmed from X. His father was so-and-so; his mother, a woman from Y. He (psychological subject) was born in such and such a year (psychological predicate). When he was three years old, he lost his father, . . ." and so on in chronological order. The [Chinese] writer of annals, on the other hand, would report: "Then and then, there and there, N. N. was born." He speaks about the time and, within the realm of the time, about the place, and says about both what has occurred there. When he introduces a new person to the scene of the story, then he certainly makes a biographical digression, which, of course, refers to the past. He does the same thing when there is a question of the prehistory of a nation, entering first into the history of the Middle Empire.[53]

The Chinese truth concept is equally completely "objective." In Chinese 實 (*shih²*) means "true," "actual," "actuality," "full," "fullness." Its counterpart is 虛 (*hsü¹*), which means "empty," "idle," "false." "Truth," therefore, is "actuality" (*Realität*) in the original sense of the word *reality* (*Sachlichkeit, Sache* [*res*]), as this term is still used in Kant. In grammar 虛字 (*hsü¹ tzu⁴*) are the "empty" words, which, as "particles" or otherwise, have merely a purely relating signification. (For Chinese logography the "word" of the speech is identical to the "sign" of the writing.) In the rudimentary beginnings of "logic," found already in ancient Chinese philosophy, the "word," or the "name," has an immediate and "objective" relationship with the "thing," also.

---

53. George von der Gabelentz, "Zur chinesischen Sprache und zur allgemeinen Grammatik," *Techmers Internationale Zeitschrift für allgemeine Sprachwissenschaft*, III (1887), 106.

The order in the conceptual world of the names and the order in the world of things—which thus is an "anthropological" human world and not, for instance, the "cosmological" world of our universe—mutually condition one another. According to Yin Wen-tzu, even if the myriads of individual entities are still all there, if they are not named in the right way there is anarchy 亂 [*luan*⁴ ("turmoil," "lack of order," "confusion," "rebellion")]). Even if all the myriads of names are concatenated in the proper order, if there is no material form which corresponds to them they become "idionymous" (*eigensinnig kuai*¹ ("strange," "eccentric," but "stubborn," "evil," "cunning," too.]).[54] The 正名 (*cheng*⁴ *ming*²), the "right preservation of the names," as "logic" is called in Chinese (taken here as a normative discipline), thus has not only a "logical" but also an "ethical" significance. The fact that "irreal" names which do not refer to a thing become "idionymous" calls to mind Heraclitus' idionymous cosmos of the dreaming people, each one of whom has "his own world" in opposition to the common world of those who are awake which is valid for everyone.[55] However, in Chinese the "world" is the self-evident background or underground of all events which even in thought cannot be "multiplied." (This is illustrated in Chuang-tzu's famous "butterfly dream," where the hero does not know whether he dreamed he was a butterfly or whether he is now dreaming he is Chuang-tzu.)

In the Indo-European languages the unity of the Being concept, found primarily in the *is* of the copula which bridges the gap of the "ontological difference" and conceptually comprises all modes of Being,[56] stands opposite the cleavage of actual existence. In the Chinese language, however, the unproblematic unity of actual reality as it becomes manifest in history and historiography, and also in the form of philosophical thought, is conversely unfolded linguistically in a coexistence of Being concepts which cannot be brought together into a uniform conception, although a certain hierarchy does seem to exist for them. One should take the statements in this brief discussion not as ready-made formulas but rather as attempts at demarcating a

54. A. Forke, *Geschichte der alten chinesischen Philosophie* (Hamburg: Friederichsen, 1927), p. 424.

55. H. Diels and W. Kranz, *Fragmente der Vorsokratiker,* 8th ed. (Berlin: Weidmann, 1956), p. 89.

56. See pp. 328–29 below.

framework which must be verified in future research involving painstaking and detailed investigations in which deductive "analysis" and inductive "interpretation" must go hand in hand.

The fact that among the different forms in which the Being concept appears in Chinese we have focused attention precisely on the conceptions of yu^3/wu^2 was determined first of all by motives taken from the viewpoint of "general linguistics," which also elsewhere determines this Being concept as a correlate of a sentence construction that remains in "ontological indifference" or at least from an exterior relation. In this respect the Semitic languages are perhaps the most instructive; in these languages the "nominal sentence" (identity structure) and the "verbal sentence" (exterior relation) stand side by side. Correspondingly, we find here a tendency toward the development of a "copula" on the one hand and an "existential verb" on the other.[57] The following are examples of this tendency: the Hebrew *i̯ẹš*, the Aramaic *ᵌī̯þai* (*ᵌelāh* = "there is a God"), the Akkadian *iši*, and the Arabic *laịsa* (in the negative). We also find an originally questioning "where being" for the nonexistence: the Hebrew *ᵌai̯in* (wə *ᵌādām* *ᵌai̯in* = "and man was not yet there" [Gen. 2:5]) and the Akkadian *jānu* (ancient *ajānum*) = *laššu* (from *lā išu*). It is important to note that, while the Russian language has given up the "copula" *is*, it has created for itself a pair similar to the Chinese yu^3/wu^2 and the Turkish *var/yok*. *Jest'* is limited to the existential meaning, and *nĕt* (*njet*), which is a contraction of *ne-estĭ*, is used in the sense of the existential negation (as are wu^2 and *yok*). In so doing, the Russian language has adapted itself to the adjacent Ural-Altaic.[58]

In Chinese, 有 (yu^3) expresses the fact that something is really contained in something else and, if taken absolutely, expresses the being-there (in the world); on the other hand, 無 (wu^2) expresses the fact of not being contained in, the "privation." It is clear that the pair $shih^2/hsü^1$, which signify the "fullness" and the "emptiness," respectively, constitute the corresponding "truth" concept. "Truth" is here the "inherence" taken

---

57. Cf. Brockelmann, *Grundriss*, p. 73. Brockelmann's interpretation of the facts is partly questionable, however—for instance, his interpretation of the "existence" verb as "interjection." Furthermore, he tears apart what belongs together.

58. Cf. Ernst Lewy, "Etymologie und Sprachbegriff," *Lexis*, I (1948), 169.

as "coexistence," that is, the bodily "unity of what belongs to-gether," in opposition to the Indo-European "selfsameness" or "cor-respondence." The "truth" taken as the "unity of what belongs together" [59] is, in the pair of concepts shih²/hsü¹ as well as in the thetic yu³ or wu², "intramundane" (inesse qua co-existere) and not, as in Indo-European, "transcendental," tran-scending the "world of things present-at-hand" (inesse qua idem-esse).

In addition to these there is in the Chinese language a second "truth" concept belonging to the predicative positing or even identical with it: 是 (shih⁴ ["(being) such," "correctness"]), with its opposite, 非 (fei¹ ["not-being (such)," "(being) false"]). Both also function as "copulas." [60] Fei¹ is found in the first (and second) sentences of Lao-tzu's Tao Te Ching: "Tau⁴ k'o³ tao⁴/fei¹ ch'ang² tao⁴"—"The speech which can be said then/is not eternal speech," "Ho logos lektōs/ouk estin ho logos autos," "Ratio ratiocinabilis/non-est absoluta (perfecta) ratio" —and then, further, "Nomen nominabile/non-est absolutum nomen," where ontōs on is expressed as negation.[61] These terms are at the same time "logical" (taken as inner "agreement" or as "contradiction") and "ethical" (taken as "good" or "evil"). This is the Chinese equivalent of the "being true" (alēthes, verum) of the Western problematic concerning the transcendentals, pro-vided this "being true" is taken under the aspect of the essential "quiddity" (Was-sein) and the agathon (bonum). Therefore, this pair is the ontological counterpart of the "ontic" yu³/wu² and shih²/hsü¹.[62]

In contradistinction to this the third pair 然/否 (jan²/fou³ ["yes"/"no"]) seem to express the "dialogical" position and nega-tion. Jan² can also become an adverb with the use of suffixes corresponding to the English -ly and the Latin -ment(e); thus,

59. See p. 307 above.
60. As far as shih⁴ is concerned, see p. 328 above.
61. Cf. p. 330 above.
62. Thus, from what has been said (p. 305 above) it also follows that for the Chinese the relationship between "name" (ming³) and "thing" (wu⁴) is an "ontic," not an "ontological," one. That is also why one cannot find in Chinese an orthotēs onomatōn as cor-respondence ("adaequatio"). The Chinese expression which "perspectivistically" cor-responds to the Greek determination of word and speech correctness is hsin⁴ ("trust [subjective reliability]," "faithfulness [objective reliability]"). This is a "practical"—thus, an "ontic"—determination of the truth of speech.

it signifies the "such" of the kind or mode (in contradistinction to *shih*[4] as the "such" of the correctness).

The usually purely "logical" negation 不 (*pu*[1]) stands by itself; the simple naming of concepts is a counterpart to this. Three of Lao-tzu's six basic maxims are formed with the help of *pu*[1], and three others with the "privative" *wu*[2]. In comparison with *wu*[2], which expresses the fact that something is not actually contained in something else, the negation *pu*[1] clearly signifies here the modification of the concept—of willing, learning, and knowing (but here not taken in the usual sense), and thus of three "intellectual," or "psychic," functions which as such should be enhanced in the direction of the "authenticity" of the *ontōs on*.

If we consider Finck's eight "basic types of language structure" in their relationship to one another from the logical point of view we have developed here, then in their geographic stratification they already show a characteristic symmetry which cannot possibly rest on pure chance. We find, oriented according to the four quarters of the heavens, two groups, each containing four linguistic types. In each group, however, three of the types are united into a triad by their sentence and word construction. In the Western triad the "supposing" types are united by the principle of the "bifurcated form." In the Eastern part of the ancient world the mere concatenation of the terms of the sentence becomes the dominating principle of the construction of thought. In the north there is the "subalternating" Ural-Altaic type; in the south, the Malayo-Polynesian type, which is built up according to the opposite ordering principle and which for that reason can be called "superordinating"; [63] and between these two, the "centro-ordinating" Chinese.

Each triad is accompanied by a fourth type, which has a certain relationship to it. Finck's "group-inflecting" type belongs to the Western triad; as we have explained earlier, this type represents one of the four possibilities of combining the two sentence types which developed on the basis of the "ontological difference": "Being" and "being" internally differentiated = Nominal sentence (N); "being" differentiated in its "Being" in outer rela-

63. For example, see Ernst Lewy, "Kleinere Beiträge," *Indogermanische Forschung*, LVI (1938), 30. Misteli and Finck spoke of "stem isolation" according to a morphological characteristic connected with this "superordinating" characteristic.

tion = Verbal sentence (V). The following combinations are possible: (1) N (Bantoid); (2) N + V (Semitic); (3) N × V (Indo-European); and (4) V (Caucasian). The Eastern triad is accompanied by the "incorporating" type, which governs the North American Indian languages and which incorporates the determinations of the "verb" into the verb itself (to simplify matters, the central point of a sentence is designated generally as "verb," as was done in our discussion of Chinese sentence construction).

Within both of these triads, and between them—considering each as a whole as well as the individual languages composing them—there exist multiple relations which somehow incorporate themselves, usually in a symmetrical way, into the whole octadic system. Those who doubt this systematization may perhaps at least evaluate it "mnemotechnically." Furthermore, we wish to recall Kant's table of categories in its fourfold triad as well as the dominating role which numbers—above all, the *trias* and the *tetractys*—have played in philosophical and theological speculation, from Pythagoras and Plato, continuing through Augustine, to Hegel.

On the one hand the "incorporating" linguistic type appears as a species of the "subordinating" type, representing the "condensation" of that type into the "sentence-word." On the other hand one can compare it to the "group-inflecting" type; this type incorporates the determinations of the verb into the verb "pronominally," that is, through "representative" elements, whereas the "incorporating" type does so "bodily." The "group-inflecting" type appears to be a "refined" form of the "incorporating" one. In Georgian forms such as *m-e-l-i-s* (*melis* ["he waits for me"]) each letter has a determinate grammatical function; a form such as *da-m-i-dg-in-n-e-s* ("he will hire us") contains among its formative elements no fewer than seven grammatic categories in addition to the root, -*dg*-. The forms thus are no less "polysynthetic" than the monstrous "sentence-words" of the "incorporating" type.

In addition to the influence of geographical stratification on languages, one recognizes also a reflection of the earth's climatic zones in the distribution of the characteristic traits of the linguistic types, especially in the "position of the words." [64] In the Torrid

64. This element is dominant in the attempts made by James Byrne (*General Principles of the Structure of Language* [London: Trübner &

Zone the "superordinating" construction of the sentence and of the concepts predominates; in the north the "subordinating" type is the dominant one, found not only in the linearly articulating languages but also in the more complicated articulations of the "supposing" ones. Between these two is found correspondingly a more or less "centro-ordinating" type, represented not only by the Chinese language but also by those languages which have a genuine "verbal sentence," where the "centro-ordination" is taken over by the "elements which constitute the inflection" and thus becomes independent of the "word order." A central order raised to a higher degree is found in the Indo-European languages, where "nominal sentence" and "verbal sentence," "identity structure" and "outer relation," are united in the verb. Therefore, the Indo-European type appears in a certain manner as the center of the whole typological universe.

REMARKS CONCERNING THE TABLES

I. The "group-inflecting" type, in which Finck includes the Basque language also (and he is certainly correct in doing so), cannot be easily determined genealogically. Apparently this is a case in which a linguistic group has been pushed back, mainly by the Indo-European languages. For lack of a better term, the designation *Japhetic,* which N. J. Marr used for the ancient Mediterranean languages, has been introduced. (Use of this term is not to be interpreted as an expression of agreement with his theories.)

II, III. The present typological systems do not distinguish consistently between morphology and sentence construction. That is why a few terminological neologisms were necessary here. The label *class inflecting,* used for the Bantoid languages,

---

Son, 1885]) and Finck (*Der deutsche Sprachbau als Ausdruck deutscher Weltanschauung*) to explain the types of language structure from the temperaments of the "races." The "superordinating" structure ("[there] falls from-the-tree the-apple" or "[there] falls an-apple in-the-grass") corresponds to the "quick thinking" which is characteristic of the races living in the Torrid Zone or in a mild climate. The "subordinating" structure ("the-apple from-the-tree falls") represents the deliberate way of speaking which is characteristic of the races living in colder and more rugged climates.

SCHEMATIC, SYNOPTICAL TABLES OF THE SYSTEM OF TYPES

I. *Types labeled according to the representative language stems*

Indo-European	(Japhetic)	Ural-Altaic	(North American Indian)
Hamito-Semitic		Indo-Chinese	
Bantoid		Malayo-Polynesian	

II. *Types labeled according to characteristics of word construction and form construction*
(The numbers refer to the chapters in Finck, *Haupttypen des Sprachbaus*)

| Stem inflecting (8) | Agglutinating (5) | Incorporating (3) |

| Root inflecting (7) | Root isolating (2) |
| Class inflecting (4) | Stem isolating (6) |

Group inflecting (9)

III. *Types labeled according to sentence construction*

Verbally ordering;
the nominal sentence }
"incorporating" the
verbal sentence   Subordinating

Verbally and nominally
ordering }   Centro-ordinating   Incorporating
Stringing   Superordinating

Verbally ordering

IIIa. *Transition to IV*
(III plus four new divisions)

Coordinating and verbally }
superordinating }   Verbally super-   =   Incorporating
Coordinating   ordinating   { Subordinating
    { Centro-ordinating
    { Superordinating

IV. *The system of types represented as a continuum*

Subordinating; incorporating
Centro-ordinating
Superordinating

Subordinating
Indo-European: Centro-ordinating
Semitic: Group inflecting, superordinating
Bantoid

follows from our earlier discussion. The term *incorporating* is the principle for word construction and form construction as well as for sentence construction. For this reason, the same label for this type appears in both II and III.

III. The names as modes of "syn-tax," of "being ordered together," are formed here in a parallel way, with the exception of the labeling of the Bantoid languages as *stringing* (*anreihend*); this term of Finck's was maintained because it best summarizes both dominating characteristics of this type, namely, the "parallel coordination" of the words and the "openness" of the sentence construction.

IIIa. The nominal order (of the "nominal sentence") is a form of "parallel coordination"; the verbal order (of the "verbal sentence"), a kind of "superordination." However, the latter is at the same time, from the viewpoint of the *nomina* of the sentence, a kind of "subordination" and, taken as a whole, a form of "centro-ordination" (with the verb as "center"). Thus one can say that the "group-inflecting" type is "verbally superordinating"; the Bantoid type, "coordinating"; and the Semitic type, "coordinating" and "verbally superordinating." If one now takes into consideration the fact that the verbal superordination represents at the same time a nominal subordination and, from the viewpoint of the sentence as a whole, a "centro-ordination," the Indo-European languages, insofar as they incorporate the nominal coordination ("congruence") in the verbal superordination (subordination and centro-ordination), would then reflect the whole cosmos of the types.

IV. Whereas in II, III, and IIIa an ideal picture of the relationships between the types is projected, here the ideal types appear as points of intersection and of concentration of certain characteristics on the continuum of the world's languages. In this connection the Indo-European languages appear at the center of the whole and have the greatest number of relations in all directions; this is in correspondence with what was established in IIIa. The three types which are "supposing" (*kat' exochēn*) are here labeled with their genealogical names since they, more than all other types, constitute a historical reality.

Prospect

1. Beyond the value of the other types as ideal points of orientation in classifying the world's languages on the basis of "inner form," the question of whether or not such types can be legitimately and fully taken as phenomena of language's concrete history remains to be answered.

2. An affirmative answer to this question should open completely new possibilities for the history of language. Such an answer would then raise a further question concerning the relationship between the concrete historical language families, in which the ideal types receive a historical form, and those languages and language groups which eventually would stand outside this historical process.

3. The genealogico-ethnological groups into which the "types" are transformed in I are typologically excessive and historically expansive. Apparently they have not always dominated the total picture of the world's languages in the same way that they do today. But how can this be combined with the supposition that the system of types exhausts all the possibilities of language formation—that is, that aside from the "types" there can be only combinations of them in concrete languages?

4. The question concerning the relationship between the ideality of the types and their historical embodiment in determinate language families has a parallel in the relationship between the phonetic forms of the languages (their "sensibility") and their "inner forms" (their "intelligibility"). Schleicher applied Hegel's idea of the "exteriorization" of the "world-spirit" in nature and its return to itself in "history" to the history of language. The human spirit first "embodied" itself in concrete phonetic forms, Schleicher believed, in order to smash them in that process of the mind's "history" in which the mind comes to itself.[65] The observation of this historic fact as such in the studies of the Schlegel brothers constitutes the beginning of modern linguistics, with the distinction between the "synthetic" and the "analytic" linguistic structures as characteristic of ancient and modern European languages. Today this observation can be

65. Cf. W. Streiberg, "Schleichers Auffassung von der Stellung der Sprachwissenschaft," *Indogermanische Forschung*, VII (1897), 360 ff.

generalized in such a way that in the "inflecting" types as such there is, together with the "spiritualization" of "reality," a tendency to detach the "inflection" from the "inflected" concepts. Starting with this observation, Ernst Lewy has added a ninth type to Finck's eight, namely, the "inflection-isolating" type.[66] He is of the opinion that modern Basque can be taken as the most consistent representative of this type. I believe that this phenomenon belongs to another level, that it falls in a dimension other than Finck's eight types, if one considers this typology (as Finck does) to be a system of the "inner linguistic form" which is closed in itself. The Basque language is "inflection isolating" in relation to the "group-inflecting" type, whereas French and English are such in relation to the "stem-inflecting" type. Therefore, the "isolation" of the inflection appears to be very different in each case. At any rate, we come in this way to a relativation of our typological system. Furthermore, in the "noninflecting" types analogous facts seem to be found, although they emerge phenomenally in a very different way. In contemporary Chinese, for instance, in addition to the "synthetic," or "nondiaeretic," wu^2 and fei^1,[67] we also find the "analytic" mei^2-yu^3, and pu^2-$shih^4$. Furthermore, in "counting" and verbally "pointing" there develops a kind of obligatory "supposition" by means of the "numerative": yi^1-ke lao^3 $p'o^2$-tzu ("a head of old woman" [just as our "a head of cattle"]), $chei^4$-ke jen^2 ("this head of man"). Similarly, attempts at forming "plural forms" and a system of "pronominal forms" are also found in Chinese. Originally, all of this was completely foreign to this type. (The fact that in the modern everyday north Chinese language the monosyllabicity of the word is practically given up must probably be evaluated in another way; here a crossing with the Mongolian [Ural-Altaic] word type appears to manifest itself; however, see also the following supplement.)

66. See, for example, Lewy, "Kleinere Beiträge," pp. 29–30; *idem,* "Etymologie und Sprachbegriff," p. 180.
67. See note 41 and pp. 341–43 above.

SUPPLEMENT

Ch'iang²   *-liang²*   *-che³*   *pu⁴*   *te²*   *ch'i¹*   *szu³.*

強   梁   者   不   得   其   死

Superbus (violentus)   *non assequitur "suam" mortem.*

At the end of chapter 42 of the *Tao Te Ching* Lao-tzu makes a confession concerning his own doctrine: "What people teach, I teach too: the violent man (the arrogant one) does not find 'his death.' I wish to make this my basic doctrine."

Thus, the wisdom of the sage is basically common wisdom, the wisdom of the "people," of "people" in general, the most trivial and common knowledge. The point is, however, that, although the "people" know it, they do not really know it because they do not know it "in principle," as we might say in our "Western" language. They do not know what they know, just as children express truths without being aware of doing so (but all of this is obviously not the Chinese way of saying things).

The example of people's wisdom in which the philosopher summarizes his own doctrine takes the form of a "proverb." It expresses a "life's experience"—for example, in English, "Pride goeth before a fall." This life experience contains a warning in regard to arrogance and violence and against that mode of behavior which is opposed as sharply as possible to the two basic maxims of the *Tao Te Ching*—namely, the negative (*wei²*) *wu²-wei²*, the "not make(ing making)," and the positive *tzu⁴-jan²*, the "letting itself be unfolded (from itself)." Both of these maxims constitute the genuine and only effective "making," whereas the busy, clumsily grasping "wanting to make" of the "man of action" always establishes, at least in the final analysis, the opposite of what it thirsts after. This is a theme that runs through the whole *Tao Te Ching*, from beginning to end, and of which we Germans have a frightening case behind us! [68]

"The arrogant man [the man who does not let things take

68. See also Ernst Herzfeld, "Der Tod des Kambyses: hvāmršyuš amryatā," *Bulletin of the School of Oriental Studies* (London), VIII (1936) (*Grierson Festschrift*), 589–97. What has been said here, however, is not affected by his objections.

care of themselves 'in a natural way'] does not find his 'natural' death." This is thus the Chinese equivalent of the Indo-European expression *sua morte mori* ("of a natural death," or "to die the death destined by fate"), with which Wilhelm Schulze has dealt in his famous treatise "The Death of Cambyses." [69] Thus we have here an "elementary idea," a linguistic form of expression, which has originated independently among different peoples. The Chinese idea certainly appears to be more precise and concrete than the Indo-European expression, insofar as the "dying of one's own accord" stands clearly in opposition to the "dying through someone else" (of the man of violence). Therefore, the idea of *sua die mori*, which plays such an important role in Schulze, must be kept out of the picture here. What the ancient Indo-European and ancient Chinese worlds of ideas have in common is that the expression "one's own death" seems to exclude the idea of suicide, an idea which appeared to be obvious, even self-evident, to the European interpreters of the *sua morte mori* in the Darius inscription.

The idea that "voluntary death" as the "highest and most certain guarantee of man's freedom" [70] represents one's own genuine death is an outflow of European "subjectivism" and, from a moral point of view, its ultimate radicalization. The French existentialist Albert Camus begins *The Myth of Sisyphus* with the sentence "Il n'y a qu'un problème philosophique vraiment sérieux: c'est le suicide [There is but one truly serious philosophical problem, and that is suicide]." The discovery of this "moral subjectivism" ("Non sumus in ullius potestate, cum mors in nostra potestate sit [We are in no one's power, as long as death is in our power]" [71] occurred in the philosophy of the Stoics, who put it into practice from the time of Zeno until that of Seneca. The Stoic *sophos* thus appears as the first embodiment of Western radical individualism, the moral realization of which therefore preceded Descartes's theoretical formulation by approximately two thousand years.

The sentence in our quotation from Lao-tzu which is verified as a popular proverb—for that matter, as a very old one—has as

69. Friedrich Specht, "Die 'indogermanische' Sprachwissenschaft von den Junggrammatikern bis zum ersten Weltkriege," *Lexis*, I (1948), 255.
70. W. Schulze, "Der Tod des Kambyses," *Sitzungsberichte der Akademie der Wissenschaften* (Berlin) (1912), p. 702. See also *idem, Kleine Schriften* (Göttingen: Vandenhoeck & Ruprecht, 1934), p. 142.
71. Seneca *Epistolae*, 91 21.

its first word a "synonym compound" ($ch'iang^2$-$liang^2$-che^3, where -che^3 is a substantivizing particle).[72] This form of expression, which has become almost the normal word type in modern ordinary language, has been called a "binom" by European Sinologists, according to the algebraic "binomial" ($a + b = c$). This represents a striking comparison for this kind of concept formation insofar as the members of the expression need not be related to one another as *determinans* and *determinandum*. If one makes the characteristic "binom" conceptually explicit, then this "binom" allows, rather, for a combination of the two members by means of *and*. This *and* in the original is co-understood (*sous-entendu*).

In order to understand this, we must clarify the form of thought with which we are dealing here and which in the foregoing was designated as the "ontological indifference," a mode of expression which connects Chinese with the north Asiatic, Mongolian languages.[73] In these languages the sentence represents for our analysis a "concatenation of pure concepts," "a concatenation of conceptual meanings"; this sentence form, although articulated in itself and thus in a certain sense differentiated, is certainly not principally related to an object, as is the case with the Indo-European sentence (*supponit* ["supposing"]).[74]

It is the continuous and thorough "supposition" of concepts that first creates the condition for an "inner" word form with which we are familiar and which, without valid reason, we take as self-evident.[75] This word form comes to the fore as sharply as possible in the ancient "synthetic" Indo-European linguistic form:

> The Indo-European form, with its sharp demarcation by means of the "ending" in which the expression of the different "supposing" sentence functions are pressed together into a unity, leaving for the most part no possibility for analysis, shows in a specifically striking way the hiatus which is brought about in each case by the supposition in a series of predicates.[76]

72. George von der Gabelentz, *Chinesische Grammatik* (Leipzig: Weigel, 1881), secs. 455–77, p. 913–15.
73. Cf. esp. pp. 336–37 above.
74. Cf. pp. 310–11 above.
75. Lohmann, *Gnomon*, p. 398.
76. *Ibid.*

In the modern western European "analytic" languages, the "inner" word form has not changed in this respect.

> It is completely out of place to compare, as has been done, English to Chinese. Although the English language has, in most instances, lost the original Indo-European inflection, it nonetheless has remained a "supposing" language, something which the Chinese language is not and never has been. The supposition, just as the inflection, has merely shifted in the expression; it has for the most part been moved from the "endings" to independent small words and, properly speaking, has thus been made technically even more perfect. In the modern languages the [definite and indefinite] articles have developed into the symbol *kat' exochēn* of the supposition; its function consists precisely in relating the *nomen* to the object that the talk is about.[77]

This "system of supposition" is developed perhaps in its most perfect form in the French language, where, in addition to the definite and indefinite articles (*le pain, un pain*), we find the "partitive article" (*du pain, peu de pain*); therefore, from the viewpoint of the linguistic form, it is certainly not accidental that around 1150 medieval "suppositional logic" originated at—or better perhaps, with—the University of Paris, the mother of Western universities.

The "subalternating" linguistic form, of which the Chinese language in a certain sense represents a modification,[78] is so called by Finck because of a certain mode of the word form which in the typological comparison of languages was in the very beginning called "agglutinating" ("the subordination of relatively loosely attached determining and modifying elements under stems which signify a thing, a property, or an event or eventually contain a reference to something").[79] We will not discuss here the relationship between "word form" and "sentence form." In any event the "subordination" also determines the character of the Altaic sentence construction, which shows itself particularly in the fact that a "subordinating" construction corresponds in this domain to the concatenating *and* of the "supposing" languages. This construction has been called "*gerun-*

---

77. *Ibid.*, p. 390.
78. See pp. 336–37 above.
79. Finck, *Haupttypen des Sprachbaus*, p. 74.

dium" (although this Latin expression does not completely fit).[80] In Chinese the conjunction *erh*^{2} (radical 126) corresponds in function to the Altaic *gerundia*. For example, the following are passages from the first chapters of the *Tao Te Ching* in which *erh*^{2} occurs: (*Tz'u*^{3} *liang*^{3} *che*^{3} *t'ung*^{2}) *ch'u*^{1} *erh*^{2} *i*^{4} *ming*^{2} ("[These two are identical] when they emerge, different names [differently named]"); [81] *Sheng*^{4} *jen*^{2} . . . *wan*^{4} *wu*^{4} *tso*^{4} *yen*^{1} *erh*^{2} *pu*^{4} *tz'u*^{2}, *sheng*^{1} *erh*^{2} *pu*^{4} *yu*^{3}, *wei*^{2} *erh*^{2} *pu*^{2} *shih*^{4}, *kung*^{1} *ch'eng*^{2} *erh*^{2} *fu*^{2} *chü*^{1} ("The perfect man . . . lets the myriads of individual beings unfold themselves and places no obstacles in their way, produces [something] and does not possess it, makes [something] and does not utilize it, achieves [something] and does not insist on it"); [82] *Tao*^{4} *ch'ung*^{2} *erh*^{2} *yung*^{4} *chih*^{1} *huo*^{4} *pu*^{4} *ying*^{2} ("The Tao is empty, and, when one uses it, it does not run over"); [83] (*T'ien*^{1} *ti*^{4} *chih*^{1} *chien*^{1}: *ch'i*^{2} *yu*^{2} *to*^{2} *yo*^{4} *hu*^{1}?) *Hsü*^{1} *erh*^{2} *pu*^{4} *ch'ü*^{1}, *tung*^{4}, *erh*^{2} *yü*^{4} *ch'u*^{1} ("[What is there between heaven and earth which is similar to a pair of bellows?] [It] empties [itself] and does not exhaust itself; it moves, and always more comes out of it"); [84] *Sheng*^{4} *jen*^{2} *hou*^{4} *ch'i*^{2} *shen*^{1} *erh*^{2} *shen*^{1} *hsien*^{1}, *wai*^{4} *ch'i*^{2} *shen*^{1} *erh*^{2} *shen*^{1} *ts'un*^{2} ("The perfect man places himself [*suum corpus*] back, and he himself is in front; exposes himself [to danger], and he himself is saved"); [85] (*Shang*^{4} *shan*^{4} *jo*^{4} *shui*^{3}) *shui*^{3} *shan*^{4}: *li*^{4} *wan*^{4} *wu*^{4} *erh*^{2} *pu*^{4} *cheng*^{1} ("[*Supremum bonum simile aquae.*] Water [is] good: it is of use to the myriads of individual beings and does not compete [is not jealous]") [86]—it occupies the space which all people scorn (the lowest) and, precisely because it does not compete, it is without flaw; *Ch'ih*^{2} *erh*^{2} *ying*^{2} *chih*^{1}— *pu*^{4} *ju*^{2} *ch'i*^{2} *i*^{3}; *ch'uai*^{3} *erh*^{2} *chuo*^{4} *chih*^{1}—*pu*^{4} *k'o*^{3} *ch'ang*^{2} *pao*^{3} ("To pack and full—rather leave it [not to bring to an end as being]; to grasp and sharp—one cannot keep it for a long

80. Cf. *ibid.*, p. 82. Two additional examples of this construction are given: the Turkish *cem olup* . . . *derler* ("they joined forces and . . . said") and *gelip aydir* ("he came and said"). In Mongolian grammar these forms are labeled "*converba*," a term used in A. von Gabian, "Alttürkische Grammatik," *Porta Linguarum Orientalium* (1941).
81. Lao-tzu, *Tao Te Ching*, chap. 1.
82. *Ibid.*, chap. 2.
83. *Ibid.*, chap. 4.
84. *Ibid.*, chap. 5.
85. *Ibid.*, chap. 7.
86. *Ibid.*, chap. 8.

time"); [87] (*sheng*[1] *erh*[2] *pu*[4] *yu*[3], *wei*[2] *erh*[2] *pu*[2] *shih*[4]), *ch'ang*[3] *erh*[2] *pu*[4] *tsai*[3] ("[produces (something) and does not possess it, makes (something) and does not utilize it], is at the head and does not dominate").[88]

The concepts which are connected here by means of *erh*[2] are almost exclusively paradoxical combinations of ideas. This fact is obviously founded in the philosophy of Lao-tzu, whose thoughts are frequently expressed in the form of the paradox.[89] Von der Gabelentz compares *erh*[2] to the genitive particle *chih*[1].[90] One might say that *erh*[2] means the same for the adverbial relationship as *chih*[1] does for the adnominal: *Jih*[4] *ch'u*[1] *erh*[2] *tso*[4]; *jih*[4] *ju*[4] *erh*[2] *hsi*[1] ("The sun rises, so work; the sun goes down, so rest [With sunrise, work; with sunset, rest]"). One might compare this to *kuo*[2] *chih*[1] *fa*[2] ("state, its laws" = "the laws of the state"). Both *chih*[1] and *erh*[2] are expressions of "subordination" (the subordination of what precedes to what follows). *Chih*[1] expresses in this context a relationship between "things" (in the example given above, "law" : "state"); *erh*[2] expresses a relationship between relationships ("position of the sun" : "work" or "rest").

The combination signified by *erh*[2] can also be a purely mental one (*rationale* rather than *reale*): *Wo*[3] *yü*[4] *chien*[4] *erh*[2] *kuei*[4], *yü*[2] *erh*[2] *chih*[4], *p'in*[2] *erh*[2] *fu*[4]: *k'o*[3] *hu*[2]? ("I wish [to be] modest and yet honored [I wish insignificance and yet honor], dull and yet clever [simplicity and yet wisdom], poor and yet rich [poverty and yet wealth]: is that possible?"); [91] *Chung*[4] *jen*[2] *to*[1] *erh*[2] *sheng*[4] *jen*[2] *kua*[3] ("Ordinary people are great in number; saintly people are rare").[92] The connection, however, is never a purely "enumerative" one in which the connected members stand on the same level. As far as the pure "parallel coordination" is concerned, the "asyndetic" connection—that is, the connection without *syndesmos*, without explicit "*conjunctio*," without "conjugation"—is certainly dominant in this linguistic

87. *Ibid.*, chap. 9.
88. *Ibid.*, chap. 10. See also note 82 above. One might quote here, "Le roi regne, mais il ne gouverne pas! [The king reigns, but he does not govern!]."
89. See note 41 above.
90. Gabelentz, *Chinesische Grammatik*, sec. 619.
91. *Ibid.*, sec. 629.
92. *Ibid.*, sec. 634.

type. This is something which connects Chinese with the genuine "subordinating type," and thus, practically speaking, with the Ural-Altaic languages, in which we have earlier tried to find a genealogical point of contact with the Indo-Chinese language family. The dominance of the "asyndetic" connection, though often observed in detail, is never seen in the over-all context— particularly not in connection with its "opposite," the copulative connection of concepts in the "supposing" languages, where thinking is determined by the "ontological difference." The linguistic form for which a purely "copulative" *and* has first been verified is the Semitic one. In the introduction to the code of Hammurabi we find "the Lord of heaven and earth," just as in Genesis we find "God created heaven and earth" (*ēt haššāmajim wĕ ēt ha³āreṣ [bēl] šamē ū erṣetim*).[93] The common Semitic concatenating *wa* ("and," Arabic *wa*, and so on) is as characteristic of this linguistic form as the "expressive" *es-ti* ("is") is of the Indo-European form. The Indo-European languages have, as an ancient word for *and*, only the "enclitic" *-que;* the form of its usage as appendage to the connected words shows that it does not really signify a parallel coordination of members with equal rights. This is further confirmed by the ancient meaning *wenn* ("when"), which Wackernagel has been able to establish for the Indo-European *-que*.[94] This meaning is to be seen in the ancient Latin *absque eo esset* ("when it was without him") and other relics. The explicit coordinating connecting *and*, which is found today as one of the most frequently occurring words in all European languages, is shown to be a relatively recent creation by the fact that etymologically different words are found with this meaning—for example, the German *und,* the Scandinavian *ok* and *og,* the Slavic *i,* the Latin *et,* and the Greek *kai.* (Perhaps another even more striking phenomenon of this kind is the fact that corresponding expressions for "yes" and "no," which appear to us today as self-evident, are found only in modern Europe.) Insofar as the words meaning "and" are etymologically transparent, they suggest the signification of "attaching" and "adding" (the Latin *et* = the Greek *eti* ["still (more)"] and the ancient Indian *áti* ["beyond," "in addition to"]; the Lithuanian *iȓ* from the

---

93. Or *bēl šamē erṣetim.* Cf. A. Ungnad, *Babylonisch-Assyrische Grammatik* (Munich: Biederstein, 1949), sec. 62.

94. J. Wackernagel, "Indogermanische *-que* als alte nebensatzeinleitende Konjunktion," KZ, LXVII (1942), 1–5.

root *ar-* ["to join"]; the Teutonic *auk, ok,* and *og* perhaps = the Latin *auge* ["add to"]). Thus we are able here to recognize as such the "explicitation" of the concatenating function ($a + b +$ . . .), which first is simply "tacitly effected" in language. The "explicit" concatenation (in addition to the "article," that is to say, the marking of the logical "supposition" as such) seems to have developed particularly early in the Greek language. "It seems that in Homer asyndeta with two members are rarely found." [95] In other European languages, particularly in Latin, the simple concatenation still plays a considerable role.[96]

Nevertheless, this kind of connection obviously has a character other than that found in the languages where thinking developed in the "ontological indifference." The Vedic *diváḥ pṛthivyā ántam* ("the heaven's and earth's end") [97] is not the same as the Chinese *t'ien¹ ti⁴ chih⁴ chien¹*,[98] in which the particle *chih¹* places *t'ien¹ ti⁴* ("heaven and earth") in a genitive relationship with regard to *chi'en²* ("interspace"). One must free oneself here completely from an external mode of consideration in which facts are isolated and in which a word is a word and a form a form, even when they only externally have the same meaning or appear to be similar. In the comparative typology of the languages, mistakes have often been made by those who have not observed this. Finck, however, notwithstanding his "psychologism," which in a certain respect levels the "forms of thought" of the languages, had a sharp view on the morphological character of the languages; but his predecessors—for instance, Misteli—made such mistakes. That the ancient Indian "asyndeton bimembre" must be something other than the Chinese "binom" and completely different from the corresponding word combination in the "subordinating" languages is clear from the fact that the ancient Indian language has created in its own way a substitute for the "binom" in the so-called Dvandva composition, whose most ancient form consists in a double dual as expression for the "pairedness": *dyává-pṛthiví* ("heaven and earth") [99] = the Chinese *t'ien¹ ti⁴*. Lewy has connected the suffix of the Indo-European dual with the ending of the instru-

95. B. Delbrück, *Vergleichende Syntax,* 5 vols. (Halle: Buchhandlung des Weisenhauses, 1967), III, 186.
96. *Ibid.,* p. 187.
97. *Rig-Veda,* I, 33, 10.
98. See note 84 above.
99. This expression occurs seventy-nine times in the *Rig-Veda*.

mental-sociative combination under the basic meaning "with (the other as complementation)." [100] Thus the pair is expressed in a typical reciprocity: "with the heaven, with the earth"; "heaven's pair, earth's pair" = "a pair consisting of heaven and earth." I believe that this constitutes a typical attempt at representing the "inner form" of the concept fusion of the "binom" in a linguistic type whose "outer form" construction is built upon the general "ontological difference." This type of expression is a pronounced cross-product which developed at the boundaries of two "forms of thought"; this is clear also from the fact that this type of expression is found in the Finno-Ugric languages, too, as Lewy first showed in his masterly work *Zur finnisch-ugrischen Wort- und Satzverbindung*, and his student K. Bouda then supported with further material in his dissertation, "Ob-ugrischer Dual." [101] The fact that such a remarkable mode of expression developed precisely in the border area between the "stem-inflecting" Indo-European and the subordinating Ural-Altaic types— and in this area, from India to northwestern Siberia—definitely cannot, in my view, be understood in any other way.

What is this "binom" which is found not only in Chinese but also, in completely corresponding, significative types, in the languages of the "subordinating" structure, namely, in the Ural-Altaic languages? [102] What is this "binom," what does this mode of combining mean, and how is it related to the "form of thought" of the "ontological indifference"? In the "ontological indifference" the fundamental distinction, given in our languages through the "grammatical supposition," between a *compositum* wherein one member determines the other conceptually and a pair of words in which two concepts or two objects are connected on the same level (*a* and *b*, *a* or *b*) becomes blurred or disappears. In the "ontological indifference" not only are there such combinations as *t'ien*^{1}-*ti*^{4} ("heaven [and] earth" = "universe," "cosmos") on the one hand and expressions such as *t'ien*^{1}-*hsia*^{4} ("heaven's underside," "under the heaven" = "world

---

100. Ernst Lewy, "Zum Dual und zum Tocharischen," *KZ*, XLV (1913), 366. See also *idem*, "Kleinere Beiträge," p. 32.
101. Ernst Lewy, *Zur finnisch-ugrischen Wort- und Satzverbindung* (Göttingen: Vandenhoeck & Ruprecht, 1911); K. Bouda, "Ob-ugrischer Dual" (Ph.D. diss., Berlin-Helsinki, 1933).
102. This question is examined with regard to the Finno-Ugric languages, the most Western and therefore the most altered group, in Lewy, *Zur finnisch-ugrischen Wort- und Satzverbindung*.

[domain]"), $t'ien^1$-tao^4 ("law of heaven"), and $t'ien^1$-chu^3 ("lord of heaven" = god [catholic]") on the other; there is also, as conceptual transition between the two concepts of a composition, the possibility of combining two concepts which meet one another in the same "object." For example, ta^4 Tao^4 ("the great Tao" = "greatness-Tao," "Tao of greatness") is not fundamentally distinct from $t'ien^1$ Tao^4 ("Tao of heaven," "heavenly Tao"); and two concepts can be combined into one of higher order, such as ta^4 $hsiao^3$ ("magnitude," namely, "great and small" [conceptually combined] or "[being] great or small" [seen from the object]).

Precisely in this latter type, namely, in the "contrast binom," the "ontological indifference"—that is, the indifferent blurring of the word meaning between concept (greatness as a property of "that which is great") and object ("something that is great")—is so obvious that one can almost touch it. By putting together appropriate examples, one obtains a gradual, unobservable transition from a Dvandva composition such as $t'ien^1$-ti^4 ("heaven and earth") to the "purely conceptual" to^1-$shao^3$ ("much and [conceptual addition] little," "much or [objective 'disjunction'] little" = "quantum, set, quantity"). Consider, for instance, fu^4-mu^3 ("father-mother" = "parents"), which is equal to the Sanskrit *mātárā-pitárā* and its derivations; [103] $hsiung^1$-ti^4 ("older brother–younger brother" = "brothers" [Chinese does not have the general concept "brother," just as the ancient Indo-European language did not have the concept "parents"]); tsu^3-pi^3 and, conversely, pi^3-tsu^3 ("grandfather-grandmother" = "grandparents," "ancestors"); nan^2-$nü^3$ ("man-woman" = "the sexes"); $niao^3$-$shou^4$ ("bird-quadruped" = "animals," "the animal world"); yin^3-$shih^2$ ("to drink–to eat" = "food"); mai^3-mai^4 ("to sell–to buy" = "trade"); $ch'ang^3$-yu^4 ("grown up–young" = "adults and children"); $ch'ang^2$-$tuan^3$ ("long-short" = "length"); hao^3-tai^3 ("good-evil" = "quality").

Similarly, there is no sharp line between the contrast combination, that is, the combination with objective or conceptual opposition, and the "synonym compound." *Synonyma* are never completely equivalent: men^2-$hu^{3(4)}$ ("gate-door" [the character represents the two-winged or one-winged door, respectively] =

---

103. J. Wackernagel, *Altindische Grammatik* (Göttingen: Vandenhoeck & Ruprecht, 1930–57), II, 151. In the *Rig-Veda* this is also used to mean "earth and heaven"!

"doors," "families"), *p'eng²-yu³* ("companion-friend" = "friend," "friends"), *kuang³-to⁴* ("to think–to measure" = "to guess"). This "synonym compound" must replace the whole realm of our verbal composition with "preverbs"—for instance: "to see–to notice" = "to discover" (*er-blicken*); "to go–to reach" = "to arrive" (*an-kommen*); "*sortir-venir*" = "to appear" (*heraus-kommen*); "to produce–to bring to the fore" = "to bring forth" (*hervor-bringen*). This "preverb" was originally, in the Indo-European mother tongue, built up as a kind of spatial adverb, which later became separated into "preposition" (*über die Brücke schreiten*) and "preverb" (*die Brücke überschreiten*).[104] In Chinese, "verb" and "adverb" ("to come" and "out") have conceptually equal rank, just as do *pai²* and *ma³* in *pai²-ma³* ("white horse").[105] "White horse," or "white horses," constitutes for the Chinese the combination of the concepts "whiteness" and "horse-ness." These, however, are to be understood in "ontological in-difference"—thus, as simultaneously signifying "that which is white" and "whiteness," "horse(s)" and "horseness." "Verb" and "adverb" on the one hand and "noun" and "adjective" on the other, which Varro relates to one another in the sentence *Homo doctus scribit docte,* become blurred in the "ontological indif-ference" of the Chinese language. This quality, as a "not dis-joining of what belongs together," is a positive rather than a negative one. Certainly no translation into our linguistic form can do it justice.

The "binom" is the expression of the "ontological indiffer-ence"; unlike our "compound," and even our simple "noun" (see pp. 309 ff. above), it does not represent a conceptually mediated knowledge of objects—that is, the *ousia* of a *pragma* (the "es-sence" of a "thing"), as Plato calls it—but rather the unmediated immediacy of knowledge itself. This does not increase in a lin-ear, specifying determination (a determination of the *genus* by the *differentia specifica* and so on) but in an unfolding of the meaning according to the "fullness" of the Chinese concept of truth (pp. 339 f. above). To use an expression of Meillet, the "binom" is more expressive than its individual members but not

104. Cf. Ernst Lewy, "Etymologie und Sprachbegriff," pp. 187–88.
105. This must be kept in mind in order to understand the famous Chinese sophism according to which a white horse is not a horse. (A. Forke, *Geschichte der alten chinesischen Philosophie,* pp. 438–39. Cf. Johannes Lohmann, "Der Sophismus der Kung-Sun-Lung," *Lexis,* II [1949], pp. 3–11.)

more "exact" in the mathematical sense of the term, as is our compound in relation to its determined members. Those who believe that "meaning-fulfillment" and "greater precision" amount to practically the same thing—and thus that, strictly speaking, this formal difference is uninteresting and unimportant—are, as Finck says, "blind to meaning," "captured" by "being." [106] Since about 1850 even the greatest minds have fallen prey to this belief, and the results have been obvious. The Chinese "expressivity," as well as the Ural-Altaic "binom," finds an immediate phonetic expression in phenomena of rhyme, alliteration, and assonance (also in certain phonetic variations in initial sounds) —for example, in Lao-tzu's *ch'iang²-liang²* and in the proverb which we discussed earlier. For quite some time an ample discussion has been developing concerning this "striking" aspect of the matter in connection with Lewy's *Zur finnisch-ugrischen Wort- und Satzverbindung*. This discussion has brought to light material from all sides, from Basque to Finno-Ugric and Aryan. [107] As for the Chinese language, where the "tones" and the monosyllabicity of the word create very special conditions in this regard, the phonetic problems of the "binom," in addition to the semantic difficulties, are still almost completely unexamined. [108]

Lewy begins *Zur finnisch-ugrischen Wort- und Satzverbindung* as follows:

> When in the Magyar language two *nomina* stand in the same relationship to a verb or a *nomen*, then the suffix which expresses the

106. Eugen Finck, "Philosophie als Überwindung der 'Naivität,'" *Lexis*, I (1948), 107–27.

107. For example, H. Jacobsohn, "Tagen baren Löneborger Kind," KZ, LIV (1927), 100 ff.; *idem*, "Zum homerischen *hysteron prōteron*," KZ, LVI (1929), 1 ff.; L. Spitzer, "Singen und Sagen—Schorlemorle," KZ, LIV (1927), 213 ff.; H. Schuchardt's review of H. Urtel, "Zur baskischen Onomatopoesis," in *Literaturblätter für germanische und romanische Philologie*, XLI (1919), col. 397 ff., where Magyar literature is also quoted in connection with the "twin words" (the Hungarian *ikerszó*); J. Wackernagel, "Eine Wortstellungsregel das Pāṇini und Winklers Aleph-Beth-Regel," *Indogermanische Forschung*, LVI (1948), 161 ff.; W. Foy, on the Turkish "Hendiadyoin," *Mitteilungen des Seminars für Orientalischen Sprachen zu Berlin*, II, no. 2 (1899), 105 ff.; R. Godel, "Formes et emplois du redoublement en turc et an arménien moderne," *Cahiers F. de Saussure*, V (1945), 5. ff.

108. August Conrady, "Der altchinesische Fragesatz und der steigende Ton," *Mitteilungen des Seminars für Orientalischen Sprachen zu Berlin*, XVIII, no. 1 (1915), 261 ff. contains an important observation concerning relationships between the tones of the "binom"; but this article, too, lacks full evaluation in systematic as well as historical respects.

relevant relationship is added to each of the two *nomina,* and both are connected with an "and" expression (*s, és, meg; -is, is-* ["as well as"]; *vagy* ["or"]).[109]

This form of expression, which appears "self-evident" to the Europeanized Hungarians of today, is subsequently shown to be strictly un-Hungarian. The Hungarian language possesses connecting conjunctions corresponding to our *and* and *or,* just as it has also developed a "copula" *is* and a "definite" and an "indefinite" article; but *and* and *is* are certainly not yet obligatory. The acts which they express refer to logical basic connections which are not in need of an explicit symbolization by means of phonetic elements, insofar as speech itself always does and at the same time must express the Being of beings as well as merely connect significations in naming concatenations. Do the copula *is* and the conjunction *and* merely contain an "explicitation" of the act which is signified by them, without there being any change in the character of this act itself? One can answer this question, I believe, both affirmatively and negatively. The logical act as such does not change, but the "meaning" of the act, in relation to the one who speaks, certainly does change. In an attitude "captured by being" (Finck) and "purely objective," no essential difference can be seen; for the Magyar it is a matter of relative indifference whether he says, for "the man is good," *as ember jó van* or simply *az ember jó* or, for "gold and silver," *arany és ezüst* or *arany, ezüst.* "In reality," however, a whole world lies between these two modes of expression; it makes an essential difference not only whether or not an *and* or an *is* is found in a language but also whether or not the expression of the "copulation" or the "predication" by means of a "conjunction" or a "copula" is obligatory. In the first case the "meaning" is being conquered; in the second it has become self-evident. In each case we have an essentially different "style of thought," and it is certainly not accidental that in Europe the obligatory *and* was first introduced in Greece (see p. 357 above), where the "article" and the obligatory *is* first appeared also.[110] In this regard, too, Greece shows itself as the homeland of a "philosophy" which

---

109. Lewy, *Zur finnisch-ugrischen Wort- und Satzverbindung,* p. 1.
110. This occurred in Ionic prose. See Meillet, "La phrase nominale en indoeuropéen," p. 10.

raised the thought of man to the level of individual "consciousness."

Within the realm of the northern and eastern European "binom" there belongs obviously also the Tocharian *akmal* ("face" = *ak* ["eye(s)"] + *mal* [(probably) "cheek(s)"]), with which Wilhelm Schulze has dealt.[111]

The "contrast binom" ("good-bad" = "quality" [in general]; see p. 359 above) belongs, with the expression of the question by means of an alternative ("to wish–not to wish" = "do you wish?"; "much-little" = "how much?"), to the many "philosophical" forms of the Chinese language. The same conception, but on the level of "consciousness," is shown by Plato's *mega kai mikron*, handed down by Aristotle, and also by the *mallon kai hētton* of Plato's *Philebus* (the "comparative" is the Indo-European "contrast form"); [112] in the language of medieval philosophy, these philosophical terms offer us the *"actus signatus"* to the Chinese *"actus exercitus."* The Chinese forms constitute at the same time a convincing proof of the concrete reality of Humboldt's "inner form," which was considered in the "positivistic" era as an idle speculation.

111. Cf. W. Schulze, *Kleine Schriften,* pp. 248–57.
112. Aristotle *Metaphysics* 1081a; Lewy, "Etymologie und Sprachbegriff," p. 189.

Selected Bibliography

I. WORKS BY HEIDEGGER, WITH CORRESPONDING ENGLISH TRANSLATIONS

(Listed in approximate chronological order of first public presentation)

Die Lehre vom Urteil im Psychologismus. Ein kritisch-positiver Beitrag zur Logik (1914). Leipzig: Barth, 1914.
Die Kategorien- und Bedeutungslehre des Duns Scotus (1916). Tübingen: Mohr, 1916.
Sein und Zeit (1927). Tübingen: Niemeyer, 1927. Translation by John Macquarrie and Edward Robinson, *Being and Time*. New York: Harper & Row, 1962. With marginal pagination of the German edition.
Kant und das Problem der Metaphysik (1927). Frankfurt: Klostermann, 1951. Translation by James S. Churchill, *Kant and the Problem of Metaphysics*. Bloomington: Indiana Univ. Press, 1962.
Vom Wesen des Grundes (1928). Frankfurt: Klostermann, 1955. Translation by Terrence Malick, *The Essence of Reasons*. Bilingual edition. Evanston, Ill.: Northwestern Univ. Press, 1969.
Was ist Metaphysik? (1929). Frankfurt: Klostermann, 1955. (Postscript added to 4th ed., 1943; introduction added to 5th ed., 1949.) Lecture and postscript translated by R. F. C. Hull

and Alan Crick, "What Is Metaphysics?" In Werner Brock, *Existence and Being*, pp. 325–61. Chicago: Regnery, 1949.

Vom Wesen der Wahrheit (1930–43). Frankfurt: Klostermann, 1943. Translation by R. F. C. Hull and Alan Crick, "On the Essence of Truth." In Werner Brock, *Existence and Being*, pp. 292–324.

Einführung in die Metaphysik (1935). Tübingen: Niemeyer, 1953. Translation by Ralph Manheim, *An Introduction to Metaphysics*. New Haven: Yale Univ. Press, 1959.

Erläuterungen zu Hölderlins Dichtung (1936–44). Frankfurt: Klostermann, 1944. Translation of the second essay (pp. 31–45 in the German) by Douglas Scott, "Hölderlin and the Essence of Poetry." In Werner Brock, *Existence and Being*, pp. 270–91.

Holzwege (1936–46). Frankfurt: Klostermann, 1950. Translation of the first essay (pp. 7–68 in the German) by Albert Hofstadter, "The Origin of the Work of Art." In A. Hofstadter and Richard Kuhns, eds., *Philosophies of Art and Beauty*, pp. 649–701. New York: Random House, 1964.

Nietzsche. (Vol. I, 1936–39; Vol. II, 1939–46). Pfullingen: Neske, 1961.

Vorträge und Aufsätze (1936–53). Pfullingen: Neske, 1954.

Platons Lehre von der Wahrheit (1942): *Mit einem Brief über den "Humanismus"* (1946). Bern: Francke, 1947. Translations of both essays are in William Barrett and Henry D. Aiken, eds., *Philosophy in the Twentieth Century*, 2 Vols. New York: Random House, 1962. The essays are in Vol. II, pp. 270–340.

Was heisst Denken? (1951–52). Tübingen: Niemeyer, 1954. Translation by Fred D. Wieck and J. Glenn Gray, *What Is Called Thinking?* New York: Harper & Row, 1968.

Der Feldweg (1953). Frankfurt: Klostermann, 1953.

Aus der Erfahrung des Denkens (1954). Pfullingen: Neske, 1954.

Was ist das—die Philosophie? (1955). Pfullingen: Neske, 1956. Translation by William Kluback and Jean T. Wilde, *What Is Philosophy?* Bilingual edition. New York: Twayne, 1958.

Zur Seinsfrage (1955). Frankfurt: Klostermann, 1956. Translation by William Kluback and Jean T. Wilde, *The Question of Being*. Bilingual edition. New York: Twayne, 1958.

Der Satz vom Grund (1955–56). Pfullingen: Neske, 1957.

Identität und Differenz (1957). Pfullingen: Neske, 1957. Trans-

lation by Joan Stambaugh, *Identity and Difference.* New
York: Harper & Row, 1969.
Hebel—Der Hausfreund (1957). Pfullingen: Neske, 1957.
Unterwegs zur Sprache (1950–59). Pfullingen: Neske, 1959.
Translation by Peter D. Hertz [and Joan Stambaugh], *On the
Way to Language.* New York: Harper & Row, 1971.
Gelassenheit (1959). Pfullingen: Neske, 1959. Translation by
John M. Anderson and E. Hans Freund, *Discourse on Think-
ing.* New York: Harper & Row, 1966.
Kants These über das Sein (1962). Frankfurt: Klostermann,
1962.
Die Frage nach dem Ding (1962). Tübingen: Niemeyer, 1962.
Die Technik und die Kehre (1962). Pfullingen: Neske, 1962.
Wegmarken (1967). Frankfurt: Klostermann, 1967.
Zur Sache des Denkens (1969). Tübingen: Niemeyer, 1969.
Phänomenologie und Theologie (1971). Frankfurt: Kloster-
mann, 1971.

II. Studies on Heidegger

Alleman, Beda. *Hölderlin und Heidegger.* Zurich: Atlantis, 1956.
Biemel, Walter. *Le concept de monde chez Heidegger.* Louvain:
Nauwelaerts; Paris: Vrin, 1950.
Birault, Henri. "Existence et vérité d'après Heidegger," *Revue de
Métaphysique et de Moral,* LVI (1950), 35–87.
———. "L'onto-théo-logie hégélienne et la dialectique," *Tijd-
schrift voor Philosophie,* XX (1958), 646–723.
De Waelhens, Alphonse. *La philosophie de Martin Heidegger.*
Louvain: Nauwelaerts, 1955.
Dondeyne, Albert. "La difference ontologique chez M. Heidegger,"
Revue philosophique de Louvain, LVI (1958), 35–62, 251–93.
Kockelmans, Joseph J. *Martin Heidegger: A First Introduction to
His Philosophy.* Pittsburgh: Duquesne Univ. Press, 1965.
Langan, Thomas. *The Meaning of Heidegger: A Critical Study of
an Existentialist Phenomenology.* New York: Columbia Univ.
Press, 1959.
Levinas, Emmanuel. *En découvrant l'existence avec Husserl et
Heidegger.* Paris: Vrin, 1949.
Marx, Werner. *Heidegger und die Tradition.* Stuttgart: Kohl-

hammer, 1961. English translation by Theodore Kisiel and Murray Greene, *Heidegger and the Tradition*. Evanston, Ill.: Northwestern Univ. Press, 1971.

Ott, Heinrich. *Denken und Sein: Der Weg Martin Heideggers und der Weg der Theologie*. Zollikon: Evangelischer, 1959.

Pöggeler, Otto. *Der Denkweg Martin Heideggers*. Pfullingen: Neske, 1963.

Richardson, William J. Heidegger: *Through Phenomenology to Thought*. The Hague: Nijhoff, 1963.

Schöfer, Erasmus. *Die Sprache Heideggers*. Pfullingen: Neske, 1962.

Vietta, Egon. *Die Seinsfrage bei Martin Heidegger*. Stuttgart: Schwab, 1950.

Index to Names

Index to Subjects

Absolution, 173, 178
Acts, presentational vs. non-presentational, 140
Alḗtheia. See Truth
Analogia entis, 121, 127 n, 129, 134
Analytic of man's mode of Being, xi
Anxiety vs. fear, 36, 36 n, 43 n
Apophansis and hermeneutic, 143
Apophantic as. See As, apophantic
Ap-propriating event. See Event, ap-propriating
Architecture, Greek, 77–78
Art, 73–75; bringing about openness, 74–75; bringing into play coming to pass of truth, 78, 162; as clearing project, 75; and form and matter, 153 n, 162; in Hegel, Nietzsche, and Heidegger, 158–60; and ontological difference between world and thing, 162; poetry as essence of, 73–75, 77–78, 163. See also Work of art
Articulation and logos (Rede), 15, 48. See also Logos (Rede)
As, apophantic, 17, 19–20, 328
As, apophantic and hermeneutic, 111, 117, 139, 141, 198, 201, 209, 210, 219, 294, 296–97
As, hermeneutic, 15, 16, 19, 48; and assertion, 308; and coming to pass of ontological difference, 219; and explanation, 15; fundamental, 198, 201; in Indo-

European languages, 219; and interpretation, 308; and meaning, 308; and ontological difference, 198, 200, 201, 219, 309; and speech, 308; and subject-predicate relation, 309, 324
Assertion, 47, 70; apophantic, 110–11; and apophantic as, 110–11; and objectivation, 110–11; and speaking forth, 50–51

Be, Indo-European, 325–28; and apophantic as, 328; meaning "to exist," 327 n.34; and ontological difference, 325, 328; and signification of pure predication, 327; and supposition, 329; and truth, 328
Beginning, new: and Heidegger's later works, 235, 261–64; and historicity of Being, 252–53, 255–56; and poetic dwelling, 235–37, 239, 245–46
Being: as abiding coming to pass, 112; as abysmal groundless ground, 122–23; and anxiety, 114; and attunement, 114; and awe, 114; as being, 205; as Being in general, 205; as Beingness, 109, 205; and call of conscience, 114; and coming to pass of ontological difference, 208, 211, 217; as continuous presence, 109,

307; and hermeneutic and apophantic *as,* 198; and man's concernful dealing with things, 197; predicative and prepredicative, 197–98

Ontic vs. ontologic, 35

Ontological difference, 150, 275, 306; ambiguity of term, 204–6; classical interpretation of, 233; description of, 204–5, 214–18; as difference between Being and beings, 204–6; and distinction between ontic and ontologic truth, 197; and distinction between world and things, 162, 213–16; and essence of truth, 197; explicit in Indo-European languages but not in Chinese, 201, 232; expressed in grammatical form (in Indo-European languages), 199, 201, 309, 311, 317, 319, 320–22, 343–44; forgottenness of real meaning of, 203; and function of copula, 204; in Heidegger's early works, 206–8, 210 n.38, 217–18; in Heidegger's later works, 211–17, 218–20; and hermeneutics, 219–20; and hermeneutic structure of thought, 195; and language, 24–27, 175, 219–20; and logic, 205; and onto-logy, 205; and predication, 204; and saying of language, 213–16; and scission, 215–17; and subject-predicate relation, 195–96; and supposition, 199, 201, 204, 233, 309; and transcendence, 197, 306–7, 308–9. *See also* Being

Ontological differentiation in verb *to be,* 325–29

Ontological indifference, 200, 300 n.41, 324, 330–36, 341, 352–60

Ontological truth, 197, 208, 305–7, 308; essence of, 208; and logical truth, 73–74; and ontological difference, **197, 208**

Ontology, 305, 308; fundamental vs. regional, 116; and science, 305–6, 308; and topology of Being, 116

Ontotheology, 122, 129

Ousia (Beingness) and distinction between *essentia* and *existentia,* 109. *See also* Being

Paronomasia, Heidegger's use of, 297–301

Phenomenology, 111

Philosophy of language, 170. *See also* Language

Poet: corresponding to saying of language and its *alētheia* structure, 243; as custodian of word, 85; receiving standards from God, 245; setting standard for world of Dasein, 244; task of, in age of *Gestell,* 247–48; used by saying of language, 243

Poetic dwelling, 235–37, 239, 244, 245–49; and Being's historicity, 252–53, 255–56

Poetic language, 153

Poetizing and thinking, 86–87

Poetry: as art of language, 76; as clearing project, 75; as coming to pass of truth, 81; as disclosure of unconcealment, 81; as disclosure of world and earth, 95; as establishment of Being by means of word, 80–81; and language, 81, 95; naming the Holy, 165–66; and poesy, 77, 164; poetizing the openness, 75; as privileged form of art, 163; and truth, 75, 95; two meanings of, 75–76

Poiēsis, 135; meaning of, 150, 161–62, 167–68, 239

Poverty of Heidegger's thought, 265, 275

Practognosie, 12

Praxis, original, xii, 11–12, 15, 17, 19–20, 28–29, 117–18; and circumspection, 118; and *poiēsis,* 135; and theory, 11, 117–18